REVIVING SOCIAL DEMOCRACY

REVIVING SOCIAL DEMOCRACY

THE NEAR DEATH AND SURPRISING RISE OF THE FEDERAL NDP

Edited by David Laycock
and Lynda Erickson

UBCPress · Vancouver · Toronto

22 21 20 19 18 17 16 15 14   5 4 3 2 1

Printed in Canada on FSC-certified ancient-forest-free paper
(100% post-consumer recycled) that is processed chlorine- and acid-free.

Library and Archives Canada Cataloguing in Publication

Reviving social democracy: the near death and surprising rise of the federal NDP / edited by David Laycock and Lynda Erickson.

Includes bibliographical references and index.
Issued in print and electronic formats.
ISBN 978-0-7748-2849-9 (bound). – ISBN 978-0-7748- 2850-5 (pbk.). –
ISBN 978-0-7748-2851-2 (pdf). – ISBN 978-0-7748-2852-9 (epub)

1. New Democratic Party – History – 20th century. 2. New Democratic Party – History – 21st century. 3. Socialism – Canada. I. Laycock, David, author, editor. II. Erickson, Lynda, author, editor

JL197.N4R49 2015   324.27107   C2014-905882-9
                                                   C2014-905883-7

Canadä

UBC Press gratefully acknowledges the financial support for our publishing program of the Government of Canada (through the Canada Book Fund), the Canada Council for the Arts, and the British Columbia Arts Council.

This book has been published with the help of a grant from the Canadian Federation for the Humanities and Social Sciences, through the Awards to Scholarly Publications Program, using funds provided by the Social Sciences and Humanities Research Council of Canada.

Simon Fraser University's Publications Fund also provided a subvention to support publication of this volume.

Printed and bound in Canada by Friesens
Set in Segoe and Warnock by Artegraphica Design Co. Ltd.
Copy editor: Joanne Richardson
Proofreader: Naomi Wittes Reichstein
Indexer: Cheryl Lemmens

UBC Press
The University of British Columbia
2029 West Mall
Vancouver, BC V6T 1Z2
www.ubcpress.ca

Contents

Acknowledgments

This volume has been a long time in the making, its origins going as far back as 1995. Our first thanks go to student assistants involved in the post-2005 phase of this project: Robert Barlow, Natalie Brown, Kyall Glennie, Nigel Kinney, Brock Kuznetsov, Thanh Lam, Julie MacArthur, Scott MacLeod, and Tyler Shymkiw. We would also like to thank Christopher Kam, then an SFU MA student and now a UBC colleague, for his help designing our 1997 NDP member survey, as well as Neil Nevitte and Keith Archer for their feedback on an early draft of this survey. Steven Weldon played a crucial role in formulating the research proposal that gained financing for the last phase of our research and in helping to design our 2009 survey. We also wish to express our gratitude to federal NDP officials interviewed over the life of this project. Those who have assisted in this manner since 2008 are listed in Chapter 4. And we would like to thank the party members who participated in both the 1997 and 2009 surveys for their generosity in responding to our surveys. Their patience and enthusiasm has been highly appreciated.

We gratefully acknowledge the financial support provided for this project between 2008 and 2012 by the Social Sciences and Humanities Research Council of Canada, with SSHRC Standard Research Grant No. 410-2008-0488. Most of this money covered student research assistants' salaries. Other financial support for student research assistants from Simon

Fraser University, in the form of various small grants, is also noted with appreciation.

When the editors of this volume realized the range of potential consequences for the federal NDP stemming from the 2011 federal election, we decided to expand our project's scope and value by drawing on the expertise of more than a half-dozen colleagues spread across the Department of Political Science at SFU and Canada. We enjoyed the opportunity to work with and benefit from contributions by Éric Bélanger, Amanda Bittner, Jean-François Godbout, Frédéric Mérand, François Pétry, Mark Pickup, Steven Weldon, Colin Whelan, and Maria Zakharova.

Emily Andrew has been a strong and very effective supporter of this volume, even before it was submitted to UBC Press. We thank her for her tremendous assistance. And we thank UBC Press's anonymous reviewers, whose assessments and recommendations pushed us to make significant improvements to the original manuscript. We are left having to claim sole responsibility for any remaining shortcomings.

REVIVING SOCIAL DEMOCRACY

Introduction

LYNDA ERICKSON and DAVID LAYCOCK

With the general election of 2 May 2011, the Canadian political landscape shifted dramatically. This shift was especially remarkable for the New Democratic Party (NDP). After fifty years as a third party, it almost tripled its previous legislative contingent and became the Official Opposition in the House of Commons. Having triumphed in 103 seats, compared to the 37 it won in the 2008 general election, was indeed a significant accomplishment, but the NDP's performance in Quebec was the most astonishing development. The party went from having just a single Member of Parliament (MP) from that province to winning 59 of its 75 seats and more than tripling its share of the popular vote. In the country as a whole, the NDP popular vote rose from 18 to 31 percent, and its share of second-place finishes in constituency contests grew from 67 to 121. By contrast, its main rival in the opposition, the Liberal Party, dropped from 77 seats in 2008 to just 34 seats in 2011 as its popular vote declined from 26 to 19 percent, and its second-place finishes dropped from 123 to 76.

The extraordinary electoral results for the NDP in 2011 followed almost two decades of instability for the party. From its creation in 1961 until the early 1990s, the NDP had held a respectable, albeit minority, niche in the electorate in several regions of the country and had provided considerable policy innovation both provincially and federally. After a period of relative success in the 1980s with a federal popular vote averaging 20 percent, the party came close to electoral annihilation in the 1993 election. Its vote share dropped by two-thirds, and its 9 seats were not even sufficient to give the NDP official party status in the House of Commons. Although the 1993 election rearranged Canada's federal party system in other dramatic ways, the collapse in NDP support raised the question of both the party's future and the relevance of the political left in federal politics.

Faced with virtual extinction, the party was forced into self-examination and into deliberating about its political role and ideological direction. The Reform Party had taken on much of the western populist mantle previously held by the NDP, thus depriving the latter of a historic regional stronghold. Meanwhile, the Liberal Party was especially successful in Ontario and urban Canada, campaigning on the NDP's touchstone issues (such as medicare) and contending that only it could prevent a more extreme political right from forming the government.

In the decade that followed, federal New Democrats struggled to establish their relevance and regain support in this challenging political environment. Led by Jack Layton in the 2004 election, the federal NDP achieved a modest electoral recovery. Better results in the 2006 and 2008 elections suggested that the party had regained its position as a politically consequential third-party competitor in federal politics. Its success in 2011 confounded election prognosticators unaccustomed to NDP success, created new potentials for a continued rise in NDP support at the expense of the once-dominant Liberal Party, and allowed Canadian social democrats to think seriously about forming a federal government within several elections.

This revival from dramatic near death to Official Opposition has occurred in a context of tremendous challenge to parties of the left across the globe. Social democratic parties in particular have been under siege in recent times. The set of competitive, ideological, and support-sustaining challenges faced by these parties has led many insiders to re-examine their ideological directions, to question their parties' core programmatic commitments, and to implement policies of restraint and market friendliness unimaginable to their activist predecessors (Kitschelt 1994; Gamble and Wright 1999; Callaghan 2000; Bonoli and Powell 2004; Fishman, Jackson, and McIvor 2007; Meyer 2007; Merkel et al. 2008; Cronin, Ross, and Shoch 2011; Cramme and Diamond 2012). Some social democratic parties have re-emerged electorally successful, occasionally after a considerable makeover, while others have continued to struggle even, in some cases, after transforming themselves.

As the NDP experienced near disaster following the 1993 election, several internal efforts were mounted to redirect the party either to the centre or to the left. However, all appeared to fail. Prior to the 2004 election, from the outside the party seldom seemed capable of laying foundations for a recovery. Since then, however, the NDP has closed the gap between itself and its major rivals as its competitive party organization benefitted from a very popular leader and established a truly national presence.

As a result of this revitalization the NDP has established itself as an especially noteworthy subject of study for Canadian political scientists. But is the NDP experience of any relevance outside of Canada? In some respects the party may look too unique to be a fit subject for comparative analysis with other social democratic parties. Before 2011, unlike social democratic parties across Western Europe and in Australia and New Zealand, it had never been a major party capable of forming government. It has had the bad fortune of being the only Western social democratic party that, throughout its history, has had to compete in a system dominated by a centrist liberal party (Johnston 2008). The NDP's supportive trade unions have had less economic power than almost all of its European and Antipodean partners in the Socialist International, thus providing the party with fewer resources and less social legitimacy. The electoral success of the NDP in Canada's industrial heartland paled in comparison to that of other social democratic parties in their respective industrial centres. And the NDP's predecessor, the Co-operative Commonwealth Federation (CCF), became nationally relevant primarily because it had stronger roots in agrarian and cooperative movements than any major social democratic party in the Organisation for Economic Co-operation and Development (OECD).

While seemingly distinctive, these features – and the NDP's recent success in Quebec – do, we believe, make the party interesting to students of comparative parties and politics. Students of party systems and social democratic parties should want to know how a social democratic party can remain a relevant player and source of key policy ideas in a multi-party system when, unlike social democratic parties in Europe, it is not a dominant player in frequent coalition governments. When the CCF and then the NDP failed to displace their centre-left competitor, why did this competitor – the Liberal Party of Canada – not eventually push the NDP off the stage? Understanding how a social democratic party can survive with such variable national success, in a famously diverse country with socially progressive public opinions, should be especially useful to party scholars at a

time when social democratic parties are struggling and/or remaking themselves across the globe. Should the NDP move from opposition to government benches in Canada's next federal election, of course, the case for its
comparative relevance will be easier to make.

The distinctive features and unusual challenges facing the NDP initially
led us to undertake a major investigation of its background, experiences,
and characteristics. We began our research shortly after the NDP's disastrous election results in 1993 occasioned widespread reflection on the
party's long-term prospects. Parties of the social democratic left had shifted
from disappointing to impressive electoral results in much of the rest of the
Western world by the mid- to late-1990s, so initially we wondered why the
Canadian variant had lurched in the opposite direction. As the 1990s and
our research proceeded, we wondered whether we might end up witnessing
the federal NDP's demise. Would we end up providing an academic gloss to
this party's epitaph?

Our 1997 survey of party members provided a good start for our research, identifying key aspects of the party's self-understanding, con-
firming its distinctive ideological profile within Canada, and suggesting a
variety of potential questions to pursue. However, with each of us busy on
other fronts, we only began to devote sustained attention to studying the
federal party in 2008.[1] A second member survey in 2009 allowed us to determine whether member and activist attitudes had changed as the NDP
slowly re-established its political presence and relevance, and raised further
questions regarding which aspects of party ideology, campaigning, and organizational practice might be undergoing transformation. When the NDP
broke through to the "big leagues" in the 2011 federal election, we realized
that we needed to quickly obtain assistance from colleagues in order to
provide a more comprehensive analysis of this newly relevant party.

We and our readers are extremely fortunate that colleagues Éric Bélanger, Amanda Bittner, Jean-François Godbout, Frédéric Mérand, François
Pétry, Mark Pickup, Steven Weldon, Colin Whelan, and Maria Zakharova
answered our call for assistance. Their diverse expertise and analytical contributions to this volume first emerged in draft form in a workshop in April
2012, and the first iteration of the complete manuscript was ready several
months later. After a demanding but ultimately rewarding review and re-
vision process, we had our final volume ready.

Our book focuses on key dimensions of NDP experience over the past two
decades; the changing character of the party's discourse, policy instrument

choice, and ideology; member and leader attitudes and impacts; and the NDP's changing status and challenges as a competitor in Canadian federal politics. In the analyses that follow, we break new ground on several fronts.

First, we have collectively taken advantage of a broad range of relevant survey and other datasets, with analysis of our two NDP member surveys (1997 and 2009), Canadian Election Study (CES) survey data from elections dating back to 1984, and Comparative Manifesto Project (CMP) data from 1993 to 2011. Second, we have employed qualitative analysis of party documents, campaign platforms, and responses to parliamentary throne and budget speeches, along with elite interviews regarding party strategy and policy issues. Finally, we attempt to understand a novel shift in the federal NDP's standing, from its imperilled third-party status during the 1990s to its position as the Official Opposition in 2011. This transition has taken place against the backdrop of a reconfigured federal party system in which Conservative dominance has replaced Liberal dominance and the NDP has become much more than an also-ran.

In our efforts to understand the contemporary NDP, we use as broad a range of empirical foci and analytical methods as possible. Our hope is that, by adopting this more comprehensive and varied approach, we can offer a multifaceted analysis of value not just for those interested in the NDP but also for those wishing to learn more about the competitive dynamics in the modern Canadian party system and for students of comparative social democratic politics.

Part 1 sets the stage for our subsequent analyses of the party. The first chapter (Erickson and Laycock) explores the party's history from its 1961 origins until 2003, when the NDP selected Jack Layton as leader. The emphasis is on the period following the 1988 election – then the party's electoral high point – until the 2001 election, when the party engaged in a renewal exercise following disappointing election results in 2000. Chapter 2 (Erickson and Laycock) continues the historical account with an examination of the Layton years and the party's growing electoral success from 2004 to 2011. It focuses on Layton's leadership, electoral campaigns, the party's support base, and strategic struggles in the context of a series of minority governments. It concludes with a brief discussion of the successful 2011 election. Chapter 3 (Erickson and Laycock) takes a closer look at the NDP's experience in Quebec, where the party moved from years of frustration and political irrelevance to being the dominant vehicle for representing Quebec in the House of Commons. This first part of the book concludes with

Chapter 4 (Laycock and Erickson), which analyzes party modernization, focusing on matters of party organization, communications, fundraising, and campaign management.

Part 2 is concerned with party ideology, in particular the issue of evolution and change in NDP ideas and principles. Drawing on a variety of party documents, Chapter 5 (Laycock) assesses the key underlying normative commitments and social vision in the party's ideology since 1961. Chapter 6 (Pétry) uses a quantitative approach to look at the party's ideological evolution from 1988 to 2011 through the lens of its election campaign platforms.

Part 3 examines party opinion, issue priorities, and party appeal among members, supporters, and potential supporters. Drawing on data from 1997 and 2009 surveys of NDP members, Chapter 7 (Erickson and Zakharova) explores the demographic characteristics of party members, their ideological positions, their opinions on social democratic issues, and their views on strategic and organizational issues. They look at change over time with regard to these issues as well as at differences between the most active members and the rest. Turning to voter responses over time, Chapter 8 (Bittner) examines voter perceptions of NDP leaders, looking at the relationship between voters and the NDP from its earliest years and the role of leadership in the party's surprising success in 2011. Chapter 9 (Zakharova) examines whether the importance of policy distance versus valence factors, including voter perceptions of leaders, has been different over time for NDP voters than it has for voters for other major parties. Finally, Chapter 10 (Pickup and Whelan), in keeping with a focus on voters, looks at the dynamics of issue importance among those voters who compose the NDP's core demographic constituency. It examines whether the priorities for this constituency are different from those for other parties as well as how these priorities and differences have changed over time.

Part 4 looks ahead. It begins at Chapter 11, with Godbout, Bélanger, and Mérand's analysis of the potential for a merger between the NDP and the Liberal Party, drawing on their earlier work on the 2003 merger between the Canadian Alliance and the Progressive Conservative parties. Then Chapter 12 (Weldon) considers whether the NDP's 2011 success was a short-term phenomenon or whether it might herald a long-term change in Canadian federal politics. It does this by examining evidence from the 2011 CES to identify long-term and short-term sources of support among NDP voters.

Reviving Social Democracy concludes with an examination of shared themes and a discussion of the NDP's strategic challenges in the evolving

Canadian federal party system. These shared themes do not always lead to shared interpretive outcomes; however, providing both our complementary and our competing conclusions is the appropriate response to the plurality of methods and perspectives we employ. As for the NDP's strategic challenges – which, less than a decade ago, focused on mere survival but now deal with the prospect of real power – we are under no illusion that they will remain as we have sketched them after the 2015 election. But future strategic challenges have to come from somewhere, and it is our hope that, with this volume, we have provided important groundwork for whoever wishes to understand where the federal New Democratic Party might go next and why.

Note

1 For this, we gratefully acknowledge the support we received from a Social Sciences and Humanities Research Council Standard Grant.

References

Bonoli, Giuliano, and Martin Powell, eds. 2004. *Social Democratic Party Policies in Contemporary Europe*. New York: Routledge.

Callaghan, John. 2000. *The Retreat of Social Democracy*. Manchester: Manchester University Press.

–. Nina Fishman, Ben Jackson, and Martin McIvor, eds. 2007. *In Search of Social Democracy: Responses to Crisis and Modernization*. Manchester: Manchester University Press.

Cramme, Olaf, and Patrick Diamond, eds. 2012. *After the Third Way: The Future of Social Democracy in Europe*. London: I.B. Taurus.

Cronin, James, George Ross, and James Shoch, eds. 2011. *What's Left of the Left?* Durham: Duke University Press.

Gamble, Andrew, and Tony Wright, eds. 1999. *The New Social Democracy*. London: Blackwell.

Johnston, Richard. 2008. Polarized Pluralism in the Canadian Party System. *Canadian Journal of Political Science* 41, 4: 815-34.

Kitschelt, Herbert. 1994. *The Transformation of European Social Democracy*. New York: Cambridge University Press.

Merkel, Wolfgang, Alexander Petring, Christian Henkes, and Christoph Egle. 2008. *Social Democracy in Power: The Capacity to Reform*. London: Routledge.

Meyer, Thomas. 2007. *The Theory of Social Democracy*. Cambridge: Polity Press.

PART 1

SETTING THE STAGE

1

Party History and Electoral Fortunes, 1961-2003

LYNDA ERICKSON and DAVID LAYCOCK

Understanding the contemporary form and place of the New Democratic Party in the Canadian party system requires some knowledge of its historical background and the organizational modernization that it has undertaken. In this chapter, in order to assist in the appreciation of key internal and external pressures that currently shape the party, we trace its history prior to the leadership of Jack Layton. In the following chapter, we examine the party's history under Layton's leadership and the changes that led to its important breakthrough election of 2011. In Chapter 3, we consider the more specific history of the party in Quebec, and in Chapter 4, we look at the modernization of the party's infrastructure and its approach to election campaigns.

We begin this chapter by looking at the roots of the NDP and its early decades as a party and then tracing its electoral record to its high point in the 1988 federal election. We then discuss the background and results of the disastrous election of 1993 and conclude with an account of the decade of struggle that preceded Layton's 2003 leadership victory.

The Roots of the NDP: The Co-operative Commonwealth Federation

The NDP was formed in 1961 in response to the electoral decline of its social democratic predecessor, the Co-operative Commonwealth Federation. The new party was designed to give social democracy a more solid electoral footing by reconstituting the old CCF and anchoring it more firmly in the support of organized labour (Archer 1990). The origins of the CCF itself were in the Great Depression and in socialist principles that opposed the capitalist system (Young 1969). Created in 1932 as a federal socialist party, the CCF incorporated labour and agrarian interests, both of which suffered particularly severe economic hardship during the Depression. The party won 7 seats (with 9 percent of the popular vote) in the first general election it contested in 1935, and, by the 1945 general election, it had increased its winnings to 28 seats (and 16 percent of the popular vote).[1] Considering the party founders' high hopes and the far more impressive electoral endeavours of socialist parties in many other Western democracies between 1930 and 1945 (Przeworski and Sprague 1986; Berman 2006), these were disappointing results.

CCF support was highly regionalized from the outset, with its success largely concentrated in western Canada.[2] Its relationship with organized labour was not as strong as was that enjoyed by socialist parties in Britain and Western Europe, and CCF support from unionized workers was not very high at the polls.[3] Moreover, support among agrarian voters, while solid in some areas, did not constitute a growing constituency in the postwar period. With its electoral base narrow in regional terms, and its limited appeal to unionized workers, in the decade following the 1945 election the party's popular vote gradually declined.

The CCF began as an explicitly socialist party committed to wholesale economic change (including extensive nationalization of economic enterprises and economic planning on a broad scale) as well as generous social programs (including a universal health care system) (Young 1969). However, by the 1950s the party's focus turned more towards generous social programs, extensive business regulation, and progressive taxation and away from the eradication of capitalism. Yet, notwithstanding the CCF's shifting policy instrument choice, success at the polls was elusive.

The CCF officially recast its party principles in 1956 to emphasize the moderate character of its social democratic agenda and to expand its popular appeal. Entitled the Winnipeg Declaration of Principles of the Co-operative Commonwealth Federation, this reformation of the party's principles had little apparent effect at the polls (Morton 1977). By 1958, the party was reduced to 8 seats in the House of Commons as its vote dropped below 10 percent. Shortly after, a newly reconstituted central labour organization, the Canadian Labour Congress (CLC), proposed to the CCF that they jointly create a new political formation for the advancement of social reform. The

CCF accepted the invitation and undertook the organizational work to create a new party (Archer 1990; Knowles 1961; Morton 1977). In 1961, the founding convention of the new party adopted a name (the New Democratic Party) and a constitution that has stayed largely intact ever since.

The New Party, 1961-88

Two major objectives drove the formation of the new party. The first was to create a more contemporary image of the party, portraying it as no longer mired in the context of the 1930s but, rather, as prepared to confront the issues posed by postwar economic development and prosperity. The second objective was to intensify the party's embrace of organized labour and, thereby, to attract the votes of more union members.[4] To boost the party's connection to organized labour, the NDP Constitution provides for the direct affiliation of labour unions, giving them a powerful direct voice in party decision-making structures.[5] Such affiliation was also offered by the CCF, and, like the CCF's, the NDP's constitution includes provisions to prevent union domination. However, while the CCF made affiliation possible, the NDP directed much more energy towards encouraging it. The party did not meet its early expectations in this regard, but it was more successful than the CCF (Archer 1990). Still, even though the party was designed to provide special status to unions, as Jansen and Young (2009, 662) observe, unions have "never dominated the New Democrats to the extent that was the case in the UK or Australia."

Programmatically, the NDP continued the social democratic direction set by the CCF. Following the pattern of social democratic parties in other countries, it rejected the widespread nationalization of industry and a centrally planned economy in favour of a Keynesian welfare state that would promote employment, establish redistributive tax policies, and create a strong social safety net (Carroll 2005). As described in Chapter 5 (Laycock, this volume), the NDP's ideological core was very similar to that of the CCF, with priority given to the concepts of equality, democracy, and solidarity, along with an evolving conception of an activist state.

The 1961 transition from a rurally oriented to a more labour-oriented party would have been much harder for the NDP had its founding convention not selected T.C. Douglas as its first leader. Douglas had been Saskatchewan's premier from 1944 until 1961, when he stepped down to run for the federal party's leadership. As a premier from Saskatchewan he knew rural Canada well, but he also had an unusually strong – and social democratic – appreciation of labour issues. In Saskatchewan, his imported senior bureaucratic corps implemented what was, in the late 1940s, North America's most union-friendly labour legislation (Brennan 1984). Douglas was also a gifted orator, brought a reputation for good governance, and, despite his background as a Baptist preacher, was widely respected by the party's intellectual and industrial union wings as well as by those from the social gospel movement.

Although no major electoral breakthrough materialized in the years immediately following its creation, the NDP did appear to benefit from the exercise of reformation. It gained increasing organizational and financial support from unions and reversed the trend of declining popularity faced by its predecessor. However, as with affiliation, the party's appeal to union members was a disappointment. As Archer (1990) points out, the level of support at the polls from individual union members was not much more than it had been in the old CCF days.

Before the end of its first decade, the party faced a major internal ideological challenge. A strong left-wing faction surfaced to advocate a more radical agenda for the party, which, it believed, had to address the threat that American investment posed to the Canadian economy. This faction, which adopted the moniker "Waffle Movement," called for an independent socialist Canada and nominated its own candidate, James Laxer, for the party leadership in 1971. Laxer survived on the leadership ballot until the fourth (and final) round, when he was defeated by David Lewis. Considered too radical by the leadership of the party, the Waffle was ordered by a vote of the Ontario Provincial Council to disband as an organization within the Ontario NDP. The group decided to leave the NDP altogether to form its own socialist party (Bakan and Murton 2006).

Notwithstanding the internal dissention posed by the Waffle and the disappointing levels of support from individual union members, the NDP vote remained robust compared to that of its predecessor. By the 1980s, the party had increased its share of the popular vote by half, and for the three elections held during that decade it attracted 20 percent of the national popular vote (see Figure 1.1). Yet, given how the single-member district plurality (SMDP), or first-past-the-post, electoral system tends to over-reward front-running parties and to penalize third parties whose votes are not sufficiently concentrated, the NDP struggled to win seats. From 1962 to 1988, the ratio of seats it gained to the proportion of votes it won averaged just over 50 percent.

FIGURE 1.1
CCF-NDP popular vote, 1935-88

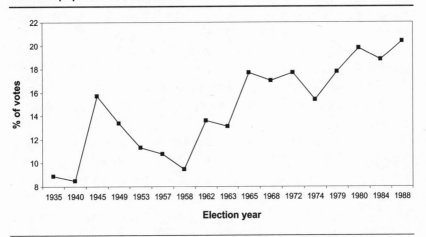

Reminiscent of its predecessor's experience, the NDP's electoral successes were not uniform across the country. By the late 1980s, the NDP, like the CCF, still attracted relatively few votes in Quebec and Atlantic Canada and was especially strong in western provinces.[6] On the other hand, in vote-rich Ontario, the NDP improved considerably on the record of the CCF, averaging 20 percent of the popular vote – double that achieved by the CCF over its lifetime. This gave the party a visible Ontario presence in the House of Commons and a more national image. Moreover, given the proportionate size of the Ontario electorate, the party's national vote was now considerably improved by its success in Ontario. Yet the NDP was still disproportionately a western party. The electoral system's tendency to exacerbate regionalism in party support meant that the NDP caucus in the House of Commons had a distinctly western Canadian image, despite its having only one leader from the west. In the three federal elections held in the 1980s, while the party received just 41 percent of its votes from western Canada, 71 percent of its seats were in western constituencies.

For much of the period prior to the 1993 election, the party's programmatic direction positioned the NDP in a relatively discrete place on the left of the federal party spectrum (see Chapter 5). The Liberals and Progressive Conservatives tended to converge at the centre, as is widely expected of major parties in SMDP systems (Downs 1957; Grofman 2004). The Liberal Party, which governed for twenty-two of the thirty-one years between 1962 and 1993, was often characterized as adopting popular policies that had been initiated by the NDP (Pétry 1995). The strategic problem that this created for the NDP was only partly solved by the party's regional strength in western Canada and its populist appeal to "ordinary Canadians."

By the 1980s, a set of more general challenges had emerged for social democratic parties (Cronin, Ross, and Shoch 2011; Merkel et al. 2008; Kitschelt 1994; Sassoon 2000), Western governments were registering persistent deficits and accumulating large debts while their economies faced mounting international competition as a result of globalization. In this context, criticisms of the expense of welfare state social programs gained political traction. As political discourse across many Western democracies shifted to the right, the commitment of social democratic parties to social protection and generous welfare state policies led to their being particular targets of criticism.

In Canada, there were some quarters in which the rhetoric of welfare state crisis was evident;[7] however, on the electoral stage, attacks on social programs had not yet become prominent in party discourse. Even Brian Mulroney, whose Progressive Conservative (PC) Party harboured more conservative instincts than did the Liberal Party, described social spending as a "sacred trust" in the 1984 election campaign (Bashevkin 2002).[8] And, during the debate about the Free Trade Agreement (FTA) with the United States, which dominated the 1988 election, Mulroney worked hard to dispel the argument that the FTA threatened social programs (Johnston et al. 1992). Moreover, while the PC Party won that election, the NDP won more MPs and popular vote than ever before.

From Boom to Bust, 1988-93

While the 1988 election marked a high point in the federal NDP's history as a competitive party, its results were both a success and a disappointment. The party attracted proportionately more voters (20.4 percent) and won more seats (43) than ever before, but it had begun its campaign with considerably higher expectations. In 1987, the party had topped the polls for a number of months. Its popularity had declined by the time the election was called, but it still continued to record strong showings in the polls (see Figure 1.2).

With a weakened and unpopular leader at the helm of the Liberal Party,[9] when the 1988 election writ was dropped the NDP's prospects for becoming the Official Opposition did not seem unrealistic (Johnston et al. 1992). Moreover, the election was primarily fought over the PC government's Free

Trade Agreement with the United States, an issue with regard to which the NDP might be seen as a natural beneficiary. Historically, the party had been identified with opposition to Canada's economic dependency on the United States, and high-profile party supporters were among the most vocal opponents of the FTA. The agreement was vulnerable to a variety of criticisms, and, by the end of the campaign, opinion opposing it was in a clear majority (ibid.).

However, the Liberals had made this a free-trade election by using their Senate majority to oppose ratification of the FTA, thus forcing the government to go to the polls on the issue. And, while the NDP clearly opposed the agreement during the election campaign, the Liberals placed even more emphasis on their anti-FTA position. In the end it was the Liberals, not the NDP, who reaped the greatest benefit from public opposition to the agreement (Johnston et al. 1992). The governing PCs profited from the split opposition and formed a majority government with 43 percent of the popular vote. The NDP's efforts to bolster its own support by focusing on social policy and its popular leader, Ed Broadbent, were only partly successful. The Liberals outpolled the NDP by 12 percentage points and won almost twice as many seats.[10]

Shortly after the 1988 election, a disappointed Ed Broadbent resigned as leader. In December 1989, at a closely fought leadership convention, Audrey McLaughlin became the first woman to lead a national party in Canada. Following the convention the party rebounded in popularity, and, by the end of 1990, it again topped the opinion polls, with over 35 percent of decided respondents supporting the NDP (Environics Institute 1990-99). Its new leader attracted more positive ratings for her leadership than did either Prime Minister Brian Mulroney or the newly elected leader of the Liberal Party, Jean Chrétien. For the first time ever, the party won a federal seat in Quebec in Chambly in a 1990 by-election.[11] Once more, however, the party's popularity faded as an election approached. Indeed, as Figure 1.2 dramatically illustrates, by the summer of 1993, the party was headed into single-digit territory.

Decline in party support at the federal level was coincident with dropping support at the provincial level, especially in Ontario, where the NDP government was under siege. Having been elected unexpectedly in September 1990,[12] Bob Rae's NDP government soon had to deal with the effects that a major recession was having on provincial finances (Tanguay 1997; Walkom 1994). Following an initial series of government missteps and embarrassments, the NDP presented its first ever provincial budget in 1991.

FIGURE 1.2
Party popularity, 1988-93

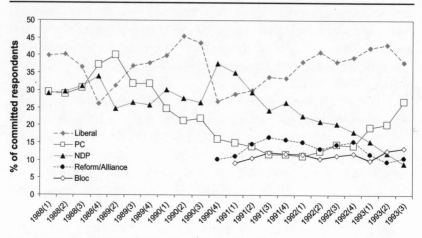

Source: Environics Institute, Focus Canada surveys, 1988-93.

With its aggressively Keynesian approach and substantial deficit, the budget was very controversial. By 1992, the increasing provincial deficit, a growing government debt, deepening criticism of its economic policies from the financial community and in the media, and sliding public support turned the government's focus towards budget cutbacks (McBride 2005; Tanguay 1997; Schwartz 1994).[13] Its controversial Social Contract, adopted in 1993, imposed a public-sector wage freeze.[14] This caused further internal party conflict and alienated major constituencies of the party, especially elements of organized labour (Jenson and Mahon 1995; Schwartz 1994). In July 1993, the provincial party's support in the polls had dropped to a mere 15 percent (Environics Institute 1990-99).

The Constitutional Conundrum

At the federal level, the situation the NDP faced was further complicated by two other factors: constitutional politics and the appearance of the new, western-based Reform Party. The constitutional politics were fought in two rounds, each of which created internal schisms in the NDP. The first round concerned the Meech Lake Accord. This accord was negotiated by the PC government and the provinces in 1987 in an attempt to meet Quebec's concerns about the constitutional changes of 1982. It proposed a number of changes to the Constitution, including recognition of Quebec as a distinct society and a revised constitutional amending formula. The Meech Lake Accord was agreed to by all provincial premiers, including the only NDP premier at the time, Howard Pawley from Manitoba. It was subsequently endorsed by the federal NDP. Partly stimulated by Quebec's support for the agreement, this endorsement reflected the party's recognition, ratified at its 1987 convention, of Quebec's "distinct status" (Cooke 2004). Initially, the accord aroused little public attention or animosity (Reid 1991); however, after the 1988 election, serious opposition began to develop. This opposition was reflected within the NDP, and one of those opposed was the soon-to-be elected leader, Audrey McLaughlin (Whitehorn 1992).[15] By the time the accord died in 1990, the NDP, during its convention, had called for a reopening of the deal, albeit while still supporting Quebec's demands for constitutional change (McLeod 1994).

A key ramification of the Meech Lake Accord's failure, with regard to the party system, was the formation of a separatist party for Quebec – the Bloc Québécois (BQ). Led by former Conservative cabinet minister Lucien Bouchard, the BQ was formed by a small group of Conservative and Liberal Quebec MPs who left their parties to promote Quebec sovereignty and Quebec interests at the federal level. Although the BQ initially refrained from calling itself a political party, in 1991 its founding convention created an official party, with an organizational infrastructure and a party creed.

The politics of the Meech Lake Accord created serious internal differences for the federal NDP. But the next round of constitutional politics resulted in even worse consequences for the party's public support.[16] This second round focused on the Charlottetown Accord, which was designed to replace the Meech Lake Accord in an attempt to appease anger in Quebec at the failure of the latter. The Charlottetown Accord was a complicated document that combined recognition of Quebec as a "distinct society" with a number of institutional changes, a social charter, limits on federal spending power, and a statement on Canada's fundamental values. The involvement of three NDP provincial premiers – Bob Rae from Ontario, Mike Harcourt from British Columbia, and Roy Romanow from Saskatchewan – meant that the negotiations that led to the Charlottetown Accord were more sensitive to NDP concerns. The role of NDP premiers in the constitutional process placed pressure on the federal party to approve the deal. Both the party's Federal Council and its federal caucus endorsed the agreement soon after it was concluded.

As with the Meech Lake Accord, public opinion initially supported the Charlottetown Accord, but this was not sustained. Right after the signing of the latter, opinion polls registered public support for the agreement at close to 60 percent (Environics Institute 1990-99).[17] However, an intense national debate on the accord ensued during the referendum campaign (Johnston et al. 1996b), and, ultimately, the Charlottetown Accord was defeated by a national vote of 55 to 45 percent. During the referendum campaign, the NDP was in the uncomfortable position of being on the same side as its two (larger) competitors from the 1988 election, most especially the governing PCs, led by the then highly unpopular Mulroney.[18] This was the side that came to be characterized as representing the "establishment" position. Some of the NDP's social movement supporters, most notably in the women's movement, became vocal opponents of the accord and were particularly disappointed in the party's position.[19] For some, the populist and protest bona fides of the party were put into question by the whole referendum experience. As Howard Pawley (1994, 181) describes it: "The rejection by the Canadian public of the Charlottetown Accord harmed the NDP more than any other party because we were seen as part of the elite of political, business, media and labour leaders."

The Reform Party Challenge
The formation of the Reform Party in 1987 posed another challenge for the NDP. The Reform Party combined regional grievances, including demands for a stronger federal voice for western Canada and resentment towards any special arrangements for Quebec, with a set of populist proposals for national institutions, a neoconservative economic agenda, and moral conservatism (Laycock 2001; Harrison 1995; Flanagan 1995). Reform contested its first election in 1988; however, having run candidates in fewer than a quarter of the constituencies in the country, and with the free-trade issue deflecting attention away from the regional alienation issue, Reform barely registered on the electoral rolls. Nationally, it won just 2 percent of the overall popular vote and no seats. Even in the west, the party only received 7 percent of the vote. Shortly after the election, however, it won a federal by-election in Alberta and its popularity in western Canada grew quickly.

The Reform Party was particularly attractive to disillusioned western supporters of the PCs. They had previously supported the PC Party because it seemed more sensitive to western concerns than the Liberals and more willing to reduce the scope of state intervention in the economy. These western PC supporters had become disenchanted by what they saw as the PC government's increasing preoccupation with Quebec and central Canadian concerns and its unwillingness to shrink the state and lower taxes (Erickson 1995). But western grievances were not limited to voters on the right. For the NDP, with much of its voter base and three-quarters of its MPs from the west, Reform's regional appeal was a real concern. In addition, Reform's populism represented an electoral threat. Based on a critique of traditional politics and traditional parties, this populism was yet another means by which Reform could draw support away from the NDP even though Reform's ideological location on socio-economic issues might otherwise seem to have little attraction for potential NDP voters. During the referendum campaign, Reform was the only party outside Quebec to oppose the Charlottetown Accord. Party leader Preston Manning was persuaded by policy advisors Stephen Harper and Tom Flanagan to break with the consensus among the "old parties" and to contend that the accord was too ambiguous on some key issues, too willing to grant "unequal" status and powers to Quebec, and left too many issues for further negotiation. Reform argued that a vote for the accord was a vote for an unknown set of future arrangements and a federal system tilted towards Quebec interests.[20] Initially, the party's position in opposition to the accord made it look as though Reform were "swimming against the stream." However, by the end of the referendum campaign, public distrust of the agreement had grown, in no small part because Reform had successfully characterized it as a bargain of the elite. This experience in the referendum campaign gained Reform visibility on the national stage and cemented its image as a populist party prepared to stand up to the establishment.

The Nearly Dead Party: The 1993 Election and the Politics of Bewilderment

The election of 1993 was held in the aftermath of the highly divisive Charlottetown Accord referendum campaign and in the context of a weak economy. Following a severe recession in 1990-91, economic recovery was slow, and even by 1993 unemployment levels remained above 11 percent through most of that election year (Gower 1996). Following their 1988 election victory, the governing Progressive Conservatives had imposed a highly visible and unpopular goods and services tax to replace a manufacturers' tax, and they expanded the FTA to include Mexico. And, although they implemented a number of conservative economic policies (including the privatization of select government corporations) and expanded the deregulation of business activity, they had presided over a growing government debt. As a result, the party was vulnerable to many-sided attacks on its economic record. The PCs' past claims that they would produce jobs and reduce the deficit now rang hollow for many voters (Frizzell, Pammet, and Westell 1994).

In the wake of disastrous polling numbers that put his personal and his party's popularity at historic lows, Brian Mulroney stepped down as PC leader in early 1993. The PCs chose a relative newcomer to federal politics from western Canada, Kim Campbell, to lead it into an imminent election. She had only been in Parliament since 1988 but had held three different cabinet posts and, given her breezy and articulate style, was seen as a potentially charismatic leader. Shortly after her selection, PC popularity increased and the party decided to focus its election campaign on her leadership and her "different way of doing politics" (Woolstencroft 1994).

In the 1993 election campaign, much of the rhetoric and debate focused on the economy and government deficit and debt. The Reform Party struck a hard line on the debt and deficits, promising to cut back social programs and taxes while reducing the deficit in three years. The PCs now faced a convincing challenge from the right. They also focused on deficit reduction but set a five-year target for deficit elimination. The Liberals took a classically centrist position, proposing a more moderate pace for deficit reduction and emphasizing job creation as key features of their economic agenda. Even the NDP felt obliged to address the deficit in its campaign (Gidengil 1994). But, while the party's campaign literature described the debt as "a real problem for Canada" and encouraged elimination of government waste, it identified "getting more Canadians working" as the primary solution to the debt problem (NDP 1993). Its election campaign focused on job creation strategies, protection of social programs, and the cancellation of the North American Free Trade Agreement as a means of attacking deindustrialization in Canada.

Within Quebec, the national question dominated much of the campaign as the BQ presented the electorate with an explicitly separatist party that was, for the first time, a credible federal political force that placed the nationalist project in the forefront of its agenda (Bernard 1994). Given the strong separatist sentiments generated by the failure of the Meech Lake Accord and the subsequent negative response in Quebec to the Charlottetown Accord, the BQ was campaigning under favourable circumstances. The popularity of leader Lucien Bouchard in Quebec was crucial to the BQ's popularity (Blais et al. 1995). The NDP had received its highest vote percentage ever in the province in the 1988 election (14 percent) and had been buoyed by its by-election success in Chambly in 1989. But, by the 1993 campaign, the NDP was back in a virtual electoral wilderness in Quebec. The election results in the province confirmed its weakness: only 1.5 percent of Quebec voters cast a ballot for the NDP.

The 1993 election campaign was characterized by a high degree of regionalism. The BQ only contested seats in Quebec, creating a distinct election dynamic in that province, while the Reform Party, although it had nominated candidates in 70 percent of the ridings in the country, ran no candidates in Quebec and did not run a full slate in three of the four Atlantic provinces (Ellis and Archer 1994).[21]

The election produced dramatic results for the party system. The governing PC Party went from holding 153 seats to winning just 2. The NDP was reduced from 43 to a mere 9 seats, three short of the 12 required for official party status in the House of Commons. While the Liberal Party was the overall victor, winning 60 percent of the seats and majority government, it did so with just 41 percent of the popular vote and a regionally narrow base of support. The most dramatic and system-restructuring inroads were made by the two new parties: Reform and the Bloc Québécois. By taking 54 out of 75 seats in Quebec, the Bloc became the Official Opposition in the House of Commons. The Reform Party's capture of most of the previous PC and some previous NDP votes in western Canada gave it 52 seats, all but 1 in the West.

In popular vote, the NDP dropped from 20 percent to just under 7 percent and to fifth place among the parties. In most ridings, the party failed to achieve the 15 percent of the popular vote required for local party associations to receive financial reimbursement from Elections Canada (Whitehorn 1994). The party's 9 seats were all in the west: 5 in Saskatchewan, 2 in British Columbia, and 1 each in Manitoba and Yukon. For the first time in its history, the NDP won no seats east of Manitoba. In its western heartland, the Reform Party had successfully wrested away the populist label once identified with the CCF/NDP (see Laycock, Chapter 5, this volume; Laycock 2001).

Analyses of the vote movements from 1988 to 1993 indicate that former NDP supporters were most likely to move to the Liberal Party. Using data from the 1993 Canadian Election Study, Johnston et al. (1994) find that 29 percent of those who voted NDP in 1988 voted Liberal in 1993. Surprisingly, given their distance from each other on the left-right spectrum, 13 percent of those who voted NDP in 1988 voted Reform in 1993.[22] Gidengil (1994) examines potential NDP voters outside Quebec – that is, survey respondents who identified with the NDP or leaned towards it, who had previously voted for it, or who had indicated an intention to vote NDP federally or provincially. She finds that, although Liberals were more likely than Reform to attract potential NDP voters, Reform attracted "as many potential NDP voters as did the NDP itself" (14). Still, the NDP was certainly not the largest source of Reform votes: "Reformers were mainly old Conservatives" (Johnston et al. 1996a, 5).

Such a dramatic decline in NDP vote meant that the party lost support in all quarters, including its core. Regionally, the party's proportion of the popular vote dropped most dramatically in British Columbia and Ontario. In British Columbia, its vote fell from 37 percent of the provincial vote to under 16 percent, a loss of more than half its proportion of the popular vote (see Table 1.1). In Ontario, which had contributed more than 35 percent of the party's overall vote in 1988, the NDP lost 70 percent of its proportion of the popular vote, dropping to 6 percent. In issue terms, the swing away from the NDP was greatest among those who showed the most support for some of the major NDP positions: anti-continentalism, being less concerned about the deficit, and being less opposed to union power (Johnston et al. 1994). Part of the reason that the party's greatest drop was among these regional and issue groups is, of course, that these were where its previous support was highest. However, this huge overall vote decline meant that the NDP's core had been hollowed out and that it faced an enormous rebuilding task.

TABLE 1.1
Change in NDP popular vote, 1988-93, by province

Province	% of vote (1998)	% of vote (1993)	% change (1988-93)
British Columbia	37.9	15.5	−21.5
Alberta	17.4	4.1	−13.3
Saskatchewan	44.2	26.6	−17.6
Manitoba	21.3	16.7	−4.6
Ontario	20.1	6.0	−14.1
Quebec	14.4	1.5	−12.9
New Brunswick	9.3	4.9	−4.4
Nova Scotia	11.4	6.8	−4.2
Prince Edward Island	7.5	5.2	−2.3
Newfoundland	12.4	3.5	−8.9

Regional Breakthrough, 1996-2000

The 1993 election substantially altered the dynamic of the party system and, with it, the competitive environment faced by the NDP. Regionalism had long been a characteristic of Canadian federal politics. However, with the Reform Party trumpeting the demands of western Canada and displaying an anti-Quebec bias (Laycock 2001), with the BQ focusing only on the interests and grievances of Quebec, and with the Liberal Party having 55 percent of its seats in Ontario, regionalism intensified dramatically (Carty, Cross, and Young 2000). In ideological terms, the Reform Party's success and the collapse of a moderate centre-right party meant that much of the momentum in the system had shifted to the right. Reform now posed the major challenge to the Liberal Party outside Quebec.

Confronted with virtual annihilation, the NDP began a process of internal examination and debate about its future directions. It would have been bad enough if the party had only to face regaining populist credentials from the Reform Party in its western Canadian stronghold; however, it also had to increase somehow its appeal relative to an ideologically centrist Liberal Party that campaigned on many of the NDP's natural issues, especially support for medicare. The party faced a struggle for recognition and support in a crowded electoral field (Carty, Cross, and Young 2000; Blais et al. 2000).

An early response to the party's circumstances came with the 1994 resignation of its leader, Audrey McLaughlin. In the past, NDP leaders had remained in office for long periods of time and, unlike those of the Liberals and Conservatives, were not replaced on the heels of electoral failure. However, the 1993 results soon drew strong criticism of the leader and her staff (Whitehorn 1997), prompting McLaughlin's decision to resign. In choosing her replacement, the party adopted a variant of a new and apparently more democratic method of leadership selection – direct primaries – with which some provincial parties had experimented. Direct primaries, in which party members vote directly for leadership candidates, had first been used by the Parti Québécois in the 1980s and then by provincial Liberal and/or PC parties in seven provinces (Carty and Blake 1999; Cross 1996).

After the NDP's 1989 federal leadership convention, the party had explored the possibility of changing its leadership selection process but had opted to retain its traditional convention system, with delegates elected from constituency associations and affiliated unions (Whitehorn 1995). After its 1993 electoral debacle, the party's need to recruit more members and to refresh its public image gave it an increased incentive to add more direct democracy to its selection process, as did its need to challenge Reform for populist credentials. Accordingly, the federal council of the party added a new dimension to the leadership contest in the form of non-binding regional and labour primaries that were to limit which leadership candidates would be placed on the convention ballot.[23]

This system was in place for the party's 1995 leadership contest. The primaries eliminated one of the four initial candidates, but, ultimately, the primary vote bore little resemblance to the final outcome. In the primaries, Lorne Nystrom, a Saskatchewan MP from 1968 to 1993, won 45 percent of the votes. Svend Robinson, a BC MP since 1979, won 32 percent. And Alexa McDonough, a former long-time leader of the Nova Scotia New Democrats with no federal legislative experience, won 18 percent (Funke n.d.). Nevertheless, at the convention the party selected McDonough. On the first and only ballot, McDonough won 33 percent of the vote, and Nystrom, with just 30 percent, was forced to drop out. Robinson had come first with 38 percent of the vote but decided McDonough would prevail on a second ballot and conceded the leadership before the next and final ballot could be held.

Beyond replacing the leadership, other demands for "renewal" and change came from all sides of the party spectrum. These were accompanied by explorations inside and outside the party for possible programmatic and organizational responses to the disastrous electoral decline (Berlin and Aster 2001; Langdon and Cross 1994; McLeod 1994; Rebick 2001; Whitehorn 1997; Laxer 1997). In late 1993, the party struck a renewal committee. It was co-chaired by Dawn Black, a former BC NDP MP and long-time party activist, and François Côté, a party activist from Chambly, Quebec. Regional renewal conferences throughout 1994 and early 1995 attracted many activists and party notables, and wide-ranging debate about policy and strategy ensued. Discussion papers were circulated, discussed at regional conferences, and debated at three major party events in Edmonton, Halifax, and Winnipeg, respectively.

The renewal committee produced three documents from this process, all presented to the October 1995 federal party convention. A short principles and mission statement stressed the party's continuing commitment to the core values of equality, democracy, community, cooperation, and (a more recent entry) sustainability.[24] It affirmed the NDP's membership in a "greater national and international movement that seeks to challenge the dominant political agenda of market globalization and resulting environmental, social and economic problems" (Martin and Riche 1996, 110).[25]

Another document proposed new internal party governance, policy development processes, and financial structures. It sought to "renew [the NDP's] founding partnership with Labour and build alliances and friendships with organizations who share [its] principles and [its] goals" (111). Changes to party policy development were to be guided by "the concepts of accountability and grass-roots control" (113), with enhanced roles for both riding associations and a national policy committee that would circulate new policy initiatives back to riding associations and build consensus across the party prior to its conventions (115-18).[26] The review committee also recommended that the federal party retain existing revenue-sharing agreements with provincial sections while allowing the federal party to raise funds directly from all members who had joined through provincial sections.[27] Finally, a policy document emphasized new initiatives in economic and social policy that could respond to what the party identified as new challenges resulting from globalization.

While the latter document provided a kind of framework for the 1997 election platform, the "mission statement" and party governance proposal had little impact on the party's regular operations, despite being adopted at the 1995 convention. The selection of a new leader at this convention effectively overshadowed the renewal committee reports and issues (NDP 1995; Dawn Black, personal communication, 9 August 2012). A major CLC/NDP review committee report in May 1996 reaffirmed the trade union federation's support for the party and its principles. It recommended more regular meetings between the federal NDP leadership and the CLC executive council as well as continuing liaisons with provincial New Democrat parties and governments. The report insisted on the trade union movement's status as "one of the founding partners" of the NDP, and it proposed a variety of other means through which labour could assert its political voice through interaction with the NDP (Martin and Riche 1996, 6-21).

In the elections that followed McDonough's selection, the NDP experienced a regional breakthrough in Atlantic Canada and regained official status in the House of Commons. However, it continued to struggle for national visibility (Nevitte et al. 2000) and votes. Just prior to the 1997 election, conditions seemed ripe for a substantial improvement in NDP fortunes. Unemployment had declined 2 percentage points since the 1993 election, but at 9 percent it remained close to double digits. The Liberals seemed vulnerable to critiques from the left (ibid.), having made cuts to unemployment benefits and restrained transfers to the provinces (which affected a number of social programs) (Maslove and Moore 1997). This gave rise to

TABLE 1.2
NDP votes and seats in the 1997 and 2000 elections, by province
and territory

Province/Territory	1997		2000	
	% of vote	No. of seats	% of vote	No. of seats
British Columbia	18	3	11	2
Alberta	6	–	5	–
Saskatchewan	31	5	26	2
Manitoba	23	4	21	4
Ontario	11	–	8	1
Quebec	2	–	2	–
New Brunswick	18	2	12	1
Nova Scotia	30	6	24	3
PEI	15	–	9	–
Newfoundland	22	–	13	–
NWT	21	–	27	–
Yukon	29	1	32	–
Nunavut	–	–	32	–
TOTAL	11	21	9	13

criticisms that the Liberals had not protected social programs as promised in their 1993 campaign. Between 1993 and 1997, the Liberal government had prioritized deficit reduction to a remarkable degree, thereby defusing the effectiveness of the deficit critique from the right.

Despite the apparent vulnerability of the Liberals to the left and the NDP focus on jobs and cuts to social programs (Whitehorn 1997), growth in NDP support was modest in most of the country, with the exception of Atlantic Canada. In Atlantic Canada, the party vote grew to 24 percent, yielding 8 seats in a region that had theretofore been no more than single-digit territory for the NDP. In the rest of the country, however, the party vote did not quite reach 10 percent of the popular vote. Nationally, the party won just 11 percent of the vote and 24 seats (see Table 1.2).

In 1997, the NDP had been unable to take advantage of Liberal vulner-abilities. Analyses of data on voter responses to the Liberals led Nevitte et al. (2000, 103) to conclude that "voters who were dissatisfied with the Liberals' performance in office were no more likely to turn to the NDP than those who were satisfied." Moreover, although the NDP did gain an addi-tional 4 seats in the west, it was not able to challenge Reform's considerable success in that region.[28] In seat-rich Ontario, the NDP's 11 percent of the popular vote yielded no seats.

Still Struggling, 2000-03
The NDP's slight electoral improvement in 1997 was reversed in the 2000 election. Its proportion of the overall vote fell to 8.5 percent, and its seat count dropped to 13, barely providing it with official party status. The configuration of the party system had been altered just prior to the 2000 election, when the Canadian Alliance was formed through the Reform Party's attempt to unite the right by attracting PC votes (Ellis 2001). While the Alliance did attract some former PC members, the PC Party itself shunned this effort at union and mounted its own national campaign for the 2000 election. The Alliance was successful in winning more support than the Reform Party had in 1997, gaining in both the west and Ontario, although its overall seat gain was only 6.

In this crowded electoral context, the NDP struggled yet again for attention during the election campaign. Its regional appeal had disappeared, and its efforts to build on the gains of 1997 failed. The party lost support in every province, but its losses were highest in Nova Scotia and Saskatchewan (3 seats in each province). The NDP campaign's strong focus on health care had been forced to compete with the Liberal campaign's emphasis on keeping the public system from being privatized by the Alliance (Nadeau, Pétry, and Bélanger 2010), and, in the end, the Liberals succeeded in attracting much of the health care vote at the NDP's expense (Blais et al. 2002). The party was concerned that progressive voters, fearing an Alliance breakthrough, would vote strategically for the Liberals. However, the apparent effects of strategic voting on the NDP were not significant. In their analysis of strategic voting in the 2000 election, Blais et al. (2002) conclude that, outside Quebec, the NDP's overall popular vote would have been only 1 percentage point higher had strategic considerations not been at issue.

Having regained party status in the House of Commons in 1997, the NDP barely retained it in 2000. So, after the 2000 election, McDonough launched a second renewal exercise, summarized in a volume that aired the party's various perspectives (Berlin and Aster 2001). This renewal process culminated in the national convention in November 2001. Once again, discussion about internal alterations to party structure and decision-making processes were overshadowed, this time by the New Politics Initiative (NPI) from the party's left. The NPI proposed disbanding the existing party and creating a new one to be driven by closer ties to social movement activists.

The NPI was intended to provide a more outspoken critique of capitalist globalization, give greater attention to environmental issues, and place more emphasis on socialist organizing and education than electoral strategy and efforts (Rebick 2001; Stanford 2011; Stanford and Robinson 2001).[29]

As an alternative to the NPI, McDonough championed a "revitalized federal party" that would pursue both a serious electoral mandate and social change. It would be a stand-alone federal party, with a new relationship with organized labour based on "one member, one vote" and intent on creating a broadened tent for progressive forces under NDP leadership (McDonough 2001). Some voices on the party's centre-right championed the "Third Way" approach, popular among many social democratic strategists elsewhere (Bastow and Martin 2003; Giddens 1999; Hale, Leggett, and Martel 2004; Pierson 2001). In the end, the party officially rejected both NPI and Third Way options at the November 2001 convention. Despite 40 percent delegate support for the NPI option, the party carried on much as before until it replaced Alexa McDonough with Jack Layton in 2003.

Notes

1 An additional seat was won by Agnes MacPhail, who was a member of the party but who won her seat under the banner of the United Farmers of Ontario-Labour.

2 Of the forty-three constituency contests the party won in the 1935, 1940, and 1945 elections, only two were outside the west. These were in the riding of Cape Breton South, Nova Scotia.

3 The close relationship between unions and the British Labour Party was a model in this regard for many Canadian socialists. The level of electoral support that Labour had received from unionized workers since the First World War was well beyond what the CCF ever gained from their counterparts in Canada.

4 Ever since the mid-1930s, the Liberal Party had harvested more union and working-class votes than the CCF.

5 The Constitution also provided for the affiliation of other groups, such as farmers' organizations and cooperatives that agree to abide by the Constitution and principles of the party.

6 The exception here was Alberta, where neither the CCF nor the NDP gained much support. The party waited until 1988 to win one seat there, in the constituency of Edmonton East, and did not gain another until 2008.

7 The Fraser Institute, created in 1974, was an early voice for the neoliberal critique of the welfare state in Canada.

8 For evidence that PC activists were less supportive of social policy issues than their counterparts among the other parties, see Blake (1988).

9 John Turner, the Liberal leader, had faced internal challenges to his party leadership, including one that occurred just six months before the election campaign started.

10 Johnston et al. (1992) and Fraser (1989) suggest that the NDP focused less on the FTA than did the Liberals because the party knew its credibility on economic issues was weak. It preferred to fight the election on social issues and the question of leadership.

11 The candidate was a high-profile consumer advocate, Phil Edmondston.

12 The 1990 election was held fewer than three years after the Liberals had won majority government and, going into the campaign, the Liberals were at 50 percent in the opinion polls. The final tally gave the NDP 38 percent of the popular vote, the Liberals 32 percent, and the PCs 24 percent.

13 According to Environics' polling in March 1992, the NDP was 14 percentage points behind the Liberals in popularity.

14 Although the government attempted to negotiate an agreement with public-sector unions, the short time frame it imposed on the negotiations and the complicated nature of the agreement being sought appeared to doom the exercise from the outset (Tanguay 1997). But some commentators lauded the government's "social contract" (see Schwartz 1994).

15 McLaughlin was elected in a by-election in Yukon in 1989, during which she had promised to oppose the accord because of her concerns about its implications for the North. She voted against the accord in the House of Commons.

16 The exception here may have been among Quebec voters.

17 This was the balance of opinion recorded among respondents who registered a view. There was, however, much uncertainty about the agreement. In the Environics poll, 36 percent of respondents did not express an opinion on the accord.

18 On questions concerning approval of "the way Brian Mulroney is handling his job as Prime Minister," the polls in 1992 were routinely recording approval levels below 15 percent (Environics Institute 1990-99).

19 The National Action Committee on the Status of Women (NAC), the most high-profile feminist organization in the country, officially opposed the accord because of the potential threat it posed to Charter rights and because of the limits it seemed to place on the federal government's spending power. Among Aboriginal groups, support for the accord was distinctly mixed (Johnston et al. 1996b). Organized labour did support the accord, although Johnston et al. found that the endorsement of organized labour had little effect in moving opinion among union members towards support for the accord.

20 Johnston et al. (1996a) also point out that, as a sectionalist party and one that was not supportive of bilingualism, Reform would benefit if the aftermath of the accord's failure was further linguistic tension.

21 In Newfoundland the party nominated candidates in 3 of the province's 7 ridings; in Prince Edward Island it ran just 1 candidate; and in New Brunswick it nominated candidates in 7 of 10 ridings.

22 Nineteen percent of the survey respondents who voted NDP in 1988 either did not vote or voted for a party other than the parties of the four major contestants. In the latter case, the National Party, headed by Canadian nationalist Mel Hurtig, was especially attractive to former NDP voters (Johnston et al. 1994).

23 There was no change to the party Constitution when this new step in leadership selection was added to the process. With no constitutional change, the formal

provisions of this document still allowed delegates at the convention to nominate and, indeed, to select a candidate who did not run in the primaries. This did not occur.

24 For a discussion of these core values in the party's evolving ideology, see Laycock (Chapter 5, this volume).

25 For the full text of this statement, as well as the 1995 review committee's recommendations on party structure and relations, see Martin and Riche (1996, Appendix D).

26 While this review committee recommendation was adopted at the 1995 convention, it is not clear from subsequent party documents or convention proceedings that its practical implementation went very far.

27 This recommendation took years to implement, with full federal party access to provincial members not secured until shortly after the 2008 election.

28 Reform added 9 western seats to its 1993 total.

29 In some ways, this proposal paralleled the formation of the party itself. The NDP was created by the CCF and the CLC when the CCF's electoral results were especially discouraging. It was an effort to strengthen organizational ties with ideological allies. For the CCF, however, the critical allies with whom it wished to strengthen ties were in the labour movement, whereas for the NPI they were among new social movement activists and sympathizers.

References

Archer, Keith. 1990. *Political Choices and Electoral Consequences: A Study of Organized Labour and the New Democratic Party.* Montreal: McGill-Queen's University Press.

Bakan, Abbie, and Philip Murton. 2006. Origins of the International Socialists. *Marxism: A Socialist Annual* 4. http://www.socialisthistory.ca/Docs/History/IS-Origins.htm.

Bashevkin, Sylvia. 2002. *Welfare Hot Buttons: Women, Work, and Social Policy Reform.* Toronto: University of Toronto Press.

Bastow, Steve, and James Martin. 2003. *Third Way Discourse: European Ideologies in the Twentieth Century.* Edinburgh: Edinburgh University Press.

Berlin, Z.D., and Howard Aster. 2001. *What's Left? The New Democratic Party in Renewal.* Oakville, ON: Mosaic Press.

Berman, Sherry. 2006. *The Primacy of Politics: Social Democracy and the Making of Europe's Twentieth Century.* New York: Cambridge University Press.

Bernard, André. 1994. The Bloc Québécois. In Alan Frizzell, Jon H. Pammett, and Anthony Westell, eds., *The Canadian General Election of 1993*, 79-88. Ottawa: Carleton University Press.

Blais, André, Elisabeth Gidengil, Richard Nadeau, and Neil Nevitte. 2002. *Anatomy of a Liberal Victory: Making Sense of the Vote in the 2000 Canadian Election.* Peterborough, ON: Broadview.

Blais, André, Neil Nevitte, Elisabeth Gidengil, Henry Brady, and Richard Johnston. 1995. L'élection fédérale de 1993: Le comportement électoral des Québécois. *Revue québécoise de science politique* 27: 15-49.

Blais, André, Neil Nevitte, Elisabeth Gidengil, and Richard Nadeau. 2000. *Unsteady State: The 1997 Canadian Federal Election.* Don Mills, ON: Oxford University Press.

Blake, Donald E. 1988. Division and Cohesion: The Major Parties. In George Perlin, ed., *Party Democracy in Canada*, 32-53. Scarborough, ON: Prentice-Hall.

Brennan, J.W. 1984. *Building the Cooperative Commonwealth: Essays on the Democratic Socialist Tradition in Canada*. Regina: Canadian Plains Research Centre.

Carroll, William K. 2005. Social Democracy in Neoliberal Times. In William K. Carroll and R.S. Ratner, eds., *Challenges and Perils: Social Democracy in Neoliberal Times*. Halifax: Fernwood.

Carty, R. Kenneth, and Donald E. Blake. 1999. The Adoption of Membership Votes for Choosing Party Leaders: The Experience of Canadian Parties. *Party Politics* 5, 2: 211-24.

Carty, R. Kenneth, William Cross, and Lisa Young. 2000. *Rebuilding Canadian Party Politics*. Vancouver: UBC Press.

Cooke, Murray. 2004. Constitutional Confusion on the Left: The NDP's Position in Canada's Constitutional Debates. Paper presented at the Annual Meetings of the Canadian Political Science Association, Winnipeg, June.

Cronin, James, George Ross, and James Shoch, eds. 2011. *What's Left of the Left?* Durham, NC: Duke University Press.

Cross, William. 1996. Direct Election of Provincial Party Leaders in Canada, 1985-1995: The End of the Leadership Convention? *Canadian Journal of Political Science* 29, 2: 295-315.

Downs, Anthony. 1957. *An Economy Theory of Democracy*. New York: Harper.

Ellis, Faron. 2001. The More Things Change ... The Alliance Campaign. In Jon H. Pammett and Christopher Dornan, eds., *The Canadian General Election of 2000*, 59-90. Toronto: Dundurn.

Ellis, Faron, and Keith Archer. 1994. Reform: Electoral Breakthrough. In Alan Frizzell, Jon H. Pammett, and Anthony Westell, eds., *The Canadian General Election of 1993*, 89-106. Ottawa: Carleton University Press.

Environics Institute. 1990-99. Focus Canada surveys.

Erickson, Lynda. 1995. The 1993 October Election and the Canadian Party System. *Party Politics* 1, 1: 133-43.

Flanagan, Tom. 1995. *Waiting for the Wave: Preston Manning and the Reform Party of Canada*. Toronto: Stoddart.

Fraser, Graham. 1989. *Playing for Keeps: The Making of the Prime Minister, 1988*. Toronto: McClelland and Stewart.

Frizzell, Alan, Jon H. Pammett, and Anthony Westell. 1994. Introduction. In Alan Frizzell, Jon H. Pammett, and Anthony Westell, eds., *The Canadian General Election of 1993*, 1-7. Ottawa: Carleton University Press.

Funke, Alice. n.d. The NDP's Previous Experience with Leadership Primaries. *Pundit's Guide to Canadian Federal Elections*. http://www.punditsguide.ca/2012/01/the-ndps-previous-experience-with-leadership-primaries/.

Giddens, Anthony. 1999. *The Third Way: The Renewal of Social Democracy*. Malden, MA: Polity Press.

Gidengil, Elisabeth. 1994. The NDP and Social Democracy in the 1990s. Paper presented to the Annual Meeting of the Canadian Political Science Association, Calgary, 12 June.

Gower, Dave. 1996. Canada's Unemployment Mosaic in the 1990s. *Perspectives.* Statistics Canada, spring, catalogue no. 75-001-XPE.

Grofman, Bernard. 2004. Downs and Two-Party Convergence. *Annual Review of Political Science* 7: 25-46.

Hale, Sarah, Will Leggett, and Luke Martell, eds. 2004. *The Third Way and Beyond: Criticisms, Futures, Alternatives.* Manchester: Manchester University Press.

Harrison, Trevor. 1995. *Of Passionate Intensity.* Toronto: University of Toronto Press.

Jansen, Harold, and Lisa Young. 2009. Solidarity Forever? The NDP, Organized Labour, and the Changing Face of Party Finance in Canada. *Canadian Journal of Political Science* 42, 3: 657-78.

Jenson, Jane, and Rianne Mahon. 1995. From "Premier Bob" to "Rae Days": The Impasse of the Ontario New Democrats. In Jean-Pierre Beaud and Jean-Guy Prévost, eds., *La social-démocratie en cette fin de siècle,* 149-72. Québec: Presses de l'Université du Québec.

Johnston, Richard, André Blais, Henry E. Brady, and Jean Crête. 1992. *Letting the People Decide: Dynamics of a Canadian Election.* Montreal and Kingston: McGill-Queen's University Press.

Johnston, Richard, André Blais, Henry E. Brady, Elisabeth Gidengil, and Neil Nevitte. 1996a. The 1993 Canadian Election: Realignment, Dealignment or Something Else? Paper presented to the Annual Meeting of the American Political Science Association, San Francisco, 28 August-1 September.

Johnston, Richard, André Blais, Elisabeth Gidengil, and Neil Nevitte. 1996b. *The Challenge of Direct Democracy: The 1992 Canadian Referendum.* Montreal: McGill-Queens University Press.

Johnston, Richard, André Blais, Elisabeth Gidengil, Neil Nevitte, and Henry Brady. 1994. The Collapse of a Party System? The 1993 Canadian General Election. Paper presented to the Annual Meeting of the American Political Science Association, New York, 1-4 September.

Kitschelt, Herbert. 1994. *The Transformation of European Social Democracy.* Cambridge, UK: Cambridge University Press.

Knowles, Stanley. 1961. *The New Party.* Toronto: McClelland and Stewart.

Langdon, Steven, and Victoria Cross, eds. 1994. *As We Come Marching: People, Power and Progressive Politics.* Ottawa: Windsor Works Publications.

Laxer, James. 1997. *In Search of a New Left: Canadian Politics after the Neoconservative Assault.* Toronto: Penguin.

Laycock, David. 2001. *The New Right in Canada: Understanding Reform and Canadian Alliance.* Don Mills, ON: Oxford University Press.

Martin, Richard, and Nancy Riche. 1996. *Report of the CLC-NDP Review Committee.* Ottawa: Canadian Labour Congress.

Maslove, Alan M., and Kevin D. Moore. 1997. From Red Books to Blue Books: Repairing Ottawa's Fiscal House. In Gene Swimmer, ed., *How Ottawa Spends, 1997-1998: Seeing Red – A Liberal Report Card,* 23-50. Ottawa: Carleton University Press.

McBride, Stephen. 2005. If You Don't Know Where You're Going, You'll End Up Somewhere Else: Ideological and Policy Failure in the Ontario NDP. In William

K. Carroll and R.S. Ratner, eds. *Challenges and Perils: Social Democracy in Neoliberal Times*, 25-45. Halifax: Fernwood.

McDonough, Alexa. 2001. A Revitalized Federal Party. In Z. David Berlin and Howard Aster, eds., *What's Left? The New Democratic Party in Renewal*, 72-79. Oakville, ON: Mosaic Press.

McLeod, Ian. 1994. *Under Siege: The Federal NDP in the Nineties*. Toronto: Lorimer.

Merkel, Wolfgang, Alexander Petring, Christian Henkes, and Christoph Egle. 2008. *Social Democracy in Power: The Capacity to Reform*. London: Routledge.

Morton, Desmond. 1977. *NDP: Social Democracy in Canada*. 2nd ed. Toronto: Samuel Stevens.

Nadeau, Richard, François Pétry, and Éric Bélanger. 2010. Issue-Based Strategies in Election Campaigns: The Case of Health Care in the 2000 Canadian Federal Election. *Political Communication* 27, 4: 367-88.

NDP. 1993. *Canada Works When Canadians Work: Canada's New Democrats Present a Strategy for Full Employment*. Ottawa: Canada's New Democrats.

–. 1995. *Convention 95* (program and official magazine). Ottawa: Canada's New Democrats.

Nevitte, Neil, André Blais, Elisabeth Gidengil, and Richard Nadeau. 2000. *Unsteady State: The 1997 Canadian Federal Election*. Don Mills, ON: Oxford University Press.

Pawley, Howard. 1994. Charting the Course for New Jerusalem. In Steven Langdon and Victoria Cross, eds., *As We Come Marching: People, Power and Progressive Politics*. Windsor: Windsor Works Publishing.

Pétry, François. 1995. The Party Agenda Model: Election Programmes and Government Spending in Canada. *Canadian Journal of Political Science* 28, 1: 51-84.

Pierson, Christopher. 2001. *Hard Choices: Social Democracy in the Twenty-First Century*. London: John Wiley and Sons.

Prseworski, Adam, and John Sprague. 1986. *Paper Stones: A History of Electoral Socialism*. Chicago: University of Chicago Press.

Rebick, Judy. 2001. No More Politics as Usual. *Rabble.ca*, 6 June. http://rabble.ca/news/no-more-politics-usual.

Reid, Angus. 1991. Canada at the Crossroads: Public Opinion and the National Unity Debate. *The Empire Club of Canada Addresses*, 316-30. Toronto, 28 Feb. http://speeches.empireclub.org/61368/data?n=16.

Sassoon, Donald. 2000. Socialism in the 20th Century: An Historical Reflection. In Michael Freeden, ed., *Reassessing Political Ideologies*, 49-66. New York: Routledge.

Schwartz, Mildred. 1994. *North American Social Democracy in the 1990s: The NDP in Ontario*. Canadian-American Public Policy Series 17. Orono, ME: Canadian-American Center, University of Maine.

Stanford, Jim. 2011. The History of the New Politics Initiative: Movement and Party, Then and Now. *Rabble.ca*, 11 November. http://rabble.ca/news/2011/11/history-npi-movement-and-party-then-and-now.

Stanford, Jim, and Svend Robinson. 2001. The New Politics Initiative: Open, Sustainable and Democratic. In Z. David Berlin and Howard Aster, eds., *What's Left? The New Democratic Party in Renewal*, 80-93. Oakville, ON: Mosaic Press.

Tanguay, A. Brian. 1997. "Not in Ontario!" From the Social Contract to the Common Sense Revolution. In Sid Noel, ed., *Revolution at Queen's Park: Essays on Governing in Ontario*, 18-37. Toronto: Lorimer.

Walkom, Thomas. 1994. *Rae Days: The Rise and Fall of the NDP.* Toronto: Key Porter.

Whitehorn, Alan. 1992. *Canadian Socialism: Essays on the CCF-NDP.* Toronto: Oxford University Press.

–. 1994. The NDP's Quest for Survival. In Alan Frizzell, Jon H. Pammett, and Anthony Westell, eds., *The Canadian General Election of 1993*, 43-58. Ottawa: Carleton University Press.

–. 1995. How the NDP Chooses. *Canadian Forum.* September.

–. 1997. Alexa McDonough and the Atlantic Breakthrough for the New Democratic Party. In Alan Frizzell and Jon H. Pammett, eds., *The Canadian General Election of 1997.* Ottawa: Dundurn.

Woolstencroft, Peter. 1994 "Doing Politics Differently": The Conservative Party and the Campaign of 1993. In Alan Frizzell, Jon H. Pammett, and Anthony Westell, eds., *The Canadian General Election of 1993*, 9-26. Ottawa: Carleton University Press.

Young, Walter. 1969. *The Anatomy of a Party: The National CCF, 1932-1961.* Toronto: University of Toronto Press.

2

Building for a Breakthrough

The Layton Years, 2003-11

LYNDA ERICKSON and DAVID LAYCOCK

There was something different about Jack Layton. Many political observers noticed this well before his untimely death produced an unprecedented outpouring of grief and support. As a veteran NDP leader, Jack Layton attracted an unusual degree of trust and admiration not just from NDP supporters but also from other party supporters. He was the first NDP leader to speak French with ease, the first NDP leader to pull his party into serious contention in Quebec, the first federal party leader to thoroughly thrash the Bloc Québécois, and, of course, the first NDP leader to become leader of Her Majesty's Loyal Opposition. In addition to these more obvious achievements, Layton moved beyond rhetoric in modernizing the federal party. He embraced the use of social media to transform federal campaigns, endorsed the extensive use of direct mail campaigns to augment party financing, and successfully won back some of the valuable populist ground lost to the Reform Party in 1993. Layton was not just the right leader at the right time; he was a necessary leader for a federal party whose viability and relevance, for more than a decade, had seemed very debatable.

Winning the Leadership

Layton was elected leader of the NDP in 2003. As part of the effort to revitalize her party, Alexa McDonough chose to step down as leader in 2002 and the party organized its first one-member, one-vote leadership selection process for January 2003. In opting for the new system, given labour's centrality in its origins and history, the party had to grapple with the question of the role of organized labour in the selection process. The solution was to allocate 25 percent of the leadership vote to party affiliates. Individual party members cast their ballots in person at the leadership convention, which was to be the media centrepiece of the selection process, or by mail-in or e-mail ballot, while affiliates sent elected delegates to the convention to cast their votes directly.

Of the six New Democrats who entered the leadership race, three were sitting members of the House of Commons. Bill Blaikie was a veteran Manitoba MP with strong support in the caucus. Joe Comartin was an MP from Windsor who, in 2000, had won the first NDP federal seat in Ontario in a decade. Lorne Nystrom was a long-time Saskatchewan MP who had been a third-place finisher behind Ed Broadbent in the 1975 leadership race and was the most centrist candidate in the race (Fraser 2003). The other three candidates were Pierre Ducasse, a young Quebecer who emphasized the importance of building the party base in Quebec; Bev Meslo, a representative of the Socialist Caucus; and Jack Layton, a long-time Toronto city councillor and urban advocate who had twice run unsuccessfully for a federal seat in his Toronto riding. In a surprising first ballot victory, Layton won with 54 percent of the vote, 29 percentage points ahead of Bill Blaikie.

Layton represented seat-rich urban Ontario, where the NDP had lost significant support in 1993 – support that, in over a decade, it had been unable to regain. Although Layton was characterized as being on the left of the party, his internal party support cut across a number of groups (Cody 2004; Lavigne 2013). In the leadership race he was endorsed by two former leaders, Ed Broadbent and Audrey McLaughlin; by a number of provincial party leaders; and by central figures in the New Politics Initiative, the "oppositional left" of the party (Topp 2010). The race not only produced a leader focused on pulling together a "big tent" team (Topp 2010, 30) but also contributed an increased membership base and added money to party coffers (Whitehorn 2004). With Layton's leadership, the party began a period of gradual growth in its electoral support, beginning with the 2004 election and culminating three elections later with the dramatic and unexpected results of 2011.

A Growing Support Base, 2004-08

The 2004 Election
Within eighteen months of his assuming the leadership of the party, Jack Layton and the NDP faced an early summer election. Compared to 2000,

when the party had dropped back to just 13 seats, the electoral landscape was now substantially changed. The once-dominant Liberal Party, which had replaced its long-time leader Jean Chrétien with former finance minister Paul Martin, was confronted with a scandal that seriously threatened its position as the "natural" front-runner in federal politics (Johnston 2000). The sponsorship scandal, as it was dubbed, involved a federal program designed to raise the profile of Canada within Quebec as a means of combating separatist sentiment (deemed to be dangerously high following the 1995 sovereignty referendum in Quebec, which very nearly achieved majority support for separation).

Amidst rumours of corruption and kickbacks in the program, Prime Minister Chrétien asked Auditor-General Sheila Fraser to investigate it. Her February 2004 report documented misuse of government money and "consistent and pervasive" non-compliance with the rules for public funding (Canada 2004). Prime Minister Martin attempted to defuse the issue by cancelling the sponsorship program, appointing an independent commission of inquiry (the Gomery Commission), firing officials ostensibly involved in the program, and generally linking the transgressions to his predecessor (Clarkson 2004). Still, the aura of scandal that surrounded the Liberal Party was not effectively dissipated by election time (Gidengil et al. 2006).

In addition to the challenges the scandal posed to the Liberal Party, there was now a strengthened threat on the right from the merger of the Canadian Alliance and the Progressive Conservative Party. In December 2003, the new Conservative Party was born when the membership of the two parties voted to support a union arranged by Stephen Harper, the leader of the Canadian Alliance, and Peter McKay, the recently selected leader of the PCs. McKay had promised one of his major challengers in the PC leadership race that he would not support a merger (Ellis and Woolstencroft 2004), and a number of high-profile Tories, including the former leader, Joe Clark, strongly opposed the union because of what they saw as the Alliance's extremism (Clarke et al. 2005). Nonetheless, the PC membership voted 90 percent in support of the merger (Bélanger and Godbout 2010). With the merged party dominated by former Alliance members, Harper readily won the weighted membership vote for the leadership against two competitors – Belinda Stronach, a businesswoman from Ontario who helped facilitate the PC/Alliance merger, and Tony Clement, a former Ontario cabinet minister from the recently defeated Ontario PC government.[1]

For the NDP, the new party configuration posed both a risk and an opportunity. On the one hand, a unified Conservative Party could be a more effective challenger in Ontario, where the NDP needed to increase its seat total if it was to gain credibility as a national party; on the other hand, if the Liberals viewed their right flank as their greatest threat and campaigned on a more conservative agenda, the NDP could have an opportunity to attract former left-Liberal voters.

In the election campaign, two central themes arose: (1) corruption and the sponsorship scandal identified with the Liberals and (2) the alleged threat to social programs and "Canadian values" posed by the Conservatives. In the context of the latter theme, preserving the public system of health care was a particularly strong focus of the Liberal campaign, reflecting the overall tenor of a platform that "lean[ed] to the right on fiscal prudence but to the left on social programs" (Clarkson 2004). The Liberal health care message was, however, complicated by the Ontario Liberal government's actions when it imposed a new tax to cover shortfalls in health care revenue (LeDuc 2005). But the Conservatives also struggled with respect to their credibility with regard to preserving public health care, notwithstanding their commitment to honour the 2003 Health Accord on health care renewal, which was committed to the principles of public health insurance (Ellis and Woolstencroft 2004).

The NDP platform put jobs in a green economy, health care, and investment in cities at the top of its list. It focused primarily on contrasting NDP promises with the Liberal record and ignored the Conservatives (Whitehorn 2004). Only later in the campaign did the party turn some of its focus to the Conservatives as opinion polls began to show them tied with the Liberals in popularity (Clarke et al. 2005). The NDP's urban emphasis featured its promise to invest in cities, which was premised on securing more seats in Ontario (LeDuc 2005). This emphasis was risky for its competition with the Conservatives in the west, especially in rural areas of Saskatchewan and Manitoba, where the NDP had been traditionally strong. The party was also at risk from the Liberal strategy that developed when the Conservatives' momentum strengthened. Warning voters to "think twice, vote once" (Clarkson 2004), Liberal ads were designed to foster strategic Liberal voting, especially among New Democratic supporters.

In contrast to its strategy in the 2000 election, in the 2004 election the NDP conducted a more national, highly visible campaign, with the new leader a major focus. Hopes for a major recovery of the party's former successes were largely placed on Layton's energetic campaigning and leadership. But his performance in the leaders' debates did not enhance his support: even among prospective NDP voters who watched the debates, less than half were more favourable towards him as a result of the debates (Compas 2004). Moreover, his performance in the French debate was not strong, although he did introduce himself to Quebec voters as someone raised in Quebec and relatively fluent in French. In the end, his leadership ratings in post-election surveys were no better than Alexa McDonough's had been when she was leader (Blais et al. 2002; Gidengil et al. 2006). Like his two predecessors, McLaughlin and McDonough, Layton lacked familiarity among the electorate, and his electoral pull suffered as a result. Still, his name was no less known than that of the Conservative leader, whose party attracted much more support, suggesting that the NDP brand itself was a more significant factor. Nonetheless, the NDP did regain support among some of its traditional constituencies, including union households and women (Gidengil et al. 2006 and see below), and, as a result, the party's showing improved substantially at the polls.

Overall, the party doubled its vote count and increased its proportion of the popular vote by more than four-fifths, from 8.5 percent to 15.7 percent (see Table 2.1). The party's proportion of the popular vote grew in every province except Saskatchewan, although in Quebec, where it had thought it might improve its appeal, its portion of the popular vote only increased from 2 to 5 percent (see Godbout, Bélanger, and Mérand, Chapter 11, this volume). The seat result was more disappointing than the popular vote result – growing by just 5, from 13 to 19. The party lost 1 seat in Nova Scotia and 2 in Saskatchewan but picked up 6 in Ontario and 3 in British Columbia.[2] In Ontario, the party's percentage of the popular vote had almost returned to pre-1993 levels.

Perhaps surprisingly, the party did not gain much support from the fallout from the sponsorship scandal; rather, it was the Conservatives who primarily benefitted (Gidengil et al. 2006). As well, the NDP appears to have lost votes to strategic calculations, mainly from potential supporters moving to the Liberals (Clarke et al. 2005). Still, Gidengil et al. (2012) find that, among their survey respondents, the proportion the party lost was only 11 percent of those who liked the NDP best of the parties. This suggests the party lost roughly 2 percentage points of its popular vote to strategic voting.[3] Given the third-party status of the NDP at the time, a larger deflection in the face of the Liberals' call for strategic voting might have been expected. However, research on strategic voting in Canada suggests that the NDP's susceptibility to it as a result of its minor party status is reduced by

TABLE 2.1

NDP popular vote and seats in the 2000 to 2008 elections, by province

Province		\multicolumn{4}{c}{Election year}			
		2000	2004	2006	2008
British Columbia	Seats	2	5	10	9
	Vote %	11	27	29	26
Alberta	Seats	–	–	–	1
	Vote %	5	10	12	13
Saskatchewan	Seats	2	–	–	–
	Vote %	26	23	24	26
Manitoba	Seats	4	4	3	4
	Vote %	21	24	25	24
Ontario	Seats	1	7	12	17
	Vote %	8	18	19	18
Quebec	Seats	–	–	–	1
	Vote%	2	5	8	12
New Brunswick	Seats	1	1	1	1
	Vote %	12	21	22	22
Nova Scotia	Seats	3	2	2	2
	Vote %	12	21	22	22
PEI	Seats	–	–	–	–
	Vote %	9	12	10	10
Newfoundland	Seats	–	–	–	1
	Vote %	13	18	14	34
All	Seats	13	19	29*	37*
	Vote %	8.5	15.7	17.5	18.2

*   Includes one seat in the Northwest Territories.

the tendency of partisans to overestimate their local candidate's chances of winning (Blais and Turgeon 2004) and the greater utility its supporters would gain (measured by the gap in positive feelings towards its candidates compared to those of other parties) from their party's success (Merolla and Stephenson 2007).

The election resulted in a minority Liberal government, with the Liberals winning just 135 of the 308 seats. The Conservatives won 99 seats, an increase of 12 over the combined number of Canadian Alliance and PC seats in 2000, although the party's popular vote was 8 percentage points below the combined percentage polled by the Canadian Alliance and PC parties in 2000. The BQ increased its seat number by 16 and its popular vote percentage by 9 points. Within Quebec, the sponsorship scandal had clearly benefited the BQ.

The 38th Parliament

In the minority Parliament that followed the 2004 election, the Liberal government needed opposition support to remain in power. For the NDP, the fact that the combined seat total of the Liberals and New Democrats was just short of a majority complicated prospects for inter-party arrangements to keep the Liberals in office in exchange for progress on NDP priorities. Indeed, Prime Minister Martin signalled early on that he was not receptive to such cooperation (Topp 2010; Lavigne 2013). Subsequently, however, facing a defeat of the government's budget in spring of 2005, the Liberals did reach an agreement with the NDP on a number of their priorities on social spending. Combined with former Conservative leadership candidate Belinda Stronach's defection to the Liberals and the support of former Canadian Alliance member and current Independent Chuck Cadman, NDP support provided the Liberals with sufficient numbers to survive the budget vote.

Yet these mildly cordial relations did not last. In particular, the Liberal rejection of NDP concerns about public health care after a Supreme Court decision on the sale of private health insurance (*Chaoulli v. Quebec [Attorney General]*)[4] frustrated the NDP (Topp 2010). At the same time, the Liberals' reputation for good government faced further scrutiny. While the November release of the Gomery Commission's phase one report on the sponsorship affair did not link the current administration to the scandal, it did refer to a "culture of entitlement" among Liberals and reminded the public of Liberal connections with corruption. Shortly after the report's release, the NDP joined the two other opposition parties in bringing down the government on a vote of non-confidence. The subsequent election was not scheduled until late January 2006, leading to a long and resource-demanding campaign period for the NDP.

The 2006 Election

Going into this campaign, the NDP had a higher public profile than it had attracted in other recent elections, partly because of its role in the spring budget and its part in triggering the election. While the party was happy to declare the budget an "NDP budget" (Whitehorn 2006; Lavigne 2013), its role in bringing down the government was more contentious, given the public aversion to another election campaign. However, for the opposition parties, defeating the government was partly a question of timing since the Liberals had already promised an election following the tabling of the Gomery Commission's second report in the spring of 2006 (LeDuc 2007).

For the Liberals, the context of the election certainly included the continuing fallout from the sponsorship scandal; but, at the same time, a robust economy and budget surpluses gave the government an opportunity to focus on its accomplishments. And, at the start of the campaign, the polls indicated the Liberals were in a reasonably strong position vis-à-vis their competition, leading the Conservatives by more than 7 percentage points in terms of voter preference (Clarke et al. 2006). For its part, the NDP began the campaign in roughly the same position as it had held in the last election in terms of popularity, and it was still concerned about losing strategic voters to the Liberals. Accordingly, the party targeted the Liberals in its campaign attacks and emphasized its defence of medicare and expanded social programs, including a national prescription drug program, better senior care, and a national daycare program (Whitehorn 2006). It also focused its campaign efforts more narrowly than in 2004, targeting fewer ridings for special resources and greater attention (see Laycock and Erickson, Chapter 4, this volume; Lavigne 2013).

The Conservative Party conducted a primarily policy-oriented campaign focused on five groups of priorities (including reducing hospital wait times, reducing the federal sales tax, and providing a family child-care tax credit), all designed to signal it was a centrist party that had moved away from the more extreme aspects of its Reform/Alliance roots (Ellis and Woolstencroft 2006). At the same time, the sponsorship scandal continued to be grist for its campaign mill, albeit not the centrepiece (LeDuc 2007). Conservative popularity grew after a shooting outside a Toronto mall that resulted in the death of a fifteen-year-old girl raised the issue of law and order, a policy area that the public associates with Conservatives. Another boost for the Conservatives came from the announcement of an RCMP investigation into possible (Liberal) government links to insider trading, which reinforced public cynicism regarding the Liberals (Clarke et al 2006). Subsequently, some on the left began to criticize the NDP strategy of focusing its partisan critiques on the Liberals. This, they argued, risked a Conservative win at the polls. High-profile Canadian Autoworker president Buzz Hargrove went so far as to publicly urge union members to vote Liberal in ridings in which the NDP was weak – an action for which his party membership was subsequently revoked (CBC 2006).

On election day, the Conservatives won a minority government with 124 seats and 36 percent of the popular vote, outpacing the Liberals' 82 seats and 30 percent of the popular vote. The NDP increased its proportion of the popular vote by just under 2 percentage points to 18, but it won an extra 10 seats. It gained seats in Ontario, British Columbia, and the North. In a reflection of the party's continuing weakness in the Prairies, once its stronghold, it lost 1 seat in Manitoba and continued to be shut out in Saskatchewan (see Table 2.1). Alberta and Quebec continued to deny the party any seats. Once more the NDP lost votes to strategic voting, notwithstanding its efforts to avoid this problem by targeting the Liberals. But, as in 2004, the overall effect was reasonably modest in percentage terms, albeit difficult to assess in terms of seats (Gidengil et al. 2012).

The 39th Parliament

The NDP emerged just short of holding the balance of power in the new minority Parliament. On the other hand, the BQ, with 51 seats, was in a considerably stronger position. As the Conservatives adopted a more conciliatory position with respect to Quebec (Bélanger and Nadeau 2009), the Bloc supported the government on a number of votes in the House. The Liberals, with the largest opposition contingent, had to deal with the selection of a new leader and subsequent internal dissention that developed as this new leader, former cabinet minister Stéphane Dion, failed to gain popular support for his party. NDP MPs found themselves frequently at odds with Conservative policies and adopted a strategy of regularly opposing the government in votes in the House, thereby distinguishing themselves from the Liberals. The Liberals were not prepared to trigger an election and so either supported the government or, for items they opposed, abstained or were absent for votes in the House (Jeffrey 2009).

In 2006, as part of its effort to enhance government accountability, the Conservative government enacted a provision for fixed elections that required federal elections to be held every four years, beginning in October 2009. However, as Conservative support in the polls approached majority government levels in the summer of 2008, and with a looming economic downturn, the prime minister called an election.

2008 Election

Going into the 2008 election, the Liberals were floundering in the polls. Attacked by Conservative ads that declared he was "not a leader" and "not worth the risk [as prime minister]" (Ellis and Woolstencroft 2009), Stéphane Dion had difficulty attracting popular support and faced internal party turmoil (Jeffrey 2009). The NDP was stagnant in the opinion polls, notwithstanding its efforts to differentiate itself from the Liberal Party by consistently opposing the Conservatives in the House. And the BQ found the Conservatives even more of a challenge as, since 2006, their conciliatory approach to Quebec had included the introduction and passage of a motion that recognized the Québécois as constituting "a nation within a united Canada."

Entering the campaign, the Conservatives emphasized their record in government and their party's leadership. Harper was characterized as a steady hand at the economic tiller, in contrast to Dion, who was portrayed as weak and ineffectual. The Liberals emphasized their proposals for a "Green Shift," a plan introduced months before the election and that involved promoting environmental technology and introducing a carbon tax to reduce dependence on fossil fuels. As economic conditions rapidly deteriorated through the election period, the Liberals also proposed a plan to deal with the growing financial and economic crisis, while, for his part, Harper was reluctant to acknowledge that economic circumstances were becoming severe.

The NDP went into the election focusing on populist policy themes that concerned protecting the middle and working classes from economic insecurity, reversing declining health care, and defending the environment. On the deteriorating economy the party's objective was to reframe the ballot question from "who will manage the economy best" to "which leader can you trust to protect you and your family in tough economic times" (Erickson and Laycock 2009). In the party's campaign strategies, two things stood out. First, like the Conservatives, the NDP focused on leadership, talking about Layton's "new kind of strong" leadership (Lavigne 2013) and presenting him not as a third-party choice but, rather, as *the* choice to replace Harper. Second, the party primarily directed its campaign attacks at Stephen Harper and the Conservatives, virtually ignoring the Liberals until the last week of the campaign. Then, in response to Liberal efforts to convince potential NDP supporters to vote strategically, the party focused some of its critique on Dion and his leadership difficulties.

The results of the election dashed the Conservatives' hopes for a majority in the House, but their minority government strength improved as they won 143 seats with a popular vote of 37.6 percent. They were just 12 seats short of a majority. The Liberals had again dropped in popular vote, to

26.3 percent, and had won only 77 seats. For the NDP the results were a good news/bad news story. The party won 7 more seats than in 2006 but increased its popular vote by less than 1 percent.

The party's largest seat gain was in Ontario, where it won 5 new seats without any increase in vote share. In Newfoundland and Labrador, the party won its first seat since 1979 and more than doubled its vote share to 34 percent. In the rest of Atlantic Canada, its support stagnated, with no change in its seats (3) or in its proportion of the popular vote. In Quebec, the party held Thomas Mulcair's seat, won initially in a 2007 by-election, and increased its popular vote by 4 percentage points, albeit only to 12 percent (see Erickson and Laycock, Chapter 3, this volume). In the Prairies, the party's popular vote barely improved, although it did gain 1 extra seat in Manitoba and made a breakthrough in Alberta, winning its first seat since 1988. It remained shut out of Saskatchewan. In British Columbia, it dropped 1 seat with a popular vote decline of 3 percentage points. As in 2006, compared to the Liberals, the party was the loser in strategic voting roulette, although again the effects on the party's popular vote were not substantial (Gidengil et al. 2012).

Party Supporters, 2004-08

During the period of Layton's leadership prior to the 2011 breakthrough, the NDP found stronger support among some expected and some unexpected groups of voters. An examination of the patterns of support for the party outside Quebec during this period illustrates this.[5]

Class and Economic Determinants

Notwithstanding the party's origins in class-based conflict and its close relations with organized labour, for much of its history the NDP has not attracted a high level of working-class support at the polls. Indeed, using a traditional measure of class based on manual and non-manual occupations, numerous attempts at finding a class vote for the NDP have failed (Pammett 1987; Nevitte et al. 2000, Johnston 2010). Studies using income as a measure of class have, on the other hand, found occasional class effects (Nevitte et al. 2000), suggesting that lower-income groups are more likely to vote NDP and that higher-income groups are less likely to do so. In looking at the voting patterns from 2004 to 2008 (Table 2.2), we see that the effect of income on NDP support was significant only in 2008.[6]

While class measures based on occupation or income are not strong predictors of NDP support, we might at least expect that union members and

TABLE 2.2

NDP vote percentage outside Quebec in the 2004 to 2008 elections, by socio-demographic characteristics

		Election year		
		2004	2006	2008
All		20	21	21
Union household	Yes	28**	29**	29**
	No	17	17	18
Income[a]	Lowest quartile	25	22	26*
	Highest quartile	19	19	14**
Sector	Private sector	18**	16**	19*
	Public sector	27	28	25
Sex	Women	22*	23*	24*
	Men	19	18	17
Religion[b]	None	30**	31**	28**
	Protestant	17*	17*	17*
Visible minority	Yes	23	18	21
	No	20	20	20
Age[c]	18 to 34	28**	20	27*
	Over 65	14	16*	15*

Note: Numbers in italic indicate variable remained significant when other significant socio-demographic variables were controlled.
* Significant at .01
** Significant at .001
a Dummy variables were created for lowest and highest quartile.
b Dummy variables were created for each religious group.
c Dummies were created for youth and senior categories.

their families would be more reliable NDP voters than would their non-union counterparts. But even union membership has had a variable history in its relationship to the party's vote.[7] However, as Table 2.2 indicates, being from a union household has, since the 2000 election, resurfaced as an important variable in the NDP vote equation. Thus, although voting for the NDP was not significantly greater among voters from union households in the 2000 election (Blais et al. 2002), in 2004 such voters were 1.6 times more likely to vote NDP than were non-union voters. This effect continued to be evident in the elections of 2006 and 2008, and in all three elections it remained significant when other socio-demographic factors were controlled.[8]

Another economic group that might be considered important for NDP support is public-sector workers. With its strong defence of a robust state sector, the NDP would seem to be a natural ally for public-sector employees. And, in the past, we see evidence of a modest impact on NDP voting from public-sector employees (Blais, Blake, and Dion 1990; Nevitte et al. 2000). In the elections of 2004, 2006, and 2008, greater party support among public-sector employees than among private-sector employees is evident (Table 2.2), but the effect of this factor on voting for the party was not particularly strong, and it did not remain significant once other relevant socio-demographic factors were controlled.

Gender

With a powerful feminist constituency in its organization, a record of affirmative action on women's roles in the party and among its candidates, and a history of strong support for women's issues such as accessible daycare and abortion rights (Bashevkin 1993; Erickson 1993; Young 2000), from its outset the NDP might have been seen as a likely beneficiary of women's votes. Yet, until virtually the end of the twentieth century, the NDP was not especially attractive to women voters. Indeed, in its early history the party was more popular among men than among women. Then, as women's support for welfare state programs became stronger than men's support, and issues of gender equality became more significant, women's partisan preferences moved to the left of those of men (Erickson and O'Neill 2002). The elections of 2004 to 2008 continued this pattern as women were more likely to support the NDP than were men. While the size of this difference varied from 3 to 7 percentage points, some gender difference was consistently evident even when other relevant socio-demographic factors were controlled.

Religion and Ethnicity

A long-standing feature of voting behaviour in Canada has been the role of religion in structuring support for the parties (Blais 2005; Johnston 2011). As a factor in shaping voting patterns over the years, religion has had especially important effects. In particular, the Liberal Party has attracted disproportionate, albeit declining, support among Roman Catholic voters (Gidengil et al. 2009). However, for the NDP, the structuring effect of religion has been in its presence or absence among voters. The party gains disproportionate support from those who say they have no religious affiliation compared to those who say they have one. On average, the former are more than 1.7 times as likely to vote for the party as are the latter. While there is also some suggestion in Table 2.2 that Protestant voters are less attracted to the party than non-Protestant voters, this relationship does not remain significant once other significant socio-demographic factors are controlled.

As with religion, the effect of ethnicity – in particular, differences between visible minorities and others – has been a continuing theme in the literature on the voting patterns of Canadians outside of Quebec. The Liberals' strength among visible minorities gave them an important base in the electorate early in the millennium, but this had shifted dramatically by the 2008 election (Gidengil et al. 2009). For the NDP, which at least partially benefitted from this movement away from the Liberals (Gidengil et al. 2006), what had been a disadvantage among visible minority voters in 2000 disappeared by 2004,[9] and, as is revealed in Table 2.2, effects on the party vote from those of visible minority background have not reappeared.[10]

Age

Beginning with the 2004 election, differential NDP support was evident in two age groups: those under thirty-five and those over sixty-five. In that election, younger voters were a full 14 percentage points more likely to support the NDP than were voters over the age of sixty-five. The party's strong support among younger voters in that election was significant even once other socio-demographic variables were controlled. In the next two elections, the party's lack of appeal to seniors was more consistent than was its support among younger voters, and, in the 2008 election, this negative relationship was more robust than was the positive relationship between younger voters and NDP support. This is indicated by the finding that, for seniors, the difference remains significant after other social factors are controlled, while this is not the case for younger voters.

Building for 2011

The 40th Parliament

Shortly after the 2008 election, and as part of its first major effort to address the growing economic crisis facing the country, the Conservative Party set out to abolish the per-vote subsidy that was paid to political parties to finance their activities between and during elections. These subsidies constituted part of the election financing reform package introduced by Jean Chrétien's Liberal government in 2003 (see Laycock and Erickson, Chapter 4, this volume). Partly implemented in order to divorce party financing from dependence on large corporate and union contributions, the new regime meant that quarterly allowances were an important source of income for the opposition parties (Jansen and Young 2011).

It was clear to all political observers that abolition of these subsidies would cripple the finances of the opposition parties. This, coupled with what the opposition saw as the Conservatives' ineffectual response to the economic challenges that were engulfing Canada, motivated these parties to attempt to defeat the Conservative minority government. To that end, they signed an agreement that laid out plans for the Liberals and NDP to form a coalition government following a defeat of the government in the House. The BQ stated that it would support this agreement until the summer of 2010.[11] The Conservative reaction was swift and ultimately effective. Attacking the NDP and Liberals for making an agreement with separatists, and acting before the opposition could move a motion of non-confidence in the House, Harper requested that Governor General Michaëlle Jean prorogue Parliament for two months. She agreed to do this.

Within a week of the governor general's decision, Liberal leader Stéphane Dion resigned. The lacklustre showing of his party in the election had virtually guaranteed his departure as leader. Michael Ignatieff, who had contested the Liberal leadership race that Dion had won, was appointed interim leader of the party and was subsequently confirmed, uncontested, as leader at a party meeting (Jeffrey 2011). Ignatieff was unwilling to continue the Liberals' commitment to a coalition with the NDP, and its demise was followed by Liberal support for the revised Conservative budget in early 2009.

The Parliament that followed was divisive and highly partisan. Much rancour resulted from the way the Conservatives treated Parliament, which, according to the opposition parties, showed their barely disguised contempt for the members of the House, notwithstanding the Conservatives' minority status. The opposition cited the government's refusal to provide House committees with information on the cost of government programs such as the proposed purchase of a new fleet of jet fighters, crime and prison legislation, and the reduction of corporate tax rates (Dornan 2011).

The fractious 40th Parliament ended with the government's loss of a confidence vote in March 2011. This followed the report of the House

Committee on Procedure and House Affairs, which declared the government in contempt of Parliament for failing to provide the House with documentation concerning the costs of major government programs. For the opposition, the government's contempt was an egregious violation of Parliament's legitimacy, while for the government the declaration of contempt was just another manoeuvre in the partisan politics of a minority government Parliament.

The 2011 Election

As a precursor to the election, using a declaration of contempt as the basis for a confidence vote was seemingly favourable to the opposition, and, indeed, in the subsequent campaign it became a centrepiece of the Liberals' critique of the Conservatives. For the NDP, however, the crusade for votes lay in generally emphasizing that "Ottawa is broken" and implicating the Liberals as well as the Conservatives in this "broken political culture" (LeDuc 2012). As well, the party platform focused on five "practical steps" the NDP would take in its first one hundred days in government, reinforcing its 2008 election theme that it was campaigning as the alternative to the Harper Conservatives, not just as a voice in Parliament. By campaigning as the alternative to the Conservatives, the NDP sought once again to challenge Liberal efforts to promote strategic voting (McGrane 2011; Lavigne 2013)

The focus on leadership in the NDP campaign, at least outside Quebec, contrasted the positive attributes of Jack Layton to the negative characterizations of Stephen Harper. And this time the party's negative attacks extended to the Liberal leader, although Harper remained their major focus. Leadership continued as a theme in the party's Quebec advertising, but the emphasis was more positive and focused on Layton. Because attacking the BQ leader could have been interpreted as an attack on Quebec, the NDP generally avoided using negative ads in that province (McGrane 2011).

Overall, Layton's popularity substantially outranked that of both Ignatieff and Harper (see Bittner, Chapter 8, this volume), but it was not until well into to the second half of the campaign that party support nationally began to reflect this and to shift significantly (see Weldon, Chapter 12, this volume). A substantial portion of this shift resulted from the NDP's popularity surge in Quebec. There, the party's support moved from averaging 15 percent (fourth place) at the beginning of the campaign to taking the lead a little more than a week before the election (LISPOP 2011;

TABLE 2.3
NDP popular vote and seats in 2011 election, by province and territory

Province/Territory	% of vote	No. of seats
British Columbia	33	12
Alberta	17	1
Saskatchewan	32	–
Manitoba	26	2
Ontario	26	22
Quebec	43	59
New Brunswick	30	1
Nova Scotia	30	3
PEI	15	–
Newfoundland	33	2
NWT	46	1
Nunavut	19	–
Yukon	14	–
TOTAL	31	103

Fournier et al. 2013). As Erickson and Laycock discuss (Chapter 3, this volume), what came to be known as the "Orange Crush" in Quebec continued until election day.

Election night results were dramatic. The NDP won 102 seats and became the Official Opposition. Its popular vote had increased nationally from 18 percent in 2008 to 31 percent, and its share of second-place seats had grown from 67 to 121. By contrast, the Liberal Party dropped from 77 seats in 2008 to 34 seats in 2011, with its popular vote declining from 26 to 19 percent and its second-place finishes dropping from 123 to 76. The NDP increased its seat total in five provinces and its vote share in all provinces except Newfoundland and Labrador. But the most dramatic developments came in Quebec, where it increased its seat count from 1 to 58 and its share of the popular vote more than threefold (Table 2.3). As Chapter 3 illustrates, although this change for the NDP in Quebec appeared suddenly, its roots can be found earlier in Quebec politics.

By comparison to Quebec, in the rest of Canada the party's success was modest, with just 8 new seats and 6 percentage points added to its share of the popular vote. Outside of Quebec the party's greatest proportional success was in British Columbia, where the party won 33 percent of the popular vote and one-third of the seats. In terms of seats, however, the party's best showing outside of Quebec was in Ontario, where it won 22 seats (21 percent of the province's seats) with 26 percent of the popular vote. With a majority Quebec contingent in its caucus, the party's image in the House and the broader public has altered radically.

The Party after Layton

Throughout the 2011 election, as a result of hip surgery Layton campaigned with a cane. In addition, his 2009 cancer diagnosis was well known. But his vigour on the election trail dispelled talk that his health was in jeopardy. It was, then, surprising for many that he became seriously ill shortly after the election and that he died within four months. This left the party facing uncertain prospects, missing the leader who had been so effective at campaigning and at modernizing the party organization (see Laycock and Erickson, Chapter 4, this volume).

Notwithstanding this uncertainty, the party opted to delay the leadership selection for seven months. Prospective candidates thus had time to become better known to the public, and the party was able to sell more memberships in Quebec, where it had very few signed-up members despite its being home to a majority of the NDP caucus.[12] The selection race attracted a number of new party members, with the result that overall party membership reached an all-time high. And, although Quebec membership did significantly increase, growing by more than a factor of six (CBC 2012), British Columbia and Ontario membership numbers (initially the highest) grew the most.[13]

For the selection process, the NDP fully embraced the one-member, one-vote system partially adopted in 2003. It abolished the provision that had reserved 25 percent of the vote for party affiliates. In effect, this further reduced the influence of organized labour, although labour organizations remained active, endorsing candidates and encouraging their members to join the party and vote in the selection process.[14] As in the 2003 leadership race, members could vote in advance, by paper ballot or online. On the day of the leadership vote, members could vote online or in person at the convention hall in Toronto.

The leadership race itself was highly competitive, with seven candidates on the first ballot (two others withdrew prior to the final vote) and a total of four ballots required to choose a majority winner. Among the candidates on the ballot were five sitting MPs: Paul Dewar, an educator from a well-known NDP family who was first elected in 2006 in Ed Broadbent's former riding in Ottawa; Peggy Nash, a labour negotiator from Toronto with strong roots and support in the labour movement who was also first elected in 2006; Nikki Ashton, a college lecturer from Manitoba who was first elected in 2008 and who, as the youngest woman in Parliament at the time, hoped to appeal to the youth vote; Nathan Cullen, a small-business owner and community organizer from British Columbia who was first elected in 2004 and who, alone among the candidates, advocated strategic co-operation with the Liberals at the local level to defeat Conservative candidates; and Thomas Mulcair, the NDP's first Quebec MP elected in a general election. The party's well-connected president, Brian Topp, entered the race early and attracted considerable support from both provincial and federal politicians (Grenier 2012), notwithstanding his lack of legislative experience.[15] His close relationship with Jack Layton and his important role in the last two election campaigns made him an attractive candidate for many New Democrats.[16] In the end, however, Thomas Mulcair defeated Brian Topp by 58 to 43 percent on the final ballot.[17] Although Mulcair had been an NDP MP since 2007, his history as a former provincial Liberal cabinet minister in Quebec, and Topp's endorsement by past leader Ed Broadbent, had led some in the party to be uneasy about him. But Mulcair also enjoyed support from the party's upper echelons, along with more caucus endorsements than any other aspirant and more endorsements from current and former NDP provincial leaders.

Since Mulcair's selection, the story for the party in the opinion polls has been variable. Early in his leadership, the NDP generally maintained a level of support close to its 2011 election vote share and regularly outpolled the Liberals (ThreeHundredEight.com 2013). However, with the selection of Justin Trudeau as leader of the Liberal Party, NDP support dropped behind that of the Liberals, often even in Quebec, where the contingent of NDP MPs is so substantial. Volatility in party popularity and electoral results appears to have become the norm in Canadian politics (Gidengil et al. 2012), often defying party management and predictability. For the NDP, which has struggled for media attention, especially during and after the Liberal leadership race, the problem of visibility is especially challenging. Media habits in covering partisan debate, which were developed when the NDP was a distinctly minority party, pose a problem for the party because it has such a short history as a major contender.

In the House of Commons, the NDP has had a mixed experience. On the one hand, three MPs have left the caucus – two from Quebec (see Chapter 3) and one (Bruce Hyer) from northern Ontario. The latter left in April 2012 to sit as an independent after having been disciplined for voting with the

Conservatives on the abolition of the long-gun registry (Fitzpatrick 2012). On the other hand, Mulcair has performed well in the House, especially in Question Period when dealing with the Senate expenses scandal (Grenier 2014). His legal background and legislative experience, first in Quebec's National Assembly and then in Parliament (since 2008), clearly helped in this regard. Some Layton loyalists who had worked closely with leadership rival Brian Topp have left the party's federal office. However, many other experienced party officials have remained, and some, most notably Ann McGrath, have returned. So there is no reason to expect reversals in the progress made by the party in modernizing its electoral apparatus. We return to this issue and other aspects of emerging dynamics in the federal party system in our final chapter.

Notes

1 For its leadership selection, the new Conservative Party adopted the weighted member vote system of the former PC Party rather than the one-member, one-vote system used by the Canadian Alliance. According to the system selected, members would vote through their constituencies, with each constituency given the same weighting. A constituency's vote would be allocated according to the distribution of votes for candidates within its riding, so that a candidate who received 40 percent of the constituency vote would receive 40 percent of the points allocated to the constituency.

2 These figures represent the change from the 2000 election results. The party had won an extra seat in Windsor, Ontario, in a 2002 by-election.

3 This figure is based on the proportion of respondents who like the NDP best.

4 *Chaoulli v. Quebec (Attorney General)* 2005 SCC 35. Here the Supreme Court decided on a case involving the sale of private insurance in Quebec, ruling that a blanket prohibition on the sale of private health insurance for publicly insured services was contrary to the Quebec Charter.

5 The data for these analyses come from the Canadian Election Studies. For information on the CES surveys, see http://www.queensu.ca/cora/ces.html. The analyses are limited to support outside Quebec. This is because of the party's low level of support in that province and because, with the existence of the BQ, the factors that influenced NDP support there differed from those that influenced it elsewhere.

6 This income effect in 2008 remained when other significant socio-demographic factors were controlled.

7 For example, for the 1970 and 1984 elections, Archer (1985) found, at best, an indirect effect on NDP voting due to union membership and union affiliation, while Johnston et al. (1992) found that, in the 1988 election, voters from union families were 1.8 times more likely to vote NDP than were those without such union attachment.

8 The other socio-demographic factors in Table 2.2 that were significant were controlled in the regression equation.

9   In 2000, according to CES data, just 3 percent of visible minority voters from areas outside of Quebec voted NDP, compared to 12 percent of those voters who were not identified as members of visible minorities.

10 For operational purposes, visible minorities are defined as those whose ancestry is non-European.

11 For the NDP perspective on how this agreement came about, see Topp (2010).

12 An interim leader, Nycole Turmel, had been recommended to the caucus by Layton prior to his death. She continued as leader until the leadership race was concluded.

13 British Columbia and Ontario were home to 30 and 29 percent, respectively, of the total membership at the February cutoff for voting memberships.

14 See, for example, the United Food and Commercial Workers endorsement of Thomas Mulcair at http://www.ufcw.ca/index.php?option=com_content&view=article&id=2726%3Andp-leadership-candidate-thomas-mulcair-gaining-momentum-as-we-head-towards-convention&catid=6%3Adirections-newsletter&Itemid=6&lang=en.

15 Topp had spent his political life as a party worker, not as a publicly elected official.

16 The seventh candidate was Martin Singh, a pharmacist from Nova Scotia who was president of the party's Faith and Social Justice Commission.

17 Topp was also born and raised in Quebec, but he has worked for the NDP in various provinces as well as in Ottawa, both as campaign director and as an advisor to Layton. He has not held elected public office.

References

Bashevkin, Sylvia. 1993. *Toeing the Lines: Women and Party Politics in Canada.* Toronto: Oxford University Press.

Bélanger, Éric, and Jean-François Godbout. 2010. Why Do Parties Merge? The Case of the Conservative Party of Canada. *Parliamentary Affairs* 63, 1: 41-65.

Bélanger, Éric, and Richard Nadeau. 2009. The Bloc Québécois: Capsized by the Orange Wave. In Jon H. Pammett and Christopher Dornan, eds., *The Canadian Federal Election of 2011,* 113-40. Toronto: Dundurn.

Blais, André. 2005. Accounting for the Electoral Success of the Liberal Party in Canada. *Canadian Journal of Political Science* 38, 4: 821-40.

Blais, André, Donald E. Blake, and Stéphane Dion. 1990. The Public/Private Sector Cleavage in North America: The Political Behavior and Attitudes of Public Sector Employees. *Comparative Political Studies* 23, 3: 381-403.

Blais, André, Elisabeth Gidengil, Richard Nadeau, and Neil Nevitte. 2002. *Anatomy of a Liberal Victory: Making Sense of the Vote in the 2000 Canadian General Election.* Peterborough, ON: Broadview.

Blais, André, and Mathieu Turgeon. 2004. How Good Are Voters at Sorting out the Weakest Candidate in Their Constituency? *Electoral Studies* 23, 2: 455-61.

CBC. 2006. NDP Dumps Buzz Hargrove. *CBC News,* 12 February. http://www.cbc.ca/news/canada/story/2006/02/12/ndp-hargrove060212.html.

–. 2012. NDP Membership Hits Record ahead of Convention. *CBC News,* 21 February. http://www.cbc.ca/news/politics/story/2012/02/21/pol-ndp-membership-numbers.html.

Canada. 2004. 2003 November Report of the Auditor General of Canada. http://
www.oag-bvg.gc.ca/internet/English/parl_oag_200311_03_e_12925.html#
ch3hd3d.

Clarke, Harold D., Allan Kornberg, John MacLeod, and Tom Scotto. 2005. Too
Close to Call: Political Choice in Canada 2004. *PS: Political Science and Politics*
38, 2: 247-53.

Clarke, Harold D., Allan Kornberg, Thomas Scotto, and Joe Twyman. 2006. Flaw-
less Campaign, Fragile Victory: Voting in Canada's 2006 Federal Election. *PS:
Political Science and Politics* 39, 4: 815-19.

Clarkson, Stephen. 2004. Disaster and Recovery: Paul Martin as Political Lazarus.
In Jon H. Pammett and Christopher Dornan, eds., *The Canadian General Election of 2004*, 28-65. Toronto: Dundurn.

Cody, Howard. 2004. The New Democrats' Search for Relevance as a Nudge Party.
American Review of Canadian Studies 34, 1: 59-79.

Compas. 2004. June 2004 Federal Debate – Major Win for Duceppe, Slim Win for
Harper, Loss for Layton. http://www.compas.ca/data/040617-2004FederalElec-
tionDebate-E.pdf.

Dornan, Christopher. 2011. From Contempt of Parliament to Majority Mandate.
In Jon H. Pammett and Christopher Dornan, eds., *The Canadian Federal
Election of 2011*, 10-16. Toronto: Dundurn.

Ellis, Faron, and Peter Woolstencroft. 2004. New Conservatives, Old Realities:
The 2004 Election Campaign. In Jon H. Pammett and Christopher Dornan, eds.,
The Canadian General Election of 2004, 66-105. Toronto: Dundurn.

–. 2006. Change of Government Not a Change of Country: The Conservatives
and the 2006 Election. In Jon H. Pammett and Christopher Dornan, eds., *The
Canadian General Election of 2006*, 58-92. Toronto: Dundurn.

–. 2009. Stephen Harper and the Conservatives Campaign on Their Record. In Jon
H. Pammett and Christopher Dornan, eds., *The Canadian General Election of
2008*, 16-62. Toronto: Dundurn.

Erickson, Lynda. 1993. Making Her Way In: Women, Parties and Candidacies in
Canada. In J. Lovenduski and P. Norris, eds., *Gender and Party Politics*, 60-85.
London: Sage.

Erickson, Lynda, and David Laycock. 2009. Modernization, Incremental Progress,
and the Challenge of Relevance: The NDP's 2008 Campaign. In Jon H. Pammett
and Christopher Dornan, eds., *The Canadian Federal Election of 2008*, 98-135.
Toronto: Dundurn.

Erickson, Lynda, and Brenda O'Neill. 2002. The Gender Gap and the Changing
Woman Voter in Canada. *International Political Science Review* 23, 4: 373-92.

Fitzpatrick, Megan. 2012. Bruce Hyer Quits NDP Caucus to Sit as an Independent.
CBC News, 23 April. http://www.cbc.ca/news/politics/story/2012/04/23/pol-ndp
-bruce-hyer.html.

Fournier, Patrick, Fred Cutler, Stuart Soroka, Dietlind Stolle, and Éric Bélanger.
2013. Riding the Orange Wave: Leadership, Values, Issues and the 2011 Canadian
Election. *Canadian Journal of Political Science* 46, 4: 863-97.

Fraser, Graham. 2003. The NDP Leadership Challenge: Re-Connecting the Left to
the Middle. *Policy Options* (February): 70-74.

Gidengil, Elisabeth, André Blais, Patrick Fournier, Joanna Everitt, and Neil Nevitte. 2006. Back to the Future? Making Sense of the 2004 Election Outside Quebec. *Canadian Journal of Political Science* 39, 1: 1-25.

Gidengil, Elisabeth, Patrick Fournier, Joanna Everitt, Neil Nevitte, and André Blais. 2009. The Anatomy of a Liberal Defeat. Paper presented to the Annual Meeting of the Canadian Political Science Association, Ottawa.

Gidengil, Elisabeth, Neil Nevitte, André Blais, Joanna Everitt, and Patrick Fournier. 2012. *Dominance and Decline: Making Sense of Recent Canadian Elections.* Toronto: University of Toronto Press.

Grenier, Eric. 2012. Crunching Numbers: On NDP Endorsements, It's Mulcair's Quantity vs. Topp's Quality. *Globe and Mail,* 19 March. http://www.theglobe andmail.com/news/politics/on-ndp-endorsements-its-mulcairs-quantity-vs -topps-quality/article534640/.

–. 2014. Approval Ratings Point to Advantage for NDP and Mulcair. *The Hill Times,* 28 April. http://www.hilltimes.com/polling-pollsters/politics/2014/04/28/approval –ratings–point-to–advantage–for-ndp–and-mulcair/38302?mcl=727&muid= 4398.

Jansen, Harold J., and Lisa Young. 2011. Cartels, Syndicates, and Coalitions: Canada's Political Parties after the 2004 Reforms. In Lisa Young and Harold J. Jansen, eds., *Money, Politics and Democracy: Canada's Party Finance Reforms,* 82-103. Vancouver: UBC Press.

Jeffrey, Brooke. 2009. Missed Opportunity: The Invisible Liberals. In Jon H. Pammett and Christopher Dornan, eds., *The Canadian Federal Election of 2008,* 63-97. Toronto: Dundurn.

–. 2011. The Disappearing Liberals: Caught in the Crossfire. In Jon H. Pammett and Christopher Dornan, eds., *The Canadian Federal Election of 2011,* 48-78. Toronto: Dundurn.

Johnston, Richard. 2000. Canadian Elections at the Millennium. In Paul Howe, Richard Johnston, and André Blais, eds., *Strengthening Canadian Democracy,* 19-61. Montreal: Institute for Research on Public Policy.

–. 2010. Political Parties and the Electoral System. In John C. Courtney and David E. Smith, eds., *The Oxford Handbook of Canadian Politics,* 208-25. New York: Oxford University Press.

–. 2011. Religion and Identity: The Denominational Basis of Canadian Elections. Paper presented to the Annual Meeting of the Canadian Political Science Association, Waterloo, ON.

Lavigne, Brad. 2013. *Building the Orange Wave: The Inside Story behind the Historic Rise of Jack Layton and the NDP.* Madeira Park, BC: Douglas and McIntyre.

LeDuc, Lawrence. 2005. The Federal Election in Canada, June 2004. *Electoral Studies* 24: 338-44.

–. 2007. The Federal Election in Canada, January 2006. *Electoral Studies* 26: 716-20.

–. 2012. The Federal Election in Canada, May 2011. *Electoral Studies* 31: 239-42.

LISPOP (Laurier Institute for the Study of Public Opinion and Policy). 2011. Voter Trends: Federal and Regional Aggregation of Poll Results. http://www.lispop.ca/ fedsupporttable.html.

McGrane, David. 2011. Political Marketing and the NDP's Historic Breakthrough. In Jon H. Pammett and Christopher Dornan, eds., *The Canadian Federal Election of 2011*, 79-112. Toronto: Dundurn.

Merolla, Jennifer L., and Laura B. Stephenson. 2007. Strategic Voting in Canada: A Cross-Time Analysis. *Electoral Studies* 26, 2: 235-46.

Nevitte, Neil, André Blais, Elisabeth Gidengil, and Richard Nadeau. 2000. *Unsteady State: The 1997 Canadian Federal Election*. Don Mills, ON: Oxford University Press.

Pammett, Jon. 1987. Class Voting and Class Consciousness in Canada. *Canadian Review of Sociology* 24, 2: 269-90.

ThreeHundredEight.com. 2013. Monthly Polling Averages. May. http://www.three hundredeight.com/p/canada.html.

Topp, Brian. 2010. *How We Almost Gave the Tories the Boot*. Toronto: Lorimer.

Whitehorn, Alan. 2004. Jack Layton and the NDP: Gains but No Breakthrough. In Jon H. Pammett and Christopher Dornan, eds., *The Canadian General Election of 2004*, 106-38. Toronto: Dundurn.

–. 2006. The NDP and the Enigma of Strategic Voting. In Jon H. Pammett and Christopher Dornan, eds., *The Canadian Federal Election of 2006*, 93-121. Toronto: Dundurn.

Young, Lisa. 2000. *Feminists and Party Politics*. Vancouver: UBC Press.

3

The NDP and Quebec

LYNDA ERICKSON and DAVID LAYCOCK

In the 2011 election, the national success of the NDP was predicated on its remarkably strong showing in Quebec. Yet, prior to that election, Quebec had presented the NDP with a long-standing strategic dilemma that, in turn, was underpinned by a substantive ideological dilemma. For a third party hoping to claim not just major party status but also national party status, the strategic dilemma was this: Should it devote scarce resources, including a major proportion of the leader's tour, to a campaign in a region that had never shown an interest in electing NDP MPs? The ideological dilemma pitted party support for Quebec's distinctiveness against the NDP's more general support for a strong central government capable of enacting substantial legislation in support of social democratic objectives.

The CCF had attempted to grapple with these challenges but it never came close to electing any Quebec MPs, and it failed to establish a competitive Quebec provincial wing. The NDP, too, failed to develop a competitive provincial wing in Quebec. For decades the federal party also experienced successive disappointments in Quebec, notwithstanding the occasional beacon of hope and a sense that many in the province shared its left-of-centre values and policy dispositions. Historically, the strategic question as to why this was the case had been indirectly answered by pointing to the party's substantive commitment to a strong central government, which, to most Québécois, seemed incompatible with support for the asymmetrical federalism minimally required to institutionally ground Quebec's existence as a distinct society within Canada.

In 2011, the NDP decided to address the strategic side of this dilemma with a gamble that involved devoting major attention and resources to Quebec – a gamble that paid off in a way no one inside or outside the party would have dared to predict. The NDP's victory in 59 of the province's 75 federal seats was stunning. It suggests that, at least temporarily, the party has discovered a way to finesse the apparent contradictions within its strategic and ideological dilemmas. In this chapter, we briefly trace the history of the NDP in Quebec and examine what happened in the 2011 campaign, focusing on the surge in the party's support.

Spurned Overtures and Electoral Failures

From its beginnings, the CCF found that its message of progressive transformation had little resonance in Quebec, where a conservative Roman Catholic culture protective of provincial powers dominated politically until the 1960s. The CCF's commitment to social democracy was anathema to the conservative instincts of the Roman Catholic Church in this province. Not long after the party was formed, the Church went so far as to warn Catholics against participation in the party, which it reviled for its socialism (Oliver and Taylor 1991). In addition to the CCF's economic and social agenda, its support for a highly centralized federation that could implement countrywide social and economic change was widely rejected in Quebec's francophone community. Robust provincial powers for Quebec governments were considered necessary to protect the French culture and its linguistic distinctiveness from being assimilated into the English culture that dominated in Ottawa and the rest of the country.

To many francophones in Quebec, the CCF also exuded a distinctly English and Protestant character that had little sensitivity towards French Canada. As Walter Young (1969, 215) observes: "[The CCF] had in it English Canadians who frankly demonstrated great ignorance and prejudice where Quebec and French-Canadian rights were concerned." CCF leaders often found themselves apologizing for insensitive or insulting comments about Québécois that were made by prominent English-Canadian CCF MPs such as Douglas Fisher and Hazen Argue (Sarra-Bournet 1986). Thus, over the years, notwithstanding its stated support for recognition of the bilingual and bicultural nature of Canada and its moderation of its strong centralism (Horn 1980), the CCF was never able to attract more than 2.5 percent of the popular vote in Quebec in federal elections (Sarra-

Bournet 1986; Trofimenkoff 1985). And, even with articulate and moderately high-profile provincial leaders like Thérèse Casgrain and Michel Chartrand, the provincial CCF never managed to surpass its banner election year of 1944, when, with 24 candidates, it won 2.6 percent of the popular vote and 1 seat.[1]

At the time the NDP was created, life and politics in Quebec were changing rapidly. A movement focused on progressive Quebec nationalism was gaining strength, and the older conservative Roman Catholic culture was in decline. This created opportunities as well as problems for the new party. On the one hand, the antipathy to social democratic policies that characterized traditional Catholic culture was rapidly eroding. This created room for the NDP to appeal to Quebec voters on the grounds that it offered them policies that fostered equality. On the other hand, the new nationalists in Quebec still looked to a strong provincial government to support and sustain the culture and distinctiveness of the francophone linguistic community. The NDP had inherited the CCF tradition of support for centralizing policies in the form of federal social programs and countrywide standards in areas such as social welfare and labour regulation. Such centralizing policies were anathema to Quebec nationalists, from devoted separatists to "soft nationalists," because they would undermine or unduly constrain Quebec's efforts to be "maîtres chez nous."

Yet, while the federal NDP supported strong federal social programs and national standards, NDP activists were also deeply dedicated to democracy and the rights of minorities. There was, then, widespread sympathy among the party's leaders and activists, if not its western Canadian voters, for the aspirations of nationalist Québécois who were concerned about the assimilation of francophones and inequities between French and English in Canada. At the founding NDP convention, a strong delegation from the Fédération des travailleurs du Québec (FTQ) spoke for the interests of Quebec nationalists. "Welcome and accommodation to French Canada" was evident on the convention floor (Oliver and Taylor 1991, 145). As a result, the convention endorsed not only equality for the French and English languages at the federal level but also recognition of Quebec as a nation. In a further acknowledgment of nationalist sentiment in Quebec, the convention renamed its National Council the NDP Federal Council and required one of its five vice-presidents to be francophone (Sarra-Bournet 1986). The convention also elected francophone Quebecers to the positions of federal president and associate-president, along with a vice-president from Quebec (Oliver and Taylor 1991).

TABLE 3.1
NDP popular vote in Quebec federal elections, 1962-2011

Year	% of vote	Year	% of vote	Year	% of vote
1962	5	1979	5	2000	2
1963	7	1980	9	2004	5
1965	12	1984	9	2006	8
1968	8	1988	14	2008	12
1972	7	1993	2	2011	43
1974	7	1997	2		

In 1965, the federal party convention adopted a resolution recommending that Canada adopt a constitutional provision that would entrench the special status of Quebec "as the guardian of the French language, tradition and culture" (cited in Cooke 2004, 8). That year also saw the establishment of the provincial Nouveau parti démocratique (NPD). With Robert Cliche as provincial leader, the Quebec wing of the party obtained almost 12 percent of the federal popular vote in the province but hardly any of the popular vote in the provincial election of the following year. In 1967, the party adopted a position paper supporting a form of asymmetrical federalism in policy fields impinging on aspects of community life central to the distinctiveness of Quebec (McLeod 1994), but subsequent elections in 1968 (federally) and 1970 (provincially) were disappointing for the party (see Table 3.1 for NDP popular vote in federal elections in Quebec). Thus, its attempt to finesse its long-standing ideological dilemma with respect to the province by accommodating Quebec concerns without weakening NDP support for robust social and economic powers for the federal government had little short-term effect (Oliver and Taylor 1991; Lamoureux 2012).

With support growing in Quebec for social democratic policies throughout the 1970s, and the NDP's sensitivity to the position of Quebec in the federation, many in the NDP thought that their party's popularity would grow in that province. But the NDP's history of support for a strong federalist state and its overwhelmingly anglophone organization and support base continued to be obstacles to such growth. Moreover, at the level of provincial politics, where much politically crucial building of community connections occurs, the NDP in Quebec continued to founder,[2] with divisions between radical nationalists and federalists (Oliver and Taylor 1991) as well as weak support from organized labour.[3]

In the late 1980s, there had been some hope that the federal party's chances of winning seats in Quebec would improve as its popularity began to grow in national polls. It had supported the 1987 Meech Lake Accord, which recognized Quebec's "distinct status," and, in that same year, the NDP had received good press in Quebec from its Montreal convention, which had unanimously recognized Quebec's "unique status" (McLeod 1994). With its prospects seemingly improved, the party organization placed more emphasis on developing NDP support in the province for the 1988 election campaign. But the 1988 election results were a clear disappointment, especially to Ed Broadbent, for whom, several years prior to the election, a breakthrough in Quebec had seemed not just necessary but possible. The NDP won none of Quebec's 75 seats, despite attracting its highest percentage of the Quebec vote ever (14 percent). Still, as Erickson and Laycock (Chapter 1, this volume) note, the party subsequently elected an MP in a 1990 by-election in Chambly.

Then came the 1993 election and the party's disastrous showing in all parts of the country, including areas of former strength. Concerned with its very survival, the party could not afford to devote many of its meagre resources to building a Quebec organization. Having won a mere 1.5 percent of the popular vote there in 1993, and having lost Phil Edmondston's Chambly seat, the party had no areas of strength on which to build. So the federal party put growth in Quebec on its back burner.

The problems facing the NDP in Quebec after 1993 were not limited to its lack of organizational resources. In 1993, the Bloc Québécois successfully entered national party competition in Canada. In ideological terms, the Bloc occupied a position on the left-right spectrum that was close to that of the NDP, thus limiting the ideological space within which the NDP could compete in Quebec on the sovereigntist/federalist dimension. On this dimension, the Liberals were more strongly positioned than the NDP, leaving it with few advantages in the electoral forum.[4] In the 1997 and 2000 federal elections, the NDP averaged just 2 percent of the popular vote in the province.

Building for Success

In the 2003 leadership race, Pierre Ducasse was the first Quebec francophone ever to run for the leadership of the NDP. His rousing appeal to build the party's Quebec base was received very positively on the convention floor (Curry 2004) at the same time as the party selected Jack Layton as its leader. Layton was born and raised in Quebec and became the federal party's first truly bilingual leader.[5] His strong commitment to fostering party support in Quebec (Lavigne, personal communication, 9 August 2012) put the province back on the party's agenda. In the 2004 election, the time the leader's tour allotted to Quebec stops went well beyond that allotted in most previous campaigns, and the party produced four TV ads in French after having made none in the 2000 election (Whitehorn 2004). Still, of the forty ridings across the country that the NDP campaign had initially targeted for success, just one was in Quebec. The party's popular vote in the province increased by only 5 percent.

The Sherbrooke Declaration

For many years, questions of party policy regarding Quebec separation and the province's role in the federation stood between the federal NDP and Quebec voters, especially those of various nationalist hues. The party's long-standing support for asymmetrical federalism had been given further substance through a consultative forum and subsequent report (Social Democratic Forum on Canada's Future), which was adopted at the party convention 1999; however, this report only addressed questions about the conditions for Quebec separation in a vague conclusion. Quebecers were to have the right to decide their future "democratically" (21). The requirements of a democratic decision were not explained.

For a party hoping to appeal to soft nationalists in Quebec without alienating its base in the rest of Canada, the question of the conditions for separation is difficult. Setting the bar for separation too high might alienate Quebecers who are ambivalent about separatism as it could easily offend their democratic sensibilities. In the rest of Canada, the public widely agrees that considerably more than a simple majority should be required to break up the country (Angus Reid 2013). This issue created a challenge for the NDP in 1999 when the Liberal government introduced its Clarity Act. This act gives the House of Commons the power to decide whether the question posed in a separation referendum is transparent and, following a vote on separation, to establish whether the results confirm that there has been "a clear expression of a will by a clear majority of the population ... that the province cease to be part of Canada."[6]

These conditions imply that a simple majority vote in a referendum could be insufficient for Canada to enter into negotiations for secession even if the referendum question was clear. The NDP proposed amendments to the bill, including one specifying that 50 percent plus one would constitute the "clear" majority requirement. Although this was not included in the final version of the bill, and even with an NDP Federal Council request to its caucus to oppose it, most NDP MPs ended up voting for the Clarity Act (Cooke 2004).

In the summer and fall of 2005, the federal party again addressed the issues of separation and Quebec's role in the federation and, pressed by its Quebec wing, released its "Sherbrooke Declaration" at a meeting of the Conseil général du NPD (section Québec) in Sherbrooke on 7 May 2005. With this, the party proposed "a new vision of federalism, with progressive and social democratic values that we share with the majority of Quebecers" (NDP 2005, 3). This vision was based on "principles of common good, collective rights, democracy, social and political involvement, respect for communities of origin, solidarity, cooperation, etc." (4). By the end of the eight-page document, the "etc." included "recognition, equality, respect, flexibility, transparency and honesty." Together, application of these principles to key areas of policy, especially social policy, meant that the NDP reaffirmed its earlier support for an "asymmetrical federalism." Quebec was to be allowed to exercise powers beyond those of other provinces in order to protect and promote its distinct society.[7]

The element of this declaration that caused the greatest controversy, however, was its provision that a successful referendum on Quebec's sovereignty could be won by a vote of 50 percent plus one. What seemed like unequivocal support for Quebec's "right to self-determination" enflamed Québécois federalists in the Conservative and Liberal parties and created unease among many other federalists outside Quebec. But, over time, as Chantal Hébert (2011) notes, the declaration became "party gospel in Quebec ... [t]he Sherbrooke Declaration was to Jack Layton in Quebec what the Liberal Red Book was to Jean Chrétien in the 1993 election." Retrospectively, it appears that in spite of its having rather incompletely addressed its "Quebec dilemma," the Sherbrooke Declaration may have played a role in finally enabling Québécois voters to see the NDP as a ballot box alternative (Lamoureux 2012). However, the positive effect of this did not materialize for another two elections.

Following the Sherbrooke Declaration, the party maintained its efforts to build a base in Quebec (Brad Lavigne, personal communication, 9 August 2012). It held a successful federal convention in Quebec City in 2006, with Thomas Mulcair (who had recently resigned as a provincial Liberal cabinet minister) as one of the keynote speakers. The NDP campaigned vigorously in the province during the two elections of 2006 and 2008. It entered these campaigns with an increasingly high-profile collection of candidates, an improved organization (under the direction of Raymond Guardia), and higher voter regard for Jack Layton (Lamoureaux 2011; Bittner, Chapter 8, this volume). For the first time, the 2008 federal campaign saw a fully funded NDP ad campaign in Quebec (Erickson and Laycock 2008; Leebosh 2011; Lavigne 2013). Despite its incremental establishment of these competitive electoral building blocks, the party continued to struggle in its efforts to gain real traction with past BQ and/or Liberal voters.

In 2007, Jack Layton successfully recruited Thomas Mulcair to run for the party in a by-election in Outremont, a borough in Montreal. Formerly a minister of sustainable development, environment and parks in the Liberal government in Quebec, Mulcair had agreed to run in Outremont even though it had long been a federal Liberal stronghold. He defeated the Liberal candidate by almost 20 percentage points. To aid the party's efforts to raise its profile in Quebec, he was appointed as one of the NDP's two deputy leaders in Parliament shortly after his by-election success.

Despite its increased focus on Quebec, the party remained in fourth place in the province through the 2008 election, with its popular vote rising to just 12 percent by election time. The popularity of the Bloc continued to hinder the NDP's success in attracting the left-of-centre vote. The Bloc attracted 42 and 38 percent of the popular vote in the 2006 and 2008 elections, respectively, winning 51 and 49 of the province's 75 seats.

By the end of 2008, two portents of future NDP success had appeared. One was clear enough: for the first time the NDP had elected a Quebec MP in a general election, with Mulcair retaining his seat in Outremont (see Erickson and Laycock, Chapter 2, this volume). The second, less obvious, portent of potential NDP strength was that, following its strenuous but unsuccessful efforts to establish a coalition with the Liberals (which included provisional support from the BQ) (Topp 2010), the NDP's polling numbers began to rise. Through 2009 and 2010, Bloc voters consistently named the NDP as their second choice (Leebosh 2011). So, while the 2008 election did not provide evidence of a major swing to the NDP, the campaign and events shortly thereafter secured Jack Layton and his party the status of political players to be taken seriously in Quebec. An Orange Wave was in no sense inevitable as a consequence, but winning conditions were beginning to accumulate.

The 2011 Election

The Campaign

The NDP began the 2011 election campaign in Quebec in roughly the same position it had occupied in 2008. It was in fourth place in terms of party popularity, and it was the preferred choice of just 15 percent of voters (Fournier et al. 2013). However, for some time internal party polling had indicated that "the New Democrats were the second choice among most Bloc voters and that Jack was seen as the best leader and best prime ministerial candidate among Quebecers" (Lavigne 2012, 101). They needed several breaks to convert such support into momentum and then actual votes.

The first major break came early in the campaign, when Layton, in his appearance on a popular Quebec talk show, *Tout le monde en parle*, successfully drew attention to the NDP as an alternative for Quebecers.[8] This appearance was followed by the first significant shift in NDP support in the province (Fournier et al. 2013). His performance in the French-language leaders' television debate ten days later was also a morale booster for the party (Therrien 2011; Lavigne 2013), although it was another five days after that before the next jump in NDP popularity (Fournier et al 2013). These two performances seemed to counteract a variety of media stories questioning Layton's leadership and the NDP's relevance to Quebec politics (Jury 2011; Bellavance 2011).

On *Tout le monde en parle*, Layton presented himself with confidence, connecting his party's values to those of Quebec in a way that finally seemed to resonate for both the television audience and the Quebec media. Journalist Yves Boisvert saw Layton's appearance on *Tout le monde en parle* as the turning point in the Quebec campaign. For Boisvert (2011), it was not a particular ringing phrase or policy appeal on the part of Layton that made the difference but, rather, his openness and sincerity: "À toutes les questions, il répondait sans brio particulier, mais avec un air sincère et sans affectation." And in the French-language debate on 13 April 2011, major Quebec media concluded that Jack Layton had come a strong second to Gilles Duceppe on his own turf (Marissal 2013; Bélanger and Nadeau 2012). Seen from Chantal Hébert's (2011) perspective: "The 2011 French-language election debate will go down as the first that a Bloc leader did not win hands down. Duceppe had to share the honours with Layton and it was an uneven split in the latter's favour." This helped to shore up Layton's already strong image as a potential prime minister.

The NDP's momentum in Quebec was heightened by creative and effective television advertisements that portrayed a vote for either the BQ or the Liberals as a futile way to address the two facts that the NDP's national campaign wished to convey: "Ottawa is broken" and "You have a choice of leaders."[9] By the third week in April, Jack Layton and the NDP seemed able to do no wrong in the Quebec campaign, while Gilles Duceppe's campaign entered its period of free fall (Bélanger and Nadeau 2012). A film clip of Layton raising a pint in a Montreal pub just after the Canadiens scored an overtime goal to force Boston into a seventh game in the Stanley Cup playoffs received repeated showings on Quebec television channels. And, on 23 April, the NDP held an unexpectedly huge rally in Gilles Duceppe's riding, which reinforced the recently reported poll results showing that the NDP had pulled in front of the BQ in Quebec (Lavigne 2012).

These positive developments – strong image-enhancing leadership performances by Layton and the novel situation of polls showing an NDP surge inside and outside Quebec – needed to be complemented by what the NDP campaign team referred to as the party's "air game." This was especially the case given that the party had no real "ground game" in the province. Outside of Outremont and a handful of other ridings in which it had had promising results in 2008, the NDP had relatively few party volunteers and little local party infrastructure. Having the financial resources to run a fully funded campaign meant, among other things, that the party could shift money to television, radio, and newspaper advertising in Quebec once there was evidence of a surge of support. In fact, by the end of the 2011 campaign, the NDP had spent $3 million on media advertising there – three times its 2008 campaign advertising expenditure in that province (Lavigne 2012).

The Results

On election night, the results in Quebec were of historic proportions. The NDP had finally broken through the barriers and achieved success in Quebec, winning 43 percent of the popular vote (an increase of more than 250 percent from its 2008 showing) and more than three-quarters of the seats. The *vague orange* (Orange Wave) swept across the whole of Quebec, with surprisingly little regional variation and with second-place finishes in 15 of the 17 ridings that the NDP did not win (Cliche 2011). Twenty-seven of the fifty-nine new MPs from Quebec were women. Among these fifty-nine winners, thirteen won in ridings in which the NDP had received less than 10 percent of the vote in 2008.

The overwhelming support for Thomas Mulcair from Quebec member-voters in the party's 2012 leadership contest suggests that he was seen as a key Quebec player in the party's *vague orange*. Quebec media commentary on Mulcair's role in this regard was extensive and largely in agreement. As André Lamoureux (2012, 242) later put it: "Indiscutablement, la victoire du NPD au Québec à l'élection fédérale de 2011 a été pilotée par le tandem Layton-Mulcair." The party's television advertisements in the final week of the campaign featured Mulcair and Layton talking about the party's major commitments and insisting that Quebec voters finally had a real alternative to the parties (including the Bloc) that had produced a dysfunctional Parliament and failed to defend Quebec's interests (Lavigne 2013).

The NDP's Orange Wave in Quebec benefitted from both the collapse of the BQ vote (from 38 percent in 2008 to 23 percent in 2011) and the disproportionate allocation of seats to front-running parties that results from the Canadian first-past-the-post election system. But, while the collapse of the Bloc vote was an important contribution to NDP success, the party was also able to attract former supporters of the Liberal Party and even some from the Conservative Party. Results from the 2011 Canadian Election Study show that 33 percent of those who had voted Liberal in 2008 voted NDP in 2011, while 31 percent of 2008 Bloc voters did so, as did 26 percent of Conservative voters (Fournier et al. 2013). Among new entrants to the electorate, the NDP won 65 percent of the vote. However, because the proportion of former BQ partisans was larger than that of each of the other groups, crossover voters from that party were most critical to the NDP success.

Fournier et al. (2013) found that demographic characteristics were not significant determinants of the NDP vote.[10] Of much greater importance was Layton's popularity among voters, especially in comparison to that of the other leaders. Further, the NDP's ideological affinity with many voters on the centre-left of the political spectrum was significant. As the party became more electorally credible, its ideological credentials became relevant and attractive to many, especially former BQ voters.

Previous BQ voters clearly wanted to prevent a Conservative majority government (Bélanger and Nadeau 2011) and appeared comfortable switching to the NDP because the leader known simply as "Jack" "offre aux électeurs québécois, bloquistes d'hier, une façon de quitter le Bloc avec un minimum de culpabilité" (Bombardier 2011). The party's position and reputation on issues such as the environment and higher corporate taxes reinforced its support among many voters. And doubts expressed during the campaign regarding the NDP's ability to square its progressive policy stances with support for at least a highly asymmetrical federalism did not seem to hurt the NDP on election night (Descôteaux 2011).

But what about sovereignty and the federalist dimension that had trumped support for the NDP in past elections? There is no evidence that support for sovereignty had declined in Quebec in 2011: among decided voters it hovered at around 40 percent (Leger Marketing 2013). And, among strong sovereigntists, the Bloc continued to be popular, although less so than in 2008. A crucial change for the NDP in 2011 involved its attractiveness to moderates on both sides of the sovereignty issue as well as the overall decline in the importance of the sovereignty dimension for vote choice (Fournier et al. 2013). The NDP had drawn support from both sides of the sovereignty divide, setting up a challenging balancing act for itself with regard to future Quebec issues.

Before the 2011 campaign began, among the NDP's candidates in Quebec only Thomas Mulcair had a significant profile outside the province. But the party had recruited a number of strong candidates who had had previous public exposure and credibility within the province. The list includes Françoise Boivin (Gatineau), Alexandre Boulerice (Rosemont-La Petite-Patrie), Marjolaine Boutin-Sweet (Hochelaga), Anne-Marie Day (Charlesbourg-Haute-Saint-Charles), Pierre Dionne Labelle (Rivière-du-Nord), Hélène Laverdière (Laurier-Sainte-Marie), Manon Perreault (Montcalm), Mathieu Ravignat (Pontiac), and Nycole Turmel (Hull-Aylmer). These candidates had prominent positions as trade unionists, journalists, social activists, and municipal councillors. Hélène Laverdière's distinguished career in international development had preceded her historic victory over Gilles Duceppe.

There is little doubt that NDP support in the province was crucially related to Jack Layton's astonishing popularity as leader, a corresponding decline in the attractiveness of Gilles Duceppe and the BQ to Québécois, and the resonance of the NDP platform with Québécois social values (Fournier et al. 2013; and see Godbout, Belanger, and Merand, Chapter 11, this volume). But the backgrounds and accomplishments of these new Quebec MPs contributed to the growing impression that Jack Layton was not simply a lone force for change but also the *chef d'équipe prometteur*. Still, the party also had to find candidates for many ridings in which its previous share of the local vote had often been in single digits. In doing this, it recruited many young and/or politically inexperienced candidates whose subsequent successes made the Quebec caucus a potentially more unpredictable unit (Cornelier 2011).

Notable among the youth corps were Pierre-Luc Dusseault, a nineteen-year-old elected in Sherbrooke; Laurin Liu, a twenty-year-old political science undergraduate at McGill (in Rivière-des-Mille-Îles); and Charmaine Borg, a twenty-year-old McGill student whose victory in Terrebonne-Blainville came after she had spent most of the campaign as a volunteer in Thomas Mulcair's riding (Bourgault-Côté 2011). The Quebec media were more likely than those in English Canada to praise the NDP candidates' youthfulness and energy, while acknowledging the steep learning curve ahead of them in Parliament (e.g., Courtemanche 2011). Many Quebec commentators who remarked on the inexperienced new NDP MPs stressed the challenge that a federalist party faced when its caucus contained a number of politically undisciplined soft nationalists (Bourgault-Côté 2011).

One of these new MPs, Claude Patry (Jonquière-Alma), left the NDP caucus to join the small BQ caucus in February 2013 when the NDP's proposed Bill C-470 affirmed that both the federal and Quebec provincial governments should have veto power over the wording of a referendum question on Quebec's sovereignty/separation. This allowed the Conservatives to contend that the NDP's Quebec caucus had a large sovereigntist contingent (Galloway 2013). Another new MP from Quebec, Lise St-Denis (Saint-Maurice-Champlain), defected to the Liberals in January 2012, noting of her voters: "Ils ont voté pour Jack Layton, Jack Layton est mort" (Presse canadienne 2012).

NDP Challenges in Quebec

Many commentators have characterized the NDP's 2011 election results in Quebec as an aberration that cannot be repeated in the foreseeable future. The most obvious element in the unique constellation of "winning conditions" for the NDP in 2011 was Jack Layton's remarkable appeal in the province. With "le bon Jack" gone, there has been much skepticism regarding whether the party can produce anything close to a repeat of the 2011 results.

Thomas Mulcair may lack some of the appeal that Jack Layton developed in Quebec during the 2011 campaign. However, he is well known and more highly regarded there than most other public figures. Crucially, in mid-2013 Quebec voters saw him as more able than any federal politician – including newly elected Liberal leader Justin Trudeau – to understand and effectively defend Quebec's interests (Hébert 2013b). This is significant because, for most of its successful twenty-year run, the BQ based most of its appeal on precisely this ability rather than on its advocacy of sovereignty (Young and Bélanger 2008). Mulcair may lack Layton's charisma, but he has been seen as a pre-eminent advocate for Quebec far longer than was the case with Layton.

One of the party's challenges in 2015 will be to develop an effective campaign that does not depend upon an out-of-the-blue Orange Wave. It will need to benefit more than either the BQ or the Liberal Party from any long-term damage done to Conservative Party credibility and/or loss of trust in Stephen Harper occasioned by integrity issues arising from, for example, the Senate expenses scandal. It will need to develop an effective ground game in the ridings that it has the best chance of holding. This will require it to mobilize its new Quebec membership to develop civil society connections and to generate media-assisted candidate profiles, both of which will make a difference in close races.

In this regard, its relations with organized labour in Quebec may turn out to be important. Among its victorious 2011 candidates are several MPs with strong ties to the labour movement, including Françoise Boivin, Nycole Turmel, and Alexandre Boulerice. Boivin is a former Liberal MP with a high profile in Quebec as a labour lawyer, and she first ran for the NDP in 2008. After her close defeat in that year, she increased her profile in the province with regular television appearances and as a program host for two different shows.[11] Turmel was a two-term national president of the large Public Service Alliance of Canada (2000-06) and, in 2010, a labour representative on the Management Committee of Financial Assets of the FTQ's Solidarity Fund.[12] After Layton's death, Turmel became interim leader of the party; when Mulcair became party leader, she was appointed parliamentary whip. Since his election, Boulerice has been an articulate NDP spokesperson in the House of Commons as the Opposition labour critic, working at developing ties between the NDP and two of Quebec's major organized labour federations – the Fédération des travailleurs et travailleuses du Québec and the Confédération des syndicats nationaux. Among his notable activities, he led a campaign to restore a tax credit for contributions to labour-sponsored economic development funds, which are far more significant to Quebec's economy than they are to those of all the other provinces combined.[13]

The NDP's Quebec membership tripled in the fall of 2011 to roughly five thousand (Smith 2011) but, with 12,300 members, came up short of the party's target on the eve of the 2012 leadership race. Although this number put Quebec ahead of Saskatchewan, it was still well behind British Columbia and Ontario in the party's membership rolls. In the latter two provinces, party members join through the provincial party organization, while in Quebec such an organization has yet to be effectively revived (Leblanc 2012).[14] The NDP has rejected the idea of diverting party resources to rebuilding a provincial party in Quebec before the 2015 election (Mas 2012), although such a rebuilding is a key long-term goal. It will, then, need to find ways to address the awkward imbalance between its Quebec membership and its Quebec caucus in the House of Commons that do not require a substantial presence in provincial politics. Although the NDP's Quebec membership numbers increased with the 2012 leadership race, this amounts to only a modest start on its objective of achieving a balance in overall party membership.

The NDP in Quebec is developing credibility as a voice for Quebec labour in federal affairs, thereby pursuing the party's traditional means of building an effective ground game and voter base. The party's new Quebec MPs are also becoming increasingly effective at channelling other social movement opposition to the Harper government agenda, whether on environmental, women's movement, or anti-poverty fronts. There are also reports that young new MPs are making good showings, whether as shadow critics for their party, as hard workers for their constituencies, or as pleasant surprises who have gone "from laughing stock to local hero" (Scott 2013).[15] All of this helps to legitimize the surprise (and surprised) NDP victors in many of the ridings in which most people had voted for "Jack" without knowing their local NDP candidates.

Perhaps the NDP's biggest challenge related to Quebec is to find a way to square its historic centralist commitments with two incompatible constituencies: (1) Quebec, with its many past BQ voters, and (2) the rest of Canada, where support for any form of asymmetrical federalism favouring Quebec is too small for comfort (see Weldon, Chapter 12, this volume). The Bloc, on the one side of the national question, and the Liberals and Conservatives, on the other, all have a clear interest in showing voters that the NDP's position is contradictory and even intentionally misleading.

The media and other parties' responses to Bill C-470, an NDP proposal that would replace the Clarity Act, suggests that this issue continues to be problematic for the party. NDP MP Craig Scott introduced the bill in the House of Commons in January 2013. It proposed an application of the logic found in the party's 2005 Sherbrooke Declaration as a response to a BQ motion to repeal the Clarity Act (Bill C-457). The NDP's bill stipulates that a 50-percent-plus-one vote on Quebec sovereignty would be legitimate and would oblige the federal government to enter negotiations with the Quebec government, but only if the referendum question were clear (Courtemanche 2013).

The BQ could not accept this alternative to the Clarity Act because it left the federal government, or the Quebec Court of Appeal, with the power to determine whether or not the referendum question was clear. However, the other federalist parties condemned it as a capitulation to sovereigntists because it recognizes the 50-percent-plus-one margin as acceptable. The only major English-Canadian daily to endorse the NDP in the 2011 election, the *Toronto Star*, joined the Conservative and Liberal parties in rejecting the NDP's attempt to square the nationalist circle (Fidler 2013). Condemnation of this NDP initiative was even harsher in the *Globe and Mail* (2013), which characterized it as "a step backward that will reopen old wounds and divisions for no reason other than to protect the NDP's gains in Quebec."

In Quebec, a *Le Devoir* columnist noted that, while C-470 was flawed in affirming a federal government veto on what constitutes acceptably clear referendum wording, the bill was a reasonable application of the party's principles of Quebec's right to self-determination, recognition of a simple majority referendum outcome, and constitutional asymmetry with respect to Quebec (Cornellier 2013 [cited in Fidler 2013]). If this view of the party's position on Quebec's right to self-determination was to be prevalent across the province, the NDP might retain a substantial portion of the 2015 federal election vote that it gained from the BQ in 2011. But such retention could cost it a substantial number of votes in other provinces, where even NDP leaders are unwilling to discuss the federal party's position on the Quebec question.

The enthusiasm with which the Conservative and Liberal parties attacked the NDP on Bill C-470 suggests that they are fully aware of how difficult it will be for the NDP to retain its 2011 voters in both Quebec and the rest of Canada if the "Quebec question" becomes salient in subsequent elections. In the 2011 election, this issue was overshadowed by issues that combined to favour the NDP in Quebec, and it was barely raised in the rest of Canada during the campaign. However, there is no reason to expect that other parties, especially the BQ and the Conservatives, would allow the NDP's Quebec dilemma to hide in the campaign shadows.

In fact, one might argue that the Liberal Party has special reasons to raise this issue. It is worth recalling that, even after legislating the Clarity Act in 1999, the Liberal Party received 40 percent of the vote in Quebec in the 2000 federal election. Should Justin Trudeau attract many young voters who supported the NDP in 2011, along with traditional Liberal federalists and perhaps even some soft nationalist votes, the Liberals might close in on the NDP's 2011 results in Quebec. The Liberal position on Quebec is strategically more attractive than that of the NDP and the Conservative Party, each of which is sandwiched between the BQ and the Liberals (see Weldon, Chapter 12, this volume).[16]

To conclude, the NDP's 2011 breakthrough in Quebec has presented it with a political challenge that it now has good reasons both to savour and to fear. With its representation from Quebec at a once unimaginable level, the federal party can now legitimately claim to have electoral and popular strength across the country. The 2011 election removed a long-time problem – failure in Quebec – in what seemed a decisive manner. On the other hand, a combination of BQ, Liberal, and even Conservative vote gains in Quebec in subsequent elections would deal a crushing blow to the NDP – just when it had finally found fertile political soil in that province. The NDP's ability to stay ahead of the Liberals nationally clearly relies on its fortunes in Quebec. As this chapter shows, predicting these fortunes and their implications is not an easy task.

Notes

We would like to thank Jean-François Godbout and Éric Bélanger for their careful review of, and suggestions concerning, this chapter.

1 Details available at *QuébecPolitique.com*, http://www.quebecpolitique.com/elections -et-referendums/elections-generales/election-generale-de-1944/. For other Quebec provincial election results, see http://www.quebecpolitique.com/elections-et -referendums/elections-generales. For more details on the CCF/NDP experience in Quebec, see Lamoureux (1985, 2012).

2 See, for example, commentary on Quebec provincial politics and the NDP, available at http://www.quebecpolitique.com/elections-et-referendums/elections -generales/election-generale-de-1998/; and http://www.quebecpolitique.com/elections -et-referendums/elections-generales/.

3 Because of the complications in provincial Quebec politics, the NDP in Quebec focused primarily on federal politics and entered provincial elections only sporadically. This situation is unique among the NDP's provincial experiences, where relative federal strength is built on a competitive provincial NDP (Erickson and Laycock 2009). Indeed, after 1994, when it ran forty-one candidates in the provincial election, the provincial party's support for Quebec independence in the following year's referendum precipitated a split with the federal NDP organization. The resulting provincial "Parti de la démocratie socialiste" fielded ninety-seven candidates in the 1998 Quebec election but none in subsequent provincial elections.

The history of the NDP in provincial politics is covered by Sarra-Boumet (1986) and Lamoureaux (1985).

4 The Liberal advantage over the NDP in this regard is well conveyed in Godbout and Høyland (2011).

5 On the importance of a party having a francophone leader if it wishes to obtain substantial votes in Quebec, see Nadeau and Blais (1993).

6 An Act to Give Effect to the Requirement for Clarity as Set Out in the Opinion of the Supreme Court of Canada in the Quebec Secession Reference 2000, available at http://laws.justice.gc.ca/eng/acts/C-31.8/page-1.html.

7 See the *Social Democratic Forum on Canada's Future* (New Democratic Party 1999), presented as a preliminary report to the Federal Council on 30 January 1999 and discussed at the National Convention of the New Democratic Party, 27-29 August 1999.

8 See interview with Jack Layton, *Tout le monde en parle*, April 2011, http://www.youtube.com/watch?v=LvY8804AKv0.

9 See, especially, two TV ads available at http://www.youtube.com/watch?v=mPcCds Zz0kI and http://www.youtube.com/watch?v=xC1ZWHY3TBU.

10 The only demographic characteristic that Fourier et al. found to be determinants of an NDP vote was university graduation. University graduates in Quebec were less likely to vote NDP.

11 See item in Wikipedia at http://en.wikipedia.org/wiki/Francoise_Boivin.

12 See item in Wikipedia at http://en.wikipedia.org/wiki/Nycole_Turmel.

13 See Pétition: Sauvons les fonds de travailleurs et travailleuses des coupures conservatrices, http://www.jappuie-boulerice.org/petition_sauvons_les_fonds_de _travailleurs_et_travailleuses.

14 The Nouveau Parti démocratique du Québec was registered in January 2014 with Pierre Ducasse listed as its leader. However, the party ran no candidates in the 2014 Quebec election.

15 The reference to local hero is to Ruth-Ellen Brousseau.

16 We wish to thank Jean-François Godbout for making this point.

References

Angus Reid Public Opinion. 2013. Canadians Would Feel Dissatisfied, Sad if Que- bec Became Independent. http://www.angus-reid.com/polls/48636/canadians -would-feel-dissatisfied-sad-if-quebec-became-independent/.

Bélanger, Éric, and Richard Nadeau. 2012. The Bloc Québécois: Capsized by the Orange Wave. In Jon Pammett and Christopher Dornan, eds., *The Canadian Federal Election of 2011*. Toronto: Dundurn.

Bellavance, Joel-Denis. 2011. Layton a la cote. *La Presse*, 7 April. http://www. lapresse.ca/actualites/elections-federales/201104/07/01-4387326-layton-a-la -cote.php.

Blatchford, Andy. 2012. NDP Will Run in Future Quebec Elections, Mulcair Says. *Toronto Star*, 17 August. http://www.thestar.com/news/canada/2012/08/17/ndp_ will_run_in_future_quebec_elections_mulcair_says.html.

Boisvert, Yves. 2011. NPD: L'effet *Tout le monde en parle. La Presse,* 4 May. http://www.lapresse.ca/debats/chroniques/yves-boisvert/201105/03/01-4395874-npd-leffet-tout-le-monde-en-parle.php.

Bombardier, Denise. 2011. Jackpot. *Le Devoir,* 30 April. http://www.ledevoir.com/politique/canada/322283/jackpot.

Bourgault-Côté, Guillame. 2011. De la jeunesse au NPD ... *Le Devoir,* 4 May. http://www.ledevoir.com/politique/canada/322558/de-la-jeunesse-au-npd.

CBC. 2011. Special Report: The Death and Legacy of Jack Layton. *CBC News,* 22 August. http://www.cbc.ca/news/politics/story/2011/08/22/f-jack-layton-death-legacy.html.

Cliche, Jean-François. 2011. Le "mystère Québec" englouti par une marée néo-démocrate. *La Presse,* 4 May. http://www.lapresse.ca/le-soleil/dossiers/elections-federales/201105/03/01-4395838-le-mystere-quebec-englouti-par-une-maree-neo-democrate.php.

Cooke, Murray. 2004. Constitutional Confusion on the Left: The NDP's Position in Canada's Constitutional Debates. Paper presented at the Annual Meeting of the Canadian Political Science Association, Winnipeg, 3-5 June.

Cornellier, Manon. 2011. Il était une fois un depute. *Le Devoir,* 9 May. http://www.ledevoir.com/politique/canada/322908/il-etait-une-fois-un-depute.

Courtemanche, Gil. 2011. Des devoirs pour le NPD. *Le Devoir,* 7 May. http://www.ledevoir.com/politique/canada/322817/des-devoirs-pour-le-npd.

—. 2013. Redéfinir la clarté. *Le Devoir,* 30 January. http://www.ledevoir.com/politique/quebec/369601/redefinir-la-clarte.

Curry, Bill. 2004. Dashing Ducasse Gives Hope for the Future. *National Post,* 16 November. http://www.canada.com/story.html?id={FBA9BD4E-58AE-4DB1-B052-A10DE66E09ED}.

Descôteaux, Bernard. 2011. Élections fédérales: La tentation néodémocrate. *Le Devoir,* 30 May. http://www.ledevoir.com/politique/canada/321664/elections-federales-la-tentation-neodemocrate.

Erickson, Lynda, and David Laycock. 2009. Modernization, Incremental Progress, and the Challenge of Relevance: The NDP's 2008 Campaign. In Jon H. Pammett and Christopher Dornan, eds., *The Canadian Federal Election of 2008,* 98-135. Toronto: Dundurn.

Fidler, Richard. 2013. The NDP Revisits the Clarity Act. Blog, posted 31 January. http://lifeonleft.blogspot.ca/2013/01/the-ndp-revisits-clarity-act.html.

Fournier, Patrick, Fred Cutler, Stuart Soroka, Dietlind Stolle, and Éric Bélanger. 2013. Riding the Orange Wave: Leadership, Values, Issues and the 2011 Canadian Election. *Canadian Journal of Political Science* 46, 4: 863-97.

Galloway, Gloria. 2013. Tory Claim of NDP's Sovereigntist Sympathies Gets New Boost with MP's Defection to Bloc Québécois. *Globe and Mail,* 28 February. http://www.theglobeandmail.com/news/politics/tory-claim-of-ndps-sovereigntist-sympathies-gets-new-boost-with-mps-defection-to-bloc-qubcois/article9149307/#dashboard/follows/.

Globe and Mail. 2013. Editorial: NDP Bid to Repeal Clarity Act Is a Bad Move for Canada. 29 January. http://www.theglobeandmail.com/commentary/editorials/

ndp-bid-to-repeal-clarity-act-is-a-bad-move-for-canada/article7936888/
#dashboard/follows/.

Godbout, Jean-François, and Bjørn Høyland. 2011. Legislative Voting in the
Canadian Parliament. *Canadian Journal of Political Science* 44, 2: 367-88.

Hébert, Chantal. 2011. Why Quebec Is Loving Jack, Leaving Gilles. *Toronto Star,*
23 April. http://www.thestar.com/news/canada/2011/04/23/hbert_why_quebec
_is_loving_jack_leaving_gilles.html.

–. 2013. Not so Fast, Don't Count Out Mulcair. *Hill Times,* 6 May. http://www.
hilltimes.com/inside-politics/2013/05/06/not-so-fast-don%E2%80%99t
-count-out-mulcair/34581.

Horn, Michiel. 1980. *The League for Social Reconstruction: Intellectual Origins of
the Democratic Left in Canada, 1930-1942.* Toronto: University of Toronto Press.

Jury, Pierre. 2011. Layton: du solide? *La Presse,* 8 April. http://www.lapresse.ca/
le-droit/opinions/editoriaux/pierre-jury/201104/07/01-4387653-layton
-du-solide.php.

Lamoureux, André. 1985. *Le NPD et le Québec, 1958-85.* Montréal: Editions du Parc.

–. 2012. Impasse historique, vague orange et nouvelle ère Mulcair: Le Nouveau
Parti démocratique et l'épreuve du Québec. *Bulletin d'histoire politique* 21, 1:
207-53.

Lavigne, Brad. 2012. Anatomy of the Orange Crush: Ten Years in the Making.
Policy Options (June-July): 93-101.

–. 2013. *Building the Orange Wave: The Inside Story behind the Historic Rise of Jack
Layton and the NDP.* Madeira Park, BC: Douglas and McIntyre.

Leblanc, Daniel. 2012. NDP Membership Blitz Comes up Short in Quebec. *Globe
and Mail,* 22 February. http://www.theglobeandmail.com/news/politics/ndp
-membership-blitz-comes-up-short-in-quebec/article549283/.

Leger Marketing. 2013. Referendum Voting Intentions in Quebec. http://www.
legermarketing.com/admin/voting_int/Referendum_Voting_Intentions_in_
Quebec2012.pdf.

Leebosh, Derek. 2011. NDP Hits the Jack-Pot in Quebec: From Decades of Work to
Overnight Success. *Policy Options* (June-July): 113-18.

Marissal, Vincent. 2011. Layton et Duceppe volent le show. *La Presse,* 14 April.
http://www.lapresse.ca/debats/chroniques/vincent-marissal/201104/14/
01-4389666-layton-et-duceppe-volent-le-show.php.

Mas, Susana. 2012. Mulcair Delays Plans for a Provincial NDP in Quebec. *CBC
News,* 4 November. http://www.cbc.ca/news/politics/story/2012/11/04/pol-tom
-mulcair-provincial-ndp-in-quebec-on-hold.html.

McLeod, Ian. 1994. *Under Siege: The Federal NDP in the Nineties.* Toronto: Lorimer.

Nadeau, Richard, and André Blais. 1993. Explaining Election Outcomes in Canada:
Economy and Politics. *Canadian Journal of Political Science* 26, 4: 775-90.

NDP. 1999. *Report of the Social Democratic Forum on Canada's Future.* http://
www.canadian-republic.ca/pdf_files/ndp_1999.pdf.

–. 2005. Quebec's Voice and a Choice for a Different Canada: Federalism, Social
Democracy and the Quebec Question. Statement adopted by the General
Council of the NDP Quebec Section. http://www.pierreducasse.ca/IMG/pdf/
Declaration_Sherbrooke_ENG_V2.pdf.

Oliver, Michael, and Charles Taylor. 1991. Quebec. In Leo Heaps, ed., *Our Canada: The Story of the New Democratic Party Yesterday, Today and Tomorrow*. Toronto: Lorimer.

Presse canadienne. 2012. Du NPD au PLC, Lise St-Denis change de camp. *Le Devoir*, 10 January. http://www.ledevoir.com/politique/canada/339943/du-npd-au-plc -lise-st-denis-change-de-camp.

Sarra-Bournet, Michel. 1986. The CCF-NDP in Quebec: The Lessons of History. *Canadian Parliamentary Review* 9: 10-13.

Scott, Marian. 2013. Fresh-Faced NDP Members Have Risen to the Challenge. *Montreal Gazette*, 13 April.

Smith, Joanna. 2011. NDP Membership Soaring in Quebec. *Toronto Star*, 14 November. http://www.thestar.com/news/canada/2011/11/14/ndp_membership _soaring_in_quebec.html.

Therrien, Richard. 2011. *Tout le monde en parle*: Jack Layton devant un public conquis. *La Presse*, 9 May. http://www.lapresse.ca/le-soleil/arts-et-spectacles/ television-et-radio/201105/08/01-4397407-tout-le-monde-en-parle-jack-layton -devant-un-public-conquis.php.

Topp, Brian. 2010. *How We Almost Gave the Tories the Boot: The Inside Story behind the Coalition*. Toronto: Lorimer.

Trofimenkoff, Susan Mann. 1985. Thérèse Casgrain and the CCF in Quebec. *Canadian Historical Review* 66: 2, 125-53.

Whitehorn, Alan. 2004. Jack Layton and the NDP: Gains but No Breakthrough. In Jon H. Pammett and Christopher Dornan, eds., *The Canadian General Election of 2004*, 106-38. Toronto: Dundurn.

Young, Lori, and Éric Bélanger. 2008. BQ in the House: The Nature of Sovereigntist Representation in the Canadian Parliament. *Nationalism and Ethnic Politics* 14, 4: 487-522.

Young, Walter. 1969. *The Anatomy of a Party: The National CCF, 1932-1961*. Toronto: University of Toronto Press.

4

Modernizing the Party

DAVID LAYCOCK and LYNDA ERICKSON

Over the last few decades, modernization has been a frequent subject in analyses of social democratic parties. It often appears as a theme in studies of contemporary conservative parties (such as those in Britain, Canada, and Australia) to help explain how they recovered their competitiveness after decisive and extended electoral failures. Attention to social democratic party modernization since the mid-1970s has shown that it has been less successful than conservative modernization. The broadly shared postwar Keynesian and welfare-state-expanding policy paradigm of social democratic parties has been on the defensive over this period as new right-wing political forces and the business advocates and/or beneficiaries of globalization set a new policy agenda. Throughout Western Europe, Australia, and New Zealand, social democratic parties scrambled to adapt, often with policies more accepting of market-led social resource distribution and less reliance on statist solutions to social problems than in the past. In this context, modernization typically signalled a shift towards centrist policy choices (or at least policy instrument choice) and more efforts to appeal beyond a core working-class constituency to the middle class. The NDP came rather hesitantly and "incompletely" to modernization; however, it has unquestionably modernized in key ways.

We must consider party modernization if we are to make sense of the NDP's electoral advances over the past decade (as described in Erickson and Laycock, Chapter 2, this volume). Party critics and loyalists (Lavigne

2013) agree that modernization has been decisive to these advances, even though they disagree regarding whether the party has sacrificed too much for this electoral progress. Understanding key aspects of the party's modernization process can also help to facilitate comparison of the NDP with other Western social democratic parties.[1]

In this chapter we address the question of modernization, paying special attention to its organizational aspects. In particular, we focus on the interaction between appeals to the electorate, campaign techniques, and intra-party organizational change. We begin with a discussion of how we can usefully conceptualize modernization in social democratic parties over the last several decades. We then focus on four key aspects of the NDP's post-2003 modernization: agency, institutions (with an emphasis on party finance), communication strategies, and organization. These four foci are primarily related to the campaign performance of the federal NDP under the leadership of Jack Layton – a campaign in which the leader's tour attained particular prominence. Finally, we consider how party modernization challenged the NDP's internal democratic governance and traditions, particularly regarding its significant centralization over the course of eight years and four federal elections.

Modernization in Contemporary Social Democratic Parties

Parties of the left have modernized in various ways since making the transition from social movements to competitive political organizations during the early years of the twentieth century. Starting with the classic work of Robert Michels (1911), analysts have offered a wide variety of explanations concerning how socialist parties have attempted to reconcile themselves to, on the one hand, the potentially antithetical imperatives of power-seeking through democratic elections and, on the other hand, the pursuit of evolving socialist and social democratic goals relating to social change (see, for example, Przeworski 1985; Przeworski and Sprague 1986; Pierson 2001; Moschonas 2002; Berman 1998, 2011). Conceived broadly, party modernization has entailed a range of strategic, organizational, and ideological decisions intended to keep social democratic parties "in the game" of competitive electoral politics in both advanced welfare states and emerging democracies.

Recent analyses of contemporary social democratic parties conceptualize modernization in a variety of ways. Some are critical (e.g., much of the academic and left-journalist commentary on Tony Blair's New Labour or on the Australian Labor Party since Bob Hawke); some offer little more than a loose way of characterizing the adoption of campaign techniques already being used by major competitors, suggesting that the party in question is playing strategic catch-up in a competitive game that it has finally taken seriously. However, some focus more usefully (and using relatively specific criteria) on the features of policy change undertaken by governing social democratic parties.

For our purposes, a blend of analytical perspectives offers the most appropriate approach to addressing modernization in the NDP. In particular, we utilize the perspectives of Merkel et al. (2008) and Padgett (2003) to facilitate a discussion of how the NDP has combined programmatic change, the promotion of new policy instruments, new methods of appealing to the electorate, updated campaign techniques, and intra-party organizational change. As mentioned, our primary focus in this chapter is on the last three phenomena (the first two are discussed in more detail in Chapters 5 and 6).

In his analysis of modernization within the Social Democratic Party of Germany (SPD) under Gerhard Schroeder, Steven Padgett (2003, 38) focuses on the "three interrelated fronts of programme, electorate and organization." He argues that the SPD's program changes were constrained by its competitive need to successfully appeal to different segments of the electorate and that the amount of power still retained by party activists limited Chancellor Schroeder's ability to liberalize the party program and government policy. Merkel et al. (2008) examine four aspects of social democratic party modernization in six European polities. They are attentive to the connections Padgett addresses but focus on political discourse, party core values, policy objectives, and policy instruments. Depending on how parties combine these four aspects of governance, they are classified as a traditional social democracy, a modernized social democracy, or a liberalized social democracy.

In a traditional social democracy, the party retains traditional policy objectives and core values such as equality and solidarity, advocating and implementing traditional policy instruments associated with an expansive universal welfare state, extensive regulation of business, and perhaps some state ownership of industry. A traditional social democratic party government, such as Sweden's, may reduce tax rates, alter some of the regulatory framework, and even make some universal program coverage less comprehensive or generous. But the basic policy objectives do not change.

In a modernized social democracy the party retains traditional policy objectives and core values but combines traditional policy instruments with newer instruments, such as carbon taxes and modestly priced additions to existing health care and economic stimulus/employment measures. In some cases, the mix of policy instruments favours shorter-term adjustments and augmentations of existing programs over the creation of major new programs. New policies are implemented with modified political discourses and campaign strategies in order to meet an altered competitive environment.

In a liberalized social democracy, the party displays new policy objectives and central emphases, with notably modified core values and new policy instruments. These are presented and implemented with modified political discourses and campaign strategies to meet altered competitive environments (Merkel et al. 2008, 227-29).

The federal NDP has not governed, so our analysis of its modernization cannot take into consideration governing records in order to assess whether its policy objectives and measures/instruments are consistent in practice (as do Merkel et al. for governing social democratic parties in Europe). We note the Padgett and Merkel et al. analyses to underscore the fact that core values, policy objectives, policy instruments, adaptive political discourses, and updated campaign strategies fit together. Their fit may not be seamless – Padgett and Merkel et al. note inconsistencies, especially for the German, French, and UK parties – but taking note of the European governing parties reminds us to search for a pattern to the federal NDP's coordination of core values, policy objectives, policy instrument choice, intra-party organization, campaign strategies, and electoral appeal.

By suggesting that this coordination follows a traditional pattern, a modernizing pattern, or a liberalizing pattern, Merkel et al. enable us to avoid choosing between "traditional" and "modernizing liberalized" social democracies, with which Padgett and many Canadian commentators on the NDP present us. However, Padgett (2003, 53-55) draws our attention to something that Merkel et al. overlook: the intra-party organizational factors that affect social democratic party modernization. Furthermore, Padgett's account of the German SPD's modernization under Gerhard Schroeder highlights the role of agency in the form of new party leadership, something that was critical to NDP modernization in the Jack Layton era.

With regard to classification, the pattern followed by Layton's NDP is something of a hybrid between the traditional and the modernized forms of social democracy, with the emphasis clearly in the latter. Like the Swedish and Danish social democratic parties in the 1990s discussed by Merkel et al. (2008), the NDP under Layton selected some new policy instruments,[2] electoral appeals, and campaign techniques, but it did not appear to do so in the pursuit of significantly altered policy objectives or underlying core values. This conclusion is reinforced by the fact that, during the time Layton led the federal party, party activists did not use conventions to criticize the leadership for having departed from the basic policy objectives that had been constructed through intra-party debate at previous conventions.

Like the Scandinavian social democratic parties, the NDP discovered that new policy instrument choices are linked to, and can be conveyed more effectively by, modified political discourse and campaign strategies. Such strategies were selected in response to an altered competitive environment, in which Conservative ascendance and Liberal and BQ decline provided a new strategic opening into which the Layton-led NDP was able to fit. Unlike Blair's "liberalizing" New Labour (Merkel et al. 2008), the NDP's addition of a new key policy emphasis – the environment – did not come at the expense of its traditional policy objective and core value mainstays.[3]

The federal NDP's modernization covered all aspects of its operations and its interaction with a rapidly shifting federal party system. In the following section, we consider institutional and organizational factors as well as matters of agency and message communication in driving modernization in the party.

Agency, Institutions, and Organization in NDP Modernization

Agency
Modernization of the party's campaign strategies, its organization, and its leadership power under Jack Layton was partly a function of the changed circumstances the NDP encountered within the federal party system following the 2004 election. Put simply, the party could not afford to continue with the historically poor showings it had experienced since 1993. A change in course had to be attempted if it was to have a future, and "modernization" in some form had worked for social democratic parties in the United Kingdom, Germany, and Australia. But to understand the overall pattern and eventual impact of the party's specific approach to modernization, one must appreciate its motivation. Here considerations of agency – specifically, of leadership – cannot be avoided.

Jack Layton became leader because he believed the federal NDP could seriously contend for power despite its dismal electoral record in the 1990s. Key advisors and office staff understood, along with Layton, that doing this would require the party's campaign performance to be "brought up to code" relative to successful, government-forming social democratic parties in Europe and Australia.[4] This would entail using research, communication, and ground-game management tools that were, for the first time in federal NDP experience, at least on par with "industry standards."[5] After the disappointing results of the 2004 election, Layton's team agreed that a clear, coherent message concerning the party's policy intentions would need to be far more effectively delivered not just during but also between elections. As soon as Layton became leader, he and his team determined that repeating the poorly organized, unfocused, and underfunded 2000 federal campaign was not an option. Bringing the party up to a competitive standard would mean changes to party fundraising, campaign organization, and ground-game delivery; election platform construction and delivery; and approach to traditional and new social media communication.[6] Becoming competitive also required careful development of new areas of party support, strategic selection of ridings on which to focus party money and efforts, and patience among party members and activists. We address this last requirement in the final section of the chapter.

Institutions: Fundraising, Public Party Finance, and Modernization
Finances have been critical to the NDP's modernization and to its successful campaign organization. Both external and internal institutional factors were key to facilitating this modernization. Externally, federal changes in campaign and party financing provisions gave the NDP a considerable financial boost, putting other aspects of its modernization agenda within reach. Internally, the party became a much more efficient fundraising organization, which, in turn, helped it to become far more proficient at planning and running competitive campaigns. We begin with the external changes.

Party Finance Rule Changes and the Federal NDP
Party financing in Canada has long been a hybrid of private and public financing. Private contributions from individuals, businesses, and organizations (such as unions) were the mainstay of party finances until 2004. While subject to disclosure requirements, these contributions were not limited. Public financing came in the form of limited tax rebates for individual contributions and partial reimbursements for the election expenses of parties and candidates.[7] In 2003, in the wake of the sponsorship scandal that threatened the governing Liberal Party, Prime Minister Jean Chrétien

introduced a series of reforms intended to deflect criticism of the government with regard to ethics issues. One part of these reforms involved substantial changes to party financing legislation, including a ban on corporate and union contributions to national parties, a limit on individual contributions,[8] and a substantial increase in the public funding of federal parties.[9] The latter included higher reimbursements for election expenses incurred by parties and candidates and a quarterly allowance for between-election financing paid to parties based on the number of votes they received in the previous election (Young and Jansen 2011).

Initially, the NDP was concerned that the ban on union contributions would have negative implications for its overall finances. Historically, unlike its major competitors, the NDP could not turn to business to provide funding for its electoral and other activities. Individuals and unions were the mainstay of NDP finances, with the latter providing about a quarter of the party's annual income (Jansen and Young 2009). However, as party financing changes came into effect in 2004, the quarterly allowances and larger election reimbursements combined to provide a more comfortable financial position for the party, especially at election time. Indeed, with the cushion of quarterly allowances making borrowing for election expenses easier, the party was able to outspend the Liberals in the 2008 election (Young and Jansen 2011).

Internal Fundraising Capacity

When Jack Layton became party leader, fundraising work was still outsourced to non-party contractors, even with a director of fundraising working in the federal party office. By 2005, the federal NDP had professionalized and brought its fundraising work fully in-house. Expertise developed by fundraising staff working day to day with other staff responsible for related aspects of party operations allowed for faster decision making and better coordination with the growing communications department. It also enabled a better understanding of which resources could be deployed in upcoming elections or even, occasionally, used for advertising between elections. An exception to this new in-house fundraising practice came in the 2011 election. When the federal party sensed that it stood a good chance to make a significant breakthrough in Quebec, its campaign team realized that fundraising there should be handled by professionals who understood how Quebec's distinct political culture shaped successful fundraising strategies. So the party contracted out this work to a Quebec firm.[10]

One crucial constraint on the modernization of party financing activities was deeply embedded in the NDP's federal party structure. In 2003, fundraising was still largely the work of provincial sections of the party. In fact, until 2009, "service contracts" between the federal and provincial parties specified that, while 15 percent of provincial fundraising monies would be transferred to the federal party office, direct federal party contact with party members – who could not join the federal party except by obtaining provincial section membership – required permission from provincial secretaries. This made anything like the kind of regular direct mail contact that secured large funds for the federal Conservatives simply impossible for the federal NDP. And without such regular direct mail and e-mail solicitation, the federal NDP struggled to have enough funds to run professionally up-to-date competitive communications operations, leader's tours, media campaigns (i.e., "air games") or strong constituency ground games from coast to coast to coast.

Following the steady increase in votes and seats in the federal elections of 2006 and 2008, the federal party office successfully negotiated with its provincial counterparts to bring these restrictive service agreements to an end. Several aspects of the new arrangements were of key importance. First, the federal party would no longer transfer money to the provincial sections to conduct vital ground-game activities between elections. With the new 2009 agreement, the federal party could hire and direct its own regional field organizers to work between elections. Their time would no longer be split between the demands of provincial sections and the federal party; even if the organizers were "locals," their loyalties, lines of communication, and strategic orientations would be to the federal party, not the provincial one. These federal party field organizers took responsibility for coordinating candidate searches, improving local campaign readiness, and generally enhancing local capacity to contest elections.

Another result of the 2009 unfettering of the federal party's fundraising and organization activities from provincial section control was that the federal party could afford to provide guaranteed revenue streams to all provincial sections. This was more important in those provinces with weaker provincial parties and fundraising infrastructure less fully developed than in Ontario, Manitoba, Saskatchewan, and British Columbia. So, for example, the 2011 federal ground game in Newfoundland and Labrador far surpassed that of 2008, resulting in notable improvements in popular vote and seats.

The federal party certainly heard complaints from numerous long-time members (who were accustomed to no more than three or four contacts from their provincial party annually) about the federal office's frequent use of direct mail solicitation. However, many members welcomed the new regimen of frequent contact from the federal party, saying, in effect: "Where have you been all these years?" And wresting control over fundraising away from the provincial sections meant that the federal office could measure its success with the new practices quite precisely. Tracking monthly intake and/or numbers of new contributors was now quite simple. This allowed the federal party to see how much better the new arrangements were for it financially and led it to conclude that the potential for new and more consistent contributors outweighed the sting of member and provincial section criticisms.

While federal NDP financing has become more modernized and effective in terms of internal revenue generation, the party faces a new challenge as a result of changes in federal government funding provisions. When the Conservative Party won majority government in 2011, one of its early policies, introduced in its first budget, involved a phase-out of the quarterly allowance system, which was to be completed by 2016 (Jansen and Young 2011) and which would leave individual contributions the overwhelming source of party revenue. Having invested heavily in building its individual donor system and substantially outperforming the other parties in attracting individual contributions, the Conservative Party was well placed to compete in an environment without quarterly allowances. On a yearly basis, individual contributions to the NDP average less than a quarter of those to the Conservative Party. This reflects both the fact that the average size of individual donations to the Conservative Party is higher than the average size of donations to the NDP and the fact that the number of Conservative contributors is substantially larger than the number of NDP contributors.[11]

Modernizing Federal Party Organization and Campaigns

The most striking thing about the NDP's performance in recent elections, besides its ascension to Official Opposition and success in Quebec, has been its highly centralized, professional, and leader-dominated campaigns. After five years and two election campaigns under Layton's leadership, by 2008 the NDP's finances and campaign delivery drew even with and then outperformed those of all but the winning party. These developments signalled that the federal NDP had made considerable progress in dealing with the

changed federal party system dynamics that had so dramatically marginalized it between 1993 and 2003. In fact, the NDP's success in stepping back
from the brink of partisan oblivion compares well to that of the other major
casualty of the 1993 election, the Progressive Conservative Party. To put it
simply: if the PC Party had made substantially more headway against its
rival on the political right, it seems quite unlikely that it would have felt the
need to merge with the Canadian Alliance in 2003.

As noted by Laycock and Erickson (Chapter 2, this volume), in the
leadership contest of 2003, Layton attracted support across the left-right
axis, with endorsements from left-wing MPs Svend Robinson and Libby
Davies, former leader Ed Broadbent, party operatives, and union activists.
He was outspoken about the need to once more make the party relevant to
Canadian voters, had a slogan promising "new energy, new leadership," and
spoke both to his campaign team and to his campaign audiences about the
need for "modernization" of the party. The party's 2002-03 leadership
campaign came on the heels of a federal election campaign in 2000 that
was run more like 308 by-elections than like a modern, coordinated, well-
financed federal election campaign.[12]

So it is perhaps not surprising that Layton's message regarding "modernization" and "relevance" resonated with members and activists across the
left-right spectrum of the party and that it did much to provide him with his
surprising first ballot victory (something not even T.C. Douglas had managed). Former national director Brad Lavigne argues that, in his leadership
campaign, Layton managed to displace the left-right axis of traditional
intra-party debate with two overlapping axes: (1) "relevant to Canadians'
daily lives/not relevant," and (2) "credible, affordable, doable/not credible
and affordable."[13] Put in other terms, he removed the party's core social
democratic values from dispute and, taking them as a given, invited his
audience – first party members, then Canadian voters – to consider whether
the party's policy agenda could make a difference to them if he became
prime minister.

The preceding narrative only emerged fully in the 2008 election campaign, which Layton began by announcing that he was running to be prime
minister. This bold stroke was linked to his modernization agenda. Becoming prime minister would require that voters take Layton and his
party seriously as a governing alternative. This could only be achieved
if the party's campaign and inter-election communication, fundraising,
leader tour planning, and coordination were "brought up to code," with all

campaign tools used to "industry standard." To Layton's team, this was not a matter of ideological choice; rather, it was a matter of becoming a serious modern political party. As James McLean (2012) argues in his detailed account of the role played by the party's "war room" in the 2006 campaign, getting others to take the NDP seriously as a political party with a capacity to govern involves, among other things, acquiring credibility among the media and, thereby, the larger public. One way of thinking about the whole modernization push under Layton's leadership is as a multi-pronged attempt to increase the NDP's media and public credibility.

The nature of Layton's party leadership victory within the context of his appeal for modernizing the party gave him the internal support the party required to modernize. Unlike Blair's modernization message and agenda in the United Kingdom's Labour Party (Russell 2005), Layton's empahsis on modernization was not seen as a threat, even by his high-profile supporters on the left.[14] They had supported him in spite of the fact that, in 2001, with their New Politics Initiative, they had suggested a rather different "modernization via social movement vehicle." These NPI activists may have been surprised by Layton's selection of "governance wing" members to key positions in the leader's office and the federal party office, but he managed to keep the vast majority of them on board with his agenda. If they criticized his policy positions and leadership style as "too centrist" or as turning away from too many of the NDP's socialist commitments, they did so almost entirely in house.

The party's domination by Layton's office and its federal office was reflected in campaign planning, with its increased focus on leader tours, more extensive use of polls, and strategic targeting of "next-tier" ridings (i.e., those in which the NDP had finished second in the previous election). This domination was also reflected in the refining of the party's message during and between elections; in the leader's heightened profile and role in conventions; in an increasingly effective use of communications and social media; and in party fundraising, which allowed for the financing of increasingly competitive campaigns.

By 2008, with greater central planning and delivery capacity than it had ever enjoyed, the NDP's federal office ran its most centralized and professional campaign ever. And polling was an important element in helping to direct campaign efforts, including an emphasis on short-term policy objectives in campaign platform construction.[15] Polling during the 2008 and 2011 campaigns focused on daily tracking polls and targeted polls in "riding clusters" in and around "next-tier" ridings. Respondents were asked standard "top-of-mind" questions to determine their issue concerns; they were also asked about their voting intentions and leader preferences. Occasional polls were conducted on request in other ridings on a one-off basis. This private polling provided federal party strategists with guidance on the use of the "strong leader" theme throughout the 2008 campaign, on its connection to the economic protection theme, and on whether the leader's tour itinerary, established well before the writs were dropped, should be readjusted in light of updated next-tier riding polling (Erickson and Laycock 2009). The process was similar in the 2011 campaign polling.

Regional and local input, while regularly solicited through the federal Election Planning Committee prior to the election, had little impact on the short-term aspects of the campaign, including tour planning, advertising content, daily national news releases, and website and party platform content. Speechwriters and the party communications office relied on local input for specific local references in the leader's daily tour stops, but there was no question that the 2008 and 2011 tours were planned and run by professional teams backed by extensive communications, war room, and other personnel in the party's headquarters.[16]

Organizational Modernization and Communication

In 2003, communications was a department of one; by 2011, the federal party office's communications department had ten employees. During federal campaigns going back to pre-Layton times, this department had been assisted largely by MPs and House of Commons caucus staff on campaign leave. From 2004 through 2011, the federal party office's IT department also grew. This made for a more smoothly run party website and better e-mail communication with party members. It also enabled close work between IT and communications staff during campaigns, so that social media such as Facebook and Twitter could do increasingly important voter contact and media outreach/messaging work. Just managing Jack Layton's impressively successful Facebook page was a full-time job for several staff.[17]

The federal NDP office did not attempt to build in-house capacity for advertising. In 2008 and 2011, a Toronto firm handled print and television advertising for the party's campaign in English Canada, while a Montreal firm handled its campaign in Quebec. Two television advertising spots in the 2011 Quebec campaign successfully captured both the party's core message and the public mood. One fifteen-second spot that did double duty as a TV advertisement and a viral YouTube video depicted a hamster running on a treadmill, with the voice-over saying: "Politics has stalled in Ottawa. It's time that this changed." The other fifteen-second spot, which featured dogs barking at each other, had a voice-over saying: "Always the same debates that lead nowhere. It's time that this changed."[18]

The NDP spent $10 million on television advertising in the 2011 campaign, including just over $1 million on online advertising. The party's communications department chose a combination of online entertainment and news sites that were likely to be viewed by various targeted demographics, and it utilized pop-up or other advertisements on these sites. This was not restricted to Canadian Internet sites: a Canadian reading the daily e-mail synopsis of news from the *New York Times* would frequently see a simple Layton-focused NDP ad and a link to a longer campaign message. The point of this and all online advertising is to "meet millennials (18-30 year olds) where they are," which is not in front of a nightly network news broadcast but online (Brad Lavigne in Blevis 2012). In light of its strong record attracting eighteen- to thirty-year-old voters since 2006 (Gidengil et al. 2012), the NDP's increased reliance on social media makes perfect modernizing sense and may have given the party a crucial extra boost in its Orange Crush in Quebec.

Traditional advertising, mainly in the broadcast media, is still important for reinforcing the main platform themes and the party's preferred "ballot question." It is crucial to use the right kinds of media to reach specific groups and demographics. Social media are not appropriate for every political advertising/communication job (Lavigne in Blevis 2012), and carefully choosing particular television shows allows the party, sometimes with apparent success, to reach demographics that have previously tilted strongly towards the Conservatives (Anderson 2012). The lion's share of the 2011 and 2008 advertising budgets, worth close to half of the total campaign budget, went to TV advertising.

A Simple Core Message

Just as the party's inter-election image had increasingly come to be dominated by the leader – strikingly so during party conventions[19] – so the party's electoral appeal came to centre on Layton's ability to "get results" for ordinary Canadians. This approach was virtually required by the gap between voters' approval of Layton and their considerably lower preference for the NDP to govern, and it was vindicated by improved NDP voting intention numbers over the course of the 2008 and 2011 campaigns.

The last two NDP campaigns featured a simpler set of themes than did its previous campaigns. Party strategists ensured that, in all of their advertising, news releases, and staged media coverage, Layton was identified as the primary protector of reasonable middle-class aspirations as represented in these themes and policy priorities. In developing the party's 2008 and 2011 platforms, the leader's office and the Election Planning Committee – also controlled by long-time Layton loyalists – stressed the need to create a pragmatic document. They wished to "change the channel" on the previous media portrayal of the NDP as a high-tax, high-spending party with no realistic sense of government revenues. The needs of ordinary Canadians were to be addressed with pragmatic and incremental policies, which Layton described in 2008 as "a very measured, step-by-step approach" (Menzie 2008, 19).

In presenting these focused policy measures as representing long-standing NDP policy objectives and core values, party strategists offered a steady stream of policy announcements whose purpose was to hold the media's focus. The focus on leader Layton, the use of a handful of simple themes, and an emphasis on making the party relevant to voters by filling its platform and Layton's tour promises with practical, affordable measures were all part of the larger modernization strategy. Launching a simple-themed, practical, policy-focused campaign that was effectively communicated through a well-financed, well-executed leader's tour and competitive air game (with TV ad buys) also took some time. Both the 2004 and 2006 campaigns were considerably less successful in this regard than were the 2008 and 2011 campaigns. With more funds, and more regional presence in its nationally directed ground game, in 2008 and 2011 it was easier to use sophisticated and expensive social media platforms and strategies, along with oft-shown TV ads, to reinforce the core messages of the platform and leader's tour.

Increasing success in the latter two campaigns was also partly a function of Jack Layton's growing political and campaign skills. Modernization, money, in-house campaigns, strategic capacity, and industry-standard communications techniques made it possible for Layton's strengths and charisma to show through. Another leader with as much charisma but without a competitive modernization agenda would not have achieved nearly as much. And, had the party not revamped its fundraising techniques, its modernization would have been less substantial. Indeed, the "whole architecture of the 2011 campaign" was based on the party's being able to spend the legal maximum of $22 million.[20] The federal party would not have been able to take advantage of the NDP's greater ideological proximity to the "median voter" in Quebec without the apparent success, in 2011, of the fundraising regimen.[21] This allowed the party to use a well-financed television advertising campaign in Quebec to make up for its organizational shortcomings on the ground in all but a handful of Quebec ridings.

Inevitably, modernization strategies for any party wishing to break into the main competitive field are expensive. Effectively demonstrating competence to a large audience requires a major cash outlay, not just a strong leader or clever party tacticians. By 2011, the federal NDP had the money needed to make modernization pay off. How or whether elimination of the quarterly allowance system, which was certainly part of the party's financial capacity, will hamper the party in the future is, of course, unknown.

The Leader's Tour

The leader's tour is an unavoidable centrepiece of national party campaigns, the primary job of which is to establish a core message on which the national and local campaigns' voter appeal can be based. With the NDP decision to focus so much on its leader, this part of the campaign became more critically important to the party's prospects than it had been in its pre-Layton days. By 2008, the tour accounted for just under 25 percent of the total campaign budget (Erickson and Laycock 2009). The well-resourced tours of 2008 and 2011 gave considerable prior attention to the details of each event, including the use of signs, favourable venues, local notables, and background research on the ridings (which aided in speech-writing).

Overall, the 2008 and 2011 tours were highly synchronized with the rest of the campaign, so that the message and presentation were more coordinated than were earlier NDP campaigns. In Merkel et al.'s (2008) terms, the campaign presented a straightforward, easily repeated set of specific policy measures whose aim was to convey support for the party's traditional policy objectives and core values. Its simple policy focus did not deliver any fundamentally new value choices or central policy objectives, though it did contain a tougher stance on law and order and supported tax breaks for businesses that created new jobs (Laycock, Chapter 5, this volume). Nor did the increased profile of the NDP's "green economy" message mean that other basic party themes and objectives had been displaced. The party was thus a blend of traditional and modernized, and, in this regard, remained well outside the category of liberalized social democratic parties.

Modernization and Party Democracy

Party modernization has clearly been a major challenge for the federal NDP. Until now, we have only alluded to the additional tensions it may have created between party members and activists, on the one hand, and the party leadership and federal party office, on the other. This deserves more attention.

Even before he won the party's leadership, Jack Layton recruited his support staff and election team from both the governance wing and the diverse social movement wing of the party. Seasoned provincial NDP administration political staffers were mixed with union and new social movement activists and organizers.[22] Both groups appreciated that there was tension between the more centralized and disciplined operations needed to become seriously competitive on the national stage and the legitimate desires of party members and activists to shape party policy and strategy.

The serious risk that such centralization poses to its members' ability to have meaningful democratic control of the party had to be acknowledged and offset in some way. By the 2008 election campaign, this was achieved through two channels. The first involved regular, in fact often weekly, communication between the national campaign headquarters and regional groupings of candidate campaign managers. Conference calls from the national campaign headquarters gave local campaign operatives and activists a clear idea of how headquarters saw the national and regional campaigns unfolding. This, in turn, gave them an opportunity to provide important feedback on how local campaigns were proceeding, which kinds of problems were being encountered, and so on. The central campaign headquarters made the crucial decisions regarding the route and agenda of the leader's tour well in advance. It also selected the key themes and specific approaches to issue framing that would be presented in the leader's tour, and it was understood that local campaigns would need to complement them.

Being kept in the loop well in advance made it easier for local campaigns to stay on message, to anticipate developments in the expected flow of the campaign, and to discipline their local troops. Avoiding surprises is dear to the heart of every local campaign organizer or manager, and experienced local volunteers feel far better working to a clear plan than participating in a sequence of ill-coordinated events and tasks. The second factor that offset potential local campaign irritation with the centralized, tightly scripted and disciplined national campaign was the central headquarters' ability to provide local campaigns with more resources for local media buys. This ability was partly due to the federal party's enhanced fundraising revenues, which came from the steady flow of direct mail and e-mail solicitations from members across the country. These increased dramatically between 2006 and 2008 and hit full stride in 2009.

Despite local and provincial annoyance at the way the federal party increasingly "treated members like ATMs,"[23] this move paid substantial dividends at the local level, allowing many individual candidates to run financially competitive campaigns. Additional funds at this level facilitated a more widespread local dimension to the national air game. This made up for significant weaknesses in the ground games of many local campaigns and allowed them to stay in synch with the messaging designed by the central headquarters. Local candidates' campaigns thus benefitted in important ways from central control of the key campaign decisions. And if the leader's tour visited a local riding, for strategic reasons carefully identified well in advance of the campaign, that local campaign almost always "got a bounce."

All of this meant that, while some local campaigns and candidates predictably chafed at the degree of central control exercised by the federal party's campaign headquarters, more local candidates appeared to have better chances of winning than had been the case before the advent of such highly disciplined and centralized campaign operations. Party activists annoyed by continual fundraising pitches from the national office and its centralized control over the campaign were nonetheless happy to see a substantial improvement in the prospects of electoral success. Whether on the left or on the right of the party, activists wanted the NDP to win.[24] Sensing that this was a real possibility did much to counter activist frustrations with centralized control of their party, which, from their perspective, should value grassroots control.[25]

Whichever other hats party activists wear, as party activists they are also power-seekers.[26] "Moral victories" and having the party act as the "conscience of Parliament" are not enough. As Erickson and Zakharova (Chapter 7, this volume) discuss, our party member survey evidence demonstrates this quite independently of whatever the federal party leadership believed.

Because Layton's desire to make his party a contender and himself prime minister was shared by party activists, it appears they were prepared to accept the diminished role in party decision making concomitant with a dominant leader and a centralized campaign. Or at least they were prepared to do so temporarily, during the unusual circumstances of Layton's leadership, in which four elections were held over eight years, putting the party on an almost constant battle footing. The NDP's historical nemesis, the Liberal Party, was staggering in the ring. Not using tools that the party could finally afford to deliver a potential knockout blow to the Liberals would be self-indulgent and, for a serious political party, irrational.

But this concession to centralized power within competitive party operations – the "Michelsian" impulse[27] – could not take the form of a continuing blank cheque for the leader and his or her team. The NDP's identity and historical experience as a democratic political movement meant that a rebalancing of member and leader/party organizational power would have to occur relatively soon. As former federal party president Brian Topp argues, the real challenge for the federal NDP as a serious contender for federal power is to find a way to balance the modern, centralized operations that go with being a contender, on the one hand, with a renewed experience of internal party democracy, on the other. Such a balance involves many factors, including serious debate at conventions and the ability of the Federal Council and other internal representative bodies to have real influence on the party's strategic decision making between elections. Party/member balance also requires that the party's stakeholder groups be included in its various deliberations. Unions, environmentalists, the lesbian-gay-bisexual-transgender (LGBT) community, women, and Aboriginal people all need to see themselves represented during and between conventions. There is no question that combining these elements of democratic party control with electoral success is an extremely tall order, that modernization tilts a party towards centralized operations, and that electoral desiderata will most likely trump those of democratic control (see Laycock and Erickson, Chapter 13, this volume).

The modernized campaign delivery described in the previous section was quite consistent with a leader-dominated party organization in which party conventions, party leadership selection processes, and policy development all reflected the influence of an increasingly popular leader who had found ways to make almost all key elements in the party feel included and effective. Beginning in 2006, party conventions gave theretofore unseen visual priority to the leader's image. At roughly this time, policy development processes culminating in biennial conventions were more carefully directed by the Federal Council than had been the case in previous leadership eras, with closer connections to the leader's inner circle, including the Election Planning Committee. Convention discussion of policy resolutions from constituency organizations and the Federal Council in pre-plenary workshops ensured both that minority voices could be heard and that embarrassing resolutions would be winnowed out prior to plenary debates observed by major media. Votes on key resolutions within plenary sessions were almost always preceded by prearranged statements given by spokespeople for groups within the NDP whose support was crucial to demonstrating the party's internal diversity.[28]

Thus, while intra-party democracy was still more alive in the federal NDP than it was in the other major parties, during Layton's era the leader and his loyalists controlled national conventions and, consequently, policy development in ways that more closely resembled leader domination of such processes by their major associates in the Socialist International. It is important to add, however, that the leader's power in the federal NDP did not attain the level achieved by Tony Blair in his "liberalization" of the British Labour Party. This is another reason for contending that Layton's NDP is best characterized as a "modernized" rather than as a "liberalized" social democratic party (Merkel et al. 2008).

Conclusion

The federal NDP went some way towards developing full "modern party" status during Jack Layton's leadership. In this chapter we review the financial, organizational, institutional, communication, and strategic dimensions of this modernization. We argue that, while this modernization did not come at the cost of significant change to the party's core values and ideology, it did unleash growing tendencies to centralize power, moving it away from party members and activists. Since this took place in an extended period of constant battle readiness – four elections in eight years – it is unclear how much of this tilt towards enhanced leader and party office power was a function of electoral requirements. But there are good reasons to believe that modernization under any electoral circumstances reduces the power of members and activists within a party (Padgett 2003; Merkel et al. 2008; Russell 2005).

Party modernization during the Layton years is difficult to disentangle from the agenda and popularity of the leader. He brought a clearer, more urgent message of modernization and relevance than the NDP had ever seen, and his team worked hard, with support from many elements within the power-seeking party, to turn this slogan into competitive reality. With crucial assistance from enhanced fundraising and a professionalized campaign strategy, Layton left the party in a historically impressive competitive position.

Notes

1 We do not attempt any systematic comparisons of this type in this volume, but we do believe that the results of our analysis help open the door to such comparative work.

2 Examples of this include changes to small business taxes and carbon tax proposals. For more detail, see Laycock (Chapter 5, this volume).

3 Our assessment of the party's modernization record has been informed by interviews with key players in its campaign and its inter-election leader's office management, especially former party president Brian Topp and former national director Brad Lavigne. Topp coordinated the NDP's 1997 and 2004 election campaign war rooms, was national director of its 2006 and 2008 campaigns, and played a major advisory role in both the 2008 attempt to form a Liberal-NDP coalition to replace the Conservatives after they lost the confidence of the House of Commons in late 2008 (Topp 2010) and in the 2011 election campaign. Lavigne was director of communications in the NDP's 2000 federal campaign, director of strategic communications for the party from 2003 to 2006, director of strategic communications for the Honourable Jack Layton from 2006 to 2009, and national director of the NDP from 2008 through April 2012, overseeing the political and administrative operations of the federal party. In 2011, Lavigne was national campaign director. We would also like to thank federal NDP staffers Ira Dubinsky, Bob Gallagher, Tara Peel, Nammi Poorooshasb, and Michael Richard for their time and provision of information in November 2008 interviews.

4 Interview with Brian Topp by David Laycock, 8 August 2012.

5 Interview with Brad Lavigne by David Laycock, 9 August 2012.

6 Interviews with Brian Topp and Brad Lavigne.

7 The basic framework of party financing regulation dated to 1974, when disclosure requirements became more systematic and stringent and when rebates and reimbursements were introduced.

8 The original limit placed on individual contributions in 2004 was, in 2006, reduced to $1,000 by the minority Conservative government.

9 Prior to 2006, a corporation or union could contribute up to $1,000 to a local party association or candidate, but in 2006 that too was banned.

10 Interview with Brad Lavigne.

11 In 2011, individual donations to the Conservative Party averaged $206.21 compared to $196.60 for the NDP; however, the number of contributors to the Conservative Party outnumbered those who contributed to the NDP by almost three to one (see http://www.punditsguide.ca/finances/).

12 Interview with Brad Lavigne.

13 Ibid.

14 This was to change later in the decade as high-profile left-wing supporters like Judy Rebick became upset by what they saw as the party's shift towards the centre.

15 Interview with Brad Lavigne.

16 This contrasts somewhat with James McLean's (2012) picture of the 2006 NDP campaign and the party war room's role in it.

17 Interview with Brad Lavigne.

18 Can be viewed at *Mark Blevis, Digital Public Affairs,* http://markblevis.com/
    brad-lavigne-on-transforming-political-communication-and-outreach/.
19 Interview with Brad Lavigne.
20 Ibid.
21 While the quarterly time period for reporting party contributions complicates
    comparing contributions from one election to another, the evidence suggests that
    the NDP was considerably more successful at fundraising in the 2011 election than
    it was in the 2008 election. In the former, during the two quarters closest to the elec-
    tion, the party raised $5.01 million from 40,301 contributors, whereas in the latter
    election the comparable numbers were $3.64 million from 36,575 contributors.
22 Interviews with Brian Topp and Brad Lavigne.
23 Interview with Brian Topp.
24 Interview with Brad Lavigne.
25 See Pétry (Chapter 6, this volume).
26 Interview with Dawn Black by David Laycock, 9 August 2012.
27 See Robert Michels's *Political Parties* (1905). In this classic study, Michels makes
    the case that political parties all operate in line with the "iron law of oligarchy,"
    which inevitably empowers senior and continuing officials in the party organiza-
    tion over either activists or elected officials, thus squeezing out serious expressions
    of grassroots control or meaningful intra-party democracy.
28 One of the authors of this chapter attended the 2006, 2009, and 2011 federal con-
    ventions. Comments here are based on personal observations at these events.

References

Anderson, Drew. 2012. NDP Making Inroads among Traditional Conservative
    Demographics. *iPolitics.ca,* 17 May. http://www.ipolitics.ca/2012/05/17/drew-
    anderson-ndp-making-inroads-among-traditional-conservative-demographics/.
Berman, Sheri. 1998. *The Social Democratic Moment: Ideas and Politics in the
    Making of Interwar Europe.* Cambridge, MA: Harvard University Press.
−. 2011. *Social Democracy's Past and Potential Future.* In James Cronin, George
    Ross, and James Shoch, eds., *What's Left of the Left: Democrats and Social
    Democrats in Challenging Times.* Durham, NC: Duke University Press.
Blevis, Mark. 2011. Audio recording of interview with Brad Lavigne. *Mark Blevis:
    Digital Public Affairs.* http://markblevis.com/brad-lavigne-on-transforming
    -political-communication-and-outreach/.
Erickson, Lynda, and David Laycock. 2009. Modernization, Incremental Progress
    and the Challenge of Relevance: The NDP's 2008 Campaign. In Jon Pammett
    and Christopher Dornan, eds., *The Canadian Federal Election of 2008,* 98-135.
    Toronto: Dundurn.
Gidengil, Elisabeth, Neil Nevitte, André Blais, Joanna Everitt, and Patrick Fournier.
    2012. *Dominance and Decline: Making Sense of Recent Canadian Elections.*
    Toronto: University of Toronto Press.
Jansen, Harold, and Lisa Young. 2009. Solidarity Forever? The NDP, Organized
    Labour and the Changing Face of Party Finance in Canada. *Canadian Journal of
    Political Science* 42, 3: 657-78.

−. 2011. State Subsidies and Political Parties. *Policy Options* (October): 43-47.

Lavigne, Brad. 2013. *Building the Orange Wave: The Inside Story behind the Historic Rise of Jack Layton and the NDP.* Madeira Park, BC: Douglas and McIntyre.

McGrane, David. 2011. Political Marketing and the NDP's Historic Breakthrough. In Jon Pammett and Christopher Dornan, eds., *The Canadian Federal Election of 2011,* 77-109. Toronto: Dundurn.

McLean, James S. 2012. *Inside the NDP War Room: Competing for Credibility in a Federal Election.* Montreal and Kingston: McGill-Queen's University Press.

Menzie, Robert. 2008. NDP Courts "Progressives." *Toronto Star,* 30 September.

Merkel, Wolfgang, Alexander Petring, Christian Henkes, and Christoph Egle. 2008. *Social Democracy in Power: The Capacity to Reform.* London: Routledge.

Michels, Robert. 1911. *Political Parties: A Sociological Study of the Oligarchical Tendencies of Modern Democracy.* 4th ed., translated by Eden and Cedar Paul. New York: Free Press.

Moschonas, Gerassimos. 2002. *In the Name of Social Democracy: The Great Transformation, 1945 to the Present.* New York: Verso.

Padgett, Steven. 2003. Germany: Modernising the Left by Stealth. *Parliamentary Affairs* 56, 1: 38-57.

Pierson, Christopher. 2001. *Hard Choices: Social Democracy in the 21st Century.* Cambridge, UK: Polity Press.

Przeworski, Adam. 1985. *Capitalism and Social Democracy.* Cambridge, UK: Cambridge University Press.

Przeworski, Adam, and John Sprague. 1986. *Paper Stones: A History of Electoral Socialism.* Cambridge, UK: Cambridge University Press.

Russell, Meg. 2005. *Building New Labour: The Politics of Party Organization.* New York: Palgrave Macmillan.

Topp, Brian. 2010. *How We Almost Gave the Tories the Boot.* Toronto: Lorimer.

Young, Lisa, and Harold J. Jansen, eds. 2011. *Money, Politics and Democracy: Canada's Party Finance Reforms.* Vancouver: UBC Press.

PART 2

THE IDEOLOGICAL EVOLUTION OF THE PARTY

5
Conceptual Foundations of Continuity and Change in NDP Ideology

DAVID LAYCOCK

This chapter provides an analysis of the changing conceptual architecture of the ideology of the federal NDP after 1988. I apply the method of analysis developed by Michael Freeden (1996), which focuses on the logic holding together "core" and key "adjacent" and "perimeter" concepts in a party's ideology. I examine how the evolving conceptual architecture of the NDP relates to shifting policy foci for the federal party and how it has used populist frames in appealing to the Canadian public.[1] In the following chapter, François Pétry uses a quantitative analysis of federal parties' campaign platforms since 1988 to provide a largely complementary account of where the NDP has located itself in relation to the other federal parties in the ideological space of federal politics in Canada.

Analyzing Conceptual Foundations of Ideological Change in Party Politics

There is no shortage of approaches in the political science literature to the study of ideological change. The most widely referenced involves the quantitative method used by the Comparative Manifesto Project (CMP), the results of which are evident in Chapter 6 of this volume. The advantage of the CMP method is that it is less subjective than other methods, and its results are more comparable across parties and systems. The key value of Michael Freeden's more normative and densely conceptual approach is its capacity to identify overarching and overlapping logics that weave together prominent policy concerns, specific kinds of voter appeals and "representational claims" (Saward 2011), and underlying normative conceptual foundations within political discourse. Using Freeden's approach, we can "drill down" below the patterns established by the CMP approach to consider whether the tectonic plates of party ideology are shifting. Policy fashions and priorities can shift rapidly, but, as Ian Budge (1994) contends, parties are not often inclined to change their ideological orientation. Freeden's approach helps us to gauge whether policy shifts signal fundamental ideological change.

Freeden proposes that we map any particular ideology using core, adjacent, and perimeter concepts. Core concepts are basic normative commitments (such as equality, liberty, or solidarity) that anchor an ideology over time. Adjacent concepts are also basic and/or normative but are less heavily weighted and not so essential to the ideology. They are often second-order normative concepts (such as conceptions of human rights) or general institutional orientations to political practice (such as participatory democracy or group representation) that are instrumental to the achievement of core conceptual objectives. Perimeter concepts are typically policy positions or symbolic features (such as proposals for a cap-and-trade system for greenhouse gas emissions, electoral reform, or medicare). They are also, in a sense, instrumental to the more basic core and adjacent concepts (Freeden 1996).

The dynamic character of any ideology results from all concepts within each zone being "essentially contestable." As Freeden puts it, essential contestability means that every ideology gives a specific meaning to, or attempts to "decontest," each key concept in its political discourse, even when these are all contested (i.e., actively debated) outside the ideology. With widely used concepts such as equality or democracy, other ideologies are especially keen to offer compelling accounts of how these key terms are best understood. For each ideology's loyal audience, "decontestation" – attaching an uncontested meaning to a concept – of these key terms is successful. (One could say, in fact, that what makes a party loyalist is her/his acceptance of a party's larger effort to decontest key concepts in social and political life.)

However, political competition among parties and organizations with distinct ideologies ensures that no party's efforts to decontest its key concepts for all citizens are successful. This means, for example, that equality will always remain an "essentially contested concept," the meaning and socio-political implications of which remain a matter of fundamental dispute within party systems and across civil society. Democratic political competition is, from this perspective, an elaborate set of efforts to gain political advantage by widening the range of citizens persuaded by specific parties' efforts to decontest key concepts that frame their views of political life.

In any ideology, the essential contestability of key concepts operates within a whole system of concepts. To put this schematically, we could say that, while party X's conceptualization of equality is distinct from party Y's, and hence contested, party X's concept of equality is internally "decontested" in terms of other key concepts in its own ideological morphology, whether in its core, adjacent, or perimeter zones. Thus, for the NDP, equality is decontested (i.e., given a party-specific meaning) via its connection to the party's decontested concepts of freedom, human rights, democracy, inclusive policy making, and medicare – to take just a small sample of the concepts influenced by the party's (evolving) understanding of equality. Any "decontestation" of equality or any other key concept is provisional and will change over time as new policies are advocated by the party and as the weight and range of core and adjacent concepts changes. Thus, understanding what any party means by equality requires us to consider how it deploys a range of related concepts.

Over time, concepts may drift from an ideology's core to an adjacent conceptual zone (or vice versa) or from an adjacent to a peripheral zone (or vice versa). Such shifts often depend on whether other major ideological challengers, including but not restricted to political parties, have altered the national policy and political agenda and created broad citizen acceptance of particular policies or institutionalized practices (like medicare) or more general foundational commitments (like pluralistic democracy). The acceptance of medicare in Canada by the 1970s meant that not just the NDP but also the Liberals and the Progressive Conservatives treated "universal access to health care" as an adjacent concept (even though it was ideologically conditioned in party-specific ways by distinctive connections to other key concepts in each party's ideology). Concepts may also drift from the core to the adjacent to the perimeter realm of an ideology's morphology, as, for example, did "state ownership of the means of production" in most socialist parties between 1917 and the end of the twentieth century.

This chapter identifies core concepts, key adjacent concepts, and policy-specific examples of perimeter concepts in federal NDP ideology. My application of the Freeden method revolves around questions pertaining to five central concepts. The first four are equality, democracy, an active state, and solidarity. In each case, I ask how they have acted as interrelated core concepts in the NDP's ideology since 1988 and whether/how their meaning has changed significantly between then and now. The fifth concept, populism, is less a concept than a label for an important dimension of NDP and most social democratic party ideologies. I consider its significance to NDP ideology and appeal since 1988 and assess whether its use as a framing device in NDP appeals has changed.

These questions derive from a substantial historical and comparative literature that establishes equality, democracy, an active state, and solidarity as fundamental normative commitments and ideological anchors in social democratic thought not only in Canada but also in other Western democracies (Berman 2006; Callahan et al. 2009; Cronin, Ross, and Shoch 2011; Freeden 1996; Martin and Riche 1996; Meyer 2007; Meyer and Rutherford 2012; Sassoon 2000; Russell 1999; Wiseman and Isitt 2007; Whitehorn 1992). The question concerning the NDP's populism derives from my earlier work on populism (Laycock 1990, 2005). The implicit hypotheses contained in these questions focus on the distinctly Canadian features of these ideological foundations while still inviting a comparative perspective.

Note that these questions do not amount to posing the perennial question that surfaces in commentary on the NDP: "Has the NDP become a left-liberal rather than a social democratic party?" (Zakuta 1969; Young 1969; Cross 1973; Morley 1984; Morton 1986; Whitehorn 1992; Carroll and Ratner 2005; Wiseman and Isitt 2007). From a Freedenite point of view, this question is too conceptually non-specific and misses the evolving and complex essential contestability operating among ideologies.

To answer these questions, I draw primarily on a variety of official party statements and materials, including federal NDP responses to parliamentary throne and budget speeches, federal campaign materials, party leader speeches, and party convention documents and internal committee reports.

The New Party: Defining Postwar Social Democracy in a 2.5 Party System

With the creation of the NDP in 1961, the concepts of equality, democracy, and solidarity carried over to the party's ideological core from that of its predecessor, the Co-operative Commonwealth Federation, as did an evolving conception of an active state. The latter entailed less state ownership than envisioned at the time the CCF was created but more than was envisioned in most Western social democratic parties of the 1960s. Among adjacent concepts, a distinctively "positive" notion of liberty and the idea of organized labour power influentially conditioned all of the party's core concepts.

Equality, democracy, and solidarity occupied centre stage throughout the decade in which Tommy Douglas led the party. They were presented through left-populist appeals that were nonetheless often characterized by a technocratic approach to the state as planner and initiator of economic activity.

Equality

The NDP expressed its concern with equality in several forms, including proposals to limit campaign expenditures, extensions of the CCF campaign for an expanded welfare state (Draft Program, the New Party, 1961, sections 1 and 2),[2] taxation that was fair to working people and not so advantageous to "the top 5 percent,"[3] secure incomes for farmers (Draft Program, the New Party, 15-16),[4] and greater power for unionized workers (Draft Program, the New Party, 20).[5] By the late 1960s, the NDP also supported the objectives of second-wave feminist efforts to reduce gender-based inequalities (McDonald 1987; Morton 1986).

Closely related to the new party's concern with equality was its understanding of solidarity. This entailed support for "workers by hand or brain," whether urban or rural, because, as economic agents, they shared fundamental challenges, and, as social beings and citizens, they shared basic needs. The party's solidaristic egalitarianism was shared by unionists and social gospellers (Allen 1971) but was conceived in primarily class terms. The party's orientation to "economic democracy," discussed below, expressed a view of solidarity that distinguished the NDP from all of its partisan rivals.

Active State

The New Party Declaration of 1961 opened with a promise to "apply new methods of social and economic planning," to implement a "Guaranteed Employment Act" that would provide jobs for all "as a matter of social right," and "to establish new industries." The NDP announced that it "differ[ed] fundamentally from the other parties." These parties had been "forced by events into increasing intervention into the economy," but they offered only "reluctant tinkering" and "pious speech" regarding "free enterprise," when "the economy [was] effectively in the hands of corporate

giants." The NDP's alternative was extensive public and cooperative ownership, with "direct public accountability and control" in "the operation of
utilities, the development of resources, the elimination of monopoly con-
centration of power, and the operation of major enterprises immediately
and directly affecting the entire nation." The party also committed to extensive national economic planning. This would entail consultation with
"all major economic groups" through an "Economic Advisory Council," a
"Federal-Provincial Planning and Development Council," a federal "Investment Board" to coordinate both public and private investments, and the
"selective repatriation of Canada's resources and industries from foreign
owners" (New Party Declaration, cited in Cross 1973, 33-35).

In all but the last proposal, the NDP echoed arguments for national
planning that had characterized federal CCF literature in the 1930s and
1940s (Laycock 1990, chap. 4). In this light, the 1969 Waffle faction's call
for the "nationalization of the commanding heights of the economy, such
as the key resource industries, finance and credit, and industries strategic
to planning our economy" ("Waffle Manifesto," in Cross 1973; see also
Erickson and Laycock, Chapter 2, this volume) was not so much a break
from the party's past as a demand that the federal party return to its new
party distinctiveness.

By the 1970s, this emphasis on extensive state ownership and national
planning had already declined. A notable exception is NDP insistence on
the creation of Petro-Canada as a condition of its support for a Liberal
minority government in 1972. The NDP remained distant from both the
Liberal and Progressive Conservative parties on such matters, shifting its
interventionist orientation more towards a combination of progressive
taxation[6] and an expansion of the federally supported welfare state.[7]

Democracy

The key to the early NDP's distinctive conceptualization of democracy is
found in its proposals for economic planning and reallocation of resources
from the wealthy to "the people." This also has its roots in the CCF's understanding of "economic democracy," which involved cooperatives and credit
unions "democratically controlled and supported by millions of Canadians"
(Cross 1973, 37), strengthened trade unions, and a strong state regulatory
and ownership presence in what it still saw as an unjust, undemocratic
market.

In this conception of economic democracy, citizens would hold state
planners accountable through parliamentary elections, and all affected

parties and economic interests would be included in economic planning exercises. A strong moral sense that corporate power was antithetical to "the people's" self-government, and hence to economic security, drove all of the early NDP's proposals for economic planning and regulation. The early federal NDP thus combined technocratic enthusiasm for economic planning with advocacy of cooperatives and other means of decentralized citizen control over economic activity.

The federal NDP also made its internal party democracy key to its appeal. Unlike the "old line parties," the NDP's democracy was new because its agenda was provided by ordinary people as members of a democratic organization. A 1976 compendium of federal party policy boasted: "Alone among Canada's political parties, [the NDP] develops and establishes its policies at regular conventions of its membership [and these policies become] the political program of the Party and form the basis of its election platform" (NDP 1976, i). NDP leaders and activists portrayed the Liberal and Progressive Conservative parties as the "Tweedledee and Tweedledum" agents of corporate Canada.

With respect to proposals for democratic political institutions and practices, compared to the CCF, the NDP offered few new ideas. However, the 1961 New Party Declaration's promotion of a repatriated constitution with an entrenched bill of rights, "equal recognition and respect for both the main cultures," stronger research capacities for opposition parties and stronger Parliamentary committees, Senate abolition, and limits on parties' campaign spending are all noteworthy (Cross 1973, 39-40).

Populism

By populism I mean an ideological appeal to, and on behalf of, "the people" against "elites" – in this case primarily corporate elites. This appeal has deep roots in Canadian social democracy, particularly in both earlier farmers' and unionized workers' movements. Analytically, there is no reason to see populism and social democracy as antithetical: populism has both left- and right-wing variants, with distinctive characterizations of the antagonism between the people and the elites (Laycock 1990, 2005).

The NDP's first two leaders both had a populist touch. T.C. Douglas was famous for folksy, cross-class appeals and humorous but hard-hitting critiques of Canada's economic and major party elites. He brought a populist appeal on behalf of medicare from its Saskatchewan roots to the national stage, insisting that Canadian governments treat quality medical care as a social right rather than as a market commodity. David Lewis, Douglas's successor in 1971, built his 1972 federal election campaign around a slogan – "corporate welfare bums" – that neatly reversed the right-wing complaint about welfare cheats and provided a punchy left-populist theme for the NDP campaign.

In this era, left populism was an "adjacent concept" in the NDP's overall ideology, crucially conditioning key core conceptual commitments and themes. The party's appeal concerning democracy was simultaneously a populist appeal. Economic democracy based on farmers' and workers' voices and needs was contrasted with a democracy that did little to convert equal voting power into social equality.

Ed Broadbent and Rising Expectations

As federal leader between 1975 and 1989, Ed Broadbent was at the helm when the NDP entered a more recognizably "modern" phase as a social democratic party. His stances on most policy issues were in the centre of the party's ideological spectrum, with the exception of his early enthusiasm for industrial democracy (Broadbent 1970). He was less inclined to push for extensive state ownership than was the Waffle faction, but he insisted that only the NDP could be trusted to protect the Canadian welfare state. Under his leadership the party proposed major federal government investments in public- and private-sector job creation, better housing for lower-income Canadians, and an employment-focused regional development program. The party promoted federal support to farmers through marketing boards, enhanced workplace health and safety and union rights, support for women's social and economic equality, medicare coverage of dental and pharmaceutical expenses, and non-profit community health clinics. Party campaigns in this period also proposed energy security through expansion of Petro-Canada (NDP 1980). Much of this was to be financed through "fair taxation," shifting tax burdens from low- and middle-income Canadians to the wealthy and corporations.[8]

In the context of a stalled economy and lingering high inflation, the NDP's 1984 campaign returned to a left-populist appeal. The 1984 party platform claims: "The future we've all been working for ... [is one with] a democratic redistribution of opportunities. Where all Canadians are given the opportunity to realize their full potential and have a greater say in the Canada our children will inherit from us" (NDP 1984, 1). This vision of democracy was "social," not just political (Broadbent 1999, 2001). It would distribute opportunities fairly, include citizens in political processes and economic decisions, and treat all citizens as legitimate claimants of rights to economic security. This deconstestation of democracy had solid roots in the CCF era and in the earlier federal NDP. It provided the intellectual substance behind the left-populist rhetoric relied on to reach a sympathetic audience that was certainly not all socialist. So the party's left populism and vision of democracy remained mutually implicated.

The active state promoted by the NDP in this era would also provide new employment through environmental, forestry, and fisheries restoration; direct funding to municipalities; marketing services for farmers; support for small businesses and cooperatives; various forms of affirmative action, targeted training, and child care assistance for Canadian women (NDP 1984, 9-10); and economic development and social services for Aboriginal peoples (8). The NDP thus decontested democracy with reference to the policy specifics of its active state.

Under Broadbent's leadership, the party continued to articulate a core social democratic conception of equality that was deeply implicated in its vision of democracy. The broad objective was a more egalitarian distribution of opportunities and socio-economic resources to benefit both "ordinary Canadians" and a wider range of previously disadvantaged groups (particularly women but also ethno-cultural minorities and Aboriginal peoples). The party's understanding of solidarity changed with the changing of its varied support base. It characterized the shared interests of "ordinary Canadians" through its concepts of equality and democracy, a populist dimension in its account of the nation's central political fault lines, and a concept of solidarity expanded to attract a changing Canadian society.[9]

From Solid Footing to Precarious Niche, 1989-93

Audrey McLaughlin's fourth-round victory at the 1989 leadership convention signalled a potential shift for the NDP. McLaughlin enjoyed support from the party's strong women's movement contingent and from various ethno-cultural minority flag-bearers and numerous public-sector unionists. Runner-up leadership candidate Dave Barrett had stronger – albeit poorly organized – trade union support.[10]

Though McLaughlin's victory and her leadership of the party through 1996 may have appeared to reflect a substantial shift in the NDP's understanding of equality, the foundations of this shift had been laid through the 1980s. The broadening of the NDP's constituency to more openly include women, Aboriginal peoples, gays and lesbians, and environmentalists in its organizational forums and policy agendas broadened the party's effective moral commitment to "equality of worth." This decontestation of equality had been changing as the party's social movement connections moved beyond industrial workers and farmers to embrace categories of visible minority, gender, and sexual identity.

The party leadership's commitment to equality of worth was signalled succinctly in a 1993 platform statement: "Only in a fair and equal society will the worth and dignity of all Canadians be respected" (NDP 1993b, 17). An understanding of equality of worth underpinned the party's more obvious promotion of equality of opportunity, which was to be established through broadly redistributive polities and efforts to include all groups in political decision making and policy development. As the 1993 campaign platform puts it: "Fairness and equality entails guaranteeing a decent standard of living, providing the opportunity to participate fully in social, political and economic life and providing the opportunity to fully develop individual talents and capacities" (NDP 1993c, 4).

The concept of equality provides the NDP with its single most important normative standard against which to judge economic and social policy choices.[11] As its effective reach changes, its implications for policy grow. To take a key example, equality of opportunity necessarily interacts with specific proposals for an active state – the former being the end to which the latter is the means. But policy change did not mean that the foundational commitment to equality was being significantly modified. The post-1988 NDP joined other Western parliamentary parties of the left in articulating a "chastened social democracy" in which an active state entailed less state ownership. It proposed fewer new Crown corporations and other direct state "implants" into the private economy and a greater emphasis on direct support for individuals and for regional organizations that could stimulate employment. These proposals came at a time when all other parties – including the fast-charging Reform Party – were tacking to the low-tax, non-interventionist right in this policy area. As Erickson and Laycock show (Chapter 2, this volume), voters did not respond positively to the NDP's isolation in the new ideological space.

Solidarity combines with equality of opportunity during this period to illustrate another aspect of the party's ideological distinctiveness. The party's solidarity with those economically vulnerable shapes NDP policy choices to enhance equality of opportunity. With increased new social movement (NSM) activist participation in the party, solidarity broadened to support group rights promotion beyond the boundaries of social class. Party members and activists supported this extension of solidarity (Erickson and Laycock 2002), but the federal party's election drubbing in 1993 suggests that it had little appeal to voters.

The NDP's understanding of democracy at this time was closely related to its commitment to increased social recognition and political inclusion for more social groups, largely with regard to "equality of opportunity."[12] In practical terms, this was to involve consultation with civil society organizations speaking for the vulnerable, both in the party and in Parliament. At a time when the Reform Party spearheaded promotion of direct democracy and rejection of any group rights, the NDP's promotion of a state-aided "politics of inclusion" for less advantaged groups did not strike a chord with a public alienated from mainstream parties and political elites.[13] The federal party's support for the Charlottetown Accord (see Erickson and Laycock, Chapter 2, this volume) had a good deal to do with its provisions for special Aboriginal and women's representation as well as the accord's attempt to bring Quebec back into the constitutional fold (Richards 1993). For many traditional NDP supporters west of Ontario, however, special status for Quebec was not acceptable (Johnston et al. 1996).

Democracy possessed adjacent rather than core status within NDP ideology in this period. However significant the rise of NSM influences on NDP thinking about democracy, they were overshadowed by the party's fight against free trade and the ascendancy of constitutional politics on the national agenda. Both of these issues had democratic implications for the party, given that its conception of democracy included economic and cultural sovereignty and national unity (NDP 1988a, 1988b; McLaughlin 1994). But the main thrust of the federal party's opposition to the Free Trade Agreement and support for the Charlottetown Accord centred on concerns about economic security and national unity.

The widening of its discursive audience as a result of NSM presence within the party corresponded with a less effective populist appeal. The party had not stopped speaking about "ordinary Canadians," but it had begun to give them more specific and pluralized characteristics and associated policy needs. Yet as "the people" take on a more plural identity, with more distinguishable policy needs expressed through an expanding language of social and group rights, it is harder to speak to them with one clear voice and against one clear elite. When "working Canadians" were the pivotal target of NDP appeals, they shared the basic pro-welfare state, anti-big-business needs prevalent in party discourse. This was relatively easy to translate into populist appeals. Such a translation became more problematic as the party attempted to embrace more group identities and distinctive rights. Over the next decade, federal leaders trying to counter-act Reform and Alliance party right populism did not manage to effect-ively convey the egalitarianism inherent in their active state working for "the people," nor did they enhance the legitimacy of the state as an agent of such democratic initiatives.

Between the 1992 Charlottetown Accord campaign and the fall 1993 election, the NDP ceded most of the effective populist terrain in federal politics to the Reform Party. From being widely perceived as a party of the west during the 1988 election, the NDP slid into being seen as old party politicians who supported an "elite" constitutional deal. The Reform Party's decision to oppose the accord placed the NDP on the other side of a popu-list political wedge, and this cost the party dearly.

The concept of an active state remained central to the party's appeal and commitments. As in the Broadbent era, the state's activism was less about expanding state enterprises and central planning agencies and more about using a fair distribution of tax burdens between "average Canadians" and the corporate elite to support a more generous array of federally initiated and funded social programs, tougher regulation of environmentally nega-tive corporate behaviour, job creation, and training and support programs for the unemployed.

The major 1993 national campaign document featured a multifaceted "jobs plan" costed by a reputable Canadian economic forecasting firm. Its central element was a proposal to rescind the Progressive Conservative's free-trade deals, yet the same option had been promoted by the Liberal Party of Canada. And the only residue of the party's once-fulsome com-mitment to centralized state economic planning was a "national invest-ment fund" to "provide venture capital through the Federal Business Development Bank to Canadian business, co-operative and community development enterprises" (NDP 1993a, 3).

Up against Liberal Dominance and Reform Ascendance, 1994-2003

The years of Liberal dominance and Reform/Alliance ascendance were hard on the federal NDP, yet the 1993 electoral debacle was followed by surpris-ingly little soul-searching. With an inexperienced leader and a tiny caucus with meagre parliamentary resources, mere survival as a national party was an achievement, and challenging policy reviews were too expensive and/ or potentially disruptive. However, by 2001, the party was strong enough, despite having dropped to 13 seats in the 2000 election, to withstand a powerful internal push to disband and create a new party with an agenda provided by left-wing trade union and NSM activists (Stanford 2011). The New Politics Initiative motion received 40 percent support at the 2001 convention. The NPI movement within the party came at a time of frustration with Liberal Party resiliency and the revival of conservatism in North America.

During this period, there seemed little ideological space available to the federal party. Almost all of the new ideological energy in national politics came from either the Reform and Alliance parties or the Bloc Québécois. The NDP's defence of existing social programs and "tax fairness" met a brick wall as the Liberal government focused on deficit and debt reduction. The Reform Party's push for more tax and program cuts effectively made it the "NDP of the right" (Flanagan 2009). That is, its impact on Liberal priorities in the 1990s was similar to the NDP's impact on Liberal priorities in the 1970s.

During the 1990s, many party activists accused McLaughlin and then McDonough of pulling the party too far to the centre or giving insufficient attention to organized labour. Yet the federal NDP was almost ignored by the media, seriously under-resourced as a political force, and dispirited as it watched the Liberal government's fiscal austerity undermine Canada's social programs while being rewarded electorally. Constructing a new synthesis of unionism, NSM thematics, and anti-globalization rhetoric demanded by NPI supporters (Stanford and Robinson 2001) was well beyond its grasp.

Nonetheless, the NPI's anti-globalization analysis and alternative policy agenda did show up in party campaign literature and leaders' responses to budget and throne speeches. The 1995 Renewal Committee statement of principles and mission, which was endorsed by the 1995 NDP national convention, identifies the party as "part of a greater national and international movement that seeks to challenge the dominant political agenda of market globalization and resulting environmental, social and economic problems" (Martin and Riche 1996, 110). By the late 1990s, the party characterized the threat to Canadian society and democracy in different terms than it had in the 1980s. Not just Canadian governments and unfair trade agreements but also the larger environment of "neoliberal globalization" were identified as counter to Canadian farmers', workers', and women's interests. This is expressed clearly in the 2000 party platform:

New Democrats were part of the popular movement against corporate globalization that culminated in the "Battle in Seattle" and the defeat of the Multilateral Agreement on Investment. Public rejection of that failed model has led to a new search for fair and democratic alternatives ... Canada should play a leading role [searching for] ... rules that will protect the rights of workers and the environment, provide for cultural diversity and ensure the ability of national governments to act in the public interest. New Democrats will ... put the interests of working families ahead of those of global corporations. (NDP 2000, 3)

Besides aligning itself with the "the popular movement against corporate globalization," the party signalled that its core ideological commitments had been retained, albeit with different adversaries and policy responses. We can discuss this with reference to equality, solidarity, an active state, democracy, and left populism.

This period sees an almost seamless extension of the previous period's understanding of equality. The 1995 Renewal Committee Report's restatement of party principles led with equality, and, given the range of associated concepts used to clarify its meaning after a year of local, regional, and national discussions on the matter, it is worth quoting in full.

We want to build a society where security, safety, health and well-being are guaranteed. We work for equality so that everyone has the opportunity for meaningful work, satisfying activity, and shared responsibility. We believe that social and economic equality can be best achieved through equitable access to reasonable income, universal quality health care and education, affordable child care and secure housing. We seek social justice for all in a society which values diversity and does not tolerate discrimination on the basis of one's race, nationality, religion, gender, language, physical or intellectual ability, sexual orientation or age. We are committed to a just and equitable distribution of wealth and to a society where all members contribute according to their ability and receive according to their needs. (Martin and Riche, 108)

This passage is notable on several grounds. While echoing Karl Marx's (1871) famous summary definition of distributive justice – "from each according to their abilities, to each according to their needs"[14] – it also speaks to both equality of opportunity and equal worth of citizens as participants in the equitable sharing of social resources. It identifies universal services and programs for health care and education, and rights to affordable housing and child care, as central to the social democratic vision of society. And it rejects the ethical legitimacy of discrimination based on race, gender, sexual orientation and a host of other minority characteristics.

Health care continues to provide a central policy focus for equality: "Every Canadian deserves high quality health care, no matter where they live or how much money they have" (NDP 2000, 4-5). Equality also grounded the right to a decent, secure, safe and well-paying job (7-8), with trade treaties properly protecting workers' social rights (18). Similarly, all Canadians were deemed to share a right to a clean environment (6-7) and to minimum social service standards across all regions (NDP 1997a, 40).

As victims of unjustifiable wage and employment gaps, women, Aboriginal peoples, and ethnic minorities deserved regulations and policies supporting pay equity or other assistance (NDP 1997a, 29-32 and 47-48). Aboriginal peoples' rights to self-government should be protected through new treaties and social programs equal to those enjoyed by non-Aboriginal Canadians (47; NDP 2000, 19). Improved unemployment benefits and training would address the government's obligations to those served poorly by the labour market (NDP 2000, 17).

Solidarity with these groups entailed assistance by an active state. For the NDP in the 1990s, there was still a necessary connection between equality deficits and state obligations to workers, including unionized workers. So the party promised to work towards "decent and fulfilling jobs that provide[d] adequate pay and benefits, the right to organize, reasonable job security, access to training ... and sufficient flexibility to balance work and family life" (NDP 2000, 8-9). In a time of dramatic budget-cutting by the governing Liberals, and demands for deeper cuts and fewer institutional foundations for equality rights from the Reform/Alliance parties, the NDP meshed democratic rights and solidarity:

> The NDP has a proud history of fighting for the democratic rights of all Canadians, regardless of their gender, skin colour, sexual orientation, or religion ... Unfortunately the progress our country has made towards the goal of equality is now threatened. Members of the Reform Party have made ill-considered public statements scapegoating immigrants, women, and minority groups. The Liberals have cut funding for shelters for battered women, child care, the elderly and disabled, degrading the ability of many to participate on an equal footing. (NDP 1997a, 48)

While the Reform Party insisted that far too many groups of state benefit-seekers were allowed access to policy-making processes (Laycock 2001), the federal NDP presented such groups as legitimately democratic agents within the policy processes of an equality-facilitating active state.

Unemployment, widening social inequalities, and Canadian sovereignty were still serious problems in the party's eyes. Though extending state enterprises gained little support in party documents (while still often advocated in resolutions at conventions), the NDP still insisted on an active state. As leader Alexa McDonough put it in her response to the 1999 Throne Speech:

> we believe in a responsive, positive and proactive role for government. We believe in a vision for 21st century Canada which includes the notion of political leadership not just by the federal government but by all levels of government working in effective partnerships with the private sector, the non-profit and co-operative sector, labour representatives, and primary producers for something that is bigger than ourselves. That is the legacy of my party's contribution to Canada. (McDonough 1999, 8)

The concept of democracy underpinning official party discourse in this period remained multidimensional. The 1995 Renewal Committee's statement of principles suggests that democracy has both intrinsic and instrumental value. At one level, democracy is what government and the party do when they are working well: both the party and the government should operate not just on the basis of accountability, openness, and citizen involvement but should do so in such a way as to enhance "the dignity and freedom of the individual" and recognize citizens' rights to "have a voice in matters that affect their lives and to have a greater control in the economy, the workplace, the community and the family" (Martin and Riche 1996, 108). In fact, the mission statement in this report affirms that the logic of democratization must extend to the party itself, with a claim that could easily have been taken from 1930s and 1940s CCF literature:[15]

> Our fundamental principles apply as much to the rebuilding of our political party as they do to our task of creating a democratic socialist society. Our party must be a model of the principles that we preach. Our actions must match our words. From an informed and involved membership and active riding associations we must move to thoughtful policy development, active dialogue, open, inclusive and democratic decision-making

and consistency between Party policies and public actions. (Martin and Riche 1996, 109)[16]

Instrumentally, democracy's value turned heavily on reducing social inequality and class or group-based power imbalances, especially those grounded in the failure of the market economy to distribute resources equitably (Martin and Riche 1996, 108). Often the party spoke of the broader economic benefits that would stem from such provision (e.g., McLaughlin 1994, 4). But the primary reason for protecting the vulnerable remained rooted in notions of justice and the sense that government is the most effective and democratic instrument with which to achieve them.

For this reason, the NDP continued to endorse including representatives of the vulnerable, the disadvantaged, and minorities in policy-making processes. This came through clearly in the discussion of its core principles of democracy, community, cooperation, and equality in the party's 1995 Renewal Committee report, especially with its recognition of "the right of individuals to have a voice in matters that affect their lives and to have a greater control in the economy, the workplace, the community and the family" (Martin and Riche 1996, 108). Numerous party documents in this period support having community businesspersons, community leaders, union leaders and workers' representatives, and, in some cases, ethnic minority group representatives on various management boards (NDP 1997a). They would provide input into the governance of the Bank of Canada, community and national investment boards, national and regional environmental boards, and a national job training board. Traditional support for credit unions as democratically controlled financial institutions was reaffirmed (NDP 2000, 9), but the party also proposed that a national securities commission represent diverse interests to establish a new regimen of corporate accountability (McDonough 2002, 4-5).

Accountability is, of course, a foundational part of what representative democracy claims to deliver. Accountability through regular federal elections is not enough: the vulnerable and less powerful also need positions within state institutions and private firms that make decisions about how to distribute social resources. This is a long-standing theme in CCF and NDP thinking. However, compared to the NDP of previous periods, McDonough's NDP tended to present these proposals for "democratization" as more about inclusive recognition of group identities and rights, and less about citizens' right of democratic participation per se. The rights of workers were not sidelined, but they competed with other strong NDP group rights claimants in party discourse: women, ethnic minorities, Aboriginals, gays and lesbians, and Québécois.

During this period, democratic inclusion entailed more enthusiastic advocacy of proportional representation than had been the case in previous periods. In her responses to the 1999 and 2001 throne speeches, for example, Alexa McDonough contended that, by helping to represent citizen interests more inclusively, proportional representation could help close the gap between electors and elected created by low voter turnout and high political cynicism (McDonough 1999, 7-8; McDonough 2001a, 1-2).

With respect to corporate globalization and Canada's free-trade deals, the party not only stressed their economic implications but also their anti-democratic implications. It argued that Canadians' rights to choose how Canada develops were being eroded by the government's decisions to transfer accountable control of our economy from citizens into corporate hands (McDonough 2001a, 1-2, 4). An NDP government would return control from the unaccountable market to the people (McDonough 2001b, 8). It would restructure Canada's trade agreements to protect environmental rights and labour rights and rebalance citizens' rights against those of corporations (NDP 2000, 12).

Senior NDP representatives seemed to appreciate that rearguard actions to protect the welfare state had become necessary due to the ascendancy of new right political forces. As Bill Blaikie (1996, 21) put it in his response to the 1996 Throne Speech: "The pressure on that [postwar] social contract is a result, partly, of an ideological trend against seeing government as a positive force in the economy and in society." The Reform Party, new right-wing think tanks, and corporate lobby groups ultimately paid little political cost for advocating the Canadian government's retreat from its previous commitments to a postwar social contract that had somewhat balanced property rights with social rights.

In this period, the federal NDP's left populism had a backwards-glancing character. Looking back, the NDP saw a succession of postwar federal governments that had used progressive taxation and regulation of business to support rights for unionized workers and expanding social programs. During this time, even centre-right parties claimed to support the redistribution of resources and opportunities from the privileged to the non-privileged (Laycock and Clarke 2002). We can thus see the NDP using an adjacent concept of "progressive postwar social contract" to backstop not just its left populism but also its concepts of democracy, the active state, and equality.

However, the centre of Canadian political gravity had shifted to the right, presenting an activist government as a problem and a less regulated marketplace with ever-lower taxes as a one-size-fits-all solution. In this context, neither left populism nor the normative idea of a social contract (which helps to legitimize it) can easily achieve much ideological traction for a social democratic party, especially when that party is distracted on multiple fronts by group recognition and rights claims. If left populism is to work for the party when ideological momentum is running in the opposite direction, the case must be made by a compelling leader. The contrast between Audrey McLaughlin and Alexa McDonough and Jack Layton here is striking.

Considering the party's use of "freedom" during this period illustrates how much the federal NDP was outside the political and ideological trajectory of the decade. The NDP's first three decades were characterized by a confident assertion of positive freedom. NDP activists felt themselves to be in the vanguard of a progressive evolution of democratic rights among equal citizens (Broadbent 1999). For three decades, the party had argued that meaningful commitments to equal freedom required governments to augment formal civic freedoms with resources that enabled citizens to exercise their freedom. The language of participatory democracy was employed to show that freedom also required citizens' active engagement in policy processes and public life generally. The NDP's Renewal Committee statement of principles sprinkled such ideas through its account of the party's core values of equality, democracy, and community (Martin and Riche 1996, 108).

By the early 1990s, however, while the federal party struggled to include an increasing range of demands for equality, the material bases of "positive freedom" in Canada were being eroded in ways that symbolic group rights recognition could not counteract. Party documents and internal discussions suggest that freedom (as meaningful autonomy) was indirectly bound up in the struggles for social recognition of group identities and rights. Nonetheless, the party also spoke about freedom in more defensive terms that were meant to shore up a weakening, less well-financed welfare state. For example, consider Audrey McLaughlin's (1995, 2) response to the 1995 federal budget:

A very important part of any country is freedom. [But] ... a mother living in poverty has no freedom. An elderly person who cannot get adequate health care has no freedom. A young person who cannot attend college, university or technical school has no freedom. The budget limits freedoms and the potential of citizenship for many groups.

This was relatively new ground for the NDP. Since the early 1960s it had seen evidence that its advocacy of "positive freedom" via expanded equality rights and expanded state-delivered social services, along with more restraints on business efforts to define the national agenda, was having an impact on both federal and provincial governments. The trajectory of federal and provincial policies was trending in what the NDP saw as the right direction. By the mid-1990s, this trajectory had been reversed. The NDP message during this period promoted the potentially inconsistent agendas of NSM advocates and social class equality advocates. These potential inconsistencies stemmed from the fact that, as much as the NDP hoped that reduction of social class inequalities would facilitate more equal "recognition" of group identities, achievement of recognition-based equality has no necessary connection to a reduction of social class inequality (Fraser 1997, 2008).

During this period the NDP showed little appreciation of the possibility that pursuit of the newer, recognition-oriented dimension of equality can take scarce political resources and public discursive attention away from the traditional, class-based emphases of social democratic parties (Cronin et al. 2011; Meyer 2007). Redoubling its advocacy of egalitarian democratization on behalf of conventional as well as new social citizenship rights may have made sense to party activists,[17] but it may also have played into the political right's increasingly successful efforts to remove class-based distributional questions from the political agenda (Laycock 2001; Erickson and Laycock 2002).

As yet there is no systematic empirical analysis of whether the NDP lost support from its more traditional electoral support base between 1993 and 2003 by giving NSM recognition concerns attention in their conventions, platforms, and leaders' public comments. Other chapters in this volume indicate that the NDP lost votes to both the Liberal and Reform/Alliance parties over this period. One could speculate that some of those who shifted their allegiances to the Reform Party were uncomfortable with the NDP's embrace of feminist, gay rights, and other NSM agendas and were attracted to Reform's openly social conservative appeal. In this sense, the shifting understanding of equality within the NDP may have cost it votes, especially with older voters and party members who, in the past, had managed to combine social conservative attitudes with support for a strong redistributive state (Erickson and Laycock 2002).

However, it seems just as likely that NDP voters in the 1988 election shifted to Reform in 1993 for regionalist reasons or – in Ontario – over their disappointment with the Rae government. If past NDP voters shifted their votes to the Liberal Party in 1993 and extended this through the next several elections, it was likely based on a desire first to punish the Mulroney Conservatives and then to prevent the more right-wing Reform and Alliance parties from gaining power.

Modernizing and Refining Appeals: The Layton Years

Jack Layton won the leadership of the party in 2003 as the most clearly to the left of all serious contenders. This allowed him, paradoxically, to pull the party's appeal closer to pragmatic, apparently more centrist, positions on many policy issues. His increasing popularity over four elections (see Weldon, Chapter 12, this volume) allowed him to modernize the party organization and campaign operations (see Erickson and Laycock, Chapter 3, this volume) and place his own leadership stamp on almost every aspect of the party's appeal. While Erickson and Laycock (ibid.) consider how the NDP modernized in terms of its internal organization and its campaigning, here I look more explicitly at whether the party "moderated" while modernizing and how its ideological morphology changed under Layton's leadership.

Jack Layton's career as a civic politician in Toronto suggested how the party could reconcile the concerns of its growing range of constituencies. He was on the forefront of civic campaigns to support the rights of immigrants, ethnic minorities, and the LGBT community, but he also built many connections with local labour leaders and small businesspeople. He championed environmental causes while keeping a high profile in the Federation of Canadian Municipalities. And he developed a reputation as a trustworthy politician able to work with political opponents to "get things done." It seemed that the broad trust that Layton enjoyed across the party enabled him to leave many social movement demands out of the political limelight. His supporters did not believe that he would let them down, even though the party's message emphasized pragmatic and incremental policy initiatives at the apparent expense of the more transformative policy goals that party activists were accustomed to seeing highlighted in campaigns.

Considering whether the federal party's core ideological message changed substantially under Layton's leadership requires us to look below the surface of its increasingly well-funded, increasingly professional leader-focused and short-term policy-focused election campaigns. We need to ask whether it was primarily continuity or primarily rupture with the recent NDP past that was offered in this package. With some interesting exceptions, the answer is continuity.

Under Layton's leadership, the party's baseline commitment to equality did not change. If anything, it continued along the same trajectory of increasing support for a wider range of "equality-seekers." This trajectory was at striking odds with the Conservative government's evident distaste for both the positions of equality-seeking groups and the costs associated with them. But equality for the Layton-led NDP was not just about supporting group rights: it also entailed enhanced federal government support for low-income housing, child care, and seniors; more affordable postsecondary education; a more comprehensive national health care system; broadband Internet service for non-urban communities; and more generous foreign aid and support for AIDS victims in developing countries (NDP 2004).

By 2011, equality was couched in terms of giving Canadian families a break, with many "practical first steps" outlined in the platform and on the campaign trail. New equality-enhancing proposals included making it easier for "working families" to reduce their energy bills, improving access to unemployment benefits, enforcing lower limits on credit card interest, and ensuring food safety (NDP 2011). Support for particular equality-seeking groups was certainly evident, with proposals for a "nation-to-nation" partnership with Aboriginal peoples, an "action plan for the rights of the disabled," and sections on women's equality and equality rights promotion for LGBT and immigrant communities (15, 17-18). These latter proposals came in a platform section entitled "Leadership for Canada," suggesting that such initiatives would express genuine Canadian values, as opposed to those informing Conservative governance. Conceptually, these proposals are based on the assumption of a post-Charter Canadian social contract.

One notable contrast between the NDP's 2011 and earlier platforms was the prominence of "tax fairness" in the latter and its absence in the former. Reform and Conservative parties had won the tax wars, in the sense that taxation had taken on a negative valence except when it involved across-the-board or targeted cuts for "average Canadians." As a consequence, it made no sense to keep reminding voters that the NDP believed in tax fairness since, in the public's mind, this had been associated with tax increases. Thus, in 2011, the NDP mentioned taxes in its platform only in targeted ways, and only as "tax breaks," as ways of "rewarding the job creators," and to endorse the idea that the Canadian corporate tax rate should be set below that of the United States (NDP 2011, 8-10). This could be construed as a decisive turn to "third way" social democracy (McGrane 2011). But it is also possible to see it as a recognition that there is no point in giving one's opponents easy targets on ground that they have successfully claimed, with overwhelming media support, over the past two decades.

Packaging the solidarity message had also taken a different form by 2011, even though, with one exception, its substance had not altered notably since 2003. This exception, which turned out to be quite politically consequential, was Layton's more enthusiastic endorsement of Québécois language and cultural rights. This came in the French-language leader's debate, 14 April 2011, but was grounded in the party's 2005 Sherbrooke Declaration (see Godbout, Bélanger, and Mérand, Chapter 11, this volume). The new element in the packaging was the 2011 platform's framing of all of its policy proposals as practical initiatives on the part of "leadership you can trust" to "give your family a break." Another new element in all of these proposals was the deserving recipient, which, except in the discussion of extensions to group equality rights, was no longer identified as "ordinary Canadians" or even as "working families" but simply as "Canadians." The message seemed to be that it was possible to acknowledge and address both special circumstances requiring special equality remedies and the shared needs of all Canadians.

If Layton was to be presented as a leader all Canadians could trust, it would not do to restrict those to whom he was obliged to govern fairly. The risk here was that some of the party's left populism would be lost if the antagonism between the morally deserving and the blameworthy, as defined in traditional social democratic terms, was no longer to be so evident. But the potential reward was greater than the potential loss, and Layton's high trust ratings meant that the party could obtain populist leverage through the leader-identification route. Layton could be trusted to work "until the job is done" for Canadians generally, not just the lucky or well-connected. The NDP seemed to understand that trust is essential for solidarity and that a trusted leader might be able to make the pursuit of equality, and a more inclusive solidarity, seem less like a zero-sum than a positive-sum game to most Canadians.

After three election campaigns, the Layton NDP team had learned that it could convey its view of an active state's positive benefits most effectively by concentrating on practical policy initiatives, not big-picture pronouncements on the state's obligation to rebalance structural relations of power in an unfair capitalist society. Like other social democratic parties, but as much as a generation later than most, the NDP had become chastened about state ownership. However, state ownership, and even progressive taxation, had only ever been a means to more normatively defined ends, each rationalized on the grounds that the market economy did not produce fair outcomes or rational aggregate decisions. The Layton-era NDP increasingly identified irrational aggregate decisions by the market in environmental terms, especially with respect to climate change. But the party still contended that many unfair results of market activity affected present-day citizens, not just future generations. Its campaign promises suggested "practical first steps" to correct market unfairness and irrationality. Not identifying final objectives in this regard did not make the NDP un-social democratic, but it did make it more competitive.

The NDP's policy critique was not restricted to inadequate government responses to market failures. The party continued to suggest that federal policy making was insufficiently inclusive and overly attentive to the "louder voices" of corporate Canada upon which David Lewis had focused. In its 2004, 2006, and 2008 platforms, the NDP gave considerable attention to initiatives to decentralize decision making in order to make it more democratic.[18] This minor shift dovetailed with its insistence on special status and jurisdiction for Quebec on linguistic matters, and for Aboriginal self-government, but it was not restricted to these two "national minorities" (Kymlicka 1996). The NDP in this period pressed equality claims and related policy remedies for Aboriginal and LGBT communities without suggesting that the government's inadequate responses in this area stemmed primarily from corporate power or market failure.

Among this period's adjacent concepts one still finds democracy, identity politics, group rights, the environment, and left populism. What makes the adjacent zone in this ideological morphology distinctive from those in previous periods is the prominence of "leadership" in this conceptual mix. As noted above, by 2011 the NDP was invoking trusted leadership in almost every conceivable policy context and placing it at the centre of its campaign appeals. Leadership thus conditioned the meaning of most key core and adjacent concepts, from solidarity to active state, from national unity with asymmetrical Quebec powers to universal health care and LGBT equality.

Leadership was a crucial part of the 2011 campaign promises to "give your family a break" through greater economic security, security from crime and health problems,[19] and the provision of an alternative to the Conservatives' lack of democratic accountability to Parliament. Pollsters had confirmed that Layton was a trusted leader. So not elevating leadership to an influential place in the party's ideological appeal would have been a serious blunder. It is not clear that Thomas Mulcair's party can make the same kind of appeal.

Conclusion

This chapter demonstrates the continuing centrality of equality, democracy, an active state, solidarity, and left populism to federal NDP ideology, from its origins through, for the most part, to the present day. It argues that one can trace consequential changes among adjacent and peripheral concepts, especially the latter (with their policy-specific contents), without being forced to accept the claim that the core components of NDP ideology have changed in fundamental ways. Even the party's gradual movement away from a commitment to large levels of state ownership can be seen, in this account, as a matter of shifting means rather than of substituting ends. The policy instruments of an evolving active state involve less state ownership and centralized planning, but the relation of other core concepts to the active state, and of key adjacent concepts to the active state, do not change in ways that suggest substantially different core commitments.

It might be argued that, as the concept of democracy moves from the core to the adjacent realm in the party's ideology after its first decade, a good deal is altered. But one could just as easily contend that democracy remains at its core through the following decades. And, even if it does experience something of a "downgrade," a distinctively social democratic concept of democracy, with clear roots in the CCF, continues to condition all core and most major adjacent concepts in familiar ways.

I also argue that left populism remains a key dimension of the federal party's ideological emphases and rhetorical delivery as a way of speaking to a broadening set of constituencies and distinguishing itself from its larger-party competitors. By the standards of contemporary social democratic parties, this allowed a relatively left-wing critique of corporate power. During Layton's tenure as leader, left populism's role in party discourse was strengthened by the high level of public trust he enjoyed, and it did not work at cross-purposes with the language and commitments of group rights as it had during the 1990s.

Unlike the analysis of CMP data in Chapter 6 (this volume), the Freedenite approach used in this chapter assigns concepts different status and weights and attaches particular significance to the logics of inter-conceptual interaction among these core, adjacent, and peripheral concepts. This approach lacks the quantifiable data that allow for the intra-party system comparative insights made possible by the CMP, and it is inevitably more subjective in assessments of key aspects, such as what belongs in the core, adjacent, and perimeter realms of an ideology, or how they relate to each other. However, the analysis employed here allows us to see both substantial continuity and significant elements of change in the NDP's ideology over the past half century, not forcing us to deny one to see the other.

It would be easy to conclude that the party's ideological flexibility under Layton's leadership was the key to its recovery through the last decade and its breakthrough in 2011. The corollary that is often added to this is that the party's ideological rigidity before Layton's leadership was responsible for its tenuous third- or fourth-party status. My analysis suggests that we need not accept this corollary, based as it is on a reading of party ideology that focuses inappropriately on perimeter (policy) choices rather than more basic core and adjacent ideological concepts. We have seen that there has been considerable continuity within these dimensions of the NDP's ideology over the past fifty years and that this continuity with regard to normative fundamentals can be maintained even as significant evolution occurs in the way that the party understands and seeks to apply such central concepts as equality.

As with the analysis of the NDP's modernization, then, it is possible to avoid misleading forced choices in categorizing the party's thought and behaviour by using an analytical framework that accepts the reality that continuity and change unavoidably complement each other in a dynamic social and political environment. From this perspective, it is appropriate to say that substantial ideological continuity has accompanied and, especially in Quebec (see Chapters 3 and 11), assisted the NDP's entry into the top tier of Canadian federal party competition.

Notes

1 I wish to thank Brock Kuznetzov for his thorough review and preliminary analysis of party manifestos and parliamentary responses to throne and budget speeches between 1989 and 2011.

2 Section 1 is entitled "Planning for Abundance"; section 2 is entitled "Security and Freedom."

3 See "1968 Speaker's Notes, Federal NDP," section 2, "Taxation," *Poltext,* http://www.poltext.org/cms/index.php?menu=2&temps=1309179382715#ancre623.

4 The Draft Program's "New Hope for the Farmer" section carefully made contact with the CCF tradition of support for cooperatives and, "where necessary, public ownership."

5 New Party, Draft Program, 1961, 20, under "National Labour Standards."

6 See the comments on the federal Carter Commission on Taxation report in the 1968 federal platform, in NDP (1968), and numerous resolutions on this matter in NDP (1976).

7 For a full compilation of party resolutions adopted as official party policy at conventions between 1961 and 1976, and those on the economy in particular, see NDP (1976).

8 This tax fairness theme is so central to the policy agenda of the party (connecting to most core and even adjacent concepts) that it may appear to warrant elevation from the perimeter to the adjacent conceptual zone. However, analytically, as a policy theme, it remains a perimeter concept.

9 This brief account of the NDP's ideological cornerstones during Ed Broadbent's leadership unavoidably overlooks his stature as an internationally respected social democratic thinker during this period and his subsequent efforts to articulate a distinctive social democratic perspective on democracy and equality. On the latter, see especially Broadbent (1999, 2001).

10 The leader of the CLC, Shirley Carr, had belatedly (after the third ballot) signalled her support for Dave Barrett, but this did not change enough delegates' minds on the close final ballot.

11 Party members indicated clearly that this was so in both our 1997 and 2009 surveys. See Chapter 7 in this volume.

12 On how this is articulated by left populism in Western countries more generally in the post-1960s period, see Laycock (2005).

13 For quantitative evidence of increased attention to such rights in the party's manifestos after 1988, see Pétry (Chapter 6, Table 6.1, this volume).

14 In Marx's *Critique of the Gotha Programme* (originally written in 1875). Available at http://www.marxists.org/archive/marx/works/download/Marx_Critque_of_the_Gotha_Programme.pdf.

15 See Laycock (1990, 146-62).

16 Details of the Renewal Committee's proposals for a "democratization" of party structures and policy development processes may be found in Martin and Riche (1996, 111-18) and are discussed briefly in Chapter 1 of this volume.

17 For more on what this distinction means in terms of party members' policy preferences, see Erickson and Laycock (2002).

18 The 2011 platform committed to "recognize and respect the vital role, expertise and necessary independence of civil society organizations" (NDP 2011, 23), which may be seen as a nod in a decentralizing direction. However, it is probably best construed as a response to the Harper governments' concerted efforts to shut such groups out of Parliamentary committee hearings and the policy process generally.

19 As François Pétry points out in Chapter 6 (this volume), by 2011 the NDP was devoting a higher proportion of its campaign platform to law-and-order issues than it had before. One should not make too much of this new wrinkle as NDP language on this matter did not endorse the hard-line changes to criminal law reform made by the Harper government. It is nonetheless worth acknowledging that Layton and his advisors had decided not to cede this category of issues to the Conservatives, given the concerns of "ordinary Canadians" over their personal and family security.

References

Allen, Richard. 1971. *The Social Passion: Religion and Social Reform in Canada, 1914-28*. Toronto: University of Toronto Press.

Berman, Sheri. 2006. *The Primacy of Politics: Social Democracy and the Making of Europe's Twentieth Century*. New York: Cambridge University Press.

Blaikie, Bill. 1996. Response to Liberal Speech from the Throne. House of Commons, 29 February. http://openparliament.ca/debates/1996/2/29/bill-blaikie-2/

Budge, Ian. 1994. A New Theory of Party Competition: Uncertainty, Ideology and Policy Equilibria Viewed Comparatively and Temporally. *British Journal of Political Science* 24: 443-67.

Broadbent, Ed. 1970. *The Liberal Rip-off: Trudeauism vs. the Politics of Equality*. Toronto: New Press.

–. 1999. Social Democracy or Liberalism in the 21st Century? In Peter Russell, ed., *The Future of Social Democracy: Views of Leaders from around the World*, 73-93. Toronto: University of Toronto Press.

–. ed. 2001. *Democratic Equality: What Went Wrong?* Toronto: University of Toronto Press.

Callahan, John, Nina Fishman, Ben Jackson, and Martin McIvor, eds. 2009. *In Search of Social Democracy*. Manchester: Manchester University Press.

Carroll, William K., and R.S. Ratner, eds. 2005. *Challenges and Perils: Social Democracy in Neoliberal Times*. Halifax: Fernwood Books.

Cronin, James, George Ross, and James Shoch, eds. 2011. *What's Left of the Left*. Durham, NC: Duke University Press.

Cross, Michael, ed. 1973. *The Decline and Fall of a Good Idea: CCF-NDP Manifestos, 1932-69*. Toronto: New Hogtown Press.

Erickson, Lynda, and David Laycock. 2002. Postmaterialism versus the Welfare State? Opinion among English Canadian Social Democrats. *Party Politics* 8, 3: 301-26.

Flanagan, Tom. 2009. *Waiting for the Wave: The Reform Party and the Conservative Movement*, 2nd ed. Montreal and Kingston: McGill-Queen's University Press.

Fraser, Nancy. 1997. *Justice Interruptus: Critical Reflections on the "Postsocialist" Condition*. London: Routledge.

–. 2008. *Scales of Justice: Reimagining Political Space in a Globalizing World.* Cambridge, UK: Polity Press.

Freeden, Michael. 1996. *Ideologies and Political Theory.* New York: Oxford University Press.

Johnston, Richard, André Blais, Elisabeth Gidengil, and Neil Nevitte. 1996. *The Challenge of Direct Democracy: The 1992 Canadian Referendum.* Montreal and Kingston: McGill-Queen's University Press.

Kymlicka, Will. 1996. *Multicultural Citizenship: A Liberal Theory of Minority Rights.* New York: Oxford University Press.

Laycock, David. 1990. *Populism and Democratic thought in the Canadian Prairies, 1910-45.* Toronto: University of Toronto Press.

–. 2005. Visions of Popular Sovereignty: Mapping the Contested Terrain of Contemporary Western Populisms. *Critical Review of International Social and Political Philosophy* 8, 2: 125-44.

Laycock, David, and Gregory Clarke. 2002. *Framing the Canadian Social Contract.* Ottawa: Canadian Policy Research Network.

Martin, Richard, and Nancy Riche. 1996. *Report of the CLC-NDP Review Committee.* Ottawa: Canadian Labour Congress.

McDonald, Lynn. 1987. *The Party That Changed Canada: The NDP, Then and Now.* Toronto: Macmillan Canada.

McDonough, Alexa. 1999. NDP Response to Liberal Speech from the Throne. 36th Parliament, 2nd session, 13 October. http://www.parl.gc.ca/HousePublications/Publication.aspx?pub=Hansard&doc=2&Language=E&Mode=1&Parl=36&Ses=2#T1810.

–. 2001a. NDP Response to Liberal Speech from the Throne. 37th Parliament, 1st session, 31 January. http://openparliament.ca/debates/1999/10/13/alexa-mcdonough-3/.

–. 2001b. NDP Response to Budget. 37th Parliament, 1st session, 11 December. http://openparliament.ca/debates/2001/12/11/alexa-mcdonough-1/.

–. 2002. NDP Response to Liberal Speech from the Throne. 37th Parliament, 2nd session, 1 October. http://openparliament.ca/debates/2002/10/1/alexa-mcdonough-1/.

McGrane, David. 2011. Political Marketing and the NDP's Historic Breakthrough. In Jon Pammett and Christopher Dornan, eds., *The Canadian Federal Election of 2011,* 77-109. Toronto: Dundurn.

McLaughlin, Audrey. 1994. NDP Response to the Speech from the Throne. Ottawa: House of Commons. http://openparliament.ca/debates/1994/1/24/audrey-mclaughlin-1/.

–. 1995. NDP Response to Liberal Budget. 35th Parliament, 1st session, 2 March. http://openparliament.ca/debates/1995/3/2/audrey-mclaughlin-3/.

Meyer, Henning, and Jonathan Rutherford, eds. 2012. *The Future of European Social Democracy.* Basingstoke, UK: Palgrave Macmillan.

Meyer, Thomas. 2007. *The Theory of Social Democracy.* Cambridge, UK: Polity Press.

Morley, J.T. 1984. *Secular Socialists: The CDCF/NDP in Ontario, a Biography.* Montreal and Kingston: McGill-Queen's University Press.

Morton, Desmond. 1986. *The New Democrats, 1961-1986: The Politics of Change.* Toronto: Copp Clark Pitman.

NDP. 1968. New Democratic Party Program. In D. Owen Carrigan, ed., *Canadian Party Platforms, 1867-1968,* 342-48. Toronto: Copp Clark Publishing.

–. 1976. *New Democratic Policies, 1961-1976.* Ottawa: New Democratic Party of Canada.

–. 1980. A Choice for Canadians: Policies of the New Democratic Party. Ottawa: New Democratic Party of Canada.

–. 1984. *A New Democratic Future: New Opportunities for Canadians Like You.* Ottawa: New Democratic Party of Canada.

–. 1988a. *Meeting the Challenge: Ed Broadbent and the New Democrats Speak up for Average Canadians.* Ottawa: New Democratic Party of Canada.

–. 1988b. *A Fair Deal for Canada: New Democrats Speak Up for Average Canadians.* Ottawa: New Democratic Party of Canada.

–. 1993a. *Canada Works When Canadians Work.* Ottawa: New Democratic Party of Canada.

–. 1993b. *Women and the Economy: A Vision of Equality.* Ottawa: New Democratic Party of Canada.

–. 1993c. *Putting People First: Rural Canada.* Ottawa: New Democratic Party of Canada.

–. 1997a. *A Framework for Canada's Future: Alexa McDonough and Canada's NDP Will Put the Needs of People First.* Ottawa: New Democratic Party of Canada.

–. 2000. *Think How Much Better Canada Could Be: The NDP Commitment to Canadians.* Ottawa: New Democratic Party of Canada.

–. 2004. *Jack Layton, NDP: New Energy – A Positive Choice.* Ottawa: New Democratic Party of Canada.

–. 2011. *Giving Your Family a Break: Practical First Steps.* Ottawa: New Democratic Party of Canada.

New Party. 1961. Draft Program: The New Party, Founding Convention. Ottawa: 31 July-4 August. http://www.poltext.org/sites/poltext.org/files/plateformes/can 1961ndp_draft_en_18072011_174709.pdf.

Richards, John. 1993. The NDP in the Constitutional Drama. In Douglas Brown and Robert Young, eds., *Canada: The State of the Federation, 1992.* Kingston: Institute of Intergovernmental Relations, Queen's University.

Russell, Peter, ed. 1999. *The Future of Social Democracy.* Toronto: University of Toronto Press.

Sassoon, Donald. 2000. Socialism in the 20th Century: An Historical Reflection. *Journal of Political Ideologies* 5, 1: 17-34.

Saward, Michael. 2011. *The Representative Claim.* New York: Oxford University Press.

Stanford, Jim. 2011. The History of the New Politics Initiative: Movement and Party, Then and Now. *Rabble.ca.* http://rabble.ca/news/2011/11/history-npi -movement-and-party-then-and-now.

Stanford, Jim, and Svend Robinson. 2001. The New Politics Initiative: Open, Sustainable and Democratic. In Z. David Berlin and Howard Aster, eds., *What's Left? The New Democratic Party in Renewal,* 80-93. Oakville, ON: Mosaic.

Whitehorn, Alan. 1992. *Canadian Socialism: Essays on the CCF-NDP.* Toronto: Oxford University Press.

Wiseman, Nelson, and Benjamin Isitt. 2007. Social Democracy in Canada: An Interpretive Framework. *Canadian Journal of Political Science* 40, 3: 567-89.

Young, Walter. 1969. *The Anatomy of a Party: The National CCF, 1932-61.* Toronto: University of Toronto Press.

Zakuta, Leo. 1969. *A Protest Movement Becalmed.* Toronto: University of Toronto Press.

6

Ideological Evolution of the Federal NDP, as Seen through Its Election Campaign Manifestos

FRANÇOIS PÉTRY

Pundits and researchers have sometimes blamed the NDP's failure to win a plurality of the vote in national elections on the radical leftist policy proposals it has advocated in elections – too radical, in any case, to appeal to moderate voters who are positioned near or at the centre of the political spectrum (Richards, Cairns, and Pratt 1991). According to a related interpretation, the NDP's historic failure to win power federally finds its root in the ability of the Liberal Party to maintain a centrist "brokerage party" image that successfully attracted the support of moderate voters at the expense of the NDP (Clarke et al. 1991). In the 2011 election, the respective roles of the NDP and the Liberals were reversed: the NDP won a larger share of the popular vote than the Liberal Party for the first time in its history. In fact, the electoral breakthrough of 2011 represents the culmination of a gradual rise of the NDP at the polls in the new millennium, from its nadir at 8.5 percent in 2000 to 18.1 percent in 2008 and 30.6 percent in 2011. This gradual rise in the polls has coincided in time with an apparent movement towards the centre in NDP ideology. The similarity might just be a coincidence. But it is sufficiently striking to raise the question: Was the electoral success of the NDP attributable to changes in its left-right ideological positions?

This chapter sets out to answer this question by looking at the ideological positioning of the NDP from 1988 to 2011. Part 1 emphasizes the theoretical importance of the fact that parties take positions on issues, and it explains the method used to position parties on said issues. Part 2 describes the changes in the positions that the NDP and the Liberal Party have taken on substantive issues over the past twenty years. Part 3 analyzes the ideological evolution over time of the NDP and the Liberal Party on a left-right composite scale built on the basis of the substantive issues examined in Part 2. I show that the Liberal Party has shifted position on the left-right axis in a haphazard fashion and that Liberal Party voters have been unsupportive of these ideological changes. By contrast, the change to the right in the position of the NDP has been deliberate, and NDP voters have supported it. In conclusion, I speculate as to whether this has helped the NDP achieve electoral gains.

Theory and Method

Party policy positions are estimated using the Comparative Manifesto Project (CMP) method, using data from party election platforms from 1988 to the 2011 election. The method extracts party positions from the content of election manifestos by means of measuring the frequency of mentions of pre-established issue categories (see Werner, Lacewell, and Volkens 2011 for an overview and definitions of categories).[1] The CMP data are very attractive to researchers because they provide the only comparable means of estimating party left-right positions over the long run.

The coding of party manifestos is based on the assumption that each party "owns" particular policy issues. Issue-ownership theory (Budge and Farlie 1983) holds that parties try to mobilize voters by selectively emphasizing in their election manifestos issues on which they hold a reputation of competence (e.g., a "tough-on-crime" attitude for the Conservative Party) while devoting less manifesto space to other issues. Voters, in turn, support the parties that they perceive as owners of the issues. In other words, parties do not compete with one another during election campaigns by taking opposite sides on the same issues but, rather, by selectively emphasizing in their manifestos the issues that resonate well with their electorates. According to the "selective emphasis" approach, what counts is not so much the substance of party manifesto statements as the relative importance that is given by each party to the issues of the day. Parties only say positive things in their manifestos about the issues that are important to them, while ignoring the issues about which they would have to say negative things.

Why analyze the content of election manifestos rather than campaign speeches, media releases, or campaign advertisements? Election manifestos are the only statements of their kind made on behalf of the whole party during an election campaign. Their content is subject to extensive prior debate and negotiation inside the party, and they are uniquely representative of what the party stands for. Election manifestos are distinctively authoritative documents on which the main election campaign themes and media comments about campaign themes are based. Most important, focusing on election manifestos allows researchers to use easily identifiable, specifically dated sets of documents that can be reliably archived and formatted for content analyses.

Two frequent criticisms levelled at issue ownership and selective emphasis are (1) that party manifestos are read by very few voters and (2) that they are vacuous statements that do not correlate with subsequent government policies. However, the fact that voters are often not informed about the details of what parties propose in their election manifestos does not mean that they are not competent to determine the ideological position of parties. Recent research has uncovered the existence of information shortcuts that demonstrably help voters to assess where parties stand on issues and whether they keep the promises they make in their election manifestos (Thomson 2011; Pétry 2014). There is also strong evidence that parties elected to power fulfill most of their campaign pledges (Rallings 1987; Pétry and Collette 2009; Naurin 2011). It appears that the belief that parties do not keep their election promises is largely a myth.

The objective of this chapter is to position the NDP and other parties on the left-right political axis and to derive some implications therefrom. The importance of the left-right axis has been demonstrated for voters (Inglehart and Klingemann 1976), experts (Benoit and Laver 2008), and political parties (Bittner and Koop 2013). Left-right appears to be the dominant partisan cleavage in countries studied by the CMP (Budge, Robertson, and Hearl 1987; see also *Electoral Studies* 2007). In Canada, the relevance of the left-right cleavage has been demonstrated in voting behaviour in federal elections (see Zakharova, Chapter 9, this volume; see also Gidengil et al. 2012 for a recent review) and in expert surveys (Benoit and Laver 2008). Research also shows that ideological competition among federal parties is primarily based on a left-right cleavage (Irvine 1987; Pétry, Collette, and Klingemann 2012).

In the analyses below, political parties are positioned on the left-right cleavage based on the RILE (right-left) scale used by CMP researchers. The RILE scale is constructed by simple addition and subtraction of percentages of mentions of a fixed number of "left" and "right" issue categories in the electoral manifestos of parties. The scale includes twenty-six CMP issue categories – thirteen categories being classified on the left side and thirteen being classified on the right side of the scale – that are listed and defined in the appendix at the end of this chapter. The identity of the left and right categories was fixed in the 1980s using exploratory factor analyses of data from individual countries (Laver and Budge 1992). The categories retained in the RILE scale were those that correlated highly with either the left or the right axis emerging from within-country factor analyses (mostly in the United Kingdom).[2]

The simplicity of the RILE method explains its popularity among researchers in numerous countries. A second advantage is that the method allows researchers to produce data that are comparable in time. Experts' surveys, which are an alternative way of positioning parties on an ideological scale, do not allow for this. Another advantage is that the results obtained in one country can be easily compared with those of other countries by consulting the CMP website.

In theory, the RILE scale ranges from -100 (extreme left) to +100 (extreme right). For example, a party manifesto whose content would only be coded in the issue category "law and order," classified on the right side of the scale, would be attributed a score of +100, while a manifesto whose content would only be coded in the issue category "welfare state expansion," classified as on the left side of the scale, would score –100. In practice, the range of RILE scale scores is much lower.

One issue raised by the use of this method is whether the mentions of CMP categories in party manifestos should be interpreted as representing the true ideological position of a party. The official stand of the CMP is that the contents of party manifestos truly reflect party ideology. However, there are reasons that a literal interpretation of mentions in party manifestos should be avoided. First, there are risks associated with a literal interpretation: statistical risks but also human coding biases (Benoit, Laver, and Mikhaylov 2009). Second, parties vary their mentions of substantial issue categories in their manifestos from one election to the next for political or tactical motives that have more to do with strategy than with ideology (Pelizzo 2003). For these reasons, it is preferable to interpret changes in the content of party manifestos as an indication of direction rather than as a literal reflection of changes in party ideology. As well, in order to take into account that changes in party manifestos may reflect short-term considerations in addition to ideological commitments, in this analysis, the scores used to measure party position on substantive issues and on the

RILE scale are averaged by adding the scores at times t and t-1 and by dividing the sum by two.[3]

Party Positions on Substantive Issues

Table 6.1 displays the evolution of the RILE issue categories that were mentioned more than 1 percent of the time on average in NDP manifestos between 1988-93 and 2008-11. The table allows us to see how the NDP has changed its stances on substantive policy issues and to understand more clearly which issue categories have been pulling NDP positions towards the right on the RILE scale and which have been pulling them towards the left. There are eleven issue categories, eight from the left and three from the right. They are ranked by decreasing order of average frequency of mention. "Welfare state expansion" clearly stands out among left categories at 14.2 percent of NDP manifesto space on average, distantly followed by "market regulation" (4.2 percent) and "education expansion" (4.2 percent). The table also reports the scores for "labour groups" (3.6 percent), "democracy" (3.5 percent), "peace" (3.3 percent), "internationalism positive" (2.7 percent), and "protectionism positive" (1.4 percent). Five remaining left RILE issue categories (not reported in the table) are mentioned 4 percent of the time on average over the period of analysis.

The table displays three right categories: "law and order" (3.8 percent), "freedom and human rights" (3.6 percent), and "incentives" (3.1 percent). Together, the nine remaining right RILE issue categories (not reported) are mentioned 5.5 percent of the time on average over the period of analysis. The percentage of mentions of the left RILE categories (41.2 percent) is almost three times larger than the percentage of mentions of the right RILE categories (16 percent) on average over the period of analysis.

The next seven columns of numbers in Table 6.1 give the percentage frequency of mention of individual issue categories in each successive period. To obtain a bird's-eye view of the trend affecting each issue category over time, the percentages in the three periods after 2000-04 are added together, and the sum is subtracted from the sum of the percentages for the same issue category in the three periods before 2000-04 (the 2000-04 period is omitted). The result of the subtraction is then divided by the sum for the first three periods. The results are reported as percentage increases or decreases over time in the last column of Table 6.1 labelled "change." The data indicate an increase in the mentions by NDP manifestos of three left RILE issue categories: "internationalism positive" (+900 percent), "market regulation" (+254 percent), and "peace" (+21 percent). And they also indicate an

TABLE 6.1

Evolution of the most frequently mentioned RILE issue categories in NDP manifestos, 1988-93 to 2008-11 (%)

Categories	Average	1988-93	1993-97	1997-2000	2000-04	2004-06	2006-08	2008-11	Change (%)
Left categories									
504 Welfare state expansion	14.2	8.6	10.9	20.9	18.3	13.0	13.6	14.2	+1
403 Market regulation	4.2	3.0	2.7	1.2	4.7	5.6	3.8	8.1	+254
506 Education expansion	4.2	3.1	4.0	5.5	4.5	3.5	4.8	4.1	-2
701 Labour groups	3.6	4.5	5.8	7.3	4.5	3.0	0.2	0.0	-82
202 Democracy	3.5	4.0	4.4	2.1	3.0	4.7	3.1	3.2	+5
106 Peace	3.3	2.9	3.5	3.2	2.1	1.5	4.3	5.8	+21
107 Internationalism positive	2.7	0.9	0.7	0.0	1.7	3.8	5.8	6.3	+900
406 Protectionism positive	1.4	2.2	2.5	1.9	1.3	0.5	0.4	0.8	-74
Remaining left categories[a]	4.0	6.2	4.8	3.1	3.5	3.6	3.2	2.8	-36
Total left	41.2	35.4	39.3	45.2	43.6	39.2	39.2	45.3	+3
Right categories									
605 Law and order	3.8	0.4	1.2	6.0	2.1	6.3	6.5	4.1	+123
201 Freedom and human rights	3.6	5.2	3.5	0.6	5.3	4.0	2.3	4.1	+14
402 Incentives	3.1	2.3	1.8	1.5	1.3	2.5	4.5	8.1	+250
Remaining right categories[b]	5.5	2.0	8.4	5.4	4.3	1.9	7.4	8.5	+11
Total right	16.0	9.9	14.9	13.5	13.0	14.7	20.7	24.8	+55
RILE score (total right minus total left)	-25.2	-25.5	-24.4	-31.7	-30.6	-24.5	-18.5	-20.5	

a The remaining left categories in the RILE scale applied to Canada are "military negative," "anti-imperialism," "nationalization," "economic planning," and "controlled economy." Each of these categories is mentioned in NDP manifestos less than 1 percent of the time on average.

b The remaining right categories in the RILE scale are " military limitation," "constitutionalism positive," "free enterprise," "protectionism negative," "economic orthodoxy," "political authority," "welfare state limitation," "national way of life positive," "traditional morality positive," and "social harmony." Each of these categories is mentioned in NDP manifestos less than 1 percent of the time on average.

increase in all the right RILE categories: "law and order" (+123 percent), "freedom" (+14 percent), "incentives" (+250 percent), and "remaining right" (+11 percent). There is a decrease in the mentions of "labour groups" (–82 percent), of "protectionism positive" (–74 percent), and of "remaining" (–36 percent) on the left. Changes between +10 percent and –10 percent are assumed to reflect stability over time; and, by this assumption, the mentions of "welfare state expansion" (+1 percent), "education expansion" (–2 percent), and "democracy" (+5 percent) have remained stable over the period. Overall, it appears that the ideological shift to the right in NDP manifestos is due primarily to an increase over time in the frequency of mentions of right issue categories (+55 percent) rather than to a decrease in the frequency of mentions of left issue categories (there is, in fact, an increase of 3 percent overall). The large increase in the mentions of "internationalism positive" and "peace" over time in NDP manifestos reveals a readiness to appear more mainstream even if the tone remains critical of established policies in this issue domain.[4] The increase over time in the mentions of all the issue categories on the right side of the RILE scale, especially "incentives" and "law and order," is also noteworthy, as is the decrease in the mentions of "protectionism positive" and "labour groups," two issue categories on the left of the RILE scale that have been traditionally associated with the NDP.

Another development in recent NDP manifestos is the shift towards a vocabulary that is more friendly towards business and trade liberalization. For example, the 2011 NDP manifesto entitled *Giving Your Family a Break: Practical First Steps* contains a section on "Practical First Steps to Reward the Jobs Creators" with pledges to cut taxes for business and to always maintain the Canadian tax rate below the United States federal corporate tax rate.[5] The change towards a more pro-business ideology is revealed in the very substantial increase in the mention of "incentives" over the period of analysis (+250 percent).

Table 6.2 presents a summary of the changes in the Liberal Party position on substantive issues over the period of analysis. The first column reports the percentage of mentions of RILE issue categories by the Liberals Party between 1988-93 and 2008-11. We see that Liberal Party manifestos have mentioned left RILE issue categories less often than the NDP (29.4 percent of the time against 35.4 percent). As expected, Liberal Party manifestos mention many left categories less frequently overall than do NDP manifestos (e.g., "welfare state expansion" and "market regulation"). Note that "labour groups positive" and "protectionism positive," which are

TABLE 6.2

Evolution of the most frequently mentioned RILE issue categories in Liberal Party manifestos, 1988-93 to 2008-11

Categories	Average (%)	Change (%)
Left categories		
504 Welfare state expansion	10.5	+78
506 Education expansion	5.1	+3
107 Internationalism positive	4.6	+37
202 Democracy	3.6	−263
106 Peace	1.6	−22
403 Market regulation	1.1	−87
Remaining left categories[a]	2.9	+29
Total left	29.4	+15
Right categories		
402 Incentives	6.2	+12
605 Law and order	2.8	−39
414 Economic orthodoxy	2.8	+125
203 Constitutionalism positive	1.3	−75
201 Freedom and human rights	1.3	−69
401 Free enterprise	1.2	−72
407 Protectionism negative	1.1	−60
Remaining right categories[b]	5.3	−25
Total right	22.0	−27
Average RILE score	−7.0	

a The remaining left categories are "military negative," "anti-imperialism," "nationalization," "economic planning," "controlled economy," "labour groups positive," and "protectionism positive." Each of these categories is mentioned in Liberal Party manifestos less than 1 percent of the time on average.

b The remaining right categories are "political authority," "national way of life positive," "traditional morality positive," "military positive," and "social harmony." Each of these categories is mentioned in Liberal Party manifestos less than 1 percent of the time on average.

featured in Table 6.1 for the NDP, no longer appear in Table 6.2 because they were mentioned less than 1 percent of the time overall in Liberal Party manifestos. At the same time, Liberal Party manifestos mention the right RILE categories more often than do NDP manifestos (22.0 percent against 16.0 percent).

The second column of Table 6.2 reports the change in the mention of each issue category calculated in the same manner as the change for the NDP was calculated in Table 6.1. We see an important increase in the mentions of "welfare state expansion" (+78 percent), the most frequently mentioned category (as it is for the NDP). This is compensated by a decrease in the mention of several left RILE categories ("democracy," "market regulation"). Overall, even though the Liberal shift to the left is due in part to increased emphasis on left categories (+15 percent), the bulk of this shift is due to a decrease over time in the overall mention of right categories (–27 percent).

Here are the main results we can draw from a comparison of the evolution of NDP and Liberal Party mentions of substantive RILE issue categories. The most remarkable result is the rapprochement over time between the NDP and the Liberal Party ideologies. This ideological rapprochement is attributed to changes in party emphases on a few substantial issues: NDP manifestos have seen an increase in the frequency of mentions of right issue categories, especially "incentives" and "law-and-order" issues. At the same time, the frequency of mentions of the same issue categories has decreased or remained stable in Liberal Party manifestos. NDP manifestos have also decreased their emphasis on "traditional" left issues categories, including "labour groups" and "protectionism positive," which, to begin with, the Liberal Party accentuated very little.

Liberal Party manifestos have also seen an increase in the frequency of mentions of "welfare state expansion," to the point at which they appear indistinguishable from NDP manifestos on this issue category. However, the fact that the frequency of mentions of left issues such as "market regulation" or "peace" has increased over time in NDP manifestos while it has decreased over time in Liberal Party manifestos reminds us that the NDP and the Liberal Party are still ideologically apart on several important substantive issues.

Party Positions on the Left-Right Scale
Figure 6.1 plots the RILE scores of the NDP that are found in the bottom row of Table 6.1. The figure also plots the scores of the Liberal Party and the Conservative Party between 1988-93 and 2008-11, of the Bloc Québécois between 1993-97 and 2008-11, and of the Reform/Alliance Party in 1993-97 and 1997-2000. Remember that the party score at each election is calculated by subtracting the total percentage of manifesto mentions of issue categories associated with the left from the percentages of right-associated issue categories. The positions of the NDP are at the bottom of the scale (negative scores on the RILE scale throughout the period). The positions of the Reform/Alliance Party are at the top of the scale (highly positive scores) and the positions of the Conservatives and the Liberals are found in the

FIGURE 6.1
Left-right ideological placement of parties over time

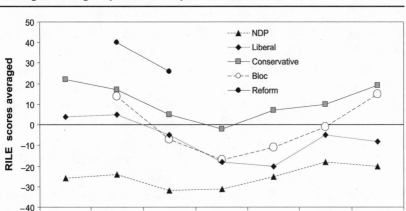

middle, with the Liberals distinctly to the left of the Conservatives (Conservative manifestos have positive scores most of the time, whereas Liberal manifestos have negative scores most of the time). At first glance, the left-right ordering of the parties is consistent with scholarly interpretations. It is also important to note that the parties distinguish themselves sufficiently to provide a clear basis for policy choice by the voters. In particular, there are no instances of leap-frogging whereby parties exchange left-right positions in successive periods.

To calculate a trend over time in the left-right scores of each party, I have averaged the RILE scores for the last three periods and subtracted the result from the average RILE score in the first three periods (the score for the middle period omitted). This method yields a net change of 6 points to the right over time in NDP manifestos, from –27 points on average between 1988-93 and 1997-2000 to –21 points on average between 2004-06 and 2008-11. By the same calculation method, there has been a net change of 12 points to the left over time for the Liberal Party (from +1 point on average before 2000-04 to –11 points on average after 2000-04). There has been a net change of 3 points to the left for the Conservative Party (from +15 points on average before 2000-04 to +12 points on average after 2000-04). This change being too small to rule out chance, it appears that the position of the Conservative Party has remained stable over the period of analysis.[6]

Several results stand out from the data in Figure 6.1. The overall ideological range of the Canadian party system (the distance that separates the NDP and the Conservative Party) has decreased over time substantially: from 42 points on average between 1988-93 and 1997-2000 to 33 points on average between 2004-06 and 2008-11. When the Reform/Alliance Party is included in the calculation, the total ideological range is much larger in 1993-97 (64 points) and in 1997-2000 (58 points) than at any subsequent time. With the disappearance of the Reform/Alliance Party after the 2000 election, the sudden widening of the ideological space that occurred between the parties in 1993 (Carty, Cross, and Young 2000) vanishes.

The average RILE score for the NDP over the entire period is –25.2 (see Table 6.1). By comparison, RILE scores for parties in the Socialist or Social Democratic family from the CMP website are as follows: PS (France 2008) –21.3; SPD (Germany 2009) –18.3; Labour (Great Britain) –1.5; Socialist (Netherlands 2010) –13.1; SAP (Sweden 2010) –32.3. This suggests that NDP manifestos are positioned left-of-centre – both on the Canadian partisan landscape and internationally – and not at the extreme left.

The diagram clearly delineates the rapprochement over time between the NDP and the Liberal Party that emerged from a comparison of Tables 6.1 and 6.2. This rapprochement was most pronounced in 2004-06. The gap between the ideological positions of the Liberal Party and the NDP has increased since. As well, after initial moves towards the left, the manifestos of the NDP, the Liberal Party, and the Conservative Party have all subsequently shifted to the right of the political spectrum. The shift to the right has been more pronounced for the manifestos of the Conservative Party after 2000-04 and for the NDP after 1997-2000. The shift to the right in the manifestos of the Liberal Party after 2004-06 occurred later and was less pronounced.

How credible is the evolution of the ideological positioning of the NDP and other parties depicted in Figure 6.1? Let us first examine whether the RILE data are free from error or biases (internal validity standard). Taking into account that the RILE scale is a "one-size-fits-all" arbitrary scale not specifically designed to coincide with Canadian party ideology, the following question arises: To what extent do the issue categories in the RILE scale correspond to the actual content of NDP manifestos? A strong percentage would reassure us of the face validity of the RILE scale when applied to the NDP. Adding the percentages of mentions of issues categories included in the RILE scale, we find that the left categories account for 35.4 percent and that the categories on the right side of the RILE scale account for

FIGURE 6.2

Left-right ideological placement of NDP by citizens and by experts

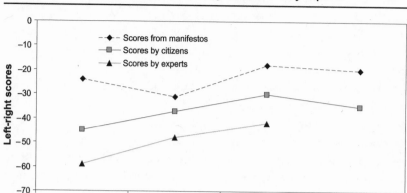

25.5 percent of NDP manifesto content overall. Thus the RILE scale accounts for 35.4 + 25.5 = 60.9 percent on average of the NDP manifesto content over the period of analysis. Put another way, the RILE scale fails to account for 39 percent of the content of NDP manifestos. This is not bad, considering that the issue categories in the RILE scale represent only half the total CMP issue categories. The RILE issue categories account for 51.4 percent of the content of Liberal Party manifestos.[7] The scale does a better job at capturing the content of NDP than Liberal Party manifestos.

To what extent are the RILE data consistent with results from surveys that ask experts or citizens to position parties on the left-right axis (external validity standard)? Both expert and mass surveys suffer important limitations that prevent their use in research concerned with party ideological evolution over time. The surveys that have been administered in Canada so far have been too infrequent and they have used methodologies that are too different to provide reliable time-series data on the evolution of party left-right positions. But their results can be used to validate the results obtained from a content analysis of party manifestos. How do the RILE data compare with data from expert surveys? Recent expert surveys position the NDP at –59 points in 1993-97 (Laver and Hunt 2000), at –48 points in 2000-04 (Benoit and Laver 2008), and at –42 points in 2008 (Pétry, Collette, and Klingemann 2012) on a standardized scale from –100 (extreme left) to +100 (extreme right) (see Figure 6.2.).

Another point of comparison for the RILE data are the judgments of the electorate as measured in election surveys. Based on data from Canadian Election Study surveys, it is calculated that Canadians placed the NDP at −45 in 2000, −35 in 2004, −30 in 2008, and −35 in 2011, respectively, on a standardized scale from -100 (extreme left) to +100 (extreme right). The data are reported in Figure 6.2.

The correlations between the RILE scale and both the expert and mass survey results are quite strong ($R = .76$ for citizens' scores; $R = .70$ for experts scores), although experts and citizens consistently position the NDP further to the left than does the RILE scale.[8] That left party positions derived from expert and mass surveys are further to the left than the positions derived from manifestos is a general feature pointed out by Klingemann et al. (2007) in their comparative study of left-right party positions in Western and Eastern Europe. Furthermore, party positions derived from expert judgments and from mass opinion are not directly comparable with party positions derived from manifesto contents. We do not know precisely on what criteria experts and laypeople base their judgments, but it is safe to assume that these criteria are different from the ones that define the RILE method. One particular difference is that, unlike party positions derived from manifesto contents that reflect today's party ideology, party positions derived from surveys are based in part on judgments about past party ideology. If, as this chapter demonstrates, NDP ideology was more to the left in the past than it is today, then we should expect that the NDP position derived from expert and mass surveys would be further to the left than the position derived from manifesto data.[9] Far from being an anomaly, the fact that surveys position the NDP further to the left than the manifesto data may reinforce the validity of using the RILE method to position the NDP on the left-right policy dimension.

While the RILE scores may better reflect the contemporary position of a party on the left-right spectrum, the question remains whether the RILE scores of the NDP and the Liberal Party reflect their supporters' left-right preferences. Figures 6.3 and 6.4 provide the answer by comparing the evolution of the left-right placement of the NDP and the Liberal Party and their supporters over time.[10] These figures demonstrate that there is a fairly good match between NDP voters and NDP manifestos positions over time ($R = .42$), although we should note that NDP supporters take up more extreme positions than the ones held by the party they support.[11] Unlike the NDP, the correlation between the Liberal Party and its supporters is negative and not statistically significant ($R = -.13$). This suggests that the NDP

FIGURE 6.3
Left-right ideological placement of the NDP and its supporters

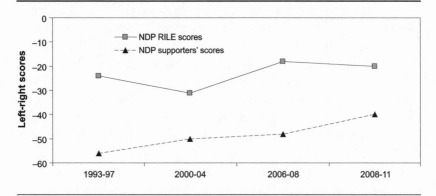

FIGURE 6.4
Left-right ideological placement of the Liberal Party and its supporters

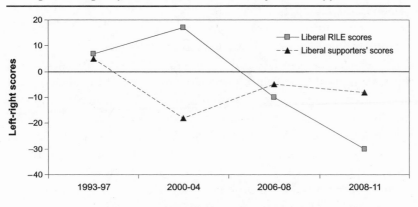

has represented the left-right preferences of its supporters more closely than the Liberal Party.[12] This may be due to the fact that the NDP has been more adept at responding to movements of opinion among its supporters than the Liberal Party has been at responding to its own supporters. Alternatively, it is possible that NDP voters are better able than Liberal Party voters to influence the left-right direction of the party they support.

Conclusion and Discussion

Three main points emerge from the analysis of the evolution over time of the ideological position of the NDP and of the Liberal Party. First, there is a gradual and fairly regular shift to the right in the manifestos of the NDP over time. Second, the NDP shift to the right is a factor in the narrowing ideological distance between the NDP and the Liberal Party. But the most important factor in this narrowing is the shift to the left in the manifestos of the Liberal Party over time. The net shift to the right in NDP manifestos is smaller than the net shift to the left in Liberal Party manifestos, even when the recent Liberal move back to the right is taken into account. This last point should serve to emphasize that the NDP achieved mainstream status without abandoning its social democratic ideological principles. Rebranding the NDP as a substitute Liberal Party may not be the only path towards electoral success.

The finding that the manifestos of the NDP and the Liberal Party have been converging over time has important theoretical implications related to selective emphasis and issue ownership. As noted above, issue ownership theory holds that parties selectively emphasize issues to mobilize voters. At first glance, judging by the differences in average frequency of mentions, the data support the theory. The NDP and the Liberal Party appear to take distinct positions on most issue categories. However, to fully qualify as being selectively emphasized, issues must not only be distinctly emphasized but also follow diverging paths in NDP and Liberal Party manifestos. Remarkably, a comparison of the data in Tables 6.1 and 6.2 shows that most issues on which the NDP and the Liberal Party take distinct positions are not diverging but, rather, converging over time. In fact, there are only five issues that are both distinct and diverging over time: "peace," "freedom and human rights," "market regulation," "economic orthodoxy," and "law and order." Those are the issue categories that truly qualify as cases of selective emphasis. The remaining issue categories are "converging" in the sense that, with time, the space given to them in NDP and Liberal Party manifestos has become more alike. A practical implication of the ideological rapprochement between the NDP and the Liberal Party is that, by making the ideological distance between them much shorter than the distance from the Conservative Party, it renders the prospect of a possible coalition more theoretically plausible (but see Jean-François Godbout, Éric Bélanger, and Frédéric Mérand, Chapter 11, this volume.).

NDP popular support gradually grew under the leadership of Jack Layton, from 8.5 percent of the electorate in 2000 to 18.1 percent in 2008 to 30.6 percent in 2011. During the same period, the Liberal Party's share of the popular vote declined, from 41 percent in 2000 to 18 percent in 2011. To what extent are the electoral success of the NDP and the electoral decline of the Liberal Party attributable to changes in their left-right ideological positions?

The data presented in this chapter strongly suggest that the electoral success of the NDP is linked to changes in its ideological position. The NDP has moved to the right at the same time as its supporters, and Canadians in general, have been moving to the right. The behaviour of the NDP followed the first rule of issue voting theory, which holds that, in order to be successful at the polls, a party must shift its ideological positions in response to shifts in the electorate (Adams et al. 2004).

However, it does not seem that the Liberal Party followed the first rule of issue voting theory. It changed ideological direction several times during the period of analysis, and, as Figure 6.2 suggests, these changes have not been in response to changes in the ideological preferences of the Canadian public or Liberal Party supporters. Its position between the NDP on the left and the Conservative Party on the right presented it with a dilemma. Before 2000-04, when the right was divided, the Liberal Party moved to the left to stop the NDP from making electoral gains at its expense. After the unification of the right, the Liberal Party was no longer free to maintain a left ideological position to compete with the NDP on issues as, by doing so, it would have opened space for the unified Conservative Party to capture some Liberal support. The Liberal Party chose the option of moving back to the right to better compete with the Conservatives, which they correctly perceived as the most immediate danger after the merger of the Progressive Conservative Party and the Alliance Party. But this opened the field for the NDP to recapture support from centre-left voters, which it has apparently done.

One last point needs to be emphasized. Without underestimating the success of the NDP, this success resulted, in part, from the recent failure of the Liberal Party to efficiently adjust its ideological position to party competition in the post-2004 party system. The failure of the Liberal Party has been first and foremost to the advantage of the Conservative Party and, to a lesser extent, to the advantage of the NDP. Evidence of this comes from CES survey data on Canadians' perceptions of party competence at solving policy issues. In 1997-2000, the Liberal Party was the most successful at channelling support based on popular perceptions of issue ownership. The Liberal Party was perceived as best at "creating jobs" and "managing the economy," "fighting crime," and "improving health care." The NDP was perceived as best at solving only one issue (social programs), and the Conservatives did not score at all (see Bélanger and Meguid 2007).

In 2008-11, the situation had almost completely reversed. The Liberal Party had lost the issue ownership advantage it enjoyed ten or fifteen years before. But this has happened to the benefit of the Conservative Party, considered by 2008 to be best at "creating jobs," "managing the economy," and "fighting crime." Meanwhile, the NDP has managed to gain issue ownership advantage only in "improving health care."

Obviously, the NDP's ability either to remain as Official Opposition or to push through to government power requires it to expand its issue ownership at the expense of the Liberal Party since it is unlikely to capture economic management or law-and-order issue ownership from the Conservatives. Whether it can do this while remaining relatively close to the Liberals ideologically and counteracting Justin Trudeau's appeal is a question that only the 2015 election can answer.

APPENDIX
Definition of Issue Categories in the RILE Scale (with their CMP codes)

103 Anti-imperialism
Negative references to exerting strong influence (political, military or commercial) over other states; negative references to controlling other countries as if they were part of an empire; favourable mentions of decolonization; favourable references to greater self-government and independence for colonies; negative references to the imperial behaviour of the manifesto country and/or other countries.

104 Military: positive
Need to maintain or increase military expenditure; modernizing armed forces and improvement in military strength; rearmament and self-defence; need to keep military treaty obligations; need to secure adequate personnel in the military.

105 Military: negative
Favourable mentions of decreasing military expenditures; disarmament; "evils of war"; promises to reduce conscription, otherwise as *104*, but negative.

106 Peace
Peace as a general goal; declarations of belief in peace and peaceful means of solving crises; desirability of countries joining in negotiations with hostile countries.

107 Internationalism: positive
Need for international cooperation; cooperation with specific countries other than those coded in *101 Special foreign relationship*; need for aid to developing countries; need for world planning of resources; need for international courts; support for any international goal or world state; support for UN.

201 Freedom and human rights
Favourable mentions of importance of personal freedom and civil rights; freedom from bureaucratic control; freedom of speech; freedom from coercion in the political and economic spheres; individualism in the manifesto country and in other countries.

202 Democracy
Favourable mentions of democracy as a method or goal in national and other organizations; involvement of all citizens in decision making as well as generalized support for the manifesto country's democracy.

203 Constitutionalism: positive
Support for specific aspects of the Constitution; use of constitutionalism as an argument for policy as well as general approval of the constitutional way of doing things.

305 Political authority
Favourable mentions of strong government, including government stability; manifesto party's competence to govern and/or other party's lack of such competence.

401 Free enterprise
Favourable mentions of free enterprise capitalism; superiority of individual enterprise over state and control systems; favourable mentions of private property rights, personal enterprise, and initiative; need for unhampered individual enterprises.

402 Incentives
Need for wage and tax policies to induce enterprise; encouragement to start enterprises; need for financial and other incentives such as subsidies.

403 Market regulation
Need for regulations designed to make private enterprises work better; actions against monopolies and trusts and in defence of consumer and small business; encouraging economic competition; social market economy.

404 Economic planning
Favourable mentions of long-standing economic planning of a consultative or indicative nature; need for government to create such a plan.

406   Protectionism: positive
Favourable mentions of extension or maintenance of tariffs to protect internal markets; other domestic economic protectionism such as quota restrictions.

407   Protectionism: negative
Support for the concept of free trade; otherwise as *406*, but negative.

412   Controlled economy
General need for direct government control of economy; control over prices, wages, rents, etc.; state intervention in the economic system.

413   Nationalization
Favourable mentions of government ownership, partial or complete, including government ownership of land.

414   Economic orthodoxy
Need for traditional economic orthodoxy (e.g., reduction of budget deficits, retrenchment in crisis, thrift and savings); support for traditional economic institutions such as stock market and banking system; support for strong currency.

504   Welfare state expansion
Favourable mentions of need to introduce, maintain, or expand any social service or social security scheme; support for social services such as health service or social housing. Note: This category excludes education.

505   Welfare state limitation
Limiting expenditure on social services or social security; otherwise as *504*, but negative.

506   Education expansion
Need to expand and/or improve educational provision at all levels. This excludes technical training that is coded under *411 Technology and infrastructure.*

601   National way of life: positive
Appeals to patriotism and/or nationalism; suspension of some freedoms in order to protect the state against subversion; support for established national ideas.

603   Traditional morality: positive
Favourable mentions of traditional moral values; prohibition, censorship, and suppression of immorality and unseemly behaviour; maintenance and stability of family; religion.

605   Law and order
Enforcement of all laws; actions against crime; support and resources for police; tougher attitudes in courts.

606   Social harmony
Appeal for national effort and solidarity; need for society to see itself as united; appeal for public spiritedness; decrying anti-social attitudes in times of crisis; support for the public interest.

701   Labour groups
Favourable references to labour groups, the working class, the unemployed; support for trade unions; good treatment of manual and other employees.

Notes

I wish to thank Lisa Birch, Benoît Collette, Dominic Duval, and the Poltext research team for their research assistance. The data for this project were collected over the years with funding from the Fonds de recherche pour la société et la culture.

1 Canadian manifestos are collected and coded by the Poltext project team in collaboration with the CMP. The scores of Canadian parties on each CMP issue category over time are posted on the project's website at www.capp.poltext.org. Each manifesto is coded separately by two trained researchers. A coding handbook explains the identification of coding units (quasi-sentences), the choice of categories, and how to cope with difficult coding decisions. At the end, the researchers compare their respective coding and reach agreement when they disagree. When agreement cannot be reached, a referee is called to settle the issue. The inter-coder agreement – that is, the percentage of agreement between the coders when they first compare their results – is usually well above 90 percent.

2 The scores of Canadian parties on the RILE scale over time are posted on the CMP website at https://manifestoproject.wzb.eu/.

3 Averaging scores in two successive elections implies that the score of a party at t-1 affects in equal proportion its score at t. Alternative forms of averaging could give smaller weights to more distant time points and/or take into account the duration of each legislative term in the smoothing formula.

4 There has been a significant increase in the frequency of mentions of "military negative" in NDP manifestos between 1988 and 2011, although the average frequency of mentions remains largely under 1 percent for that category over the period.

5 This is in contrast with promises to increase corporate taxes in earlier NDP manifestos. For example, the 1988 NDP manifesto *A Fair Deal for Canada* contains a pledge to introduce tax increases for profitable corporations.

6 The Conservative scores are based on the manifestos of the Progressive Conservative Party before 2004. Starting with 2004, the scores are based on the manifestos of the Conservative Party, resulting from a merger between the Reform/Alliance Party and the PC Party.

7 By comparison, the RILE scale accounts for 57 percent of Conservative Party manifesto content and 39 percent of Bloc manifesto content.

8 Franzmann and Kaiser (2006) propose an alternative method for analyzing CMP data – one that produces NDP scores that are closer to expert survey results than

the scores on the RILE scale. Their method focuses exclusively on "positional" issue categories, on which the parties take opposite views (e.g., "for" or "against" tougher crime measures or "for" or "against" an increase in military expenditures) while ignoring "valence" issue categories, on which parties take the same view (e.g., all parties stand for democracy or peace). When applied to Canadian party ideology, the method positions the NDP further to the left than the RILE method and produces an NDP trajectory that moves less towards the centre of the ideological space over time than the trajectory produced by the RILE method. The Liberal Party trajectory produced by the Franzmann and Kaiser method is very similar to the trajectory produced by the RILE method.

9   Recent expert surveys position the Liberal Party closer to what its position was on the RILE scale twenty years ago than to its current position on the scale.

10 Self-placement data from CES surveys are used to locate party supporters. The CES surveys ask respondents to place themselves on a 1-to-10 left-right scale. For comparison purpose, the CES data have been transformed linearly into the –100 to +100 RILE metric and averaged over two elections.

11 Klingemann et al. (2007) also find that parties of the left in Europe are further to the left, whereas supporters of centrist parties are more moderate.

12 Note that the convergence of views is strongest between the Conservative Party and its supporters ($R = .85$)

References

Adams, James, Michael Clark, Lawrence Ezrow, and Garrett Glasgow. 2004. "Understanding Change and Stability in Party Ideologies: Do Parties Respond to Public Opinion or to Past Elections?" *British Journal of Political Science* 34: 589-610.

Bélanger, Eric, and Bonnie M. Meguid. 2007. Issue Salience, Issue Ownership, and Issue-Based Vote Choice. *Electoral Studies* 27: 477-91.

Benoit, Kenneth, and Michael Laver. 2008. *Party Policy in Modern Democracies*. London: Routledge.

Benoit, Kenneth, Michael Laver, and Slava Mikhaylov. 2009. Treating Words as Data with Error: Uncertainty in Text Statements of Policy Positions. *American Journal of Political Science* 53, 2: 495-513.

Bittner, Amanda, and Royce Koop, eds. 2013. *Parties, Elections, and the Future of Canadian Politics*. Vancouver: UBC Press.

Budge, Ian, and Dennis Farlie. 1983. Party Competition-Selective Emphasis or Direct Confrontation: An Alternative View with Data. In Peter Mair, ed., *Western European Party Systems*, 267-305. London: Sage.

Budge, Ian, David Robertson, and Derek Hearl, eds. 1987. *Ideology, Strategy, and Party Change: Spatial Analysis of Post-War Elections Programmes in Nineteen Democracies*. Cambridge, UK: Cambridge University Press.

Carty, R. Kenneth, William Cross, and Lisa Young. 2000. *Rebuilding Canadian Party Politics*. Vancouver: UBC Press.

Clarke, Harold, Jane Jenson, Lawrence LeDuc, and Jon Pammett. 1991. *Absent Mandate*, 2nd ed. Toronto: Gage.

Electoral Studies. 2007. Special Symposium: Comparing Measures of Party Positioning: Expert, Manifesto, and Survey Data. Special Issue (Vol. 26).

Franzmann, Simon, and André Kaiser. 2006. Locating Political Parties in Policy Space: A Reanalysis of Party Manifesto Data. *Party Politics* 12, 2: 163-88.

Gidengil, Elisabeth, Neil Nevitte, André Blais, Joanna Everitt, and Patrick Fournier. 2012. *Dominance and Decline: Making Sense of Recent Canadian Elections.* Toronto: University of Toronto Press.

Inglehart, Ronald, and Hans-Dieter Klingemann. 1976. Party Identification, Ideological Preference, and the Left-Right Dimension among the Western Mass Publics. In Ian Budge, Ivor Crewe, and Dennis Farlie, eds., *Party Identification and Beyond: Representations of Voting and Party Competition*, 243-73. New York: Wiley and Sons.

Irvine, William. 1987. Canada 1945-1980: Party Platforms and Campaign Strategies. In Ian Budge, David Robertson, and Derek Hearl, eds., Ideology, *Strategy and Party Change: Spatial Analyses of Post-War Election Programmes in 19 Democracies*, 73-95. Cambridge, UK: Cambridge University Press.

Klingemann, Hans-Dieter, Andea Volkens, Judith Bara, Ian Budge, and Michael McDonald. 2007. *Mapping Policy Preferences II: Estimates for Parties, Electors and Governments in Central and Eastern Europe.* Oxford: Oxford University Press.

Laver, Michael, and Ian Budge, eds. 1992. *Party Policy and Government Coalitions.* London: Macmillan.

Laver, Michael, and William Hunt. 2000. *Policy and Party Competition.* London: Routledge.

Naurin, Elin. 2011. *Election Promises, Party Behaviour and Voter Perceptions.* New York: Palgrave MacMillan.

Pelizzo, Roberto. 2003. Party Positions of Party Direction? An Analysis of Party Manifesto Data. *West European Politics* 26: 67-89.

Pétry, François. 2014. A Tale of Two Perspectives: Election Promises and Government Actions in Canada. In Elisabeth Gidengil and Heather Bastedo, eds., *Canadian Democracy from the Ground Up: Perceptions and Performance.* Vancouver: UBC Press.

Pétry, François, and Benoît Collette. 2009. Measuring How Political Parties Keep Their Promises: A Positive Perspective from Political Science. In Louise M. Imbeau, ed., *Do They Walk the Talk? Speech and Action in Policy Processes.* New York: Springer.

Pétry, François, Benoît Collette, and Hans-Dieter Klingemann. 2012. Left-Right in Canada: Comparing Data from Party Manifesto Content and Expert Surveys. Paper presented at the annual congress of the Canadian Political Science Association, University of Alberta, Edmonton.

Rallings, Colin. 1987. The Influence of Election Programmes: Britain and Canada 1945-79. In Ian Budge, David Robertson, and Derek Hearl, eds., *Ideology, Strategy, and Party Change: Spatial Analysis of Post-War Elections Programmes in Nineteen Democracies.* Cambridge, UK: Cambridge University Press.

Richards, John, Robert Cairns, and Larry Pratt, eds. 1991. *Social Democracy without Illusions: Renewal of the Canadian Left.* Toronto: McClelland and Stewart.

Thomson, Richard 2011. Citizens' Evaluation of the Fulfillment of Election Pledges: Evidence from Ireland. *Journal of Politics* 73: 187-201.

Werner, Annika, Onawa Lacewell, and Andrea Volkens. 2011. *Manifesto Coding Instructions*, 4th ed. Berlin: Wissenschaftszentrum Berlin für Sozialforschung.

PART 3

PARTY ACTIVISTS, LEADERS, AND VOTERS

7

Members, Activists, and Party Opinion

LYNDA ERICKSON and MARIA ZAKHAROVA

Party members are important resources for political parties. In elections, they are the backbone of local campaigns: they distribute election materials to voters' doorsteps, provide personnel for phone campaigns, deliver campaign signs, and staff local offices.[1] Beyond elections, members populate parties' organizational structures and act as their potential ambassadors outside of campaigns. Given the historical roots of the NDP as a mass party that celebrates the importance of party democracy and defines its delegate conventions as the "supreme governing body of the party," party members are also symbolically important for the NDP. Internal party opinion at odds with the party leadership can therefore complicate party decision making on policy and programmatic priorities and discourage members from participating in election campaigns.[2] Accordingly, understanding the NDP entails knowing who composes its membership as well as appreciating key dimensions of both their loyalty and attraction to the party, and their ideological tendencies and policy preferences.

In this chapter, we examine the backgrounds and political opinions of the party members, including their views on traditional social democratic commitments and the strategic directions their party should take. We do this using the results of a member survey undertaken in November 2009 (see appendix at end of this chapter). In addition, in order to provide some insight into internal party dynamics, we use the results from a member survey carried out by the 1997 study of the Canadian Social Democracy in

Transition (CSDT) survey to explore whether member opinion has changed over the last decade (see appendix). We conclude by examining whether contemporary member opinion as found in the 2009 survey is differentiated internally by levels of member activism. The core of our analysis, the 2009 survey data, consists of a sample of 1,171 members. The survey was conducted at a time when an immediate election was not anticipated and when the party leadership was not at issue.[3] Thus, the short-term factors that tend to attract more transient members were not in play. As a result, the 2009 sample represents the more long-term members who tend to populate parties between periods of high membership mobilization (Cross and Young 2004). It also largely reflects the distribution of the party's membership across the country.

Party Members: Who Are They?

NDP members' age and income characteristics appear to be similar to those of other federal parties. This means that they are older and more affluent than the general electorate (Cross and Young 2004). Seventy-three percent of our respondents were 55 or older, and their median household income was $70,000 per year, almost $4,000 above the median income of Canadian households documented in the 2006 census. In addition, fully 62 percent said they had a university or a postgraduate/professional degree. By comparison, in the 2006 census, 23 percent of the adult population aged 25 to 64 had a university degree (Statistics Canada 2009). On the other hand, the gender of the 2009 respondents more closely reflected the population: 51 percent of our respondents were male and 49 percent were female. This is in contrast with the gender distribution Cross and Young (2004) found in the Conservative, Canadian Alliance, and Bloc Québécois parties they surveyed in 2000, where men were substantially overrepresented.[4] Reflecting the party's historical relationship with organized labour, a high proportion of the sample were, or had been, union members. Thirty percent said they were current union members, with public-sector unionists twice as numerous as those in private-sector unions. A further 25 percent of the sample said they had been union members before they retired.

As suggested above, our sample was composed of many long-time party members. Sixty-two percent had belonged to the NDP for more than twenty years. In terms of party activity, they were most likely to participate in party affairs financially – by contributing funds to the party or a candidate – with 91 percent having done so in the last five years. Fifty-seven percent had worked for the party in a federal or provincial election campaign in the last five years, and roughly the same proportion had attended a local constituency meeting during that time. Seventy-seven percent of them donated money to that campaign, 65 percent displayed a party yard sign, 55 percent attempted to directly persuade someone to vote for the federal party, and a third of them distributed party election materials. These members represented an important mainstay of the party's outreach efforts in the 2008 election and probably in its 2011 campaign efforts as well.

Recruitment, Attraction, and Loyalty

The ways in which members are recruited to parties, and the reasons members continue to support these parties, are relevant to party continuity. Moreover, they are likely to differ across parties. In this respect, our respondents reflected characteristics we would expect of members of a more ideological party with a long history as a minor competitor on the electoral stage. First, a comparatively high proportion said they were self-motivated in joining the party. As Table 7.1 demonstrates, seven in ten of the members said they initially joined the party on their own initiative

TABLE 7.1
NDP membership incentives

Were you asked to join or did you decide on your own to become a party member?	(%)		
• Someone from party suggested I join	31		
• I decided on my own	69		

Reasons for supporting the NDP by level of importance	Level of importance (%)			
	Very important	Somewhat important	Not very important	Not at all important
• Leader of the party	35	49	12	4
• Core party ideas or platform	85	14	–	–
• Family has always supported NDP	19	20	19	43
• Trade union support for the NDP	20	33	24	22
• Don't like other parties	29	38	24	11

rather than being asked to do so. This figure is 10 percentage points higher than the proportion Young and Cross (2002) found among their sample of Canadian party members surveyed in 2000.[5]

Second, the party's ideology – that is, its core ideas as reflected in the platform – is crucially important for members' support for the party and greatly surpasses the importance of other factors for members' allegiance. When presented with a list of reasons for supporting the federal NDP, more than four-fifths of our respondents said that the "party's ideas or platform" were very important for them personally, whereas the leader of the party was very important for just 35 percent and their dislike of other parties was very important for only 29 percent. That their families had always supported the NDP was least important. An indication of the connection between organized labour and the NDP is evident in our finding that trade union support for the party was somewhat or very important for more than half of the respondents.

Given that ideological issues are so important to NDP members, loyalty at the voting booth may have posed a serious dilemma for them in recent elections. With the consolidation of the right in the merger of the Canadian Alliance and the Progressive Conservative parties, arguments concerning the need for strategic voting among "progressives" were mounted. By the 2008 election, strategic voting campaigns designed to defeat the Conservatives had gained considerable attention in the press (*Toronto Star* 2008) and on the Internet (Thompson 2008). As noted in Chapter 2 (Erickson and Laycock, this volume), after the merger of the PC and Alliance parties, the NDP was more vulnerable to strategic defections from its prospective voters than were other parties.

Given their intense dislike of the Conservative Party, our NDP members could also have been especially vulnerable to the appeals for strategic voting. When asked to indicate their feelings about the various parties, using a scale from 0 to 100, where 0 means really dislike and 100 means really like, these members gave the Conservative Party an average score of just 11.[6] Yet, in the 2008 election, relatively few succumbed to the calls for strategic voting. Among those who voted in that election, 91 percent said they voted NDP (see Table 7.2), although some 21 percent said they had considered voting for a different party. Among them, the majority (56 percent) said they had considered voting for the Liberals, suggesting the pull of strategic voting. Thirty-seven percent said they had considered voting for the Green Party.

TABLE 7.2

Members' voting loyalty, 2008 election

	Loyalty	%
Party voted for in 2008*	NDP	91
	Liberal	6
	Conservative	1
	Green	2
Considered voting differently (NDP voters only)	Considered another party	21
	Considered not voting	3

* Includes only those who said they voted.

Party on the Left?

To begin our analysis of the ideological dispositions of party members, we looked at where our respondents placed themselves on a general left-right scale and whether they saw themselves close to or at some distance from the federal party on this dimension. On a scale from 1 to 9, with 1 on the left and 9 on the right, the average score the 2009 respondents assigned themselves was 2.85. When characterizing their party on this same scale, almost half the respondents (49 percent) placed the federal party on their right, giving the party an average score of 3.49.[7] By comparison, a decade earlier in the CSDT study, although the respondents assigned themselves similar scores on the same left-right scale (2.90), they placed their party much closer to themselves. The average score they assigned to their party was 3.07.[8] This change in perceptions of the party's positioning was also evident among respondents to national election surveys of the same time period. In the Canadian Election Study of 1997 and that of 2008, respondents were asked to assign the parties a position on a left-right scale that ranged from 0 to 10. On that scale, respondents assigned the NDP a mean score of 3.40 in 1997 and a mean score of 3.68 in 2008.

Consistent with their self-placement on the left-right ideological scale, the 2009 party members were overwhelmingly committed to equality. When asked to choose between freedom and equality, 83 percent chose equality, defined as "Nobody is underprivileged and ... social class differences are not too strong," compared to just 17 percent who chose freedom, defined as "Everyone can live in freedom and develop without hindrance." These results were virtually identical to those from the 1997 survey, in which 84 percent chose equality and 16 percent chose freedom.

On the other questions we posed relevant to welfare state issues and priorities, our respondents also demonstrated strong and consistent support for positions on the left. With respect to state provision of social goods, the 2009 respondents were again highly supportive of a strong, universal welfare state. Once again, this echoed results from our 1997 survey. When asked to rank themselves on a 7-point scale between the option that "individuals should take more responsibility for providing for themselves" versus the position that "the state should take more responsibility to ensure that everyone is provided for," 60 percent opted for a position on the state responsibility side and a mere 20 percent for the individual responsibility

TABLE 7.3
Members' opinions on welfare state issues

Welfare state issues	Opinion	
General	% on individual responsibility side	% on state responsibility side
Individual versus state responsibility		
• 2009 respondents	20	60
mean score: 4.72		
• 1997 respondents	20	57
mean score: 4.73		
Universalism	% agree strongly or agree	% disagree strongly or disagree
Health care user fees		
• 2009 respondents	8	83
• 1997 respondents	9	85
Canada Pension Plan should be voluntary		
• 2009 respondents	4	92
• 1997 respondents	7	91
Welfare issues	% agree strongly or agree	% disagree strongly or disagree
Much talk of "welfare abuse" is exaggerated		
• 2009 respondents	63	26
• 1997 respondents	79	15

side. Twenty percent placed themselves in a neutral position (see Table 7.3). They strongly rejected proposals to pull back from the universalism of health care through user fees (83 percent disagreed with the statement that health care user fees should be instituted as a cost control measure) and to make participation in the Canada Pension Plan voluntary (92 percent disagreed with the proposal to make the plan voluntary).

Only on welfare abuse did our 2009 respondents indicate much ambivalence about provisioning by the welfare state, and they did so in slightly greater proportions than their 1997 counterparts. When asked whether "talk about 'welfare abuse' was exaggerated," just over a quarter of the 2009 respondents (26 percent) disagreed, compared to only 15 percent of the 1997 respondents. Still, this does not signal substantial dissention in the ranks about programs for the disadvantaged. Moreover, the respondents' answers to a question on the appropriate goals for social democratic governments attest to the strength of members' support for the disadvantaged. They were asked to rank the importance of various goals of social democratic governments, including reducing poverty, increasing resources for training unemployed people, increasing public support for health care, increasing public support for child care, and spending more on public education. Seventy-two percent chose reducing poverty as their first or second priority, and the mean ranking for this choice was 1.94 (see Table 7.4). By comparison, the mean ranking for increasing public support for health care was 2.55.

On more specifically economic topics we asked our respondents their position on three issues: government ownership, equality of incomes, and the accumulation of wealth. With respect to government ownership, using a 7-point scale we asked our respondents to choose between the options "private ownership of business and industry should be increased" (scored 1) versus "government ownership of business and industry should be increased" (scored 7). In choosing increased government ownership, the members would be reflecting their party's roots in socialist discourse on transforming property relations rather than the practices of most contemporary social democratic parties. Such parties, both in Canada and elsewhere, have downplayed issues of government ownership (see Laycock, Chapter 5, this volume) and, typically, have not challenged private ownership in domestic economies (Block 2011; Cronin, Ross, and Schoch 2011). Our 2009 respondents, however, leaned to a more traditional social democratic position on government ownership, showing relatively strong support for more of it. On the 7-point scale, 54 percent opted for the public ownership side, while

TABLE 7.4
Members' social policy priorities

Social policy priority	% ranking item as most important	Mean score
Reducing poverty		
• 2009 respondents	57	1.94
• 1997 respondents	64	1.82
Increasing public support for health care		
• 2009 respondents	28	2.55
• 1997 respondents	15	2.85
Spending more on education		
• 2009 respondents	14	3.04
• 1997 respondents	10	3.28
Increasing resources for retraining unemployed people		
• 2009 respondents	11	3.44
• 1997 respondents	10	3.26
Increasing public support for child care		
• 2009 respondents	8	3.48
• 1997 respondents	3	3.66

35 percent took a neutral position. Just 11 percent chose the private owner-ship side. In 1997, support for more public ownership was somewhat less, as 42 percent supported increased government ownership, compared to 24 percent who supported more private ownership (see Table 7.5).

With respect to income distribution, again our respondents showed strong support for traditional social democratic norms. Using a 7-point scale to choose between whether "incomes should be made more equal" (scored 1) versus "there should be greater incentives for individual effort" (scored 7), 68 percent opted for greater equality versus 16 percent who opted for individual incentives. This distribution was virtually unchanged from our 1997 survey results. At the same time, rejecting the option of greater incentives did not mean that these members held a zero-sum view of the economy. Responding to a 7-point scale ranging between "people can only accumulate wealth at the expense of others" (scored 1) and "wealth can grow so there's enough for everyone" (scored 7), 57 percent of the respondents chose the growth alternative. In 1997, 59 percent chose the same option.

TABLE 7.5
Members' opinions on economic issues

Economic issue	Opinion	
General		
Increase private ownership vs. increase government ownership	% on private ownership side	% on public ownership side
• 2009 respondents *mean score:* **4.80**	11	54
• 1997 respondents *mean score:* **4.75**	24	42
Incomes should be more equal vs. greater incentives for individual effort	% on incomes more equal side	% on individual effort side
• 2009 respondents *mean score:* **2.84**	68	16
• 1997 respondents *mean score:* **2.91**	68	18
People can only accumulate wealth at the expense of others vs. wealth can grow so there's enough for everyone	% on wealth accumulates at others' expense side	% on wealth can grow side
• 2009 respondents *mean score:* **4.60**	27	57
• 1997 respondents *mean score:* **4.68**	27	59
Employment issues		
(Un)employment Insurance should be harder to get	% agree or strongly agree	% disagree or strongly disagree
• 2009 respondents	4	90
• 1997 respondents	8	80
Unemployed should take any job vs. right to refuse job	% on take any job side	% on right to refuse job side
• 2009 respondents *mean score:* **4.71**	20	58
• 1997 respondents *mean score:* **4.88**	19	62

We also asked our respondents questions about unemployment policies. The first one concerned employment insurance. A long-standing aspect of social protection supported by social democratic parties has been provision of insurance for unemployed workers (Esping-Anderson 1990). However, the extent of employment insurance protection supported by social democratic parties across different countries has been variable. This differential protection has often reflected priorities for policies that facilitate labour market entry and activation as opposed to simply unemployment payments.[9] In the Canadian context, as federal unemployment insurance has been increasingly restricted in the last two decades, the NDP has been a strong critic of such cutbacks. In keeping with the party's position, our members showed virtually unanimous opposition to the proposition that employment insurance should be harder to get. Ninety-percent disagreed with this proposition, with half disagreeing strongly. Moreover, when asked to choose on a 7-point scale between "unemployed people should have to take any job available or lose their unemployment benefits" (scored 1) and "unemployed people should have the right to refuse a job they do not want" (scored 7), respondents' mean scores were 4.71, with 58 percent opting for the right to refuse a job. In comparing these results with the 1997 survey, it is clear that members' opinions on unemployment policies have not substantially shifted.

Equity issues that focus on expanding opportunities for historically disadvantaged groups outside traditional class concerns are another set of issues that have appealed to contemporary social democratic parties as an extension of their historical concern for equality. As Erickson and Laycock (2002) note in their analysis of the 1997 members, equity policies are frequently criticized for creating an unfair playing field in the labour market and are potentially divisive for social democratic parties in a shrinking working-class labour market. But in both 1997 and continuing in 2009, party members strongly rejected the general argument that "we worry about equality too much in Canada." In each of 1997 and 2009, members also showed high levels of support for extending "employment equity policies beyond the public sector to enterprises that do business with the public sector" (see Table 7.6.). Still, the membership showed some ambivalence concerning such policies. When asked whether "employment equity programs create reverse discrimination," 42 percent either agreed with or were neutral about this proposition. Notwithstanding a further decade of party support for such policies, this figure is unchanged from the results in 1997.

TABLE 7.6
Members' opinions on equity issues

Equity issue	% agree strongly or agree	% disagree strongly or disagree
We worry about equality too much in Canada		
• 2009 respondents	9	82
• 1997 respondents	11	82
Government should extend employment equity to companies doing business with government		
• 2009 respondents	70	11
• 1997 respondents	73	14
Employment equity creates reverse discrimination		
• 2009 respondents	22	58
• 1997 respondents	27	58

The overall picture of the party membership that emerges from these survey questions is of a group firmly planted on the left of the spectrum. Members' strong commitment to traditional social democratic policies has not notably altered over a decade, and few areas of problematic internal division seem evident. However, party members' views on government ownership have not been reflected in the federal party's electoral agenda, which has tended to avoid focusing on state ownership, and they see their party as more centrist than they see themselves.

Green Politics
In the last decade, green politics posed complications for the NDP. With a strong constituency of post-materialist supporters within the party (Erickson and Laycock 2002), the NDP has included environmental issues in its platform for some time, giving them increasing priority in recent years (see Laycock, Chapter 5, this volume). Yet the party has faced considerable inter-party competition for the support of environmentally oriented voters. The Green Party has gained increased credibility among the public,[10] and, in 2008, the Liberal Party proposed a "Green Shift," including a carbon tax as a central part of its election platform. When the NDP rejected a carbon tax and proposed instead a cap-and-trade alternative in 2008, its position

was queried in many environmental quarters (CTV 2008; Silver 2009). At the provincial level, in BC politics, the NDP's critique in the 2009 provincial election campaign of the provincial Liberals' adoption of a carbon tax provoked a negative reaction in the environmental community (CBC 2009) and was internally controversial.[11]

To get a sense of where the party members were positioned on environmental issues we included three questions about the environment in our 2009 survey. To begin, we asked our respondents to characterize themselves in terms of the green dimension in politics, defined as attaching "great importance to the state of the environment." Using a scale on which "Least Green" was scored 1 and "Most Green" was scored 7, respondents gave themselves a mean ranking of 5.34. When asked to place the federal parties on this same scale, they placed the Green Party slightly closer to themselves than they did their own party. Respondents gave a mean score of 5.73 to the Green Party compared to 4.93 to the NDP. On the other hand, notwithstanding the Liberals' "Green Shift" of 2008, the NDP respondents gave that party a mean score of just 3.4.

On specific environmental policies, the respondents demonstrated considerable support for strong environmental positions. Sixty-six percent agreed that a carbon tax should be implemented, and fully 86 percent said, "We should do much more for environmental protection, even if it means considerably lower personal consumption." These responses suggest a membership that is more "green" than its party. They may signal either a possible source of internal dissent or an opportunity for new leader Thomas Mulcair to place more emphasis on environmental issues at the expense of traditional social democratic redistributionist issues. At the same time, since members do not feel particularly close to the Green Party (see note 7), widespread defection to that party may not be a serious threat to the NDP vote base.

Strategy

The federal NDP faces a number of strategic options as an electoral force. One of these concerns its relations with organized labour, and another involves relations with its provincial wings, while a third concerns its positioning in electoral competition. On the last, the party's ideological placement and its relationship with the Liberal Party are most critical. The 2009 survey included questions that allow us to explore party opinion on all these strategic issues.

Relations with Labour

The relationship of the NDP to unions has long been a contested issue. While the links between the party and organized labour have never been as strong as those between labour and social democratic parties in Australia and many parts of Western Europe, they have often attracted critical comment in the press and sometimes from within the party.[12] And these critiques persist, despite changes in the relationship that have signalled a diminished role for unions in the party.[13] As noted by Erickson and Laycock in Chapter 2, changes to electoral financing legislation beginning in 2004 led to a banning of union contributions to the party and severed the financial relationship between unions and the party (Jansen and Young 2009). As well, more recently the special provision for weighting union votes in the leadership selection process was eliminated with the adoption of a one-member, one-vote leader selection system.

To assess sentiment among the membership about the role of unions in the party, the 2009 questionnaire asked respondents two questions about party links to organized labour. First, they were asked whether labour influence in the party should be increased, be decreased, or stay the same. Then they were asked whether the party should "place more emphasis on its links with trade unionists" or whether it should "place more emphasis on its links with members of social movements." Notwithstanding the apparent decline in labour's influence in the party and the large contingent of respondents who have or have had membership in a union, there is little appetite among them to expand labour's influence. A majority of respondents (54 percent) said that labour's influence in the party should stay the same, while a further 30 percent said it should actually decrease (see Table 7.7). Moreover, when asked to choose whether the party should emphasize its links with labour or its links with social movements, the overwhelming preference was for social movements. More than four-fifths of the respondents said the party should place its emphasis on links with social movements, not labour. These results signal a drop in support for the party's connections with labour unions. In 1997, 28 percent of the survey respondents said the party should emphasize its links with organized labour rather than with members of social movements. In 2009, a mere 13 percent took this position. Even among union members, both current and retired, support for placing more emphasis on social movements versus unions was high, reaching almost 80 percent among current members and even higher (88 percent) among retirees.

Federal-Provincial Party Relations

A second strategic issue facing the federal NDP concerns relations with its provincial counterparts. The NDP is alone among the major parties in Canada in requiring members to join the provincial wing as well as the federal wing of its party.[14] Because of ideological and other differences between federal parties and their provincial wings, and given the differences between the strategic circumstances of federal and provincial politics, other parties have largely severed these formal ties between federal and provincial wings. The requirement that NDP supporters join the federal party through their provincial wings has been a topic of internal discussion, with proposals to eliminate it raised at several conventions. Among

TABLE 7.7
Members' opinions on party strategies

Party strategy	Opinion (%)
Role of unions	
Labour influence on party decision making	
• Increase or greatly increase	16
• Stay the same	54
• Decrease or greatly decrease	30
Links with labour versus social movements	
• Emphasize links with labour	13
• Emphasize links with social movements	87
Federal-provincial linkages	
Should members be required to join provincial organization?	
• Allow direct federal membership	55
• Require provincial-federal membership	45
Positioning the party	
Relations with Liberals	
• Engage in riding-level coalitions	47
• Always nominate own candidates	53
Power-seeking versus policy emphasis	
• Focus on being conscience of Parliament	27
• Strive to become government	74
Moving towards the centre	
• Move closer to the centre	16
• Stay where the party is	84

the 2009 respondents, a more independent federal party was the preferred choice. When asked whether members should be allowed to join the federal party directly or continue to be required to join their provincial organization, a majority (55 percent) chose the first option.

Electoral Strategies

Our survey posed three questions regarding positioning the party vis-à-vis its competitors. First, respondents were asked whether they should "engage in riding-level coalitions with Liberals" to defeat the Conservatives or "always nominate their own candidates and not engage in riding-level coalitions." Second, they were asked whether the party should "embrace [its] role [as the conscience of Parliament] and focus its resources on being an influential voice in Parliament" or "continue to seek more responsibility and strive to become government." Then they were asked whether the federal party would "best serve its members' interests by moving closer to the centre of the ideology spectrum" or by staying "roughly where it is in the ideological spectrum."

With 84 percent saying that the party should stay roughly where it is on the ideological spectrum, party members were overwhelmingly opposed to moving closer to the centre of it, and a majority, albeit a small majority (53 percent), opposed riding-level coalitions with the Liberals. However, they were strongly in favour of the party striving to become government (74 percent) and did not see its role as the "conscience of Parliament" as sufficient. Thus, even before the party achieved its considerable success in 2011, a robust majority of NDP members supported efforts to become government. Notwithstanding the overwhelming majority that opposes movement to the centre, the strong support for power-seeking may mean the party leadership has some flexibility in the electoral strategies that it might pursue without backlash from its membership.

Party Organization

Democracy for the Ranks

Given the emphasis on internal democracy at the historical roots of the NDP, we might expect that members' opinions on party organization would display preferences for member-driven decision making. Indeed, our survey demonstrates robust support for aspects of a strong role for members; however, at the same time, there is evidence of ambivalence on some mechanisms for member input. Party members do not see their role as simply

TABLE 7.8
Members' opinions on party organization

Party organization issue	% agree strongly or agree	% disagree strongly or disagree
The role of party members is to support the decisions made by the leadership	22	56
Only a few party members have the knowledge necessary to make policy	19	63
Party convention should have the final say on important issues	42	38
A member referendum for decision making in the party would be a good thing	47	21
Regular party members like me should play a greater role in developing the national election platform	58	8
I can have a real influence on party decision making when I am actively involved	60	15
The party leadership doesn't pay a lot of attention to ordinary party members	27	38
A problem with the party today is that the leadership is too strong	10	57

Note: Percentages include neutral and "don't know" responses.

supporting the leadership, and they clearly reject the view that "only a few party members have the knowledge to make policy." In response to the statement "The role of party members is to support the decisions made by the leadership," just 22 percent agreed or strongly agreed, while 56 percent disagreed or strongly disagreed. Sixty-three percent rejected the position that only a few party members have the knowledge to make policy, and just 19 percent agreed with it (see Table 7.8). Regarding mechanisms for member input, twice as many respondents support as oppose member referenda (47 percent to 21 percent). Yet, on the question of whether party conventions should have the final say on important issues, the convention is supported by just a small plurality. Forty-two percent agreed that the convention should have the final say, while 38 percent disagreed.

When asked whether "regular party members like me should play a greater role in developing the national election platform," 58 percent agreed or strongly agreed and just 8 percent disagreed. This suggests there may be some unease about the status quo with respect to the development of the party's election platform; some of this could be a consequence of the party's having run four federal election campaigns in less than eight years. This tightly packed sequence allowed far less opportunity for member input into platform emphases than would typically be available in regular four-year cycles. Somewhat inconsistently, however, on another question about influence in party decision making, 60 percent agreed or strongly agreed with the statement "I can have a real influence on party decision making when I am actively involved." Just 15 percent disagreed or strongly disagreed with the statement.

The Role of Leadership

As discussed by Erickson and Laycock in Chapters 2 and 3, during Layton's tenure, a strong leadership focus emerged, especially during election campaigns. We asked two questions to determine whether members were uneasy about strong leadership. The results suggest some ambivalence but not widespread dissatisfaction. When asked whether they agreed with the statement "The party leadership doesn't pay a lot of attention to ordinary party members," 27 percent of the respondents agreed or strongly agreed, while 38 percent disagreed or strongly disagreed. Twenty-three percent said they were neutral on this issue, and 12 percent said they did not know. On the other hand, when presented with the statement "A problem with the party today is that the leadership is too strong," merely 10 percent agreed or strongly agreed, and 57 percent disagreed or strongly disagreed. One-third took a neutral position or said they did not know. Overall, member opinion on party organization tends to reinforce the view that members may accord the leadership a degree of flexibility as it pursues electoral success.

The Activists

Dimensions of Activism

Within any party, activism among members is likely to range considerably, from those who buy their membership but engage in few other activities to those whose party activism is a consuming enterprise. For the NDP and its leadership, it is important how opinion is distributed among and between levels of activism. If the most active members are more radical in their ideology and less pragmatic regarding strategies than the rest of the membership, party leaders may find it more difficult to move towards the political centre in order to capture votes. They may find that, in response to a more centrist party agenda, activist members spark internal criticism, raise contentious issues at conventions, or fail to actively support the party at election time. In this section, we explore some characteristics of NDP activists, beginning with factors shaping lower or higher levels of activism. We then look at whether and how more active members differ from less active ones with regard to their left-right placement, their loyalty to the party, their views on socio-economic issues, and their opinions on party strategy.

The 2009 survey included a battery of questions (twenty-four in all) that assessed members' levels of activity within the party, ranging from donating funds and persuading others to join the NDP to holding various offices within the party organization. Members were asked to indicate whether they had participated in each type of activity within the last five years, more than five years ago, or never. In order to develop a summary scale to measure general activity levels among members, we ran an exploratory factor analysis on all twenty-four questions. Exploratory factor analysis is a statistical technique that reveals underlying relationships within a set of measures. Using these relationships between measures, factor analysis identifies latent variables – that is, underlying constructs that summarize a group of measures – and indicates which variables best measure these constructs. Our analysis identified just one latent variable and found that nine questions best measured it. The types of activities covered in these questions are attendance at a nomination meeting, fundraising for the party, work on provincial or federal election campaigns, voting for national convention delegates, leadership convention attendance, being a delegate for a national policy convention, being a table officer in a constituency association, and being a member of an NDP provincial council. These activities mainly refer to "middle-level" activism. They do not include seeking a political career at the federal or provincial level, but they still cover activities that would be undertaken by a very active member of the party organization.[15]

Because some of the nine questions were found to be more central to the activity factor we had identified, we used the factor scores of the variables to weight the variables when we constructed our scale.[16] The respondents' scores on this activity scale ranged from –1.30 to 2.55 with a mean of 0.[17] Figure 7.1 displays the distribution of activity levels among the survey respondents based on these activity scores. The distribution is decidedly skewed, with the high peak below –1, pointing to the conclusion that a large part of the membership is relatively inactive. Using the distribution of the

FIGURE 7.1

Activity levels of survey respondents based on activity scores

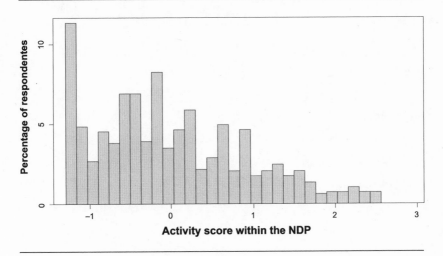

scores as a guideline, we divided the members into three groups: those with the scores of 0 or lower were coded as "Not active" (63.45 percent of all respondents); individuals with scores above 0 but below 1 were coded as "Active" (24 percent); finally, those with the scores of 1 or higher were coded as "Very active" (12.55 percent).

Which Factors Lead to Activism?

In looking at the demographic characteristics of our three groups of members, we found relatively few substantial differences between members who are more or less active in the party. However, in keeping with previous research (Whiteley 2011), we did find that more active members tended to have somewhat higher levels of education: 73 percent of the very active had a university or postgraduate degree compared to 65 percent of the active and 59 percent of the non-active members. We also found that the percentage of males was higher in the most active group (58 percent) compared to the other two (52 and 50 percent), but the difference was small. And a difference in average age for the most active was apparent but similarly small. The average age of the most active members was 59, compared to 62 in both other groups (see Table 7.9). Finally, a small difference in the proportion of visible minorities in the most active group was apparent. Three percent of the most active group indicated they were from a visible minority, whereas

TABLE 7.9
Activists' demographic characteristics

	Very active	Active	Not active
Education (%)			
Some elementary school	0	1	2
Some high school	4	6	7
High school diploma	7	12	11
College/technical diploma	16	17	21
University degree	38	30	28
Postgraduate degree	35	35	31
N	140	269	689
Gender (%)			
Male	58	52	50
Female	42	48	50
N	139	265	689
Average age	58.6	61.7	62.1
(SD)	(14.71)	(13.69)	(14.95)
N	140	265	678
Ethnic composition (%)			
Visible minority	3	8	6
White	97	92	94
N	140	261	680
Average income (000s)	94.83	75.96	76.68
(SD)	(55.31)	(46.83)	(45.90)
N	131	237	615

8 percent and 6 percent of the active and least active groups, respectively, did so. The one area in which there was a substantial difference between the most active group and the other two concerned the average household income they recorded. The most active members had a significantly higher average household income ($95,000) compared to active or non-active members ($76,000 and $77,000, respectively).

In terms of party recruitment, we found that the most active members were, perhaps surprisingly, somewhat less likely to have decided on their own to join the party and more likely to have been asked to join than were less active members (see Table 7.10). Still, a majority of all activist groups were self-motivated to join. Also of interest, active members were the *least* likely to have joined the party to support a candidate in a leadership race or

TABLE 7.10
Activists' incentives for joining the party

	Very active	Active	Not active
Were you asked to join or did you decide on your own to become a party member? (%)*			
• Someone from party suggested I join	39	32	29
• I decided on my own	61	68	71
N	149	279	727
What triggered your decision to join? (%)**			
• Wanted to support a candidate in leadership race	4	19	13
• Wanted to support someone in nomination race	4	10	10
• Other	92	71	77
N	141	258	638

*   Significant to .05.
** Significant to .001.

a nomination race, although again, for all three activist groups, it was *not* the mobilization for leadership or candidate races that triggered their decision to join the party.

Activist Opinion

How did our three groups of activists view themselves and the federal NDP on the left-right scale? Table 7.11 displays the summary statistics for each group. First, there was a clear tendency for more active members to place themselves further to the left than their less activist colleagues. Interestingly, more activist members also placed the federal NDP further to the left. The

TABLE 7.11
Members' placement scores on the left-right scale

Level of activity	Self (SD)	*N*	Federal NDP (SD)	*N*
Very active	2.54 (0.98)	144	3.22 (1.39)	144
Active	2.72 (1.29)	269	3.40 (1.41)	270
Not active	2.96 (1.35)	690	3.58 (1.53)	693
TOTAL	2.84 (1.31)	1,103	3.48 (1.49)	1,107

Note: The scale consists of 9 integer points, ranging from 1 "Left" to 9 "Right."

most active members placed themselves on average at 2.54 on a 10-point scale, with 1 being furthest left. The average self-placement for less active members is 2.72, and the least active members place themselves at 2.96. The most active group placed the federal NDP at 3.22; active members placed the party at 3.4 and the least active placed it at 3.57. As a result, the differences between the means for self and party are virtually the same at each level of activism.

Also of interest is the size of the standard deviations within each group in both questions. Standard deviations measure the variation in scores from the average, or mean, score of a group. A small standard deviation means there is a small range of values in the group. Among our members, the standard deviation decreases with levels of activism. This indicates that, as the levels of activity increased, the opinions tended to become more homogenous – either because less active members had more varying opinions or perhaps because less active members were less aware of the left-right spectrum compared to more active members and so their placements on these scales were made more randomly. Nevertheless, despite these variations in average placements and the spread of their distributions, in general the differences among the three groups of members in terms of their ideological positions and views of the federal NDP were rather small.

But what about differences between levels of activism and the other indicators of opinion on traditional social democratic issues and party strategy discussed above? Are more active members more radical on these kinds of political opinions, as some might predict (May 1973; Kitschelt 1989)? In order to develop scales to examine this question, we ran another exploratory factor analysis, this time using twelve of the questions relevant to state provision, welfare, and equity issues described earlier. The results suggested two broad scales:one concerning equity issues and the other concerning the economy.[18] The equity scale included respondents' reactions (strongly agree, agree, neutral, disagree, or strongly disagree) to the following statements:

• We worry about equality too much.
• Affirmative action is reverse discrimination.
• The government should extend its employment-equity policies beyond the public sector to enterprises that do business with the private sector.

The scale on the economy included respondents' views on access to employment insurance, income equality as opposed to incentives for individual

TABLE 7.12
Members' average scores on equity and economy scales

Level of activity	Equity (SD)	N	Economy (SD)	N
Very active	0.60 (0.51)	127	1.22 (0.70)	140
Active	0.87 (0.59)	233	1.56 (0.80)	256
Not active	0.90 (0.59)	542	1.66 (0.83)	604
TOTAL	0.85 (0.59)	902	1.58 (0.82)	1,000

Note: Equity scale ranges from 0 to 3; economy scale ranges from 0 to 5.

effort,[19] increased government as opposed to private ownership of business and industry, state versus individual responsibility for one's personal welfare, and whether unemployed people should have the right to refuse a job they do not want without losing unemployment benefits. The equity scale ranges from 0 to 3, and the economy scale ranges from 0 to 5, with lower scores on both scales corresponding to more "left-wing" views (i.e., greater support for equity issues and for government provision).

Using these scales, we found more evidence that the most active members were more left-wing in their views, with the average score on the economy among the most active group 1.22 compared to 1.56 for the active members and 1.66 for the least active (see Table 7.12). On the equity scale, the scores are .60, .87, and .90, respectively, for the three groups. Again, the most active members tended to have the most homogeneous opinions (i.e., the standard deviations in their scores were smaller compared to the other two groups). But, as with the members' ratings of themselves and the party on the left-right scale, the differences among the three groups on both these scales were quite small.

On issues of party strategy, somewhat larger differences between the three activist groups emerged on at least some of the questions. The percentage of the most active members who said the NDP should strengthen its connection with unions rather than social movements was almost twice as high (21 percent) compared to the less active or not active members (13 and 11 percent, respectively), although, even among the most active members, support for strengthening union connections rather than social movement connections was distinctly low (see Table 7.13). When the question of the party's union connections was framed only in terms of the party's relationship with organized labour (whether its role should decrease, increase, or stay the same), the differences in responses between the three groups were negligible.

TABLE 7.13

Activists' opinions on party strategy

	Very active	Active	Not active
Links with labour versus social movements (%)			
• Unions	22	13	11
• Social movements	79	87	89
N	137	255	639
Chi-square = 10.16 (p < .01)			
Strategic cooperation with the Liberals on federal level (%)			
• Cooperate	28	38	55
• Not cooperate	72	62	45
N	136	248	630
Chi-square = 44.68 (p < .001)			
Power-seeking vs. policy-seeking emphasis (%)			
• Policy-seeking	15	26	29
• Power-seeking	85	74	71
N	137	254	640
Chi-square = 10.69 (p < .01)			
Moving towards the centre (%)			
• Move closer to centre	11	18	17
• Keep current position	89	82	83
N	135	251	625
Chi-square = 3.14 (p = 0.21)			
Independent vs. joint required membership (%)			
• Join federal NDP directly	30	54	61
• Joint membership required	70	46	39
N	139	255	636
Chi-square = 42.42 (p < .001)			

The question of strategic cooperation with the Liberals elicited the biggest difference between activist groups.[20] On the one hand, the most active members firmly rejected the proposal that the party should form coalitions at the riding level with Liberals (72 percent said no), while a small majority of the least active group (55 percent) said the party should form coalitions. Active members also rejected cooperation with Liberals but in smaller proportions (62 percent). At the same time, when asked whether the federal NDP should seek more responsibility and strive to become government or embrace its role as the "conscience of Parliament," the vast majority of members in all three groups chose the power-seeking strategy, but this time the most active members were more likely to agree that the party should seek power (85 percent) compared to the active or least active members (71 and 74 percent, respectively). There was also considerable unanimity with regard to rejecting the proposal that the party should adopt a more centrist ideology, with virtually no differences among the three groups on this point: more than 80 percent of respondents in each category agreed that the party should stay roughly where it was on the ideological spectrum.

The combination of these results is interesting. Specifically, the most active members had more consistent opinions: they largely rejected co-operation with the Liberals, and they overwhelmingly agreed that the NDP should stay at its current position on the left-right spectrum. The majority of the least active members, however, said the NDP should cooperate with Liberals, but they did not want the party to move towards the centre. At the same time, a large majority of members in all three groups both rejected moving the party's ideology towards the centre and strongly supported party efforts to become government. Regardless of the extent of their activism, most members apparently want the NDP to seek power without sacrificing its core principles for the sake of getting the seats in Parliament.

The largest differences among the three groups emerged when we looked at the question related to party membership rules. In particular, the most active members were the most opposed to changing the current rule that individuals can join the federal NDP only through their provincial party. More than two-thirds of the most active members said the party should keep the rule of joint membership. The majority of respondents in the other two groups were more willing to relax this rule and allow people to join the federal NDP directly (54 percent in the active group and 61 percent in the least active group). These differences may be explained by the fact that our "activity" variable captures members' levels of activity at the provincial level as well as at the local and federal levels.

On questions about party organization, we found a pattern similar to the one we identified on strategy – that is, there were differences between the most active and less active, but the differences were typically not large (see Tables 7.14 and 7.15). Moreover, many of the differences between three groups of activists are most evident in the extent to which less active members chose a neutral position or said they don't know. Still, some features of activist opinion on party organization stand out. First, with respect to most aspects of party democracy, support tends to *increase* with levels of activism (Table 7.14), except support for member referenda, which *declines* with

TABLE 7.14
Activists' opinions on party democracy

	Very active	Active	Not active
*Role of party members to support decisions of leadership (%)**			
• Agree strongly or agree	19	21	26
• Disagree strongly or disagree	67	61	52
N	144	270	694
*Only few members have knowledge to make policy (%)***			
• Agree strongly or agree	13	20	20
• Disagree strongly or disagree	74	66	60
N	144	275	680
*Party convention should have final say on important issues (%)***			
• Agree strongly or agree	47	44	40
• Disagree strongly or disagree	40	· 40	37
N	146	270	694
*A member referendum a good thing (%)***			
• Agree strongly or agree	35	45	50
• Disagree strongly or disagree	36	24	16
N	146	274	692
*Regular party members should play greater role developing platform (%)***			
• Agree strongly or agree	60	61	57
• Disagree strongly or disagree	14	11	6
N	145	275	679

*   Significant to .01.
** Significant to .001.

levels of activism. Second, in terms of their views about current party structure, the most active members show especially high levels of efficacy in terms of party decision making (Table 7.15). When combined with the demographic finding that the most active members had higher levels of education and income, this result – that the most active members had the strongest sense of political efficacy – is consistent with the civic voluntarism model of activism developed by Verba, Schlozman, and Brady (1995). This model links personal resources and perceived efficacy to levels of political activism and civic engagement.

TABLE 7.15
Activists' opinions on party organization

	Very active	Active	Not active
*Can influence decision making when involved (%)***			
• Agree strongly or agree	74	62	55
• Disagree strongly or disagree	10	20	14
N	145	275	690
*Party leadership does not pay attention to members (%)***			
• Agree strongly or agree	32	31	25
• Disagree strongly or disagree	42	43	35
N	145	273	692
*Party leadership too strong (%)***			
• Agree strongly or agree	11	14	8
• Disagree strongly or disagree	66	60	54
N	145	275	681

* Significant to .01.
** Significant to .001.

Overall then, we have found some differences of opinion between members with substantially different levels of party activism. Activists are somewhat left of other party members: they tend to characterize both themselves and their party as further left on the ideological spectrum, and their scores on economic and equity issues are similarly further to the left. But these groups do not inhabit different ideological countries: the differences among them tend to be small. Similarly, although more active members are clearly more opposed to the idea of strategic cooperation with the Liberals, there are virtually no differences among activist groups regarding opinions on power-seeking. The vast majority of respondents, regardless of their levels of activism, want the NDP to seek power and not just be "the conscience of Parliament." Moreover, regardless of their level of activism, a majority of the respondents do not want the NDP to move closer to the centre of the left-right spectrum, thereby sacrificing its social democratic agenda.

Conclusion

The NDP members we surveyed had long-time ties to the party and were comparatively affluent, well-educated individuals, and a majority were or had been union members. They demonstrated remarkable loyalty at the ballot box, even in the face of strategic pressures to vote Liberal in order to defeat a party (the Conservatives) they strongly disliked. The attraction of the NDP for its members is strongly rooted in the party's ideas and platform. Although close to a majority saw themselves as further left than the party on the ideological spectrum, and recently the party itself has placed somewhat less emphasis on certain aspects of social democratic policies (including public ownership) than the members support (see Laycock and Pétry, Chapters 5 and 6), nonetheless the members continue to affirm the appeal of the party's ideas and platform. The NDP's core ideological commitments, which Laycock discusses in Chapter 5, still appear to be successful in holding its membership base.

Notwithstanding changes in party organization and structure over the last decade, and the party's increasing popularity among the electorate (see Erickson and Laycock, Chapters 2 and 4, and Weldon, Chapter 12, this volume), the nature of opinion within the NDP appears to have changed little over that time. The differences in policy preferences and priorities between members in 1997 and members in 2009 were typically very small. One issue on which there was some movement in opinion among the membership concerns the party's relations with organized labour. In 1997, a strong majority said they would rather emphasize the party's links to social movements than its links to labour. By 2009, support for the labour option had dropped even more, leaving few to champion strong labour connections. The direction of opinion in this regard appears to reflect the movement of the party away from some of its labour roots.

Opinion differences between activists and non-activists were, in most respects, also small. Only on the question of requiring members to join the federal party through their provincial wings, and on the issue of strategic cooperation with the Liberals in nominations at the local level, were important differences between activists and non-activists revealed. While a push towards strategic cooperation by the leadership would create internal controversy, in other respects our survey findings suggest that the leadership has considerable room to manoeuvre on policy and strategy as it seeks electoral success. Both activists and the general membership strongly support the party's efforts to form the first federal NDP government, and few among them believe that the leadership has hijacked power in the party in search of electoral success. Indeed activists, who tend to be more on the left of the party, are the most likely to deny that the party leadership is too strong. Even though the charismatic Jack Layton was replaced by Thomas

Mulcair, there is little in our survey data to suggest that party activists are on the verge of precipitating the kind of division seen in the late 1960s, with the Waffle movement, or in the early 2000s, with the New Politics Initiative. The only possible move by the party leadership that might trigger this kind of internal division would be one to merge with the Liberal Party. And the odds of this happening soon now seem very low, for reasons explored in Chapter 11 by Godbout, Bélanger, and Mérand.

APPENDIX
The Surveys and Scales

The Canadian Social Democracy Survey, 1997
In 1997, 3,879 surveys were mailed to NDP members and activists from British Columbia, Saskatchewan, Manitoba, and Ontario. A total of 1,440 questionnaires were returned, giving a response rate of 37 percent. The sample distribution in regional terms included 35 percent from British Columbia, 15 percent from Saskatchewan, 15 percent from Manitoba, and 36 percent from Ontario. For more details of the survey, see Erickson and Laycock (2002).

The NDP Member Survey, 2009
In November 2009, a questionnaire was sent to 5,000 party members randomly selected at party headquarters from the total party membership. The questionnaire was accompanied by a letter of support from the party's national director. With 1,171 of the questionnaires completed and returned, the return rate for the questionnaire was 23.4 percent.

The largest proportion of the returns came from Ontario (31 percent), followed by BC (29 percent), Saskatchewan (16 percent), and Manitoba (7 percent). The figures from the party's membership list indicated the distribution of members was 31, 24, 18 and 7 percent respectively for these four provinces. The returns from Quebec were very few (a mere 6 responses). There were no responses from Newfoundland, although 6 percent of the responses overall came from Atlantic Canada. The party membership figures at the time of the survey indicated that 2 percent of their federal members came from Quebec, while 7 percent came from Atlantic Canada.

Notes
1 For a discussion of the literature on the effects of local campaigns in elections, see Cross and Young (2011).
2 This suggestion of some influence from party members is at odds with the cartelization hypothesis in comparative politics (Katz and Mair 1995), which argues that contemporary party leaders have become fully divorced from party members. The

cartelization model is, however, contested both theoretically (Kitschelt 2000; Koole 1996) and empirically (Loxbo 2013).

3 The Conservative Party was in a minority position in government, but because there had been three elections in the previous five and a half years, there was little public appetite or opposition party support to go to the polls soon.

4 In their study, Cross and Young (2004) found the gender composition of the NDP membership to be similar to the distribution we found. They also found the gender distribution among Liberals to be relatively similar to that found in the population. By contrast, male members composed 67, 68, and 64 percent, respectively, of their Conservative, Alliance, and BQ respondents.

5 Our findings are at odds with Young and Cross's findings on the NDP. They found that only 51 percent of NDP members were self-motivated.

6 By comparison, the average scores they gave the Liberal and Green parties were 34 and 37, respectively. For the NDP, their average score was 78.

7 Relatively few – 21 percent – placed the party to their left on the scale.

8 In order to see if the regional differences in the two samples made a difference in the results, the 2009 results were calculated with respondents from the same provinces in which the 1997 survey was conducted. The results were virtually the same.

9 Hou, Nelson, and Stephens (2008) found, in their comparative study of the relationship between the partisan nature of governments and decommodification and labour activation policies, that social democratic polities tend to have higher overall levels of decommodification policies, including sick-pay and pension provisions, but not higher levels of unemployment insurance.

10 In the 2008 election, the leader of the Green Party, Elizabeth May, participated in the national leaders' debates and the party won an unprecedented 6.8 percent of the popular vote.

11 In the leadership race the provincial NDP held in 2011, a number of front-running candidates recanted on their opposition to the tax.

12 See, for example, *Vancouver Sun* (2011) and LeBlanc (2011a). The Conservative Party has attempted to use the NDP-organized labour connection as a critique of the NDP. Speaking of the leadership selection process, the Conservative Party argued: "All we do know is that the process allows affiliate members like union bosses to have a direct say in the process [of leadership selection] while ordinary Canadians are locked out ... The influence of big unions and special interests in the NDP is yet another worrying example of their big government union agenda" (LeBlanc 2011b).

13 Jansen and Young (2009) stress that, while the relationship between the NDP and organized labour has been restructured, it continues to involve cooperation between the two political players.

14 The exceptions to this are found in Quebec and the North. In Quebec, the ties between the federal and provincial party were severed in 1989, and the federal party established the Nouveau Parti démocratique-Section Québec/New Democratic Party Quebec Section. In Nunavut and the Northwest Territories, where non-partisan politics is practised at the territorial level, members simply join the federal party.

15 We re-ran the factor analysis on just these nine variables. The results indicated that the first principal component explained 90 percent of the variance in the answers

to these questions. This confirmed that these variables effectively summarized the major aspects of party activism.

Our original factor analysis also revealed a second principal component for another five questions from the series, which included seeking the party's nomination in a provincial election; being a provincial candidate; being a federal candidate; being a provincial MLA, MPP, or MNA; and being a member of an NDP federal council. The answers to these questions appear to indicate whether a person has sought out leadership positions on various levels of party organization. When we ran factor analysis on only these questions, the first principal component explained 48 percent of the variance in the answers. On this dimension, the vast majority of the respondents scored 0 or below, indicating that a relatively small number of people (9 percent) had undertaken these kinds of leadership roles within the NDP.

16 Factor scores indicate the relative relationship of each question to the activity factor. Rotated factor scores were used.

17 The coding of the variables was as follows: 1 = "in the last five years," 2 = "more than five years ago," and 3 = "never." As a result, lower original activity scores indicated higher levels of activity and vice versa. In order to make the interpretation of the scores more intuitive, we have reversed the signs of the scores (essentially creating a variable with an opposite sign to that of the original scores). This has not changed the nature of the activity scores but has made their interpretation less confusing. We conducted the same transformation for the scores on the second type of activity.

18 These results are based on the rotated component matrix.

19 This question had a similar factor loading on the equity factor and the economy factor. Because it seemed substantively closer to the questions on the economy, we included it in our economy scale.

20 We did not ask members about the option of an NDP-Liberal party merger. See Chapter 10 regarding the strategic calculations involved in such an option.

References

Block, Fred, 2011. Reinventing Social Democracy for the 21st Century. *Journal of Australian Political Economy* 67: 5-21.

CBC. 2009. Environmental Groups Disagree with BC NDP's Stand on Carbon Tax. *CBC News*, 13 April.

Cronin, James, George Ross, and James Schoch. 2011. *What's Left of the Left: Democrats and Social Democrats in Challenging Times*. Durham, NC: Duke University Press.

Cross, William, and Lisa Young. 2004. The Contours of Political Party Membership in Canada. *Party Politics* 10, 4: 427-44.

–. 2011. Explaining Local Campaign Intensity: The Canadian General Election of 2008. *Canadian Journal of Political Science* 44, 3: 553-71.

CTV. 2008. Suzuki Slams NDP, Tories, Backs Dion's Carbon Tax, 18 May.

Erickson, Lynda, and David Laycock. 2002. Postmaterialism versus the Welfare State? Opinion among English Canadian Social Democrats. *Party Politics* 8, 3: 301-25.

Esping-Andersen, Gøsta. 1990. *The Three Worlds of Welfare Capitalism*. Princeton: Princeton University Press.

Huo, Jingjing, Moira Nelson, and John D. Stephens. 2008. Decommodification and Activation in Social Democratic Policy: Resolving the Paradox. *European Journal of Social Policy* 18, 1: 5-20.

Jansen, Harold, and Lisa Young. Solidarity Forever? The NDP, Organized Labour, and the Changing Face of Party Finance in Canada. *Canadian Journal of Political Science* 42, 3: 657-78.

Katz, Richard S., and Peter Mair. 1995. Changing Models of Party Organization and Party Democracy: The Emergence of the Cartel Party. *Party Politics* 1, 1: 5-28.

Kitschelt, Herbert. 1989. The Internal Politics of Parties: The Law Curvilinear Disparity Revisited. *Political Studies* 37: 400-21.

–. 2000. Citizens, Politicians, and Party Cartellization: Political Representation and State Failure in Post-Industrial Democracies. *European Journal of Political Research* 37, 2: 149-79.

Koole, Ruud. 1996. Cadre, Catch-All or Cartel? A Comment on the Notion of the Cartel Party. *Party Politics* 2, 4: 507-23.

LeBlanc, Daniel. 2011a. Mulcair Draws Line in NDP Sand, Describes Telling Union Boss "No." *Globe and Mail*, 26 October.

–. 2011b. Federal NDP Rejects Special Role for Unions in Selecting Leader. *Globe and Mail*, 8 September.

Loxbo, Karl. 2013. The Fate of Intra-Party Democracy: Leadership Autonomy and Activist Influence in the Mass Party and the Cartel Party. *Party Politics* 19, 4: 537-54.

May, John. 1973. Opinion Structure of Political Parties: The Special Law of Curvilinear Disparity. *Political Studies* 21: 135-51.

Silver, Robert. 2009. The NDP's Evolving Climate-Change Policy. *Globe and Mail*, 12 August. http://www.theglobeandmail.com/news/politics/second-reading/evolving-ndp-climate-policy/article1345017.

Statistics Canada. 2009. 2006 Census: Educational Portrait of Canada. http://www12.statcan.ca/census-recensement/2006/as-sa/97-560/table/t2-eng.cfm.

Thompson, David. 2008. Strategic Voting 2.0: How the Web Has Changed Our Ability to Target, and Swap, Votes. *The Tyee*, 9 October. http://thetyee.ca/Media check/2008/10/09/StratVote/.

Toronto Star. 2008. 7,000 Ready to Swap Votes, 14 October. http://www.thestar.com/news/politics/federalelection/2008/10/14/7000_ready_to_swap_votes.html.

Vancouver Sun. 2011. Affiliated Unions Have Too Much Clout with NDP. *Vancouver Sun*, 11 September. http://www2.canada.com/vancoversun/news/editorial/story.html?id=d8fcd5b0-5367-4e83-b694-9ce5a0e102e2.

Verba, Sydney, Kay Lehman Schlozman, and Henry E. Brady. 1995. *Voice and Equality: Civic Volunteerism in American Politics*. Cambridge, MA: Harvard University Press.

Whiteley, Paul. 2011. Is the Party Over? The Decline of Party Activism and Membership across the Democratic World. *Party Politics* 17, 1: 21-44.

Young, Lisa, and William Cross. 2002. Incentives to Membership in Canadian Political Parties. *Political Research Quarterly* 55, 3: 547-69. doi: 10.1177/106591290205500303.

8

Party Leaders in the NDP

AMANDA BITTNER

Thomas Mulcair took over the leadership of the NDP in March 2012, after months of campaigning, debates, and supposition about who might best fill the void left by Jack Layton. Known for his combative, scrappy tendencies, credited in large part for the party's success in Quebec in the 2011 election, and expected to "move the NDP towards the centre" (*Globe and Mail* 2012), the new leader won amidst much talk of the importance of political presence for a prospective leader. Of course, Mulcair's political presence is important only if perceptions of his personality traits actually matter to the general public.

Previous research indicates that voter perception of the personality traits of party leaders plays a key role not only in determining individual vote choice but also in influencing the outcomes of elections (Bittner 2011). However, for years, scholars' understanding of the NDP has been fundamentally different from their understanding of the other major national parties. The Liberal and Conservative parties in particular have been described as brokerage parties focused on appealing to a broad base of voters (e.g., Carty and Cross 2010), while we tend to think of the NDP as a programmatic party, focused more on ideological concerns and party platforms. This distinction might suggest that, for the NDP, leaders are not as important with regard to attracting the support of voters as are the leaders of the other major (non-policy driven) parties. And it might even suggest that the party itself has not focused on leadership, preferring to channel its attention towards developing policies and staying true to its ideological base.

That NDP leaders may not be as important to their supporters (or voters in general) as are leaders of other parties might seem to be counterintuitive, especially given the role that Jack Layton is said to have played over the last few years. Indeed, some suggest that it is to Jack Layton that we can attribute recent NDP successes, especially the previously unheard-of support for the party that was achieved in the 2011 federal election (Coletto 2012). Was Layton's winning personality unusual in comparison to those of past NDP leaders or in comparison to those of leaders of other national parties? Were perceptions of his personality a major factor that influenced voters to decide to cast ballots in favour of the NDP in 2011? And was his impact different from the impact of leaders in the past?

This chapter assesses voter perceptions of NDP leaders over time, using data from the Canadian Election Study (CES) from 1984 to 2011. By examining the role of leaders over time, we should be able to gain a better understanding of the relationship voters have had with NDP leaders over the past thirty years. Furthermore, we should be able to shed important light on the party's success in the 2011 election and also gain a sense of what the future may hold.

The Importance of Party Leaders

While scholars have debated the importance of leaders' personalities in Canadian elections for some time (see, for example, Blais et al. 2002; Brown et al. 1988; Clarke et al. 1991; Gidengil, Everitt, and Banducci 2006; Johnston et al. 1993; Johnston 2002), there has been very little consensus about exactly how important leaders are in the minds of voters, especially in comparison to other considerations (such as the economy, party platforms, and other issue-related concerns). Recent longitudinal and comparative analysis (e.g., Bittner 2010, 2011) consolidates and extends some of this past work and suggests that leaders might be more important than we have previously believed, be it in Canada or cross-nationally. Other chapters in this volume note the increased focus on leadership within the NDP, but it is also the case that leaders have mattered to voters for quite a while and that the academic literature has only started to understand the role of leaders in the minds of voters.

In fact, this most recent research suggests that party leaders matter more than just about everything else, with the exception of partisanship, in the minds of voters (Bittner 2011) and that the importance of leaders applies across both parties and national political contexts. There are plenty of reasons that we ought to expect leaders to matter. First, as Blais et al. (2002, 165) note in the Canadian context, "an election is not just about choosing which party will form the government, it is also about who is going to be Prime Minister"; therefore, who the leader will be *ought* to be important as he or she will be holding the top job in the country. Second, media coverage of election campaigns tends to focus a great deal on the party leaders and the horse race, which may lead voters to weigh the leaders more heavily when they enter the ballot box on election day (e.g., Mendelsohn 1993; Gidengil et al. 2000). Third, it may be that deciding how we feel about leaders is relatively "easy" in comparison with deciding how we feel about complex policy issues. Rahn et al. (1990) suggest that sorting out how we feel about candidates and leaders should be possible even for those who have very little information on or interest in politics since the judgment process is similar to activities we perform regularly: we are constantly deciding how we feel about those we encounter, and, in many ways, assessing party leaders should be no different.

In this regard, it is important to consider potential differences across parties because this can give us a better sense of the conditions under which leaders influence voters. For the NDP, which has traditionally been thought to be a party that does not focus heavily on promoting its leader, looking at the role of leaders is particularly relevant because it points to potential linkages between party activities and voter perception. If leaders matter in the electoral game, and the NDP does not play according to those rules, then the party is going to have a difficult time winning seats. If the rules are different for different types of parties, however, then perhaps a greater focus on policy and platform makes sense from an organizational standpoint.

Should We Expect Leadership to Matter in the NDP?
In his assessment of Canadian federal electoral politics in the early 1960s, Desmond Morton (1986, 34) notes: "For voters then and for the next four years, the dominant issue seemed to be the contrasting personalities of John Diefenbaker and his Liberal opponent, Lester Pearson." This supports (at least anecdotally) the notion that leaders have played an important role in elections for quite some time. However, he also notes that the NDP's ability to participate in the personality contest at the time was limited: "The NDP might willingly match the cocky, aggressive personality of its leader against his two rivals but image contests are extravagantly expensive ... [and] the leader's tour had to be done on the cheap" (35).

The costs of a leader-focused campaign, especially advertising, travel for leader tours, and national messaging strategies may have been an impediment for the NDP over the years, but it is also possible that the party has simply been more interested in focusing on platforms and issues. Issues linked to medicare (especially in the early days of the party), social justice more broadly, job creation and resource development, gender equality, social programs, homelessness, and the environment have all been raised by the NDP during elections over the last fifty years. While the other major parties have also discussed issues and policies in their platforms over time, there is a sense, especially among academics, that the role of policies and platforms is simply different in an "ideologically flexible" brokerage party than it is in programmatic parties (Cross 2004, 7). Young and Cross (2002, 552) sum up the traditional view of Canadian political parties:

> For the most part, the dominant image of Canadian political parties has been the brokerage model, which observes that Canadian parties lack strong ideological foundations, shift policy positions routinely, and are preoccupied with stitching together coalitions across significant political cleavages. Within brokerage parties, there are few opportunities for policy innovation or debate, with the result that the parties have little to offer potential members in the way of purposive incentives.

The NDP, however, has not traditionally been seen as a brokerage party. As Erickson and Zakharova show in Chapter 7 of this volume, for NDP members, the party's core ideas and platform are very important to their continuing support. Moreover, a commitment to left-leaning ideology and social democratic values has been important to members in the party for quite some time. This is evidenced by the party's periodic reassessment and self-analysis and by the associated tension between "principle and pragmatism, between a party of principle which many social democrats think of as the NDP and a pragmatic party which is the big, one-stop-shop party in Canada" (Berlin and Aster 2001). There is some sense that a "big-tent" party (or one-stop-shop party) is more likely to rally around a particular leader, focusing more on selling the image of the leader and the party than on selling a particular set of policy choices. Therefore, it makes sense that the NDP, known for its strong ideological foundations and close ties to labour, would be less focused on leaders and that, as a result, leaders might matter less in the minds of their voters.

There is some debate, however, about whether or not the label "ideological party" can really be applied to the NDP (e.g., Brodie and Jenson 1991). The importance of ideology was raised on a number of occasions during the most recent NDP leadership race as candidates battled over where the party should be situated on the left-right spectrum. These battles included discussions over potential mergers with the Liberal Party (e.g., Coyne 2012; Salutin 2012).

While the potential move to the centre has been a rhetorical issue for the NDP, it is not at all clear that this is something that will simply "start" now that Thomas Mulcair is sitting in the big chair. A number of authors have argued that a move to the right by the NDP has been taking place for years (Bittner and Koop 2013; Carroll and Ratner 2005). Laycock, in Chapter 5 of this volume, and Pétry, in Chapter 6, suggest some such movement, although they contend that fundamental changes to party ideology have not occurred. If, in recent years, the NDP has been making efforts to move to the centre and to appeal to a wider base, then perhaps the role of the leader has also become more important during this time.

Data and Analysis

In order to assess perceptions of NDP leaders in Canada and the importance of those perceptions to vote choice, I draw upon data from the CES from 1984 to 2011 (Lambert et al. 1984; Johnston et al. 1988; Johnston et al. 1993; Blais et al. 1997; Blais et al. 2000; Blais et al. 2006; Gidengil et al. 2008; Fournier et al. 2011). Included in the analysis are questions about leader personality traits, leader thermometers, vote choice, and a number of control variables – ideological left-right self-placement, issue attitudes, socio-demographic variables, and partisanship.

I begin by assessing overall voter feeling towards the leaders of all three major parties as well as voter perception of their personality traits, focusing on their character and competence.[1] I then focus on perceptions of NDP leaders specifically, comparing the perceptions of NDP partisans to those of non-NDP partisans (including both partisans of other parties and non-partisans in general), and I follow this by assessing perceptions of NDP leaders according to voter level of political sophistication, comparing those who are "most knowledgeable" about politics to those who are "least knowledgeable." I then go on to provide multivariate analyses of the impact of perceptions of leaders on vote choice, assessing the role of leaders in comparison to other factors, such as ideological beliefs and issue attitudes. By

FIGURE 8.1

Feelings towards leaders over time (compared to mean rating of all leaders)

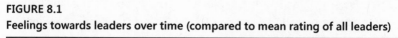

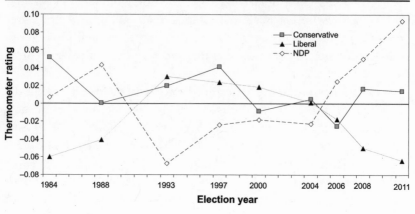

examining voter perception of leaders longitudinally, we should be better able to understand the importance of NDP leaders in Canadian elections – for voters in general and for NDP supporters in particular.

Perceptions of Party Leaders

Between 1984 and 2011, feelings about the leaders of the three major parties fluctuate substantially. This is not surprising, given that, in that twenty-five-year period, twenty party leaders were at the helm of six competitive national parties (Liberal, Conservative, NDP, Bloc, Reform/Alliance, and Green). This total includes four NDP leaders, five Liberal Party leaders, and six Conservative Party leaders.[2] Where someone stands on the leader thermometer is one of the most frequently asked questions in election studies around the world, and it has formed the basis of numerous studies that examine the impact of leaders in elections (e.g., Aarts, Blais, and Schmitt 2010; Clarke, Ho, and Stewart 2000; Gidengil et al. 2000; Jones and Hudson 1996). Figure 8.1 tracks mean thermometer ratings of the leaders of the three major national parties in Canada, comparing those means to the average rating of leaders across all national parties in a given election year (marked at 0 on the *y* axis).[3] Thermometer ratings (originally ranging from 0 to 100) are scaled to a 0-1 format, where 1 reflects most positive ratings and 0 reflects most negative ratings.

As Figure 8.1 makes clear, Ed Broadbent had very favourable evaluations in the 1980s, especially compared to John Turner, but following his departure and until 2006, the NDP leader was consistently rated lower than the leaders of the other major national parties. In 2006, Layton's popularity rose substantially, surpassing Broadbent's 1984 popularity levels, and he consistently scored higher than the leaders of the other parties. In 2008 and 2011, Layton's popularity ratings surpassed those of his competitors by more than any lead any other leader had obtained over the past two and a half decades.

When we look in more detail at evaluations of specific personality traits, we again see that the patterns of perceptions are varied over the years as leaders change, but once more Layton was perceived very positively, especially as voters became familiar with him over time.

Figures 8.2 and 8.3 track voter mean perception of leader competence and character across the three major parties, comparing them to the average across all major party leaders competing in a given election. As Figure 8.2 makes clear, until 2006, the NDP leader was generally perceived to be less competent in comparison to his or her competitors. This pattern is consistent with patterns established cross-nationally and over time, in which leaders of left-leaning parties are perceived less positively on the competence dimension than are leaders of conservative parties (Bittner 2011).

FIGURE 8.2
Ratings of leaders' competence over time (compared to mean rating of all leaders)

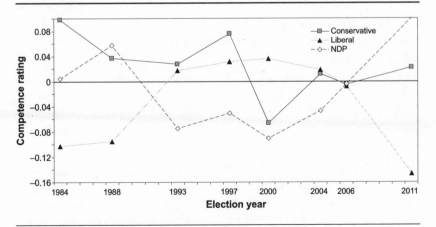

FIGURE 8.3
Ratings of leaders' character over time (compared to mean rating
of all leaders)

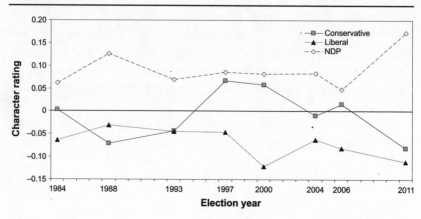

However, it is important to note not only that Broadbent achieved higher competence ratings than the other two leaders in 1988 but also that, after 2004, Layton did as well. He tied Martin and Harper in 2006 and surpassed Ignatieff and Harper by quite a large margin in 2011.[4]

When it comes to evaluations of leader character, NDP leaders have generally done quite well across the board. This is also consistent with past research, which indicates that leaders of left-leaning parties are generally perceived more positively on the character dimension than other party leaders (Bittner 2011). This same research also found that evaluations of leader character are more weighty when it comes to the decision to vote for a party than are evaluations of leader competence: when they enter the ballot box, voters care more about honesty and trustworthiness than they do about intelligence and strength of leadership. Again, it is worth noting that not only were Broadbent and Layton perceived more positively than were the leaders in between them (McLaughlin and McDonough) but also that Layton's ratings in 2011 were substantially higher than the ratings of Ignatieff and Harper. Quite simply, on each of the measures assessing perceptions of party leaders, Layton consistently outshone his competitors, especially in the 2011 election. This suggests that, if leaders do have an impact on vote choice, Layton's popularity ought to have served his party well in the most recent election (or, at a minimum, it would not have detracted from the decision to vote for the NDP).

FIGURE 8.4

Ratings of NDP leaders by partisanship (compared to mean rating of all leaders)

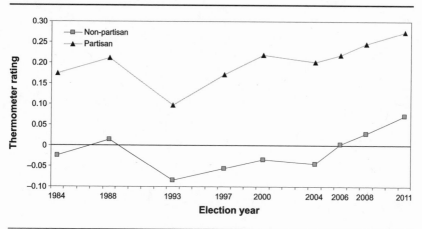

When we examine feelings about NDP leaders over time, comparing NDP partisans to all others,[5] it is fairly clear that partisans generally feel quite a bit more positively about their leaders than do other Canadians. Figure 8.4 tracks thermometer ratings of NDP leaders from 1984 to 2011. The upper line tracks feelings among NDP partisans, while the lower line tracks feelings among all others – including both partisans of other parties and non-partisans. While partisans generally view their leader more positively than do others, the fact remains that the lines have similar peaks and valleys, indicating that both partisans and non-partisans are able to differentiate across leaders over time and that there are similar patterns in the impressions gleaned by all Canadians. Furthermore, note that Broadbent (in 1988) and, especially, Layton (after 2004) were perceived quite positively by non-NDP partisans, achieving thermometer ratings higher than the average for all national party leaders (as indicated by the 0 line on the *y*-axis).

When it comes to ratings of the character and competence of NDP leaders among partisans and all others, the patterns again are similar, although not quite as evenly matched as those seen for thermometer ratings (see Figure 8.5). Put simply, partisans perceive NDP leader personality traits in a more positive light than do other Canadians.

All respondents perceive NDP leader character (dashed lines) more positively than they perceive NDP leader competence (solid lines). While NDP

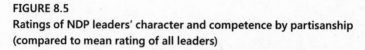

FIGURE 8.5
Ratings of NDP leaders' character and competence by partisanship
(compared to mean rating of all leaders)

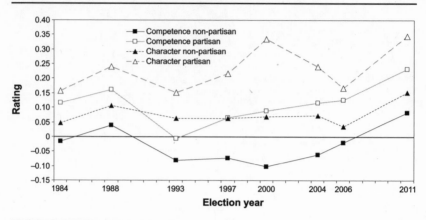

partisans view their leaders' traits more positively across the board, and while all voters generally perceive NDP leader character more positively than they perceive NDP leader competence, on average, NDP partisans also generally view their leaders' competence more highly than non-partisans perceive NDP leader character traits.

Also important to note is where ratings of NDP leaders stand in comparison to those of the other national party leaders. The 0 on the *y*-axis marks the average across all party leaders, and, as is fairly clear, NDP partisans (lines marked with a triangle) view their leaders more positively than what is the average for all leaders. Even NDP partisans' ratings of Audrey McLaughlin's competence in 1993 sit at the average for all leaders, indicating that partisans are fairly positive about their leaders in general. However, also notable is that non-partisans viewed the character of all NDP leaders in this twenty-five-year time period in a positive (above average) light as ratings never dipped below the 0 line. Furthermore, competence evaluations of both Broadbent (1988) and Layton (2011) among non-NDP partisans were above the 0 line as well, indicating that those two leaders were perceived more positively by voters who would naturally lean towards supporting one of the other major parties. Both Broadbent and Layton stand out as having been popular and well-respected not only by NDPers but also by Canadians in general.

FIGURE 8.6
Ratings of NDP leaders by level of political knowledge (compared
to mean rating of all leaders)

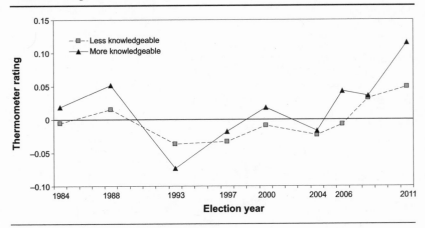

Comparing the perceptions of partisans with those of non-partisans is
an important step, but another crucial question concerns whether leader
evaluations are "informed" and "reasoned" or whether Canadians assess
leader personality traits in a vacuum, using them as a shortcut at the ballot
box because they lack more "important" or "relevant" types of information.
In order to better understand patterns in how Canadians perceive their
leaders, I divided all respondents into groups according to their levels of
political knowledge, as measured in the CES over time through answers
to factual questions. Respondents were coded into terciles according to
how many correct answers they gave, and I compared the attitudes of the
one-third who are most knowledgeable with the one-third who are least
knowledgeable. As the data demonstrate, the patterns noted above continue even across knowledge levels. As seen in Figure 8.6, among the less
knowledgeable, ratings of NDP leaders are generally less positive, hovering
closer to the average than among the more knowledgeable. Among the
most knowledgeable, Broadbent consistently rated higher than the average for all leaders, as did Layton. Even McDonough rated higher than average among the more knowledgeable in the 2000 election.

Ratings of NDP leader character and competence have also hovered closer
to the average for all leaders among the less knowledgeable, as is shown in
Figure 8.7. The more knowledgeable respondents provided substantially

FIGURE 8.7
Ratings of NDP leaders' traits by level of knowledge (compared to mean rating of all leaders)

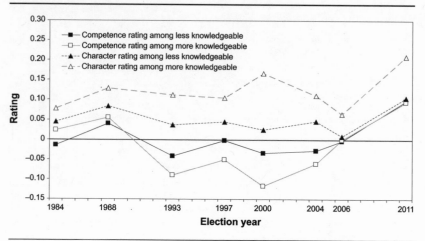

higher character ratings and generally lower competence ratings as well, especially for the years between Broadbent and Layton. These data suggest that it is not simply partisans who perceived Broadbent and Layton positively, or simply those who were ignorant about politics, but, rather, that all voters were partial to those two leaders, rating them higher than the average across all national party leaders. That the most knowledgeable were even more likely to do so provides further support to the notion that there was something special about these two most popular NDP leaders. The question is whether leader popularity had an impact on the decision to vote for the party.

Impact of Leader Character and Competence on Vote Choice

In order to assess the impact of perceptions of leaders on vote choice, the data were pooled and a series of logistic regression analyses were performed for the decision to vote for each of the three main parties. Table 8.1 presents these results, with columns for vote choice for each of the New Democratic, Liberal, and Conservative parties from 1984 to 2006.[6] In addition to the variables of interest (evaluations of leader character and competence), the model includes a series of control variables: partisanship, ideological left-right self-placement, and attitudes on three main issue dimensions – social liberalism (as measured through attitudes towards abortion), taxes versus

TABLE 8.1

Impact of leaders' character and competence on vote choice

	NDP		Liberal		Conservative	
	Odds ratio	(SE)	Odds ratio	(SE)	Odds ratio	(SE)
Leader evaluations						
Conservative character	0.324***	(0.0982)	0.163***	(0.0399)	27.900***	(7.9140)
Conservative competence	0.546**	(0.1550)	0.608**	(0.1400)	9.872***	(2.7710)
Liberal character	0.350***	(0.1010)	16.400***	(3.7860)	0.251***	(0.0621)
Liberal competence	0.445***	(0.1280)	6.948***	(1.7590)	0.396***	(0.1000)
NDP character	10.690***	(3.5840)	0.615*	(0.1560)	0.190***	(0.0548)
NDP competence	4.849***	(1.4310)	0.415***	(0.0976)	0.806	(0.2120)
Socio-demographic variables						
Married	0.912	(0.1130)	0.877	(0.0915)	1.284**	(0.1430)
Woman	1.374***	(0.1620)	1.064	(0.1050)	0.904	(0.0935)
University graduate	0.855	(0.1060)	1.077	(0.1100)	1.092	(0.1150)
Employed full time	0.978	(0.1290)	1.106	(0.1220)	0.954	(0.1100)
Age	0.924*	(0.0387)	1.074**	(0.0374)	0.996	(0.0362)
Partisanship and ideology						
Conservative partisan	0.183***	(0.0424)	0.213***	(0.0412)	5.596***	(0.8250)
Liberal partisan	0.516***	(0.0787)	4.692***	(0.5660)	0.389***	(0.0531)
NDP partisan	12.620***	(2.1910)	0.195***	(0.0431)	0.137***	(0.0305)
Other partisan	0.086***	(0.0277)	0.101***	(0.0273)	0.138***	(0.0307)
Left-right ideological self-placement	0.267***	(0.0772)	1.023	(0.2310)	2.003***	(0.5000)
Issue attitudes						
Major campaign issue	0.665*	(0.1510)	1.192	(0.2180)	1.639***	(0.3140)
Issue: taxes versus spending	1.331	(0.2360)	1.094	(0.1540)	0.909	(0.1360)
Issue: social liberalism	1.508*	(0.3210)	1.103	(0.1800)	1.108	(0.1830)
Constant	0.199***	(0.0961)	0.110***	(0.0435)	0.191***	(0.0804)

Logistic regression analysis; odds ratios presented, standard errors in parentheses.
$N = 3,328$.
*$p < .1$, **$p < .05$, ***$p < .01$.

spending, and the major campaign issue (as determined through an examination of media coverage of the campaign).[7]

It is important to note that, for all three parties, vote choice is influenced by voter impressions of leader character and competence. The table presents odds ratios and standard errors, thus facilitating greater ease in interpreting the results. Those who give NDP leaders' character a rating of 1 on the 0-1 scale are ten times more likely to vote for the party than are those who give the leaders a rating of 0 (odds ratio of 10.69). Those who give the most positive rating of leader competence are nearly five times more likely to vote for the NDP. Similar patterns emerge when it comes to vote choice for the other two major parties, and the odds ratios are even larger. Voters are more likely to vote for a party if they perceive the party's leader in a more positive light on the two trait dimensions. The data also indicate that the impact of leader traits on vote choice is larger for the Liberal and Conservative parties than it is for the NDP. This is consistent with past findings indicating that leaders matter more for "main" parties than they do for "third" parties (Johnston 2002; Bittner 2010, 2011).

While impressions of leaders may have a larger impact on vote choice for the Liberal and Conservative parties, the substantially larger impact of partisanship on votes for the NDP is notable. NDP partisans were nearly thirteen times more likely to support their party, while the odds ratios for Liberal and Conservative partisans on vote choice for their own parties were 4.7 and 5.6, respectively. Partisanship had the largest impact on the decision to vote for the NDP, indicating that, of the major national parties, NDP partisans are likely to support their party regardless of how they feel about who is at the helm.[8]

All other variables included in the models had a substantially smaller impact on vote choice in comparison to either leader evaluations or partisanship. Among socio-demographic indicators, women are more likely to vote for the NDP than are men, and those who are older are slightly less likely to vote for the NDP than are those who are younger. But the odds ratios are not very large. When it comes to ideology or issue attitudes, the impact of these variables on vote choice is also small. Right-leaning respondents are less likely to support the NDP, while those who hold more socially liberal attitudes are more likely to support it. But again, these odds ratios are not very big. Further, they are not bigger than the impact of ideology or issue attitudes on vote choice for either the Liberal or Conservative parties. These data suggest that ideology and issue attitudes are not substantially more important than other types of factors that influence vote choice for the NDP (see Zakharova, Chapter 9, this volume, for similar conclusions on ideology).

Indeed, further analysis provides additional support for the contention that issues and ideology are not really more "important" factors in determining support for the NDP than in determining support for other parties,

at least not in the last twenty-five years. When we run the same multivariate analysis for each election in question (minus 2008 and 2011), the results
are no different. In comparison to leader evaluations and partisanship,
ideological self-placement is not particularly influential with regard to vote
choice for the NDP. In examining the impact of the above-listed three issue
areas (social liberalism, taxes versus spending, and the major campaign
issue) across these nine elections, only eight issue area coefficients reached
statistical significance for the NDP, while, for the Conservative Party, issues
had a statistically significant impact on vote choice ten times in this same
time frame. The importance of issues for Liberal vote choice was much
lower, with only four issues having a statistically significant impact (data
not shown).[9]

Impact of Feelings towards NDP Leaders on Election Results
Given the data limitations, it is difficult to pinpoint the (possibly) changing
impact of leader traits within the NDP over time. In particular, the data
prevent us from getting a real sense of whether or not Layton's perceived
strengths of character and competence provided an electoral boost for the
party. Indeed, it is conceivable that positive evaluations of Layton's personality traits may have drawn non-partisans and partisans of other parties to
support the NDP. While there are plenty of reasons not to focus too heavily
on thermometer ratings to get a sense of the importance of leaders (see
Bittner [2011, 16-18] for a more detailed discussion of the problems with the
measure), when there are no other options, it seems reasonable to employ
what we have available.

In order to assess the electoral impact of evaluations of party leaders of
the three main parties from 1984 to 2011, the average thermometer rating
of the three candidates was calculated for each year in order to establish a
fictional "neutral" or baseline candidate. Then, using the results of logit analyses conducted for each year (with vote for the NDP as the dependent
variable), simulations were run to determine the change in probability of
voting for the NDP based on the average ratings that the three real leaders
were actually given in each election (thus I essentially compared the real
leader to the fictional baseline character).[10] Figure 8.8 tracks the results,
illustrating the NDP net gain from evaluations of Conservative leaders,
Liberal leaders, and NDP leaders over time as well as the sum of the three
(the total net effect of feelings towards leaders). Where the lines fall below
the horizontal 0 line in a given election, the NDP lost ground as a result of
evaluations of leaders.

FIGURE 8.8
Net NDP gain from evaluation of leaders of three main parties

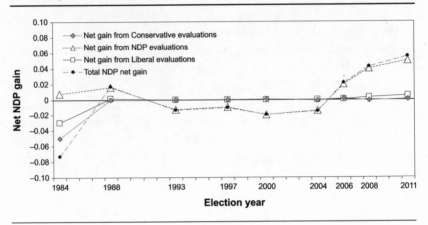

As is clear from Figure 8.8, the NDP gained vote share as a result of Broadbent's popularity in 1988 and lost ground from 1993 to 2004 as a result of evaluations of McLaughlin and McDonough. In 2006, the pattern shifted again, and the party benefitted from positive evaluations of Layton. Leader effects on the electoral outcome range from 0 to 2 percent (either positive or negative) between 1984 and 2004, and then rise as high as 5.5 percent in 2011, the year in which evaluations of leaders provided the largest boost.[11]

Given the nature of the electoral system and the fact that voters are not directly voting for the party leader (as they do in a presidential system), it is difficult to know how decisive an impact leaders may have had on the distribution of seats in the House of Commons. A nearly 6 percent boost in the popular vote might offer a 6 percent boost in the seat share in a more proportional electoral system, but the same kind of calculation cannot be made in Canada. In the 2011 election, the NDP obtained slightly more than 30 percent of the popular vote. Had it obtained 25 percent of the national vote share instead, presumably it would have had fewer seats in the House of Commons, but it is difficult to say how many fewer as this would depend on the distribution of that vote share across ridings. The fate of the Bloc Québécois in the most recent election demonstrates how a regionally concentrated vote share can drastically affect a party's fortunes. The Bloc lost only 6 percent of the national vote share in the 2011 election over the 2008 election, but it lost 43 seats. Many of these seats went directly to the NDP.[12]

Evaluations of leaders do play an important role in determining the outcome of an election. And, in 2011, they may have played a decisive role.

Conclusion

Analysis of data from the CES over time suggests that voters have indeed considered party leaders at the ballot box. Further, the data suggest that the importance of leaders extends not only to leaders of the main brokerage parties but also to the decision to vote for the NDP over time. Canadians do not appear to judge the NDP more on ideology or policy bases than they do other parties, and voters react to party leaders regardless of whether or not they are partisans of the leader's party. When the NDP has had popular and well-respected leaders, it has done better on election day; when it has had less popular leaders, it has done less well. These results suggest that, if the NDP's goal is to form Official Opposition and/or government, then it needs to take leadership selection seriously as voters of all stripes consider party leaders when they decide which party gets their vote.

The NDP's recent success in the national election suggests that it has been doing something "right" over the last few years. Since Layton took over the helm, the NDP's fortunes have consistently climbed, gaining ground in each election. The reasons for this seem to be complex and interdependent, and would likely include shifts in the party's electoral platform (Bittner and Koop 2013; Laycock, Chapter 5, and Pétry, Chapter 6, this volume) and the modernization of the party's approach to campaigning (Laycock and Erickson, Chapter 4, this volume). The changing dynamics of the party system, including the decline of the Liberals as an electoral force, would also appear to be important in this regard. However, as the evidence in this chapter suggests, Layton's increasing popularity among partisans and non-partisans alike (as seen in Figures 8.4 and 8.5) must also be considered in any account of the NDP's current, unprecedented position.

Notes

I would like to thank Mark Winward and Susan Piercey for their excellent research assistance.

1 Recent analysis of cross-national data suggests that it makes the most sense to think about personality traits as falling within two main "umbrella" dimensions: competence and character (Bittner 2011). The competence dimension broadly includes traits such as "leadership," "competence," and "intelligence," while the character dimension includes traits such as "integrity," "empathy," "honesty," and "trustworthiness." Because the dimensions themselves do not change, even if the

specific traits within them might differ slightly from year to year, looking at traits in this way allows us to consider evaluations of leader character and competence, regardless of the changes that have taken place in the question format. This will allow us to gain a better understanding of evaluations and the impacts of those evaluations.

2 This includes the five Progressive Conservative leaders since 1984 and Stephen Harper, who, in 2004, was elected leader of the Conservative Party (which resulted from the merger of the Canadian Alliance and Progressive Conservative parties in 2003).

3 Thus, while I present means only for the Conservative, Liberal, and NDP leaders, they are compared to the average ratings of leaders of all major parties competing in a given election.

4 Note that respondents were not asked to evaluate leader traits in the 2008 CES; thus data are missing for that year.

5 Partisanship was measured through the classic Canadian question: "In federal politics, do you usually think of yourself as a: Liberal, Conservative, NDP, Bloc Québécois, Green Party, or none of these?" This was recoded as a binary variable, so that those self-identifying as NDP partisans were coded as 1 and all others were coded as 0.

6 Recall that respondents were not asked to evaluate leaders' traits in the 2008 CES; therefore, that year is not included in the analysis. In addition, in 2011, those voters who were asked to evaluate a leader on the competence dimension were not asked to evaluate that same leader on the character dimension; therefore, 2011 respondents are excluded from the pooled multivariate analysis as well.

7 The setup mirrors that of Bittner (2011). All variables included in the model are coded on a 0-1 scale, with the exception of age, which is coded into quintiles. Dependent variables (vote choice for a given party) are coded where 1 = vote for party and 0 = vote for any other party, including independents and "other" parties. Non-voters are excluded from the model. Evaluations of leaders are coded so that values of 1 reflect the highest possible evaluations and evaluations of 0 reflect the lowest possible evaluations. Socio-demographic and partisanship variables are primarily binary variables, where 1 reflects individuals belonging to the category (e.g., woman = 1, man = 0). Ideological left-right self-placement is coded so that 1 is most right-leaning and 0 is most left-leaning. Issue attitudes are coded in the opposite way, so that 0 is most right-leaning and 1 is most left-leaning (e.g., those in favour of easiest access to abortion in the "social liberalism" issue dimension would be coded 1). Model includes dummy variables for each election year, but those variables are not shown in the table. For more information about coding of variables, including issue attitudes, see Bittner (2011).

8 Note, however, that, because this analysis excludes 2008 and 2011 (the years in which Jack Layton's popularity exceeded that of all other leaders both past and present), the results may not be as generalizable across all years as one might hope. It is quite conceivable that the impact of partisanship may have been smaller and the impact of leader traits may have been bigger with Layton at the helm.

9   It may seem surprising that issues or ideology are not more important for explaining NDP vote choice than they are for explaining that of the other two main (brokerage) parties. On one level, it might be considered as counter-intuitive, given that we have this "sense" that the NDP has been so issue-focused over the years, as programmatic parties are wont to be characterized. It is possible that the overwhelming importance of partisanship for explaining NDP vote choice has dominated the importance of all other variables, but it also may be that the left-right rhetoric behind the federal "unite-the-right" campaign in the last two decades has meant that issues and ideology have become associated with the Conservative Party rather than with the left-leaning NDP.

10 See Bittner (2011, Chapter 6) for a similar setup. Control variables in the model include the same variables seen in Table 8.1; however, evaluations of leader competence and character were left out and replaced with overall thermometer ratings.

11 This range is consistent with the range of the electoral effect of leaders found elsewhere, including Canada, the United States, and the United Kingdom (e.g., Bittner 2011; Bartels 2002; Graetz and McAllister 1987; Johnston 2002).

12 Note that, in the calculation of the NDP's net gain as a result of leader evaluations, I focus solely on evaluations of the three main parties in English Canada. Evaluations of Gilles Duceppe are not included in the model, even though much of the NDP's gain in this election came from Quebec.

References

Aarts, Kees, André Blais, and Hermann Schmitt. 2011. *Political Leaders and Democratic Elections*. Oxford: Oxford University Press.

Bartels, Larry M. 2002. "Beyond the Running Tally: Partisan Bias in Political Perceptions." *Political Behavior* 24, 2: 117-50.

Berlin, Z. David, and Howard Aster. 2001. *What's Left? The New Democratic Party in Renewal*. Oakville, ON: Mosaic.

Bittner, Amanda. 2010. Personality Matters: The Evaluation of Party Leaders in Canadian Elections. In Cameron D. Anderson and Laura B. Stephenson, eds., *Voting Behaviour in Canada*. Vancouver: UBC Press.

–. 2011. *Platform or Personality? The Role of Party Leaders in Elections*. Oxford: Oxford University Press.

Bittner, Amanda, and Royce Koop, eds. 2013. *Parties, Elections, and the Future of Canadian Politics*. Vancouver: UBC Press.

Blais, André, Elisabeth Gidengil, Richard Nadeau, and Neil Nevitte. 1997. The 1997 Canadian Election Study. Dataset. http://www.queensu.ca/cora/ces.html.

–. 2000. The 2000 Canadian Election Study. Dataset. http://www.queensu.ca/cora/ces.html.

–. 2002. *Anatomy of a Liberal Victory: Making Sense of the Vote in the 2000 Canadian Election*. Peterborough, ON: Broadview.

Blais, André, Elisabeth Gidengil, Neil Nevitte, Patrick Fournier, and Joanna Everitt. 2006. The 2004-2006 Canadian Election Study. Dataset. http://www.queensu.ca/cora/ces.html.

Brodie, Janine, and Jane Jenson. 1991. Piercing the Smokescreen: Brokerage Parties and Class Politics. In Alain-G. Gagnon and A. Brian Tanguay, eds. *Canadian Parties in Transition: Discourse, Organization and Representation*. Scarborough, ON: Nelson Canada.

Brown, Steven D., Ronald D. Lambert, Barry J. Kay, and James E. Curtis. 1988. In the Eye of the Beholder: Leader Images in Canada. *Canadian Journal of Political Science* 21: 729-55.

Carroll, William K., and R.S. Ratner, eds. 2005. *Challenges and Perils: Social Democracy in Neoliberal Times*. Halifax: Fernwood Books.

Carty, R. Kenneth, and William Cross. 2010. Political Parties and the Practice of Brokerage Politics. In John C. Courtney and David E. Smith, eds., *The Oxford Handbook of Canadian Politics*. Toronto: Oxford University Press.

Clarke, Harold, Jane Jenson, Lawrence LeDuc, and Jon H. Pammet. 1991. *Absent Mandate: Interpreting Change in Canadian Elections*. 2nd ed. Agincourt, ON: Gage.

Clarke, Harold D., Karl Ho, and Marianne C. Stewart. 2000. Major's Lesser (Not Minor) Effects: Prime Ministerial Approval and Governing Party Support in Britain since 1979. *Electoral Studies* 19: 255-73.

Coletto, David. 2012. Layton's Legacy is Authenticity. *Hill Times*, 19 March. http://www.hilltimes.com/opinion-piece/politics/2012/03/19/layton's-legacy-is-authenticity/30099.

Coyne, Andrew. 2012. NDP Should Hold onto Its Sensibilities; Party Should Bring the Middle to the Left. *National Post*, 14 February.

Cross, William. 2004. *Political Parties*. Vancouver: UBC Press.

Fournier, Patrick, Fred Cutler, Stuart Soroka, and Dietlind Stolle. 2011. The 2011 Canadian Election Study. Dataset. http://ces-eec.org/pagesE/surveys.html.

Gidengil, Elisabeth, André Blais, Richard Nadeau, and Neil Nevitte. 2000. Are Party Leaders Becoming More Important to Vote Choice in Canada? Paper presented at the Annual Meeting of the American Political Science Association, Washington, DC. 31 August–3 September.

Gidengil, Elisabeth, Joanna Everitt, and Susan Banducci. 2006. Gender and Perceptions of Leader Traits: Evidence from the 1993 Canadian and 1999 New Zealand Elections. Paper presented at the Conference on Women and Leadership, University of Toronto, May.

Gidengil, Elisabeth, Joanna Everitt, Patrick Fournier, and Neil Nevitte. 2008. The 2008 Canadian Election Study. Dataset. http://www.queensu.ca/cora/ces.html.

Globe and Mail. 2012. Editorial: Mulcair Is NDP's Best Hope of Winning Election. 25 March. http://www.theglobeandmail.com/news/opinions/editorials/mulcair-is-ndps-best-hope-of-winning-election/article2380754/.

Graetz, Brian, and Ian McAllister. 1987. "Popular Evaluations of Party Leaders in the Anglo-American Democracies." In Harold D. Clarke and Moshe M. Czudnowski, eds., *Political Elites in Anglo-American Democracies*. DeKalb, IL: Northern Illinois University Press.

Johnston, Richard. 2002. "Prime Ministerial Contenders in Canada." In Anthony King, ed., *Leaders' Personalities and the Outcomes of Democratic Elections*. Oxford: Oxford University Press.

Johnston, Richard, André Blais, Henry Brady, Elisabeth Gidengil, and Neil Nevitte. 1993. The 1993 Canadian Election Study. Dataset. http://www.queensu.ca/cora/ces.html.

Johnston, Richard, André Blais, Henry E. Brady, and Jean Crete. 1988. The 1988 Canadian Election Study. Dataset. http://www.queensu.ca/cora/ces.html.

–. 1992. *Letting the People Decide: Dynamics of a Canadian Election*. Stanford: Stanford University Press.

Jones, Philip, and John Hudson. 1996. "The Quality of Political Leadership: A Case Study of John Major." *British Journal of Political Science* 26, 2: 229-44.

Lambert, Ronald D., Steven D. Brown, James E. Curtis, Barry J. Kay, and John M. Wilson. 1984. The 1984 Canadian Election Study. Dataset. http://www.queensu.ca/cora/ces.html.

Mendelsohn, Matthew. 1993. Television's Frames in the 1988 Canadian Election. *Canadian Journal of Communication* 19, 2: 149-71.

Morton, Desmond. 1986. *The New Democrats, 1961-1986: The Politics of Change*. Toronto: Copp Clark Pitman.

Rahn, Wendy M., John H. Aldrich, Eugene Borgida, and John L. Sullivan. 1990. A Social-Cognitive Model of Candidate Appraisal. In John A. Ferejohn and James H. Kuklinski, eds., *Information and Democratic Processes*. Urbana: University of Illinois Press.

Salutin, Rick. 2012. Cullen and Nash Struggle for NDP's Soul. *Toronto Star*, 10 February.

Young, Lisa, and William Cross. 2002. Incentives to Membership in Canadian Political Parties. *Political Research Quarterly* 55, 3: 547-69.

9

Valence Politics, Policy Distance, and the NDP Vote

MARIA ZAKHAROVA

Over the last two and a half decades, the NDP's vote share in Canadian federal elections has fluctuated considerably. It went from 20 percent in 1988 to its lowest point, below 7 percent, in 1993, to its high point of 30.6 percent in 2011. Which factors can explain such changes in the party's vote share from one election to the next? In this chapter, I explore the role of policy distance and valence politics in short-term changes to voter support for the NDP over more than two decades of elections.

Policy Distance, Valence Politics, and Short-Term Change

Models that explain voting behaviour and voter choice often include (but are not limited to) such factors as party identification, voters' socio-demographic characteristics, their levels of political sophistication, policy distance between voters and particular parties, and non-policy (or valence) variables. Some of these factors are more long-term features that are un-likely to help explain short-term phenomena. For example, party identifi-cation – that is, voters' sense of attachment to a particular party – has been widely used as a variable in explaining voter preferences in Canada (Bélanger and Meguid 2008; Scotto, Stephenson, and Kornberg 2004; Gidengil et al. 2012). But, as Campbell et al. (1960, Chapters 6 and 7) argue in their book on voting behaviour in the United States, which is the classic reference on party identification, the phenomenon of party identification is relatively stable and not readily modified or changed. In the Canadian context, Anderson and Stephenson (2010, 21) argue, "recent findings suggest the ongoing importance of partisanship as a key explanatory factor underlying the stability of Canadians' vote choices." As a result, party identification would not likely account for dramatic changes in the NDP's vote share from one election to the next.

Voters' socio-demographic characteristics and levels of political information, which have had demonstrable effects on voting preferences in Canada (Kanji and Archer 2002; Bittner 2010), may have changed over the last two decades, but these changes were relatively slow. They were, for example, not very substantial between 2000 and 2004, when the NDP vote share nearly doubled, or between 2008 and 2011, when the NDP vote share grew by almost 70 percent.

While party identification and socio-demographic changes may not readily explain short-term shifts in voter support, policy distance may have more potential to do so. Policy distance refers to the distance between positions of an individual and a party on some policy continuum. Sometimes this is conceptualized as a composite left-right spectrum (Downs 1957; Adams, Merrill, and Grofman, 2005); at other times it is broken down into specific issues (Clarke et al. 2009; Sanders et al. 2011). A foundational concept for spatial models of voting behaviour, policy distance assumes that both parties and voters have positions along a policy continuum and that individuals choose the party or a candidate that is closest to their own (Downs 1957). According to this approach, if a party changes its position so that another party is closer to a voter's place on the policy continuum, that voter's support for the original party should change. Similarly, if voters change their position on a policy continuum so that it is closer to that of a different party, their support for their original preference should also change. Although parties' policy shifts over time are seldom large enough to completely rearrange the political landscape, they do nonetheless occur (McDonald, Mendes, and Kim 2007), as do shifts in voter opinion. Accordingly, policy distance could be a factor affecting short-term change in levels of voter support for a party.

Still, the effects of policy distance on changes in party support may be limited. As many authors have pointed out, the assumptions the policy model makes about voter behaviour can be problematic (Popkin 1991; Sniderman, Brody, and Tetlock 1991; Rahn 2000; Brader 2005). People may, for example, base their voting decisions on other considerations, such as liking or disliking a candidate or a party (Sniderman, Brody, and Tetlock

1991; Rahn 2000; Brader 2005), leader image (Blais et al. 2003), or a politician's or a party's perceived competence (Clark and Leiter 2013; Pardos-Prado 2012).

People's feelings of liking or disliking parties or candidates, as well as their perceptions of leader competence, are linked to the concept of valence (Stokes 1963). The term "valence" is often used in connection with one of the following two phenomena: (1) valence issues and (2) candidate and/or party valence. Valence issues are those on which the electorate has consensus. For example, in any election there would be a consensus among voters on the desirability of a strong economy, low unemployment, and a low crime rate. Research in this area usually has an emphasis on voter perception of party or leader competence in dealing with particular valence issues (Green 2007; Johnston and Pattie 2011). For its part, candidate and/or party valence is often used in models of party positioning and voting behaviour, and it refers to a collection of positive qualities associated with a party or a candidate, such as candidate charisma and competence or party unity and integrity (Adams et al. 2011; Stone and Simas 2010). Valence-based theories of voting behaviour imply that people vote largely on the basis of considerations that are not related to policy. Unlike party identification, these considerations may readily change from election to election since, in developed democracies, party leaders change often, as do the aspects of leader or party competence that are emphasized in different election campaigns. In other words, it would seem that valence judgments may be especially helpful in explaining short-term fluctuations in a party's vote share.

The questions, however, are: How much is a party's vote share affected by valence attributes, and how much is determined by voters' policy calculations? And are these effects stable, or do they vary from one election to the next? This chapter examines the extent to which people vote for the NDP based on calculations of policy distance between their positions and those of the NDP as compared to the impact on their NDP vote choice of the party's valence attributes in the 1988, 1997, 2004, 2008, and 2011 federal elections.

Given the NDP's status in federal politics (at least until the 2011 election) as a perennial "third party" (Bélanger 2004) that has long anchored the left of the party spectrum in Canadian parliaments (see Laycock, Chapter 5, this volume), it might be hypothesized that the effects of valence judgments and policy distance on the NDP vote would differ from those on the Liberal or Conservative voting choice. Valence effects may be lower and the effects of ideological distance may be higher for NDP voters because the party was not perceived to be likely to form governments. Thus, the qualities of a particular leader may have mattered less than the kinds of policies that the party has long been promoting. I therefore also compare the effects of valence and policy distance on the vote for federal Liberal and conservative parties to those on the vote for the NDP.[1]

Conceptualizations of Valence

The concept of valence, as first introduced by Donald Stokes (1963), is concerned with "valence issues." Responding to the dominance of spatial models in the literature on voting behaviour, Stokes introduced the notion of "valence" issues as opposed to "position" issues. Specifically, he refers to valence issues as those that involve "the linking of the parties with some condition that is positively or negatively valued by the electorate" (373). Thus, a particular party may win votes because it is associated with low unemployment or high economic growth; other parties may lose votes because they are associated with corruption or war. In other words, the electorate has a consensus on valence issues, as opposed to the varying policy distance associated with position issues.

Following this logic, a large body of literature in political science explores the impact of valence issues (or "valence politics") on voting behaviour (Bélanger and Meguid 2008; Green and Jennings 2012; Green and Hobolt 2008; Green 2007; Clarke et al. 2011; Clarke, Scotto, and Kornberg 2011; Clarke et al. 2009; Sanders et al. 2011; Pardos-Prado 2012). Many of these studies incorporate the idea of "issue ownership" – that is, the notion that certain parties are perceived by the electorate as being more capable than others of dealing with particular valence issues. In this area of valence research, the term "valence" often appears in the context of "valence politics" – that is, the notion that people choose their representatives largely on the basis of their judgments of party or leader competence in dealing with valence issues. Accordingly, parties and candidates that are perceived as being more competent in resolving valence issues tend to win elections. Specifically, in the Canadian context, Bélanger and Meguid (2008) and Clarke, Scotto, and Kornberg (2011) argue that voters largely base their electoral choice on their perceptions of party and leader competence in dealing with the most salient valence issues.

Another branch of the literature expands Stokes's original valence concept from valence issues into factors related to characteristics of parties and leaders – that is, candidate and/or party valence (Adams et al. 2011; Clark

2009; Clark and Leiter 2013). In this approach, valence refers to party and leader characteristics that provide electoral advantage but that are not related to party or leader policy positions. This includes leader images; voters' emotional responses to parties and leaders; and perceived qualities of competence, party unity, and integrity. The research in this area demonstrates that party vote shares can be substantially influenced by leader image (Clark 2009). In addition, Green and Jennings (2011) find a strong effect from perceived party competence in dealing with what voters identify as the most important problems facing the country. Consistently with this latter interpretation of valence politics, I treat valence judgments as people's perceptions of a leader or party's non-policy-related qualities (e.g., liking or disliking the party and leader) as well as their perceptions of leader or party competence with regard to dealing with the most important issue of the day.

Data and Methods

My analyses of valence and policy effects use data from five Canadian Election Studies (1984, 1997, 2004, 2008, and 2011).[2] Although the CES have been conducted for almost every general election since 1965, many of the surveys do not include the variables required in my model, particularly those measuring policy distance between the respondents and parties. Thus, my choice was limited to these five datasets. I ran the analyses on respondents from all Canadian provinces in all of these elections. In order to run the analyses, I modified the data so that, for each election, each respondent appeared as many times as there were main parties (usually three). Therefore, the units of analysis in the final data set are each individual's assessments of each party in a given election.[3] Following the methodology of Bélanger and Meguid (2008), I ran logistic regression analyses separately for each party for each election, with the goal of assessing the effects of valence judgments and policy distance on the probability of voting for that party.

Measuring Valence

To test the effects of valence judgments versus policy distance, it was necessary to create a single valence indicator from a number of measures of different valence components. The first of these valence components – party and leader evaluations – were measured using the questions about a respondent's feelings for the party on a scale from 0 (strongly dislike) to 100 (strongly like) and feelings for the party leader (measured on the same scale). The second component of valence judgments is perceived party competence. In order to measure it, I looked at a survey question that deals with the first interpretation of valence politics (above) concerning the questions of issue ownership (Bélanger and Meguid 2008; Clarke et al. 2009; Clarke et al. 2011a; Clarke, Scotto, and Kornberg 2011; Pardos-Prado 2012). In particular, I used the question that asks a respondent to indicate which party is the most competent to deal with the most important problem for that individual. Unlike the researchers who deal with the issue ownership questions, I did not identify what issues individuals deemed the most important. Since I am treating valence as non-policy-related characteristics of parties and leaders, one of which is competence, I only used the information on which party the individual viewed as most competent, regardless of the issue. Based on answers to that question, for that individual I created a dummy variable, with the value of 1 corresponding to the party that had been chosen as the most competent and 0s for all other parties. Finally, since some of the surveys also included the question assessing leader competence on a scale from 0 (incompetent) to 100 (very competent), for the elections in which this question was asked these responses have also been incorporated into the measure of valence judgments.

It is worth mentioning that many Canadian Election Studies contain a question on one's party identification, which Clarke and his colleagues consider to be one of the key components of valence politics. However, "party identification" may be interpreted by respondents in a policy-related sense: it might not necessarily bring to mind a party or leader's positive non-policy-related qualities but, instead, might appeal to one's political orientation. For this reason, it has been excluded from the current measure of party valence.

To explore whether creating a single valence indicator from these items was reasonable, I ran a principal component factor analysis (see Pétry, Chapter 6, this volume) for an explanation of this statistical technique) on the three to four components that were measured in each survey (feelings for the party, feelings for the party leader, which party is the most competent at dealing with the most important problem, and, for the surveys in which it was available, assessment of leader competence). The objective was to see whether the measures were related to one another in a way that would suggest that there was a common underlying factor in the valence judgments the respondents made of each party. The analysis confirmed the assumption that all of these items measured a common latent construct, with the first factor accounting for 64 to 90 percent of the variance in these variables.[4]

Measuring Policy Distance in the Canadian Context

To determine the extent to which people use a calculus of policy distance as opposed to valence-based judgments when making their voting choices, I devised a measure of policy distance. In the Canadian context, ideological distance seems to be conceptualized mainly in terms of distance between an individual and a party on specific issues. For example, Johnston, Fournier, and Jenkins (2000, 1,149) measure the distance between the Canadian electorate and parties on "the place of Quebec in the larger nationality, Canada-US relations, and aid to ethnic and racial minorities" for the 1993 election and "the Quebec issue and willingness to pay taxes" for the 1997 election. In a similar way, Gidengil et al. (2001, 496) treat policy distance among the parties in the specific domains of two salient issues in the 1990s in Canada – the Quebec question and the trade-off between the size of taxes and the number of social programs. Another way of looking at policy distance would be to place voters and parties on a left-right continuum, using voter self-placement. Despite the relative simplicity of the left-right concept of spatial proximity, few studies employ it in the Canadian context. Moreover, Gidengil et al. (2012, 15) argue that "Canadians typically do not have a very clear grasp of concepts like 'left' and 'right.'" The analyses that follow test this claim by examining how well the distance on the left-right policy continuum can predict voting choice in Canada over the course of several elections.

It is important to distinguish between perceived (or subjective) and actual (objective) policy distance. Perceived policy distance is measured using people's own placements of themselves and the parties. Arguably, this distance may be influenced by one's valence judgments of parties and leaders. In other words, when individuals like a leader or a party, they may place this leader or party closer to their own position. This is known as an assimilation effect (Merrill, Grofman, and Adams 2001). To exclude this effect, a more objective measure of distance should be used. However, to produce a measure of objective distance, an estimate of actual party positions is required. Warwick (2010, 13) shows that "respondents, on average, place political parties on the left-right scale in a fashion that appears to be largely consistent with expert placements." Accordingly, I treat respondents' aggregate party placements in each election study as actual positions of the parties. Objective distance is then calculated as an absolute distance between these party positions and each respondent's self-placement.

Results

Before examining the effects of policy versus valence factors in NDP support, it is important to consider the validity of measuring policy distance in Canada by asking respondents to place themselves and the parties on the left-right spectrum. One way to address this issue is to look at whether CES respondents place the parties on the left-right spectrum in a way that reflects other, potentially more objective, placements. If their placements are similar to objective placements, it is reasonable to assume that their self-placements are also relatively reliable. The results confirm the validity of measuring policy distance in Canada using respondent placements on the left-right spectrum. Specifically, respondents on average place the three main parties that contested the elections under study in the correct order on the left-right spectrum in every election that has been analyzed. They placed the NDP on the left, the Liberal Party in the middle, and the Conservative (or PC in 1984 and Reform in 1997) Party on the right. As an example, Figure 9.1 demonstrates the distribution of respondents' placements of the five political parties in Canada for the 2011 election. It shows, in particular, that the majority of respondents placed the Conservative Party on the right, the Liberal Party in the middle, and the NDP on the left of the political continuum. This order matches the ratings of the parties on the left-right scale according to the Comparative Manifesto Project[5] (see Table 9.1 and Pétry, Chapter 6, this volume).[6]

When we turn to the effects of policy and valence over the five elections, the results of the logistic regression analyses performed for each of the parties suggest that both valence judgments and policy distance play a role in determining the vote choices of Canadians. However, valence effects are clearly the most important. (Table 9.2 demonstrates the coefficients for all parties across the five elections.) The valence effect is statistically significant in all cases ($p < .01$), while the effect of policy distance is significant in 8 cases out of 15 ($p < .05$). Both effects are in the expected direction in all cases: the valence effects are a positive sign, and the effects of policy distance are negative. The coefficient for the effect of valence judgments among all major parties ranges from 1.15 for the NDP in the 2011 election to 2.53 for the NDP in 1984, with an average value of 2.03. It is noteworthy that both the lowest and the highest value of the valence effects among all

TABLE 9.1
Left-right placements of the major parties in Canada by CES respondents and CMP team

Year	Party	CMP ratings[a]	CES respondents[b]
1984	NDP	−31.9	3.00
	Liberal	−16.2	4.19
	PC	12.3	5.14
1997	NDP	−31.8	3.36
	Liberal	6.3	5.41
	Reform	40.4	5.96
2004	NDP	−17.6	3.38
	Liberal	−12.2	5.07
	Conservative	14.4	6.28
2008	NDP	−20.7	3.52
	Liberal	5.2	5.00
	Conservative	9.1	6.92
2011	NDP	−19.0	3.42
	Liberal	−13.0	5.02
	Conservative	19.0	7.17
	Bloc Québécois	−1.0	3.62

a   CMP scale ranges from −100 to 100.
b   CES scale ranges from 1 to 7 in 1984 survey and from 0 to 10 in 1997, 2004, 2008, and 2011 surveys.

parties were for the NDP vote. The effect of policy distance ranges from −.2 for the Liberal Party in the 1997 election to −.46 for the Conservative Party in 2011, with an average of −.33 across all elections for all major parties.[7]

To illustrate the effects these results suggest, I calculated the predicted probabilities of a vote for the NDP for various values of the policy distance and valence scores for the 1984 election when the effect of valence variables on votes for the NDP was highest at 2.53, and the effect of policy distance was at −0.46 (see Table 9.2). If a person has one of the lowest valence scores for the NDP (−2), his or her predicted probability of voting for the NDP is negligible (.0007). If one has given one of the highest ratings for the NDP (1.9), one's predicted probability of voting for the NDP is .91. For an average valence score of 0 for the NDP, the probability of voting NDP is .10. To compare, the effect of policy distance is substantially weaker: if someone has a minimal distance score for the NDP of 0.01, then his or her predicted probability of voting for the party is only .26. If someone is at the average

FIGURE 9.1
Distribution of CES respondents' placements of major parties in 2011
Canadian federal election

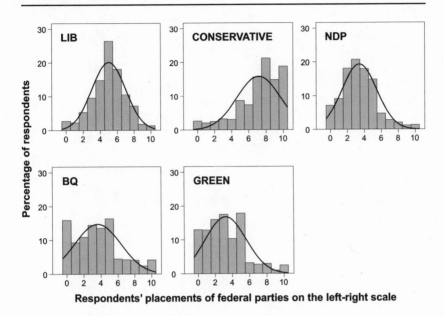

Respondents' placements of federal parties on the left-right scale

distance from the NDP of 1.3, he or she has a .20 probability of voting for it. At 4 points away from the NDP, which is near the maximum value of distance measured among respondents in that election, the probability of voting for the NDP is .10. Figure 9.2 demonstrates plotted predicted probabilities of voting for the NDP for various valence scores and values of objective distance, with 95 percent confidence intervals. The graphs show that the effect of valence on the probability of voting has a much larger magnitude compared to that of objective distance.

In terms of the NDP vote, it is hard to identify any common pattern of effects across the five elections. First of all, valence appears to have had a stronger effect on the NDP vote compared to that of the other two mainstream parties in two elections (1984 and 1997). However, in the other three elections, it had the lowest effect compared to that of the other two parties (2004, 2008, and 2011). Policy distance had a stronger effect on the NDP vote compared to the other two parties in 1984. In 1997, policy distance had almost the same effect on the NDP vote as on the Reform

TABLE 9.2
Effects of valence and policy distance on the vote choice in Canada

	NDP		Liberal		PC/Con/Reform	
	Beta	(SE)	Beta	(SE)	Beta	(SE)
1984						
Valence	2.53***	(0.19)	1.73***	(0.13)	2.42***	(0.15)
Distance	−0.46***	(0.11)	−0.2	(0.11)	−0.27*	(0.11)
Intercept	−1.6***	(0.19)	−0.74***	(0.15)	−0.57***	(0.19)
N	979		972		1,003	
Pseudo R^2	0.41		0.26		0.44	
1997						
Valence	2.29***	(0.25)	1.6***	(0.12)	1.94***	(0.15)
Distance	−0.34**	(0.12)	−0.2**	(0.07)	−0.07	(0.09)
Intercept	−1.38***	(0.28)	−1.11***	(0.15)	−1.11***	(0.19)
N	484		988		705	
Pseudo R^2	0.4		0.26		0.36	
2004						
Valence	2.24***	(0.2)	2.39***	(0.17)	2.45***	(0.18)
Distance	−0.14	(0.09)	−0.07	(0.08)	−0.2	(0.11)
Intercept	−1.81***	(0.24)	−1.49***	(0.18)	−1.08***	(0.22)
N	708		801		759	
Pseudo R^2	0.37		0.41		0.46	
2008						
Valence	1.79***	(0.16)	1.91***	(0.15)	2.3***	(0.16)
Distance	−0.16	(0.1)	−0.28**	(0.09)	−0.27**	(0.1)
Intercept	−1.78***	(0.2)	−1.15***	(0.15)	−1.12***	(0.25)
N	819		830		839	
Pseudo R^2	0.26		0.31		0.51	
2011						
Valence	1.15***	(0.20)	1.47***	(0.20)	2.24***	(0.26)
Distance	−0.35**	(0.12)	−0.22	(0.12)	−0.46**	(0.14)
Intercept	−0.86***	(0.29)	−1.00***	(0.23)	−0.26	(0.34)
N	336		338		341	
Pseudo R^2	0.17		0.22		0.51	

$*p < .05, **p < .01, ***p < .001.$

FIGURE 9.2
Plotted predicted probabilities of voting for the NDP for various valence scores (top) and for values of objective distance to the NDP (bottom) in the 1984 federal election

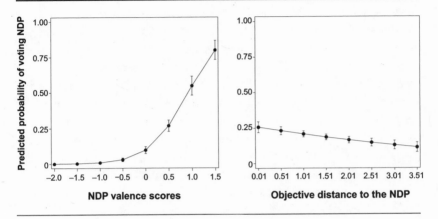

Party vote. In the election of 2004, the effect of distance is not statistically significant in any of the cases. In the 2008 election, the distance effect is not significant in the case of the NDP, but it is significant for the Liberals and Conservatives.

The voting patterns in the 2011 federal election in Canada were similar to those during the previous elections: the effects of valence and distance were present, were in the expected direction, and were statistically significant for all three major parties.

Discussion

The findings in this chapter suggest several conclusions with respect to electoral choice in federal politics in general and with respect to the relevance of policy and valence issues for the NDP in particular. First of all, contrary to Gidengil et al. (2012), the analyses suggest that a majority of Canadians can meaningfully use the left-right policy continuum to assess the parties. In particular, the results indicate that Canadians generally are able to place parties in the same order as does the Comparative Manifesto Project, which uses analyses of what parties actually promise the electorate in their election manifestos. The results also suggest that many Canadian voters appear to pay attention to the parties' positions on the left-right spectrum and, to some extent, consider the distance between their own ideological position and that of a party when deciding for whom to vote. Fitting with the spatial model explanation of voting behaviour, the results suggest the relevance of party positioning on the left-right spectrum.

However, the effect of policy distance on voting choice varies from one election to the next and is not always present for every party. For example, in the 2004 election, which was held shortly after the sponsorship scandal erupted (see Erickson and Laycock, Chapter 3, this volume), policy distance was not significant for any of the three parties. It seems that questions of corruption related to the incumbent government eclipsed the effects of people's assessments of their policy distance from the parties. It is interesting that voters apparently ignored their policy distance not only relative to the Liberal Party but also relative to the two other parties. Compared to the effects of policy distance, the impact on voting choice of the valence characteristics of parties and leaders is more consistent. Valence attitudes are generally formed via an emotional route (Zuwerink and Devine 1996) and are easily accessible to the voter. Since emotions play an important role in guiding human behaviour (Fazio, Powell, and Williams 1989, 154), they will often influence the voter's choice. At the same time, assessment of policy distance between one's own position and that of the parties perhaps requires more rigorous thinking. Moreover, when campaigns focus on leaders or are dominated by scandal (such as the sponsorship scandal of 2004), policy distance assessments may be crowded out and not be as readily accessible in the voter's mind. This is not to say that policy distance does not matter for voting behaviour in Canada – on the contrary, it matters in most elections – however, its effects are not as consistent as are those of the valence judgments. Valence plausibly offers a partial explanation of the changes in the NDP vote over the last two decades, given that leaders have changed from one election to another. In particular, the increase in NDP support, with the increasingly charismatic leadership of Jack Layton, indicates a valence effect (see also Bittner, Chapter 8, this volume). However, the results of 2011 also suggest a more complex situation in which policy distance was also a factor.

These 2011 results are interesting in the context of the 2008 results. Note that, in 2008, voter distance from the NDP on the left-right spectrum did not have a statistically significant effect on vote choice. Based on the assessments of the CES survey respondents, the NDP has been moving more towards the centre of the left-right spectrum (from 3.36 in 1997 to

3.42 in 2011, where 1 is furthest left and 10 is furthest right). In 2008, the party was actually located at 3.52. The difference in the results of 2008 and 2011 could be interpreted in the following way: in 2008 the NDP had not yet captured support from many of the voters that locate themselves around the centre-left of the left-right spectrum, although "technically" the party had moved closer to them, because many of these voters still lacked confidence in the party and its leader. However, by 2011, the NDP had managed to win the confidence of a larger proportion of the centre and centre-left voters and more of their votes went to the NDP. The data support this explanation: in 2008, only 20 percent of people who located themselves at 4 on the 10-point left-right scale voted for the NDP, and only 20.63 percent of those who located themselves at 5 did so. In 2011, both proportions of these groups of NDP voters had risen by one-third: 33.33 percent of those who located themselves at 4 and 32.45 percent of those who located themselves at 5 voted for the NDP. Accordingly, the shares of the Liberal Party dropped among these voters. This suggests that the Orange Crush of the 2011 federal election can be explained by the combination of the charismatic leader Jack Layton and the party's being able to attract Liberal voters because of its perceived move towards the centre of the left-right political spectrum in earlier elections. The perceived weakness and/or unattractiveness of the leader of the NDP's main competitor on the centre-left, the Liberal Party, may also help to explain the "valence advantage" that the NDP had over the Liberals in 2011.

This chapter also reveals a surprising negative result: there is no particular trend in the effects of valence and distance for the NDP compared to the other two major parties. In other words, the effects on the NDP are not consistently different from the effects on the other two parties. It appears that NDP voters use the same combination of rational calculations and valence perceptions to make their voting choice as do supporters of the other two main parties. The overall variation from one election to the next in the patterns of valence and distance effects on voting choice suggests that the balance of the two is influenced by the election campaign, the issues surrounding it, and the personalities of the party leaders. NDP voters seem to be affected by these factors as much as the voters for the other two main parties.

Notes

1 I have treated different parties as the "main" conservative party depending on their levels of popularity in a given election. In the 1984 election, it was the Progressive Conservative Party; in 1997, it was the Reform Party; and in 2004, 2008, and 2011, it was the Conservative Party.

2 These studies were conducted by Lambert et al. (1986), Blais et al. (1998), Gidengil et al. (2009), and Fournier et al. (2011).

3 The analyses were then clustered by individual in order to avoid bias due to the fact that observations are not independent from one another.

4 In the subsequent analysis of the effects of valence judgments I used the factor scores for each individual for every party and its leader as his or her valence judgment score for that party. In other words, in the end each respondent had a separate score measuring that individual's valence judgment for each party.

5 CMP data has been collected by Budge et al. (2001), Klingemann et al. (2006), and Volkens et al. (2012).

6 Because the CMP left-right scale ranges from -100 to 100 and does not match the metric of the CES scales, only the order of the parties is comparable, not the specific numbers. CES scales range from 1 to 7 (in the 1984 and 1997 elections) or 0 to 10 (in the 2004, 2008, and 2011 elections).

7 I have included only statistically significant cases in the calculation of the range and average values, $p < .05$.

References

Adams, James F., Samuel Merrill III, and Bernard Grofman. 2005. *A Unified Theory of Party Competition: A Cross-National Analysis Integrating Spatial and Behavioral Factors*. New York: Cambridge University Press.

Adams, James F., Samuel Merrill III, Elizabeth N. Simas, and Walter J. Stone. 2011. When Candidates Value Good Character: A Spatial Model with Applications to Congressional Elections. *Journal of Politics* 73, 1: 17-30.

Anderson, Cameron D., and Laura B. Stephenson. 2010. The Puzzle of Elections and Voting in Canada. In Cameron D. Anderson and Laura B. Stephenson, eds., *Voting Behaviour in Canada*, 1-42. Vancouver: UBC Press.

Bélanger, Éric. 2004. Antipartyism and Third-Party Vote Choice: A Comparison of Canada, Britain, and Australia. *Comparative Political Studies* 37, 9: 1054-78.

Bélanger, Éric, and Bonnie M. Meguid. 2008. Issue Salience, Issue Ownership, and Issue-Based Vote Choice. *Electoral Studies* 27, 3: 477-91.

Bittner, Amanda. 2010. Personality Matters: The Evaluation of Party Leaders in Canadian Elections. In Cameron D. Anderson and Laura. B. Stephenson, eds., *Voting Behaviour in Canada*, 183-210. Vancouver: UBC Press.

Blais, André, Elisabeth Gidengil, Richard Nadeau, and Neil Nevitte. 1998. The 1997 Canadian Election Survey. York University, Institute for Social Research (distributor), ICPSR 2593; Université de Montréal, Faculté des artes et des sciences, Département de science politique.

Brader, Ted. 2005. Striking a Responsive Chord: How Political Ads Motivate and Persuade Voters by Appealing to Emotions. *American Journal of Political Science* 49, 2: 388-405.

Budge, Ian, Hans-Dieter Klingemann, Andrea Volkens, Judith Bara, Eric Tanenbaum. 2001. *Mapping Policy Preferences: Estimates for Parties, Electors, and Governments 1945-1998*. Oxford: Oxford University Press.

Campbell, Angus, Philip E. Converse, Warren E. Miller, and Donald E. Stokes. 1980. *The American Voter*. Chicago: University of Chicago Press.

Clark, Michael. 2009. Valence and Electoral Outcomes in Western Europe, 1976-1998. *Electoral Studies* 28, 1: 111-22.

Clark, Michael, and Debra Leiter. 2013. Does the Ideological Dispersion of Parties Mediate the Electoral Impact of Valence? A Cross-National Study of Party Support in Nine Western European Democracies. *Comparative Political Studies*, June. doi: 10.1177/0010414013488537.

Clarke, Harold D., Allan Kornberg, Thomas J. Scotto, Jason Reifler, David Sanders, Marianne C. Stewart, and Paul Whiteley. 2011. Yes We Can! Valence Politics and Electoral Choice in America, 2008. *Electoral Studies* 30, 3: 450-61.

Clarke, Harold D., David Sanders, Marianne C. Stewart, and Paul F. Whiteley. 2009. *Performance Politics and the British Voter*. Cambridge: Cambridge University Press.

Clarke, Harold D., Thomas J. Scotto, and Allan Kornberg. 2011. Valence Politics and Economic Crisis: Electoral Choice in Canada 2008. *Electoral Studies* 30, 3: 438-49.

Downs, Anthony 1957. *Economic Theory of Democracy*. New York: Harper and Row.

Fazio, Russell H., Martha C. Powell, and Carol J. Williams. 1989. The Role of Attitude Accessibility in the Attitude-to-Behavior Process. *Journal of Consumer Research* 16, 3: 280-88.

Fournier, Patrick, Fred Cutler, Stuart Soroka, and Deitland Stolle. 2011. The 2011 Canadian Election Study. Dataset. http://ces-eec.org/pagesE/surveys.html.

Gidengil, Elisabeth, André Blais, Neil Nevitte, and Richard Nadeau. 2001. The Correlates and Consequences of Anti-Partyism in the 1997 Canadian Election. *Party Politics* 7, 4: 491-513.

Gidengil, Elisabeth, Joanna Everitt, Patrick Fournier, and Neil Nevitte. 2009. Canadian Election Study, 2004-08 panel dataset (computer file). Toronto: York University. Institute for Social Research (producer); Montréal: Université de Montréal, Canadian Election Study (distributor).

Gidengil, Elisabeth, Neil Nevitte, André Blais, Joanna Everitt, and Patrick Fournier. 2012. *Dominance and Decline: Making Sense of Recent Canadian Elections*. Toronto: University of Toronto Press.

Green, Jane. 2007. When Voters and Parties Agree: Valence Issues and Party Competition. *Political Studies* 55, 3: 629-55.

Green, Jane, and Sara B. Hobolt. 2008. Owning the Issue Agenda: Party Strategies and Vote Choices in British Elections. *Electoral Studies* 27, 3: 460-76.

Green, Jane, and Will Jennings. 2012. The Dynamics of Issue Competence and Vote for Parties In and Out of Power: An Analysis of Valence in Britain, 1979-1997. *European Journal of Political Research* 51, 4: 469-503.

Johnston, Richard, Patrick Fournier, and Richard Jenkins. 2000. Party Location and Party Support: Unpacking Competing Models. *Journal of Politics* 62, 4: 1145-60.

Johnston, Richard and Charles Pattie. 2011. Tactical voting at the 2010 British General Election: Rational Behaviour in Local Contexts? *Environment and Planning* 43, 6: 1323-40.

Kanji, Mebs, and Keith Archer. 2002. Theories of Voting and Their Applicability in Canada. In Joanna Everitt and Brenda O'Neill, eds., *Citizen Politics: Research and Theory in Canadian Political Behaviour,* 160-84. Toronto: Oxford University Press.

Klingemann, Hans-Dieter, Andrea Volkens, Judith Bara, Ian Budge, and Michael McDonald. 2006. *Mapping Policy Preferences II: Estimates for Parties, Electors, and Governments in Eastern Europe, the European Union and the OECD, 1990-2003.* Oxford: Oxford University Press.

Lambert, Ronald D., Steven D. Brown, James E. Curtis, Barry J. Kay, John M. Wilson. 1986. The 1984 Canadian Election Study. Dataset. http://www.queensu.ca/cora/_files/_CES/ces1984.dta.zip.

McDonald, Michael D., Silvia M. Mendes, and Myunghee Kim. 2007. Cross-Temporal and Cross-National Comparisons of Party Left-Right Positions. *Electoral Studies* 26, 1: 62-75.

Merrill, Samuel, III, Bernard Grofman, and James Adams. 2001. Assimilation and Contrast Effects in Voter Projections of Party Locations: Evidence from Norway, France, and the USA. *European Journal of Political Research* 40, 2: 199-221.

Pardos-Prado, Sergi. 2012. Valence beyond Consensus: Party Competence and Policy Dispersion from a Comparative Perspective. *Electoral Studies* 31, 2: 342-52.

Popkin, Samuel L. 1991. *The Reasoning Voter: Communication and Persuasion in Presidential Campaigns.* Chicago: University of Chicago Press.

Rahn, Wendy M. 2000. Affect as Information: The Role of Public Mood in Political Reasoning. In Arthur Lupia, Mathew D. McCubbins, and Samuel L. Popkin, eds., *Elements of Reason: Cognition, Choice, and the Bounds of Rationality,* 130-52. Cambridge, UK: Cambridge University Press.

Sanders, David, Harold D. Clarke, Marianne C. Stewart, and Paul Whiteley. 2011. Downs, Stokes and the Dynamics of Electoral Choice. *British Journal of Political Science* 4, 2: 287-314.

Scotto, Thomas J., Laura B. Stephenson, and Allan Kornberg. 2004. From a Two-Party-Plus to a One-Party-Plus? Ideology, Vote Choice, and Prospects for a Competitive Party System in Canada. *Electoral Studies* 23, 3: 463-83.

Sniderman, Paul M., Richard A. Brody, and Phillip E. Tetlock. 1991. *Reasoning and Choice: Explorations in Political Psychology.* Cambridge, UK: Cambridge University Press.

Stokes, Donald E. 1963. Spatial Models of Party Competition. *American Political Science Review* 57, 2: 368-77.

Stone, Walter J., and Elizabeth N. Simas. 2010. Candidate Valence and Ideological Positions in US House Elections. *American Journal of Political Science* 54, 2: 371-88.

Volkens, Andrea, Onawa Lacewell, Pola Lehmann, Sven Regel, Henrike Schultze, and Annika Werner. 2012. *The Manifesto Data Collection: Manifesto Project (MRG/CMP/MARPOR).* Berlin: Wissenschaftszentrum Berlin für Sozialforschung.

Warwick, Paul V. 2010. Bilateralism or the Median Mandate? An Examination of Rival Perspectives on Democratic Governance. *European Journal of Political Research* 49: 1-24.

Zuwerink, Julia R., and Patricia G. Devine. 1996. Attitude Importance and Resistance to Persuasion: It's Not Just the Thought That Counts. *Journal of Personality and Social Psychology* 70, 5: 931-44.

10

The Issue Priorities of NDP Supporters

How Different Are They?

MARK PICKUP and COLIN WHELAN

In this chapter, we examine the dynamics of the issue priorities of those who compose the electoral base of the federal NDP and compare them to the dynamics of the issue priorities of the bases of other Canadian federal parties. We do so in order to explore whether the issue priorities of the electoral constituency from which the NDP derives its support differs from those of the other parties' electoral constituencies. If so, how substantial are these differences? And in what ways do they differ? In some cases, differences in issue importance might be a matter of degree, in which case when an issue shifts in importance the shift is similar for all Canadians. But there may be some issues that set the NDP base apart from the bases of other partisans. If this is the case, the dynamics of the importance of key NDP issues for the NDP base would be independent of the dynamics of the importance of these issues for other partisans.

We examine the dynamics of the importance that the base of each national party has placed on eight key issues since the first session of the 27th Parliament (1966) up until the end of the prorogation of the 2nd session of the 40th Parliament (2009). We find for some issues that there is much common movement in issue priorities across the bases of the different parties. This is as expected (Wlezien 2005) and reflects the changing salience of these issues to Canadians over time.

We also find distinct differences in the issue priorities of the bases of the different parties. These differences have been growing over time, particularly since the emergence of the Reform Party in the 35th Parliament. On issues such as social welfare, the environment, health, and foreign trade, the NDP base increasingly places a distinctly greater importance than do the bases of other parties. On tax policy and reform, the NDP base places a distinctly lower importance, both in comparison to its views on other issues and in comparison to the bases of other parties.

Potential Implications of Distinct Issue Priorities

The question of whether issue priorities separate the NDP base from the bases of other parties has important implications for issues pertaining to party and electoral politics in Canada. It also has potential implications for public policy. The relative distinctness of different parties' bases will affect how those parties conduct election campaigns and what policy proposals they highlight. If the NDP base gives greater priority to a particular issue than do other party bases, then the party is in a position to potentially benefit from being seen to own that issue. Being associated with particular issues gives parties opportunities to expand their vote share if they can make them more salient for potential supporters. Understanding the issues that party supporters think are most important also helps us to understand the prospects for party mergers. Furthermore, it helps us understand the types of policies a party would be likely to pursue if it were to form the government.

The extent to which a party's base is distinct in what issues it views as priorities places the party in a position to benefit from an emphasis on corresponding policies. It is well established that voters see certain parties as owning particular issues and that these opinions inform vote choice, both in other countries (Clarke et al. 2004; Green 2007; Green and Hobolt 2008; Green and Jennings 2012) and in Canada (Johnston et al. 1992; Bélanger 2003; Clarke, Scotto, and Kornberg 2011). Significantly, however, this effect is moderated by the extent to which voters prioritize these issues (Fournier et al. 2003; Van der Brug 2004; Bélanger and Meguid 2008). In other words, issue ownership matters only insofar as supporters, or potential supporters, see the issue as important. Thus, in understanding vote choice, it is important to understand not only the dynamics of issue ownership but also the partisan dynamics of issue priorities. In this chapter, we shed light on the latter.

The incentive to prioritize and thereby own an issue has implications for how the NDP (and the other parties) conducts itself during an election campaign. If a party is identified with certain key issues, it has an incentive to frame the election in terms of those issues (Petrocik 1996; Soroka 2002;

Petrocik, William, and Hansen 2003). Specifically, it will want to influence the agenda of the election campaign so as to reflect those issues on which it has established itself as the leader.[1]

The distinct issue priorities of different parties' bases also have implications for possible party mergers, as discussed by Godbout, Bélanger, and Mérand (Chapter 11, this volume) and by Weldon (Chapter 12, this volume). If the bases of two parties are largely in agreement on issue priorities, there is a greater chance that the two could successfully merge than there would be if there was no such agreement. In their analysis of the Progressive Conservative Party/Canadian Alliance merger, Bélanger and Godbout (2010) draw on Harmel and Janda's (1994) framework to identify the factors that motivate political parties to implement organizational change. Bélanger and Godbout argue that, in the Canadian system, there may be two such motivations: vote seeking and policy seeking. Though traditional analysis of party politics tends to assume that politicians themselves are vote maximizers (Duverger 1954; Downs 1957; May 1973; Cox 1997), any decision to merge would require approval of each party's membership. Party members in general will be less sold on the potential of increasing vote share through a merger if it produces a party that will not prioritize and address the issues they care about. This means that the degree of similarity between issues that the two parties' supporters care about will be an important consideration in any merger decision.

Finally, the priorities of a party's base, relative to other party bases, tell us something about the policies a party would implement if it formed the government. It is generally established that parties largely pursue the policies preferred by the median voter (Downs 1957; Powell 2000; Soroka and Wlezien 2010). To the extent that this is the case, it is the issue priorities of all (or at least a majority) that inform public policy. However, for strategic, ideological, or policy-seeking reasons, parties may also/instead respond to a narrower group of interests, such as their partisan base (see Cox 1997; Persson and Tabellini 2004). Party supporters offer scarce resources, such as active campaign participation and party donations, that the governing party leadership may be dependent upon (see, for example, Kitschelt 1988; Miller and Schofield 2003; Panebianco 1989). Moreover, the preferences of the partisan base are likely to reflect a party's policy objectives more accurately than is the average voter. To the extent that this is the case, it is necessary to know the distinctiveness of the party base's issue priorities in order to understand which issues the party will be motivated to pursue if it forms the government (Pickup, Hobolt, and Whelan 2013).

The remainder of this chapter proceeds as follows. In the next section, we describe how we operationalized the concepts of issue priority and party base, and then outline the data used in our analysis. The following section describes the method of analysis we utilized in estimating the dynamics of the issue priorities of the base for each of the national parties of Canada. This is followed by a section outlining the results of our analysis. We conclude with some comments regarding the implications of our findings.

Definitions and Data

To examine the issue priorities of Canadian parties' electoral bases, we collected Canadian public opinion data from 1965 to 2009. We use the individual-level responses to fourteen Canadian election studies and eighty-five commercial polls from Gallup and Environics.[2] These data allow us to explore, over an extended period of time, the issue priorities of the party base for each of the Canadian national parties: the New Democratic Party, the Liberal Party of Canada, the Progressive Conservative Party of Canada, and the Reform Party/Canadian Alliance/Conservative Party of Canada.[3]

We define party base as each party's core constituents. By this we mean those Canadians who, by virtue of their socio-demographic characteristics, are most likely to vote for that party. This definition is chosen because we cannot simply use the opinions of those who, in each survey, indicate they would vote for the party. Using a party's voters as its core constiutuency is problematic because, as a party becomes more/less popular over time, more/fewer individuals will indicate they will vote for it. This will result in a change in the opinions of this group, not necessarily because any individual changed his or her opinion, but simply because the composition of the group has changed. The method we use to identify core constituents and their issue priorities is described more fully in the next section.

To determine the issue priorities of each party's base, we look at responses to what is known as the most important problem/issue question. These are (usually) open-ended questions such as: "What do you think is the most important issue/problem facing Canada today?" Some variant of this question was consistently included in polls and the election studies throughout the period of our analysis. Significantly, it provides a measure of issue salience relative to all other issues as each respondent can only provide one answer.

Some part of the over-time changes in responses to this question likely reflects the changing salience of an issue in the nation as a whole (Wlezien 2005). However, to the extent that there are differences between the bases of different parties, these differences reflect differences in priorities. Many of the issues commonly identified by respondents clearly relate to a set of policies. For example, "the environment" as an issue relates to a particular set of governmental policies. These might include carbon pricing, environ- mental assessment regimes, or regulations on pollutants, to note a few examples. Therefore, the extent to which the NDP base identifies the en- vironment as the most important problem more often than do the bases of other parties reflects, in large part, the differing policy priorities of typ- ical NDP supporters.

The issues included in the analysis are: social welfare; environment; health; inflation, prices, and interest rates; foreign trade; unemployment; national budget and debt; and taxation, tax policy, and tax reform. This set of issues reflects those that have come to be emphasized by the NDP base as well as those economic issues that a substantial portion of all Canadians commonly identified as the most important.

Method of Measuring Partisan Policy Priorities

We are interested in the opinions of the base of each party. There are a number of potential ways to define a party base in order to examine its issue priorities. As mentioned above, it is problematic simply to use vote intention because the group expressing such an intention can change in composition from poll to poll. We are seeking to identify the opinions of the consistent base of party supporters.

To a lesser extent, this same problem of composition applies to simply using the opinions of those who indicate they identify with each party in each poll. Given the current phenomenon of partisan dealignment (Dalton and Wattenberg 2002; LeDuc 2007; Weldon, Chapter 12, this volume), the composition of party identifiers also changes over time with the popularity and fortunes of the parties. Partisan dealignment also means that the ex- tent to which party identifiers represent the typical base of supporters for the party has decreased over time.

To address these problems, we define the party base as the party's core constituents. The core constituents of a party are those with the demo- graphic characteristics that make them the most likely to support the party in an election. We start by measuring the demographics of a party's voters in a given Canadian election cycle, and we use those demographics to iden- tify its core constituents in each poll through to the following electoral cycle. For the first electoral cycle, we use the 1965 Canadian Election Study.[4]

An electoral cycle is defined as the period from one election to the next. The first electoral cycle in the period of study starts with the completion of the 1965 election and finishes with the 1968 election.

For every commercial poll within a single electoral cycle, the same set of demographic values is used for a given party. In other words, we hold the composition of each party's core constituents constant and then estimate the opinions of these core constituents for each party. For example, a poll conducted in the period between the 2000 and 2004 elections would use the demographics of the core constituents in the 2000 election. Because the values of the demographics used to produce the predictions remain the same throughout the electoral cycle, changes in the predicted opinions on issue priorities are due entirely to changes in the opinions of this demographic group. The method ensures that the changes cannot be due to a change in the composition of this group. At the beginning of a new electoral cycle, the demographics for each party are reassessed, based on the vote intentions of the respondents in the next election study. This allows for the real possibility that the composition of the core constituents for each party might change from one electoral cycle to the next.

To construct usable demographic profiles, we developed a coding scheme for the applicable demographic survey questions that is common between the CES and each commercial (Gallup/Environics) poll. This is done so that the same demographic variables from the election study that are used to define a party's core constituents (the party base) can then be used to predict the opinions of the party base using the commercial polls. The variables and the common coding scheme used for each electoral cycle are outlined in the web appendix (see https://circle.ubc.ca/handle/2429/641). The demographic variables used include age, income, education, province, gender, union membership, community size, language, occupation, and employment status. These demographic profiles would tell us, for example, what percentage of NDP voters were from each province, what percentage were female, or what an NDP voter's average income was for that electoral cycle. To measure these core constituents' changing opinions over time, the "most important problem" question in each poll was recoded into a series of dummy variables, each indicating whether or not a particular problem was identified as the most important by a given survey respondent. A dummy variable is a variable that takes either a value of 0 or a value of 1. For example, a social welfare dummy variable was created so that, if some respondent indicated that social welfare was the most important problem facing the country, he or she would have a value of 1 for the social welfare dummy variable and 0 for every other problem mentioned. Because a dummy variable only takes on one of two values (0 or 1), it is also called a binary variable.

For every commercial poll, each of the dummy variables was regressed on the set of demographic variables in the poll using a penalized logit regression model. A logit model is a regression that predicts a binary outcome. The penalized logit is used to correct for separation, which occurs when the value of the dependent variable is perfectly predicted for a range of one or more of the independent variables. This is a problem because, for many of the most important problem responses, there were few survey respondents giving that answer. For example, if only individuals from Quebec in a survey listed bilingualism as their number one issue, the dependent variable (mentioned bilingualism as the number one issue) would be 0 for *all* cases from outside Quebec. Therefore, a regression that included Quebec as one of the independent variables would have to be estimated with a penalized logit.[5]

The equation estimated in a logit model predicts the probability that a respondent with a given set of values on the demographic covariates will list the given problem as most important. Thus, the estimation of the penalized logits for each commercial poll gives us models that allow us to predict the proportion of respondents, with a particular demographic profile, who identify a particular issue as the most important facing Canada.

Using the prediction equations for a commercial poll from a particular electoral cycle, we plug in the demographic characteristics of a core NDP constituent. As described above, these characteristics were calculated using the election study preceding the electoral cycle. This gives us an estimate (a point estimate and a standard error) of the proportion of typical NDP constituents (i.e., the party base) that identify each issue as the most important problem at the time the commercial poll was conducted in the electoral cycle. Again, for example, this gives us an estimate of the proportion of core NDP constituents that indicated social welfare as the most important problem facing the country. This was done for each commercial poll during the electoral cycle, so we have an estimate of the proportion of core NDP constituents that would indicate a particular issue as the most important problem facing Canada at each point throughout the cycle that a commercial poll was conducted. We also applied this procedure using the values of the demographic variables for a typical Conservative constituent[6] and a typical Liberal constituent.

To sum up, the process can be thought of in three steps: (1) we identify the demographics of the party base; (2) for each issue in each poll in that cycle, we determine how demographics predict whether a respondent thinks that issue is the most important; and (3) we then apply the demographic profiles from the CES to each issue in each poll to obtain estimates – for each party, each issue, and each poll – of what proportion of the party base thinks that issue is the most important problem facing Canada.

We repeated our procedure for each electoral cycle, with the result that we have an estimate of the proportion of each party's base that is predicted to indicate each issue as the most important at various points in time (niney-nine different months) over the forty-four-year period. In other words, for each party and each issue we have a time series. As we did not have polls for every month in this time period, we have a monthly time series with missing values. We apply to these time series what is known as a filter to reduce the random error inherent in such predictions and to fill in missing values. The filtering algorithm is essentially the same as a sound engineer might use to reduce the "noise" and to impute the missing information in a radio signal with a lot of static and gaps.[7]

We then use our "cleaned up" values to produce averages for each parliamentary session – thirty-two in total. For our eight key issues, this gives us the average proportion of each national party's base that identified that issue as the most important during each parliamentary session from 1966 to 2009.

Results

To determine whether our estimates of the proportion of each party base that identified each of the eight key issues as the most important indicates any differences in issue priorities across the national federal parties, we plot our results. Each of the eight key issues is plotted separately.

For two of the issues, the movement over time is nearly identical for the bases of all parties. These issues are: inflation, prices and interest rates, and unemployment. This suggests that the importance of these issues is largely driven by their salience at any given point in time. Given the established connection between economic conditions and public opinion in Canada (Erickson 1988; Johnston 1999), the salience of these issues is likely driven by objective economic conditions – inflation and unemployment rates.

For social welfare and the environment, there is certainly common over-time movement for each party's base. However, since the emergence of the Reform Party, there are distinct differences between the bases of each party.

FIGURE 10.1

Issue priorities of Canadian parties, 1966-2009

Parliamentary session	Start date	End date	Governing party	Prime minister
27.1	1966.01.18	1967.05.08	Liberal	Lester B. Pearson
27.2	1967.05.08	1968.04.23	Liberal	Lester B. Pearson/ Pierre Trudeau
28.1	1968.09.12	1969.10.22	Liberal	Pierre Trudeau
28.2	1969.10.23	1970.10.07	Liberal	Pierre Trudeau
28.3	1970.10.08	1972.02.16	Liberal	Pierre Trudeau
28.4	1972.02.17	1972.09.01	Liberal	Pierre Trudeau
29.1	1973.01.04	1974.02.26	Liberal	Pierre Trudeau
29.2	1974.02.27	1974.05.09	Liberal	Pierre Trudeau
30.1	1974.09.30	1976.10.12	Liberal	Pierre Trudeau
30.2	1976.10.12	1977.10.17	Liberal	Pierre Trudeau
30.3	1977.10.18	1978.10.10	Liberal	Pierre Trudeau
30.4	1978.10.11	1979.03.26	Liberal	Pierre Trudeau
31.1	1979.10.09	1979.12.14	Progressive Conservative	Joe Clark
32.1	1980.04.14	1983.11.30	Liberal	Pierre Trudeau
32.2	1983.12.07	1984.07.09	Liberal	Pierre Trudeau/ John Turner
33.1	1984.11.05	1986.08.28	Progressive Conservative	Brian Mulroney
33.2	1986.09.30	1988.10.01	Progressive Conservative	Brian Mulroney
34.1	1988.12.12	1989.02.28	Progressive Conservative	Brian Mulroney
34.2	1989.04.03	1991.05.12	Progressive Conservative	Brian Mulroney
34.3	1991.05.13	1993.09.08	Progressive Conservative	Brian Mulroney/ Kim Campbell
35.1	1994.01.17	1996.02.02	Liberal	Jean Chrétien
35.2	1996.02.27	1997.04.27	Liberal	Jean Chrétien
36.1	1997.09.22	1999.09.18	Liberal	Jean Chrétien
36.2	1999.10.12	2000.10.22	Liberal	Jean Chrétien
37.1	2001.01.29	2002.09.16	Liberal	Jean Chrétien
37.2	2002.09.30	2003.11.12	Liberal	Jean Chrétien
37.3	2004.02.02	2004.05.23	Liberal	Paul Martin
38.1	2004.10.04	2005.11.29	Liberal	Paul Martin
39.1	2006.04.03	2007.09.14	Conservative	Stephen Harper
39.2	2007.10.16	2008.09.07	Conservative	Stephen Harper
40.1	2008.11.18	2008.12.04	Conservative	Stephen Harper
40.2	2009.01.26	2009.12.30	Conservative	Stephen Harper

▶

ISSUE: Inflation, prices, and interest rates

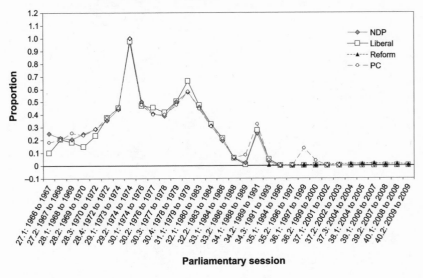

Parliamentary session

ISSUE: Unemployment

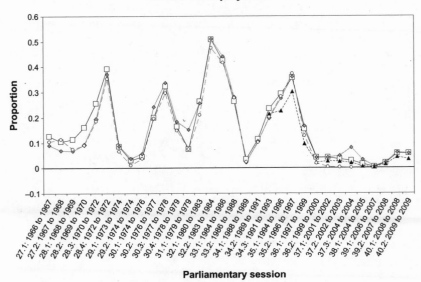

Parliamentary session

ISSUE: Social welfare

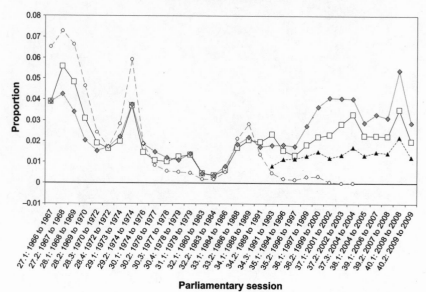

Parliamentary session

ISSUE: The environment

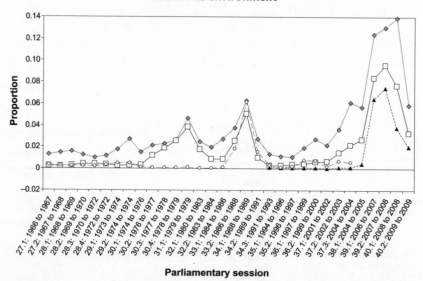

Parliamentary session

- ◆ NDP
- □ Liberal
- ▲ Reform
- ○ PC

ISSUE: Health

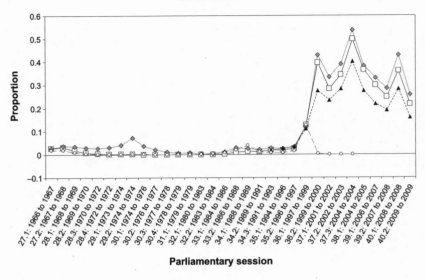

Parliamentary session

ISSUE: Foreign trade

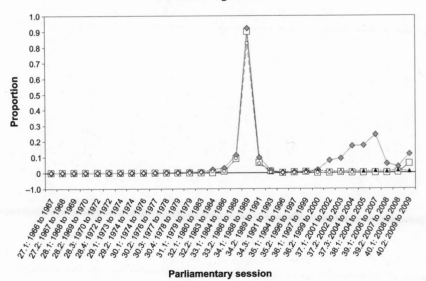

Parliamentary session

—◆— NDP
—□— Liberal
---▲--- Reform
— ○ — PC

248

ISSUE: Taxation, tax policy, and tax reform

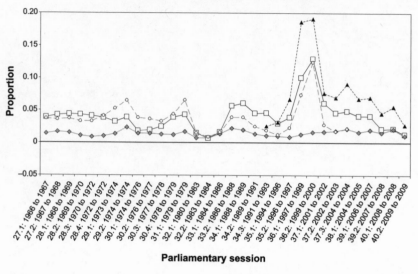

Parliamentary session

ISSUE: National budget and debt

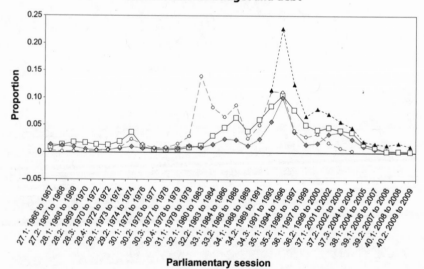

Parliamentary session

—◆— NDP
—□— Liberal
----▲---- Reform
— ○ — PC

These issues are clearly more of a priority for the NDP base relative to the Liberal Party base and even more so relative to the Conservative Party base. In these regards, the issue of health is similar to that of social welfare and that of the environment, but the differences are less distinct.

Prior to the Free Trade Agreement, foreign trade was not much of an issue for the base of any party. During the debate over the FTA, foreign trade became about equally salient for all party bases before disappearing as an issue. However, since the 36th Parliament (September 1997 to October 2000), foreign trade has become a distinct issue priority for the NDP base relative to that of any other party. This probably reflects the rise of foreign trade as an issue that taps into the growing concern within the NDP over increased globalization. This concern has also been expressed in party platforms and leaders' statements in Parliament (see Laycock, Chapter 5, this volume; Pétry, Chapter 6, this volume).

The NDP base is also distinct from the base of any other party on the issue of taxation, tax policy, and tax reform. In this case, though, the distinction is that this is clearly *not* an issue priority for the NDP base,[8] while it is for the constituents of other parties. This is true even when it is a very important issue for the bases of all other parties – in particular, the base of the Conservative Party. Bear in mind that such a finding does not require the NDP base to consider that tax issues have no importance. It simply means that, relative to the other parties, NDP constituents are much less likely to consider it the *most important* issue facing the country. On the issue of national budget and debt, it is the PC and Reform Party bases that have been distinct (at different points in time) from the bases of other parties by placing a particular emphasis on this issue.

Generally, the dynamics of the issue priorities of each party base reveal important differences between the parties. It is notable that these issue priority differences have become much stronger (and in some cases have only existed) since the emergence of the Reform Party.

The issues on which the NDP base distinguishes itself, by identifying them as distinctly important, reflect differences in the policy preferences of such individuals. The NDP base is distinct in the priority it places on social welfare, the environment, health, and foreign trade. It is also distinct in the low priority it places on tax policy and tax reform.

Conclusion

This chapter examines the dynamics of the issue priorities of the federal NDP base and compares them to the dynamics of the issue priorities of the bases of other Canadian federal parties. We find that most issue priorities are affected by the salience of an issue during a given period of time. When issues such as inflation, prices and interest rates, and unemployment become important, they become important for all Canadians. This is also true for issues such as social welfare, the environment, and health, but, as of late, the NDP base distinguishes itself in consistently placing a greater emphasis on these issues than do the bases of other parties. On other issues, the NDP base is even more distinct. The dynamics of the importance of foreign trade and the lesser importance of tax policy and tax reform as issues for the NDP base are distinct from those of the bases of other parties. Again, this has become more evident in recent years.

In terms of the implications of these findings, it is on issues of social welfare, the environment, health, and foreign trade that the federal NDP is now in a position to distinguish itself. The party is in a good position to take the lead on these issues both in Parliament and during election campaigns, thus "owning" these issues more than it has in the past. If the party is successful in doing this, to the extent that Canadians come to see these issues as priorities, the NDP can benefit electorally.

Using CES data, Weldon (Chapter 12, this volume) finds that, in the 2011 federal election, the levels of expressed importance of issues for vote choice were broadly similar on key issues among Liberal, Green, and NDP voters. The starker differences were between those voters and Conservative voters. This suggests that there is a basis for voters from these parties to converge towards one option. However, this result runs against the grain of our findings here. The methodological difference is significant, though. We seek to measure the proportion of each party base that lists an issue as the most important. In our data, a respondent can only list a single issue as the most important, but he or she can list any issue he or she wishes.[9] In the data used by Weldon, respondents can rate the importance of a fixed set of issues. Rather than measuring how important an issue is to an individual member of a party's base, our measure captures whether it is a top priority for a significant portion of the party base – that is to say, its relative importance over other possible considerations. Another important methodological distinction is that we are examining issue priorities over a forty-four-year period, ending in 2009, while Weldon examines issue priorities in the 2011 election. By our measure, we do find increasing divergence of party bases over time, as each party base prioritizes the political landscape in increasingly different ways.

This (increasing) divergence across the bases of the national parties also has implications for the types of policies an NDP government (or maybe even a government with the NDP as a coalition partner) would likely pursue. Such a government might place greater emphasis on social welfare, the environment, health, and foreign trade (as an issue of globalization) than might a Liberal or a Conservative government. It might also be expected to place relatively less emphasis on tax policy and reform.

Looking to the future, it is useful to note the issues that Canadians as a whole identify as most important. To get a sense of current public opinion, we can examine the responses to the monthly Nanos (2012) poll question, covering the period from January 2007 to September 2012: "What is your most important NATIONAL issue of concern?" Prior to September 2008, health care and the environment usually topped the list of most important issues. Since that point in time, jobs and health care have been trading positions as first and second on the list.

Employment is not an issue with which the NDP can easily identify itself. The party and its base may differ from other parties regarding how to increase employment, but the bases of all parties agree equally on the issue's importance. The environment, on the other hand, is an issue on which the NDP has a distinct advantage. The NDP base has consistently identified this issue as more important than have the bases of other parties. Health care falls somewhere between employment and the environment. The NDP base has recently identified health care as more important than have other party bases but not to the same degree as the environment.

As long as the economy, in particular jobs, dominates the federal political agenda, the NDP will be at a disadvantage. Canadians are relatively homogenous in the degree to which they view this issue as important, and the NDP is not in a strong position with regard to it. Having never formed government at the national level, the NDP also does not have a record of achievement to which it can point.[10] If/when the economy improves and issues such as health and the environment again top the political agenda, the NDP will be in an advantageous position to take the lead on these issues and, potentially, may even be seen as the party best suited to address them.

Notes

1 Exogenous shocks to the salience of issues in campaigns can also help or hurt the prospects of parties associated with those issues. Clarke, Scotto, and Kornberg (2011) find this to be the case in the 2008 Canadian election, in which the sudden

salience of economic issues generated by the financial crisis benefitted the Conservatives at the expense of the Liberals. For a further discussion of the short-term factors influencing party choice, see Zakharova, Chapter 9, this volume.

2 The analysis in this chapter is based, in part, on Environics Institute Survey Research Microdata files, which contain anonymized data collected in the Focus Canada 2010 study. All computations performed on these microdata were prepared by Mark Pickup and Colin Whelan, and the responsibility for their interpretation is entirely that of the authors. Gallup data files were obtained through the Canadian Opinion Research Archive, Queen's University (available at http://www.queensu.ca/cora/).

3 Because the Bloc Québécois is restricted to Quebec, most national surveys do not have sufficient numbers to conduct the analysis we propose.

4 Investigators: Philip Converse, John Meisel, Maurice Pinard, Peter Regenstreif, and Mildred Schwartz.

5 Penalized logits are problematic to evaluate with standard goodness of fit measures, so to evaluate the prediction accuracy of the penalized logit, we estimate ROC curves for each logit run. Overall, the penalized logits perform well. The standard statistic used to assess ROC curves is the area under the curve, ranging from 0.5 (equivalent to chance alone) to 1 (perfect prediction). The mean for all issues over all surveys was 0.762, which is a moderately strong ROC value. Some individual issues had quite strong ROC values: trade at an average of 0.883 and welfare at an average of 0.842. The weakest predictions were for unemployment at an average of 0.700. The standard errors are in all cases reasonably small and do not introduce a great deal of uncertainty into the estimates of the curves. The web appendix includes a complete table of summary statistics for the ROC curves. Note, however, that despite the similar 0-1 scale, interpretation of this statistic is not comparable to interpretation of a typical R^2 measure.

6 Prior to the 1993 election, this means Progressive Conservatives. After 1993, we model PC constituents and Reform constituents separately. After 2000, the new Conservative Party is treated as a continuation of Reform.

7 The estimates and their standard errors were input into a Bayesian Kalman filter (Green, Gerber, and De Boef 1999; Jackman 2009, chap. 9) to produce a smoothed time series that both reduced the uncertainty in the estimates and interpolated values for the months without estimates. Interpolation estimates values of the time series for months that we do not have a poll, using the poll information from months preceding and following the months without polls. In this interpolation procedure, the standard error of the estimates from each Gallup/Environics/CES poll is used to indicate our confidence in the estimate. This means that estimates with large standard errors have little to no effect on the final interpolated time series values, while estimates with small standard errors have the greatest effect. We also have a temporal overlap between Gallup and Environics polls, which we can use to estimate and control for systematic (constant) differences in polls from the two firms.

8 It is worth noting that "fair tax" reform has been a theme – albeit not the top priority – in NDP platforms since the 1960s. See Laycock, Chapter 5, this volume.

9 The issues named by the respondents are subsequently recoded into a smaller number of categories.

10 However, it can point to the achievements of provincial NDP governments on such issues.

References

Bélanger, Éric. 2003. Issue Ownership by Canadian Political Parties, 1953-2001. *Canadian Journal of Political Science/Revue canadienne de science politique* 36, 3: 539-58.

Bélanger, Éric, and Jean-François Godbout. 2010. Why Do Parties Merge? The Case of the Conservative Party of Canada. *Parliamentary Affairs* 63, 1: 41-65.

Bélanger, Éric, and Bonnie M. Meguid. 2008. Issue Salience, Issue Ownership, and Issue-Based Vote Choice. *Electoral Studies* 27, 3: 477-91.

Clarke, Harold D., David Sanders, Marianne C. Stewart, and Paul Whiteley. 2004. *Political Choice in Britain*. Oxford: Oxford University Press.

Clarke, Harold D., Thomas J. Scotto, and Allan Kornberg. 2011. Valence Politics and Economic Crisis: Electoral Choice in Canada 2008. *Electoral Studies* 30, 3: 438-49.

Cox, Gary W. 1997. *Making Votes Count: Strategic Coordination in the World's Electoral Systems*. New York: Cambridge University Press.

Dalton, Russell J., and Martin P. Wattenberg. 2002. *Parties without Partisans: Political Change in Advanced Industrial Democracies*. New York: Oxford University Press.

Downs, Anthony. 1957. *An Economic Theory of Democracy*. New York: Prentice Hall.

Duverger, Maurice. 1954. *Political Parties: Their Organization and Activity in the Modern State*. New York: Wiley.

Erickson, Lynda. 1988. CCF-NDP Popularity and the Economy. *Canadian Journal of Political Science* 21, 1: 99-116.

Fournier, Patrick, André Blais, Richard Nadeau, Elisabeth Gidengil, and Neil Nevitte. 2003. Issue Importance and Performance Voting. *Political Behavior* 25: 51-67.

Green, Donald P., Alan S. Gerber, and Suzanna L. De Boef. 1999. Tracking Opinion over Time: A Method for Reducing Sampling Error. *Public Opinion Quarterly* 63, 2: 178-92.

Green, Jane. 2007. When Voters and Parties Agree: Valence Issues and Party Competition. *Political Studies* 55, 3: 629-55.

Green, Jane, and Sara B. Hobolt. 2008. Owning the Issue Agenda: Party Strategies and Vote Choices in British Elections. *Electoral Studies* 27, 3: 460-76.

Green, Jane, and Will Jennings. 2012. Issue Competence and Vote Choice for Parties in and Out of Power: An Analysis of Valence in Britain, 1979-1997. *European Journal of Political Research* 41, 4: 469-503.

Harmel, Robert, and Kenneth Janda. 1994. An Integrated Theory of Party Goals and Party Change. *Journal of Theoretical Politics* 6, 3: 259-87.

Jackman, Simon 2009. *Bayesian Analysis for the Social Sciences*. London: John Wiley and Sons.

Johnston, Richard. 1999. Business Cycles, Political Cycles and the Popularity of Canadian Governments, 1974-1998. *Canadian Journal of Political Science* 32, 3: 499-520.

Johnston, Richard, André Blais, Henry E. Brady, and Jean Crête. 1992. *Letting the People Decide: Dynamics of a Canadian Election.* Montreal: McGill-Queen's University Press.

Kitschelt, Herbert. 1988. Organization and Strategy of Belgian and West German Ecology Parties: A New Dynamic of Party Politics in Western Europe? *Comparative Politics* 20, 2: 127-54.

LeDuc, Lawrence. 2007. Realignment and Dealignment in Canadian Federal Politics: Canadian Parties in Transition. In Alain-G. Gagnon and A. Brian Tanguay, eds., *Canadian Parties in Transition,* 3rd ed., 163-78. Peterborough, ON: Broadview.

May, John D. 1973. Opinion Structure of Political Parties: The Special Law of Curvilinear Disparity. *Political Studies* 21, 2: 135-51.

Miller, Gary, and Norman Schofield. 2003. Activists and Partisan Realignment in the United States. *American Political Science Review* 97, 2: 245-60.

Nanos Research. 2012. National Issue: Jobs up as Top National Issue of Concern, 17 September. http://www.nanosresearch.com.

Panebianco, Angelo. 1989. *Political Parties: Organization and Structure.* Cambridge, UK: Cambridge University Press.

Persson, Torsten, and Guido Tabellini. 2004. Constitutions and Economic Policy. *Journal of Economic Perspectives* 18, 1: 75-98.

Petrocik, John R. 1996. Issue Ownership in Presidential Elections, with a 1980 Case Study. *American Journal of Political Science* 40, 3: 825-50.

Petrocik, John R., William L. Benoit, and Glenn J. Hansen. 2003. Issue Ownership and Presidential Campaigning, 1952-2000. *Political Science Quarterly* 118, 4: 599-626.

Pickup, Mark, Sara Hobolt, and Colin Whelan. 2013. The Conditionality of Government Responsiveness: The Impact of Minority Status and Polls in the Canadian House of Commons. Paper presented at the 2013 meeting of the Canadian Political Science Association, Victoria, BC, 4-6 June.

Powell, G. Bingham. 2000. *Elections as Instruments of Democracy: Majoritarian and Proportional Visions.* New Haven: Yale University Press.

Soroka, Stuart N. 2002. *Agenda-Setting Dynamics in Canada.* Vancouver: UBC Press.

Soroka, Stuart N., and Christopher Wlezien. 2010. *Degrees of Democracy: Politics, Public Opinion, and Policy.* Cambridge, UK: Cambridge University Press.

van der Brug, Wouter. 2004. Issue Ownership and Party Choice. *Electoral Studies* 23, 2: 209-33.

Wlezien, Christopher. 2005. On the Salience of Political Issues: The Problem with "Most Important Problem." *Electoral Studies* 24: 555-79.

PART 4

NEW GAME, NEW PARTY?

11

Uniting the Left?

The Potential for an NDP-Liberal Party Merger

JEAN-FRANÇOIS GODBOUT, ÉRIC BÉLANGER, and FRÉDÉRIC MÉRAND

Since the 2 May 2011 federal election, there has been much talk about a merger between the New Democratic Party and the Liberal Party of Canada. Supporters of this option attribute the current electoral success of the Conservative Party to the joining of the forces of the right (the Canadian Alliance and the Progressive Conservative parties) in 2003. Since more than 60 percent of Canadians who participated in the last federal election did not vote Conservative, many believe that a merger of the centre and left parties would make the victory of a progressive party much more likely. Before becoming Liberal Party leader, Justin Trudeau publicly defended the idea (Bellavance 2012), although he has understandably been coy on this issue since then. Jean Chrétien has also been a supporter of this scenario. According to him, if the Liberals had merged with the Co-operative Commonwealth Federation (the predecessor of the NDP) back in 1956, "they would be in government today." The former prime minister added confidently: "It will happen some day."[1]

Some political parties have merged in recent years in different countries, most notably in the United Kingdom (Social Democrats and Liberals in 1988), South Korea (Democratic Justice Party, New Democratic Republican Party, and Reunification Democratic Party in 1990), France (creation of the right-of-centre UMP in 2002), the Netherlands (Protestant parties GPV and RPF in 2003), and Germany (*Die Linke*, created in 2007 by former Eastern Communists and a splinter faction from the Social Democrats).

While party fusion remains a rare event in consolidated democracies, it can occur under specific conditions (Mair 1990; Bélanger and Godbout 2010). First, a merger must necessarily unite parties (and voters) that share similar ideological positions. Second, these parties have to suffer from under-representation in the legislature, a situation that is more likely to occur in non-proportional electoral systems such as the Canadian single-member district plurality voting system. Third, parties are more likely to merge when the fusion will provide additional partisan supporters, votes, and financial contributions. Finally, and perhaps most important, a merger between two parties often arises from the perceived need by the two parties to create a new, more attractive political brand.

The most recent party merger in Canada, between the Canadian Alliance and Progressive Conservative parties in 2003, is a case in point. Both parties and their voters shared a common ideology on the right of the political spectrum. The Alliance and the PC were also underrepresented in the House of Commons. The former Reform Party – renamed the Canadian Alliance in 2000 – was perceived by many voters as too extreme, so a merger with the more moderate and established Progressive Conservative Party helped create a new political brand. For its part, the PC Party had some serious financial difficulties in the years leading up to the 2003 merger, so uniting with the Canadian Alliance was a question of survival. In short, then, all of the necessary conditions were present for a merger to occur between the PCs and the Canadian Alliance. But what about the NDP and the Liberals today? Should we also expect a merger between those two parties in the near future?

This chapter answers this question in three analytical steps. First, we look at the institutional pressures exerted on political parties by the Canadian electoral system. Current discussions about an NDP-Liberal merger take place against the backdrop of a recent consolidation of the Canadian party system around three main parties, only one of which sits on the right. While the single-member district plurality voting system favours the co-existence of two major parties, Canada is characterized by strong regional dynamics that complicate the prospects of a "liberal-democratic party." Second, we consider the hypothesis of an electoral realignment that would result from the creation of a new party. Turning to voter preferences, we evaluate whether, under present circumstances, counting on a realignment of the electorate along a dominant right-left dimension is a reasonable bet for "progressive" forces to make. We find that regional cleavages may create coordination problems for party leaders. Third, we analyze more closely the strategy of party leaders, especially in terms of resources and branding. We look at the experience of Canada's right wing to identify the factors that might encourage or hinder a merger of the New Democrats and the Liberals.

Our main conclusion is that, in the current electoral system, with stable voter preferences and from the point of view of party supporters, a merger between the two progressive parties is neither desirable nor likely. However, we think that the evolution towards a two-party system is possible in the long term, on the condition that an institutional reform increases the representation of regional interests, particularly those of Quebec, in Parliament.

Explaining the Multiparty System in Canada

We begin our analysis by reviewing the main theories put forward to explain the roots of Canada's multi-party system. Until the 1921 election, the Canadian political landscape was largely dominated by two major players, the Liberal and Conservative parties, which elected most MPs.[2] This all changed with the 14th Parliament when the Progressive Party won 59 seats in the House of Commons. Almost all of the Progressive members were from rural and western ridings, although the party also made important gains in Ontario. The election of Progressive members transformed the Canadian party system permanently. Not only did it precipitate the formation of the first minority government in Canadian history, but it also signalled the arrival of several important new parties in the political system. Parties like Alberta's Social Credit and the CCF became permanent fixtures in the House of Commons well into the 1960s. The party system consolidated somewhat with the creation of the NDP in 1961. However, the presence of the Social Credit in Alberta and later in Quebec, and the arrival of the Bloc Québécois and the Reform Party in the 1993 election, confirmed once again the high volatility of the Canadian party system (for a recent review, see Bélanger 2007).

The enduring presence of more than two parties in a simple-majority single-ballot system remains a puzzle for scholars of Canadian politics today. Duverger's Law predicts that, in this type of voting system, third parties will be marginalized because they will be unable to bring together at the local level the plurality of votes necessary to allow them to win at least more than a handful of seats. In each riding, there is a competition for the median voter, which favours the two dominant parties, whereas proportional systems allow a greater number of parties to get their candidates elected as MPs. According to Duverger (1951), the electoral system in

Canada should thus lead the House of Commons to be organized by only two major parties, as in the case of the US Congress.

Like all laws, Duverger's Law has exceptions. India, which also has a first-past-the-post electoral system, but where the vote is concentrated regionally, is perhaps the best-known example. The frequent presence of successful third parties at the federal level has led some scholars to consider Canada as another exception to Duverger's Law (see the discussion in Bélanger and Stephenson [2014]). There has also been an increase in the number of political parties in all democratic countries in recent years, including in those, like Canada, that have first-past-the-post electoral systems (Grofman, Blais, and Bowler 2009). So, while logical in theory, a merger may not always appear logical in practice.

In the most comprehensive study of Canada's unique party system to date, Gaines (1999) identifies several possible explanations for the failure of Duverger's Law in the Canadian context. He explains that conventional theory on strategic behaviour by party elites and by voters predicts that, under most circumstances, bipartisanship should hold at the local level (with single-member districts). This is explained by strategic voting on the part of voters and strategic withdrawals by politicians who want to minimize the opportunity costs of running campaigns.

In Canada, one could postulate that a two-party equilibrium exists at the level of constituencies. The presence of a multi-party system at the federal level would then be the consequence of regional disparities between the main competing parties – that is, local electoral contests would generally be fought between whichever two of the main parties are most popular locally, while the other major party's candidates would receive very little support. This might even hold if the ridings contain as many as four major parties (or five in the case of Quebec between 1993 and 2000). In this case, voters would simply decide to support the two candidates who have the greatest chance of winning; as a result, a local form of bipartisan competition would set in. Yet, although it makes sense to assume that the election of several parties in the House of Commons may be the result of a competition between different pairs of parties with strong regional ties, Gaines (1999) himself finds no evidence to support the claim that *local* bipartisan competition held at the riding level in the elections between 1935 and 1993.

Johnston and Cutler (2009) propose an interesting alternative explanation to account for the enduring presence of a multi-party system in the Canadian context. They claim that the consolidation of the party system never really occurred in Canada because of the domination of the Liberal

Party (see also Johnston 2008). The authors argue that this party's electoral success is explained by its centrist location on the left-right axis combined with its position on the question of Quebec-Canada relations. Because it was traditionally perceived as the defender of Quebec interests, the Liberal Party was able to win around 75 percent of the seats in that province from 1900 to 1980. This advantage also explains why the Liberals never really felt threatened by the arrival of the CCF in the 1935 election or later, in 1961, by the arrival of the NDP. Unlike in the United Kingdom and Australia, the growth of the left was never serious enough to warrant the consolidation of the centre-right into one major party (like the Conservatives in the United Kingdom or the Liberal-National coalition in Australia), precisely because the Liberals could always rely on a strong delegation of MPs from Quebec to provide them with almost half of the seats necessary to form a majority government. This last point explains why a tacit "ends-against-the-middle" alliance between the Progressive Conservatives and the NDP to oppose the Liberals was never seriously considered as an option (Cox 1997).

The importance of the regional cleavage in Canada is not new. Up until the 1920s, elections were fought between the Conservatives and the Liberals, which represented heterogeneous regional, social, and economic interests in Parliament. However, both parties were divided on the role of Canada in the British Empire and on religion (Johnston et al. 1992). As we saw, this party system was progressively modified by the advent of various regional parties. The presence of these new parties was attributable partly to the feeling of alienation in the regions: in the West for the Progressive Party, the Social Credit, and the CCF; and in Quebec for Laurier's Liberals during the First World War, the Bloc Populaire in the 1940s, and the Ralliement Créditiste in the 1960s. Furthermore, the existence of strong provincial parties, such as the Parti Québécois in Quebec or the Social Credit Party in Alberta, paves the way for the later emergence of *national* regional parties, such as the Bloc Québécois and the Reform Party, which contributes even more to the fragmentation of the party system (Johnston and Cutler 2009). As long as certain issues, like the national question in Quebec or the alienation of another region in Canada, have the potential to mobilize a significant portion of the electorate, it will be difficult for political elites to consolidate the party system into two main parties, as in the case of the United States.

The theoretical arguments put forward to explain the roots of the Canadian multi-party system can thus be summarized as follows. First, the routine presence of more than two major parties can be explained by the fact that the Liberals have for a long time been perceived as a moderate party on questions of economic redistribution and on the different regional conflicts in the federation. The fact that the Liberals dominated the centre guaranteed the presence of more than two parties because a tacit alliance of both ends (the NDP on the left and the PC on the right) against the middle was unlikely to occur. In addition, the Liberals were viewed, until recently, as the party best able to balance the various regional interests, being perceived outside of Quebec as the party that could best handle Quebec issues while being perceived inside Quebec as the party that was the most moderate when it came to responding to western grievances.

Now, given that the party system consolidated in 2003, with the merger of the Canadian Alliance and the PC Party, perhaps there is a window of opportunity for the unification of the centre and the left in the near future. Indeed, this project could be facilitated by the fact that the Liberal Party is no longer the dominant party in Canadian politics as well as by the fact that the last remaining regional party, the Bloc Québécois, almost disappeared from the House of Commons in the 2011 election.

For supporters of a merger, such a project is justified – even if in the short term a number of voters may change allegiance – because the new party would stop dividing the progressive vote and allow the defeat of the Conservative Party. By combining the various voters who are hostile to the Conservatives, it would be possible to mobilize a good portion of Canadians who voted for the opposition parties during the last election. The merger would also create a medium-term draw of voters by reconfiguring the Canadian political space around two strong poles: one on the right and one on the left. The Greens could be added to this new left party; although they were only able to elect one MP, they attracted about 4 percent of the vote in 2011 (7 percent in 2008), which represents a significant block of progressive voters.

However, this scenario rests on a problematic assumption. The logic of a merger of progressive forces in Canada assumes a one-dimensional political space separating right and left. That dimension is based on different views of the role of the state in economic redistribution (Noël and Thérien 2008). However, as already alluded to above, the Canadian federation is characterized by strong regional dynamics, which, along with socio-economic issues, creates a bi-dimensional policy space in Canadian politics (see Flanagan 1998; Hinich, Munger, and De Marchi 1998; Johnston 2000, 2008; Godbout and Høyland 2011). In the following section, we move to an empirical analysis to show that the presence of these two dimensions in the electorate can generate important coordination problems for party leaders.

Do Voters Want a Liberal-Democratic Party?

A successful alliance of progressive forces presupposes that, following a merger, most former NDP and Liberal supporters would vote for the new party. The available evidence suggests that the shift in support may not be automatic. A Harris-Decima poll conducted at the beginning of September 2011 suggests that only 24 percent of Canadians were favourable to a merger of the two progressive parties, while 63 percent were opposed. No majority favoured this idea: neither among NDP voters nor among Liberal voters; neither in Quebec nor in the rest of Canada.[3] Another survey conducted by the Canadian Election Study (CES) team after the 2011 election also shows that an NDP-Liberal merger would not necessarily attract more supporters. Respondents who said they had voted for the Liberal Party were asked what would have been their second choice: 54 percent of these Liberal voters said they would have voted for the NDP, while 17 percent would have chosen the Conservative Party. The proportions are slightly different for NDP voters, 35 percent of whom indicated that their second choice would have been the Liberal Party, followed by the Conservative Party (18 percent), the Green Party (14 percent), and the Bloc Québécois (14 percent). Using calculations that do not take into account the political effects of the creation of a new party, a loss of almost half of the traditional voters is predicted if both parties merge. Why is that so? Two factors can be identified: (1) voter movement along the left-right axis; and (2) the Quebec question.

The Left-Right Dimension

Were a liberal-democratic party to be created, former Liberal voters would have to accept casting their ballot for a party that would probably be slightly further to the left, while NDP voters would have to accept supporting a party that would be more centrist. In a recent study, which analyzes the different electoral programs of the political parties, Cochrane (2010) suggests that the Liberal and NDP ideological positions are not as close as one might think. In fact, on the left-right spectrum, the NDP is closer to the Bloc Québécois than to the Liberals. Some Liberal supporters may be alarmed by what they consider to be the radical positions of the NDP and vice versa. The electoral benefits for the centre-left of a party merger could thus be reduced if these voters do not recognize themselves in the new party.

Further evidence of the policy distance that separates the two parties can be seen in Table 11.1, which summarizes the NDP and Liberal partisans' views of each other's party on the left-right dimension. For comparative purposes, the table also reports similar scores for PC and Canadian Alliance members in 2000. Three points are worth mentioning. First, NDP and Liberal identifiers' self-placement scores are relatively close (a gap of only 0.10), which indicates that their left-right views are compatible; second, the same is true for PC and Alliance members back in 2000 (a gap of 0.10); third, both partisan groups perceive an ideological gap (of 0.19) between their party and the other one. While certainly not a large difference, it nonetheless represents close to one-fifth of the total range of the left-right scale used in the table, and it is nearly double the gap observed on the self-placement scale.

By comparison, this gap was much smaller for PC identifiers in 2000, a perceived difference of only 0.01 with the Canadian Alliance, even though for Alliance identifiers the gap was much larger (0.18) and comparable to the NDP/Liberal identifiers in 2011. Overall, the gap between a partisan group's mean self-placement and the perceived placement of the other party is practically twice as large among NDP identifiers as among Liberal identifiers (0.20 versus 0.12, respectively). Note an important difference here: the same gap is much smaller for Alliance and PC identifiers in the 2000 survey (0.11 and 0.04, respectively).

We can, of course, expect some regional variation in these various perceptions of policy placements. Since we focus here on party identifiers only, breaking down these perceptions by regions gives us estimates based on tiny samples (typically fewer than fifty respondents). Still, looking at regional breakdowns is interesting even if it remains somewhat tentative. The results indicate that NDP identifiers and Liberal identifiers stand a bit closer ideologically in Quebec and the west than in Ontario and the Atlantic provinces. It is in Quebec that perceptions of the parties' left-right positions are the closest and in the Atlantic provinces that they are the most distant. In sum, the regional picture of these policy perceptions is mixed: while there is some hope for an ideological rapprochement in Quebec between NDP and Liberal Party identifiers, there might be some significant ideological tensions that may arise in other parts of the country (especially Atlantic Canada) were the two parties to attempt to merge.

TABLE 11.1

Mean scores of self-reported ideological placement and party ideological placements in 2011 and 2000 (party identifiers only)

	Self-placement	Placement of their party	Placement of the other party
NDP identifiers (2011)	0.35	0.36	0.55
	(0.01)	(0.02)	(0.02)
	n = 113	*n* = 106	*n* = 104
Liberal identifiers (2011)	0.45	0.52	0.33
	(0.01)	(0.01)	(0.01)
	n = 228	*n* = 224	*n* = 218
PC identifiers (2000)	0.66	0.71	0.70
	(0.03)	(0.03)	(0.04)
	n = 161	*n* = 148	*n* = 162
CA identifiers (2000)	0.76	0.83	0.65
	(0.02)	(0.02)	(0.02)
	n = 244	*n* = 246	*n* = 222

Notes: Standard errors in parentheses; data are weighted. The ideological placement question comes from the post-electoral mailback wave in 2011 and from the pre-electoral wave in 2000. The question in 2011 uses an eleven-point scale (0-10, from left to right, rescaled to 0-1), while the 2000 question uses a three-point scale (from left to right, rescaled to 0-1 for consistency reasons). Party identification is taken from the pre-electoral wave.

Source: 2011 and 2000 Canadian Election Studies.

The policy distance – both *real* and *perceived* – between the NDP and Liberal parties constitutes a significant obstacle to a merger (see also Loewen and Owen 2011). In particular, the perceived difference between NDP and Liberal Party identifiers implies that a merged party would have to cover much more ground ideologically. This was not the case for the Alliance/PC parties. PC voters basically saw no difference between their own party and the Canadian Alliance. For the Alliance and the PC, the perceived distance was much smaller in 2000, and this finding holds in the 1997 Canadian Election Study as well (see Bélanger and Godbout 2010).

The Regional Dimension

A second obstacle to an NDP-Liberal Party merger has to do with the particular situation of Quebec, where the vote at the federal level is usually determined less by the left-right axis than by the national question. The NDP won 59 seats in Quebec in the 2011 federal election because it offered an alternative to the Bloc Québécois that was ostentatiously not the Liberal Party, which has brand issues in the province. According to CES data, close to one-third of former Bloc voters supported the NDP in 2011, although note that the "Orange Wave" was also due, in part, to former Liberal and Conservative voters in Quebec supporting the NDP (Fournier et al. 2013).

Liberal support has been in free fall in Quebec for many years, from 44 percent in the 2000 federal election to 21 percent in 2006 and hitting 14 percent in 2011. However, it is important to note that the election of Justin Trudeau as the new Liberal Party leader appears to have reversed this trend in the province, at least temporarily. During 2013, the Liberals were polling at their highest in a decade, receiving between 30 percent and 40 percent of voting intentions in Quebec. Still, the NDP remained highly competitive in the province, ahead of the Bloc and the Conservative Party, while the popularity of the Liberal Party has declined slowly but steadily since Justin Trudeau won the leadership race in the spring of 2013 (see Bellavance 2013).

As Bélanger and Godbout (2010) note, one of the main reasons for the merger between the Canadian Alliance and the PC was to create a new political brand, mainly because the former remained too extreme for a majority of the electorate, even after the party changed its name and platform and selected a new leader in time for the 2000 election. In the case of the Liberal Party and the NDP, it is the more moderate party that has a brand problem in Quebec (not the other way around). The NDP risks losing support in the province if it is associated with a party that has been perceived as hostile to Quebec nationalism since Pierre Trudeau's repatriation of the Canadian Constitution without Quebec's consent at the beginning of the 1980s and the Chrétien government's adoption of the Clarity Act in the years following the 1995 referendum on Quebec sovereignty. For these reasons, for many Quebec nationalists, voting for the federal Liberal Party is simply not an option (Bickerton 1997). For example, only 7 percent of 2011 Bloc voters mentioned the Liberal Party as their second choice, whereas 61 percent mentioned the NDP (2011 CES). Thus, the Liberal Party's actions of the past three decades with regard to the accommodation of Quebec's interests constitute an important image problem for that party in Quebec – and a significant obstacle to a potential NDP-Liberal fusion. The selection of Justin Trudeau as the new party leader did nothing to change that perception, mostly because Trudeau has embraced his party's usual hardline stance on sovereignty.

This regional cleavage also manifests itself among NDP and Liberal voters in terms of their second preference, as expressed in the 2011 CES survey. In Quebec, only 25 percent of NDP voters indicated the Liberal Party as their second choice, compared to 41 percent outside Quebec. About 38 percent of them actually had the Bloc Québécois as their second preference. As for Liberal voters in Quebec, 48 percent of them mentioned the NDP as their second choice, which is relatively close to the proportion of 55 percent found outside Quebec, but 24 percent of these Liberal voters indicated having no second preference at all (compared to only 17 percent in the rest of Canada). These figures provide further evidence of the relative gap between the two voter groups in Quebec – a gap that might prove difficult to overcome following a merger of the two parties.[4]

Is an Electoral Realignment Possible?

In sum, as in the 2004 election, which immediately followed the merger of the PC with the Canadian Alliance and in which the new Conservative Party only increased its share of the vote by 4 percentage points compared to the Alliance's 2000 vote share of 25 percent, a significant number of former Liberal and New Democratic voters would probably not support a liberal-democratic party in the short run. In the rest of Canada, many moderate Liberal voters might vote for the Conservative Party, while the more progressive elements might find a new home with the Greens. In Quebec, the resurgence of the Bloc Québécois, or perhaps of another nationalist party, cannot be ruled out in the face of a new party associated with Pierre Trudeau, Jean Chrétien, and Stéphane Dion. In the current state of public opinion, nothing suggests that a merger of these two parties would lead to a progressive victory in the next federal election.

While present voter preferences do not seem to augur well for the project of an NDP-Liberal merger, the argument for the unification of progressive forces in Canada must also take into account the political effects related to the creation of a new party. These are difficult to anticipate since they are based on the hypothesis of an electoral realignment following a party merger. In the following paragraphs, we evaluate the plausibility of this hypothesis by looking at the data available in order to better understand the political preferences of Canadians.

Conveniently enough, the 2011 and 2000 CES surveys each asked two questions that can be associated, respectively, with economic redistribution (the left-right dimension)[5] and with the place of Quebec in Canada (the regional dimension): (1) "Where would you place yourself on a 0-10 scale

FIGURE 11.1
Two-dimensional policy placements of party voters in 2011

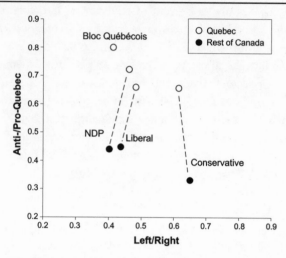

Notes: Data are weighted. The anti-/pro-Quebec placement question comes from the post-electoral wave. The left/right placement question comes from the post-electoral mailback wave. Scores have been rescaled to 0-1.

Source: 2011 Canadian Election Study.

[i.e., the left-right self-placement score of party identifiers]?" and (2) "How much do you think should be done for Quebec?" For the latter, the interviewees were given the following list of possible answers: much more, somewhat more, about the same as now, somewhat less, much less. We have recoded both scales to run from 0 to 1 (for a similar method, see Johnston [2008]). Figure 11.1 represents the average location of interviewees who indicated that they voted for the Liberal Party, the NDP, the Conservative Party, and the Bloc Québécois, and whether these voters lived in Quebec or outside the province. Figure 11.2 reproduces the same graph with data from the 2000 survey, with Canadian Alliance, Progressive Conservative, Bloc Québécois, Liberal, and NDP voters.[6]

Figure 11.1 shows that, in 2011, the positions on the question of redistribution (the horizontal axis) are mostly comparable in Quebec and in the rest of Canada. Interviewees who stated that they voted for the Conservative Party were further to the right (ideologically) in this dimension in both regions, followed by the Liberal Party and the NDP towards the left end of the spectrum. That said, in Quebec the position of the latter two parties on this dimension is slightly more to the right than in the rest of the country

FIGURE 11.2
Two-dimensional policy placements of party voters in 2000

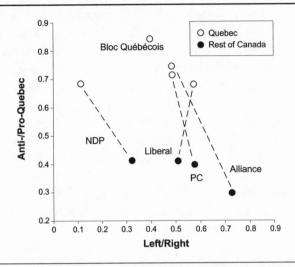

Notes: Data are weighted. Both the anti-/pro-Quebec placement question and the left/right placement question come from the pre-electoral wave. Scores have been rescaled to 0-1.
Source: 2000 Canadian Election Study.

(and Quebec Conservative supporters position themselves slightly more to the left). It can also be observed that Bloc Québécois voters are on average more polarized on this dimension than are the voters for other parties.

Clearly, the greatest distance between voter preferences in Quebec and the rest of Canada lies in the second dimension, related to the place of Quebec in the federation. Because the Conservative Party would have been able to form a majority government without the support of any MPs from Quebec in 2011, it could decide to completely ignore the demands of voters from this province, particularly on the national question. The Tories could choose to represent only the interests of conservative voters from the rest of Canada, who are more polarized on this second dimension. Figure 11.2 confirms more or less the same placement in 2000 by showing the relatively small distance between the positions of PC and Alliance voters on the first dimension outside of Quebec.

If we assume that the merger between the PC and the Alliance was conducted mostly without having to worry about nationalist voters in Quebec, we can see that the combined preferences of Conservative Party supporters were similar, although PC supporters were closer to the Liberal position.

However, the key point to take away from this plot is not related to the placement of party supporters on the first dimension; rather, it is associated with the difference between PC and Alliance supporters on the question of Quebec. Unlike the new Conservative Party, New Democratic and Liberal parties cannot afford to ignore Quebec in their electoral strategies. They will need to elect MPs in this province to form a majority government. The more the New Democrats and Liberals distance themselves from the average preferences of Quebecers on this dimension, the more they risk alienating an important proportion of the province's electorate, which could bring back support for the BQ or a similar nationalist party.

Examining the case of Quebec in more detail, we can see that the average position of Bloc voters on the national dimension is relatively distant from those of NDP and, especially, Liberal voters. Although the NDP took some of these Bloc voters in 2011, a competing political party would always be tempted to play the "national card" to divide the left-wing (or right-wing) vote during an election. The example of the 2008 federal election is suggestive. By announcing cutbacks in the cultural area, the Harper Conservative government had not counted on being the object of a particularly vociferous campaign by a coalition of Quebec artists. This issue partly explains the recovery of the BQ in the polls during the last few weeks of the election campaign. According to Bélanger and Nadeau (2009), the argument of a "culture in peril" helped the Bloc avoid major electoral losses, which only materialized in the following election to the benefit of a party other than the Conservatives – the NDP.

In short, supporters of a merger will have to find a way to deal with the regional diversity of a federal country (Gagnon and Iacovino 2008). This is difficult since such a party would have to bring together the anglophone urban voters of the Liberal, NDP, and Green parties with voters in western Canada who traditionally support the NDP and those from Quebec who are driven by the national question. The example of the Progressive Conservatives in the 1993 election should serve as a cautionary example. By mobilizing Quebec nationalists and conservative voters in western Canada, both disappointed by the constitutional accord of 1982, Brian Mulroney succeeded in winning more than 75 percent of the seats in the House of Commons in the 1984 election. However, this coalition of divergent interests, who did not agree at all on the question of Quebec's place in the Canadian federation, eventually gave birth to two parties (the Bloc Québécois and the Reform Party), which came to replace the Progressive Conservatives in Parliament (see Bickerton 1997).

Party Strategies: Will the Merger Happen?

While we have observed obstacles that would make an NDP-Liberal merger rather challenging, the idea is not about to disappear, mainly because of the systemic bias to bipartisanship in a first-past-the-post electoral system. The real issue, then, is whether party leaders and activists will support a merger. At the time of writing, Liberal leader Justin Trudeau and NDP leader Thomas Mulcair rule out a merger, but heavyweights in both parties continue to promote the idea. Will this party fusion take place, if not now, at least after another Conservative victory? Based on the experience of the merger of the Canadian Alliance and PC parties, Bélanger and Godbout (2010) have identified several factors that can explain a merger of political parties in the Canadian context. Are these conditions present in the current political context?

First, Bélanger and Godbout found that a political party organization that is running a financial deficit will be more open to a merger project. The question here is whether the reform of party financing rules adopted by the Conservative government will affect the two main opposition parties' budgets.[7] Evidently, the NDP seems more confident of obtaining stable funding from its members than does the Liberal Party, although the situation has improved for the Liberals since Justin Trudeau became leader. Both parties should therefore be lukewarm towards a merger if they believe that they can enjoy an advantage in raising money in the near future. Just before the 2011 election, the NDP had around $5.7 million in net assets and an operating surplus of 2.4 million dollars, whereas the Liberal Party had net assets of $4.6 million and a balance of available funds of just $1.6 million.[8] The Liberals have run important deficits since 2003 (Young and Jansen 2011), whereas the NDP has operated under better financial conditions. New Democrats were even able to purchase a $4 million building in Ottawa to house their headquarters and generate revenues by renting office space (see Ryckewaert 2012).

The fact that the Liberals, like the PCs in 2003, find themselves financially under pressure thus meets one of the conditions for a merger; although one should note that, in early 2003, the Canadian Alliance was threatened with losing some of its financial backing if it did not get on board with the merger (Segal 2006), a situation that the NDP does not currently appear to be facing. But once again, the arrival of Justin Trudeau has changed the picture somewhat. Between March and June 2013 after the leadership race, the Liberal Party was able to attract more than 38,000 individual donors (compared to 23,000 between January and March 2013).

The party also raised more than $3 million during that period, an increase of $2.3 million over the previous quarter.[9] Obviously, this new-found wealth greatly lowers the incentive for the Liberal Party to merge with the NDP.

Second, the ideological convergence of MPs facilitates a merger. In the case of the Alliance-PC merger, the sticky question of Quebec was not an issue due to the near disappearance of the Progressive Conservative Party in that province and the absence of Alliance MPs east of Ontario. In that case, the merger was basically conducted without Quebec. The Liberal-Democratic Party, by contrast, would rely a great deal on MPs from Quebec. The election of Outremont MP Thomas Mulcair as party leader has tightened the grip of the Quebec caucus on the NDP, while the Liberal Party retains only a few prominent faces in Quebec (Justin Trudeau, Marc Garneau, and Stéphane Dion). In recent years, the NDP has adopted a number of positions that are favourable to a special status for Quebec, including with regard to language rights, an issue that remains touchy for the Liberal Party. The new party would run the risk of being divided over the national question (the centralizing vision of Ontario MPs versus the more decentralist vision of Quebec MPs; opposition to "special status for Quebec" in western Canada versus insistence on this issue among Québécois MPs and party activists).[10] As we have seen, this tension between MPs explains, in large part, the difficulties the Progressive Conservative Party encountered at the beginning of the 1990s and its electoral debacle of 1993.

Third, a merger between two political parties is more likely to occur when both parties are underrepresented in Parliament. That is, for a merger to become the parties' preferred option, the advantage ratio (i.e., the percentage of seats divided by the percentage of votes) must be inferior to one for both parties. This is what happened in the case of the Alliance and PC parties. What about the case at hand? As Figure 11.3 shows, the advantage ratio of the Liberal Party in 2011 has dropped to 0.58, down from 0.94 in 2008 (it stood above 1.0 in previous elections). The decline of the Liberal Party in the Province of Quebec is even more startling. The party has been systematically underrepresented in the province since the 1984 federal election.

With the Liberals now being clearly underrepresented not only in Quebec but also across Canada, one can understand that a merger with the NDP has become a more attractive option for them. How about the NDP? Before the 2011 election, its advantage ratio was always well below 1. It was at 0.40 in 2004, Jack Layton's first election. Since then the NDP's ratio has been constantly on the rise. It has now crossed the 1.0 threshold for the first

FIGURE 11.3

Seat to vote advantage, Liberal and NDP (CCF), 1935-2011

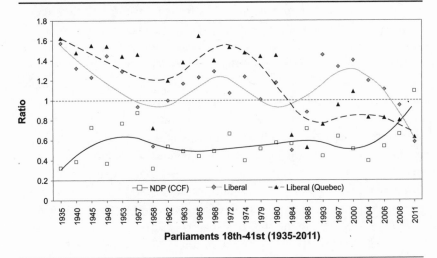

Parliaments 18th-41st (1935-2011)

time in its history and stands at 1.09 following the outcome of the 2011 election. From the point of view of parliamentary representation, the New Democrats, unlike the Liberals, do not have an immediate incentive to merge; they are currently overrepresented and the electoral system works to their advantage. Not surprisingly, pro-merger voices have been heard more loudly in the Liberal Party than in the NDP since 2011.

Finally, the electoral strategies of party leaders should be considered. With the merger of the Canadian Alliance and the Progressive Conservative parties, it became possible for the new party, now relieved of a banner too heavily associated with western populism, to make important gains in Ontario, Quebec, and the Maritime provinces. The question for the Liberal Party is whether its leftward tilt would risk loss of votes for its merged successor party in Ontario. For the NDP, the question is whether its Liberal association would cost votes in Quebec, where, as we have noted, the Liberal brand is far from being rehabilitated. From this point of view, for the NDP it might even be necessary to find a new name with no historical baggage in order to reflect an entirely new identity for the merged party. Unlike the Alliance-PC merger, which offered a more moderate brand to the electorate, a merger between the NDP and the Liberal Party risks polarizing even more potential supporters from Quebec and the rest of Canada on the national question.

274 *Jean-François Godbout, Éric Bélanger, and Frédéric Mérand*

Conclusion

A merger of progressive forces faces a contradiction between the first-past-the-post electoral system, which favours bipartisanship, and the increasingly heterogeneous political preferences of the Canadian population. The electoral system is conducive to a merger of the Liberal Party and the NDP, and perhaps the Green Party, but the heterogeneity of the electorate, notably on the issue of Quebec, makes it difficult to write a coherent political program likely to win a majority of seats.

Short of a reform of the electoral system, which is unlikely, there is a short-term solution favourable to progressive parties. As we have seen, voting in Canada is highly concentrated on a regional basis, similar to voting in India, although to a lesser extent. The NDP is solidly implanted in British Columbia, Saskatchewan,[11] and Manitoba. The Liberal Party has historically high support in Ontario and Atlantic Canada, where the NDP generally does less well, although the NDP has pockets of support in this area as well. The last election gave the NDP a clear advantage in Quebec, even if its base there is still fragile. Rather than a merger, the prospects of an electoral alliance on the basis of a division of the electoral map (as in France, where the Socialist Party "reserves" a number of safe ridings for its Green government partner and the UMP does the same for the New Centre Party) or a preliminary coalition agreement (as has occurred in India or Germany) represent potential strategies to defeat the Conservatives in the next election.

In the longer term, we would argue in favour of an institutional reform that would allow a better reflection of the regional diversity of the country in Parliament. The history of our political party system underscores the inability of its federal parliamentary institutions to represent regional interests. The appearance of third parties in Parliament in the 1920s corresponds precisely with the consolidation of party discipline in the House of Commons. To create a real bipartisan system on a left-right axis, it would be necessary to soften party discipline, allowing MPs to dissociate from their party's positions when they go against the interests of their ridings or, as the case may be, their "nation." A reform to make the Senate elected, for example, would allow a real representation of the regions in Parliament. In this context, Conservative senators and Liberal Democrats might form regional coalitions and vote against their colleagues in the Lower Chamber. This softening of party discipline would not be a problem since, by virtue of the principle of ministerial responsibility, the risk of Senate votes causing the government to fall is non-existent. But it would have the advantage of allowing voters to express their preferences on regional or national issues in the Upper Chamber, without contaminating the left-right debate in the Lower Chamber necessary for the reconstitution of the Canadian political space.

Yet, in the end, it may well be that a merger – or even an electoral alliance as suggested by Nathan Cullen – of the NDP and the Liberal Party will simply never happen. We have seen that the possibility of a merger scenario's being acceptable is slightly higher within Liberal than within NDP ranks. The New Democrats' comparative lack of enthusiasm for a fusion of their party with the Liberals (see also Pétry, Chapter 6, this volume) stems from many reasons, some of which are clearly highlighted by our analysis. First, we have seen that NDP partisans are less attracted to the Liberal Party, notably because of their perception of a significant policy distance between the two parties – a greater gap than Liberal identifiers perceive. Second, when we move the focus to the more broadly defined group of voters, we observe that, while NDP and Liberal voters across the country appear closer on the left-right dimension than party identifiers would indicate, Quebec Liberal voters hold views that are less accommodating towards Quebec than those held by Quebec NDP voters. Hence, a merger might potentially alienate some nationalist NDP voters and pave the way for the return of the BQ (or a similar nationalist party). It might also create a clash over Quebec-centric issues among the merged party's caucus, as occurred within the Progressive Conservative Party after the failure of the Meech Lake Accord, which partially led to the creation of the BQ.

The third factor reducing the odds of a merger is that there is no immediate incentive for the New Democrats to merge since, unlike the Liberals, they do not face internal party finance pressures, they are currently overrepresented in Parliament, and acquiring the Liberal brand would probably diminish their support among nationalist Quebec voters. And finally, the recent selection of Justin Trudeau as leader of the Liberal Party has greatly improved its popularity (and finances) across the country. It seems very unlikely today that the supporters of the Liberal Party would agree to an electoral alliance with the NDP, primarily because they are much more confident about their chances going into the next election. With Justin Trudeau polling ahead of Stephen Harper and Thomas Mulcair, it appears that the post-election blues of 2011 have been replaced by cautious optimism, and talks of party merger have all but disappeared from the media.

Taking all these considerations into account, the NDP might just as well stay its course and hope that it can re-establish its recent rising trajectory. Figure 11.3 certainly indicates that the representation of the Liberal Party in Parliament has been in decline, whereas the NDP has seen a surge in its representational advantage, most notably because it did so well in Quebec in the 2011 election. Of course, the NDP needs to grow outside of Quebec, and a merger would possibly help the party there. But again, the delicate issue remains with this province. The NDP needs to consolidate its new support base in Quebec as well because the gains it made in 2011 remain fragile. These gains were mostly due to Jack Layton's positive image and to some fatigue with the BQ's dominance (Bélanger and Nadeau 2011; Bittner, Chapter 8, this volume). The fact that the NDP shared the profile of the Bloc on several key issues such as increasing spending on health care and the environment, and increasing corporate taxes, facilitated the migration of voters from the Bloc to the NDP (Fournier et al. 2013). Consolidation of the NDP's new voting base in Quebec is possible, and would probably be easier to achieve, without a merger with the Liberals. The party's leader, Thomas Mulcair, is well positioned to continue the work of Jack Layton with regard to building a bridge with Quebec. Then, a slight movement of the NDP towards the centre of the left-right spectrum might just be the missing element to provoke a major and lasting electoral realignment in Canada. The key to the NDP's success will be to find the right balance between these two overarching goals.

Notes

1 See "Ex-PM Jean Chrétien Predicts NDP-Liberal Merger," *CBC News*, 6 September 2011, http://www.cbc.ca/news/politics/story/2011/09/06/pol-chretien-merger.html. See also Bryden (2012).

2 Some minor parties, such as the Labour Party, won a handful of seats in several elections prior to 1921.

3 See "Majority Oppose Liberal-NDP Merger," *Harris/Decima*, September 2011, http://www.harrisdecima.com/news/releases/201109/1224-majority-oppose-liberal -ndp-merger.

4 The data indicate no substantial variation among the other regions of Canada in terms of the second preferences of these voter groups. The only notable difference is that 36 percent of NDP voters in the west mentioned the Liberal Party as their second choice, a proportion that is a bit lower than in the other two regions outside Quebec (41 and 43 percent in Atlantic Canada and Ontario, respectively) but that remains significantly higher than what is observed among Quebec NDP voters (25 percent).

5 In Canada, the left-right distinction has typically been understood as being about equality and, hence, governmental redistribution of social resources (Cochrane 2010).

6   Unfortunately, the 2000 CES survey only uses a 3-point scale for the left-right place-
    ment. That said, results from the 1997 CES survey (which uses a 10-point scale) do
    not differ significantly from the 2000 CES results. We have decided to use the 2000
    CES here because it is the last survey made before the 2003 Alliance-PC merger.
7   To recall, the 2011-12 Conservative budget announced the phasing out of the per-
    vote state subsidy over a period of four years. The state allowance to political
    parties, which has been in place since 2003, will thus be completely gone by fiscal
    year 2015-16.
8   See Elections Canada, http://www.elections.ca/fin/pol/asset/2010/Liberal_2010.
    pdf and http://www.elections.ca/fin/pol/asset/2010/ndp_2010.pdf.
9   See Elections Canada, Financial Reports, http://www.elections.ca/WPAPPS/WPF/.
10 Even Jean Chrétien, a major supporter of the NDP-Liberal merger, acknowledges
    that such diverging views on the Quebec question constitute a major, though not an
    insurmountable, obstacle to the merger (Bryden 2012).
11 Although the NDP gained no seats in Saskatchewan in 2011, its share of the popu-
    lar vote was 32 percent. Over time, the NDP's vote share in Saskatchewan has regu-
    larly matched its Manitoba and British Columbia vote shares. However, given the
    idiosyncratic way in which electoral boundaries were redrawn in the 1980s in
    Saskatchewan, it has been extremely hard for the NDP to capitalize on its Saskatoon
    and Regina urban votes since all seven ridings in Saskatoon and Regina now have
    substantial rural components that vote heavily for the Conservatives. New urban
    ridings for both cities will be re-established in time for the 2015 federal election.

References

Bélanger, Éric. 2007. Third Party Success in Canada. In Alain-G. Gagnon and A.
    Brian Tanguay, eds., *Canadian Parties in Transition*, 3rd ed., 83-109. Peter-
    borough, ON: Broadview.

Bélanger, Éric, and Jean-François Godbout. 2010. Why Do Parties Merge? The Case
    of the Conservative Party of Canada. *Parliamentary Affairs* 63, 1: 41-65.

Bélanger, Éric, and Richard Nadeau. 2009. The Bloc Québécois: Victory by Default.
    In Jon H. Pammett and Christopher Dornan, eds., *The Canadian Federal
    Election of 2008*, 136-61. Toronto: Dundurn.

–. 2011. The Bloc Québécois: Capsized by the Orange Wave. In Jon H. Pammett and
    Christopher Dornan, eds., *The Canadian Federal Election of 2011*, 111-37.
    Toronto: Dundurn.

Bélanger, Éric, and Laura B. Stephenson. 2014. The Comparative Study of Canadian
    Voting Behaviour. In Luc Turgeon, Martin Papillon, Jennifer Wallner, and
    Stephen White, eds., *Comparing Canada: Methods and Perspectives on Can-
    adian Politics*. Vancouver: UBC Press.

Bellavance, Joël-Denis. 2012. Trudeau évoque la fusion avec le NPD. *La Presse*, 15
    March. http://www.lapresse.ca/actualites/politique/politique-canadienne/201203/
    15/01-4505674-justin-trudeau-evoque-la-fusion-avec-le-npd.php.

–. 2013. Sondage: Le PLC et le NPD à égalité au Québec. *La Presse*, 22 October.
    http://www.lapresse.ca/actualites/politique/politique-canadienne/201310/22/
    01-4702239-sondage-le-plc-et-le-npd-a-egalite-au-quebec.php.

Bickerton, James P. 1997. Crime et châtiment: Le Parti progressiste-conservateur du Canada entre 1984 et 1993. *Politique et Sociétés* 16, 2: 117-42.

Bryden, Joan. 2012. Liberal-NDP Merger Would Create "Political Stability," Chrétien Argues. *Globe and Mail*, 16 April.

Cochrane, Christopher. 2010. Left/Right Ideology and Canadian Politics. *Canadian Journal of Political Science* 43, 3: 583-605.

Cox, Gary W. 1997. *Making Votes Count: Strategic Coordination in the World's Electoral Systems*. Cambridge: Cambridge University Press.

Duverger, Maurice. 1951. *Les partis politiques*. Paris: Armand Colin.

Flanagan, Thomas. 1998. *Game Theory and Canadian Politics*. Toronto: University of Toronto Press.

Fournier, Patrick, Fred Cutler, Stuart Soroka, Dietlind Stolle, and Éric Bélanger. 2013. Riding the Orange Wave: Leadership, Values, Issues, and the 2011 Canadian Election. *Canadian Journal of Political Science* 46, 4: 863-97.

Gagnon, Alain-G., and Raffaele Iacovino. 2008. Canadian Federalism and Multinational Democracy: "Pressures" from Quebec on the Federation. In Herman Bakvis and Grace Skogstad, eds., *Canadian Federalism: Performance, Effectiveness and Legitimacy*, 2nd ed., 334-54. Toronto: Oxford University Press.

Gaines, Brian. 1999. Duverger's Law and the Meaning of Canadian Exceptionalism. *Comparative Political Studies* 32, 7: 835-61.

Godbout, Jean-François, and Bjørn Høyland. 2011. Legislative Voting in the Canadian Parliament. *Canadian Journal of Political Science* 44, 2: 367-88.

Grofman, Bernard, André Blais, and Shaun Bowler, eds. 2009. *Duverger's Law of Plurality Voting*. New York: Springer.

Hinich, Melvin J., Michael C. Munger, and Scott De Marchi. 1998. Ideology and the Construction of Nationality: The Canadian Elections of 1993. *Public Choice* 97, 3: 401-28.

Johnston, Richard. 2000. Canadian Elections at the Millennium. *IRPP Choices* 6, 6: 4-36.

—. 2008. Polarized Pluralism in the Canadian Party System. *Canadian Journal of Political Science* 41, 4: 815-34.

Johnston, Richard, André Blais, Henry E. Brady, and Jean Crête. 1992. *Letting the People Decide: Dynamics of a Canadian Election*. Montreal and Kingston: McGill-Queen's University Press.

Johnston, Richard, and Fred Cutler. 2009. Canada: The Puzzle of Local Three-Party Competition. In Bernard Grofman, André Blais, and Shaun Bowler, eds., *Duverger's Law of Plurality Voting*, 83-96. New York: Springer.

Loewen, Peter, and Taylor Owen. 2011. Doing the Math on a Merger. *Toronto Star*, 21 September.

Mair, Peter. 1990. The Electoral Payoffs of Fission and Fusion. *British Journal of Political Science* 20, 1: 131-42.

Noël, Alain, and Jean-Philippe Thérien. 2008. *Left and Right in Global Politics*. Cambridge, UK: Cambridge University Press.

Ryckewaert, Laura. 2012. NDP's 2003 Decision to Buy $4-million Building at Laurier Avenue West and Bank Street Ensures Party's "Financial Viability." *Hill Times*,

23 January, http://www.hilltimes.com/news/2012/01/23/ndp's-2003-decision
-to-buy-%244-million-building-at-laurier-avenue-west-and-bank-street/29366.
Segal, Hugh. 2006. *The Long Road Back: Creating Canada's New Conservative
Party.* Toronto: HarperCollins.
Young, Lisa, and Harold Jansen, eds. 2011. *Money, Politics, and Democracy: Can-
ada's Party Finance Reforms.* Vancouver: UBC Press.

12

The 2011 Election and Beyond

STEVEN WELDON

The dramatic surge for the New Democratic Party in the 2011 Canadian federal election campaign took many long-time observers of Canadian politics by surprise. Though the NDP hovered around 15 percent in public opinion polls at the start of the campaign, just one month later the Orange Crush propelled the party to over 30 percent of the popular vote and Official Opposition status with 103 seats in the House of Commons. Caught up in the NDP's wake, the Liberals and Bloc Québécois floundered badly, retaining just 34 and 4 parliamentary seats, respectively.

The first indication of this shift in Canadian federal politics came on 18 April 2011 – three weeks into the official campaign and only two weeks before the election – when three leading polling firms showed NDP support jumping to about 25 percent and into a second-place tie nationally with the Liberals.[1] Coming just a few days after the leaders' debates, most commentators attributed the jump to Jack Layton's strong performance in the debates. Indeed, despite the fact that the NDP was trailing the Conservatives overall, a plurality of respondents in the same polls believed that Layton would make a better prime minister than Stephen Harper. Still, pundits remained sceptical the NDP could maintain that level of support through the final weeks of the campaign. Some pointed to recent elections in which high support for Layton and the NDP during the campaign failed to materialize on election day; others argued that the party's supporters, who tended to be younger, were less likely to turn out and vote; some suggested that the NDP's support was only tepid and that, ultimately, many supporters would cast a strategic vote for the Liberals at the ballot box. Few, if any, foresaw a growing surge that the NDP would ride to a historic best, securing a third of the seats in Parliament.

As we look to the future, a key question is whether the 2011 election will be a short-lived success for the NDP or whether it constitutes a more fundamental transformation in Canadian federal politics. The NDP appears to have crossed one major hurdle already with the selection of Thomas Mulcair to replace Jack Layton as its leader. Can the NDP with Mulcair at the helm build on its triumph under Layton? If so, how will it affect the other major parties' electoral fortunes, especially the Liberals and BQ but also the Conservatives and the Greens? To answer these questions, we need to develop a better understanding of the reasons for the NDP's surge in the 2011 election. That is, we need to understand how likely the NDP is to retain its current supporters in future elections and gauge its potential to attract new voters.

Drawing on the 2011 Canadian Election Study, I systematically examine the long- and short-term sources of party support and vote choice. On the one hand, the results indicate that the NDP has much work to do to shore up and consolidate its base. Much of its support in 2011 came from first-time NDP voters who made their decision during the election campaign, flirted with a different party up to the last minute, and appear to have been swayed by their affection for Jack Layton more than the NDP's formal policy positions.

On the other hand, the NDP appears primed to grow its support beyond the 30 percent threshold from 2011. Voters for other parties, including the Conservatives, were most likely to say that the NDP was their second choice, and they expressed a relatively high willingness to vote for the party in the future. Perhaps more important, the NDP stands poised to replace the Liberals as the de facto alternative to the Conservative Party. The Liberals have long benefitted from NDP supporters casting strategic votes for the Liberals with the hope of preventing a Conservative government. However, as I show below, the NDP also benefitted from this type of strategic voting in 2011, largely at the expense of the Liberals.

As we look ahead to 2015, the NDP may be able to capitalize even more in this respect. The extent to which it can do so will likely determine whether we see a fundamental transformation in Canadian federal politics. Over four distinct party systems, the Liberal-Conservative split has dominated Canadian federal politics since Confederation. That era may be coming to an end, replaced by a system dominated largely by the Conservatives on the right and the NDP on the left.

In the following section, I provide a brief overview of recent trends in Canadian federal elections. I then seek to identify the NDP's core voters and distinguish them from voters who had previously voted for other parties but came to support the NDP over the course of the 2011 election campaign (i.e., swing voters). In doing so, I compare the NDP with the other four major federal parties. This analysis indicates how relatively few of the NDP's voters are core voters who can be relied upon to consistently vote for the party. The analysis also underscores the importance of the campaign itself to the NDP's fortunes in 2011. I also examine several long-term factors that affect vote choice, including social demographic cleavages, partisan attachments, and past voting behaviour. I then consider more short-term factors that go into the voting calculus. Finally, I examine the role of strategic voting, focusing just on the respondents who report switching their vote to the NDP from the Liberals, BQ, or Greens since the 2008 election.

Changes in the Canadian Party System, 2000-11

The dramatic change in the Canadian party system and rise in support for the NDP may have taken many by surprise, but it has its roots in events nearly a decade earlier (Gidengil et al. 2012). This includes the sponsorship scandal, which undermined the Liberals' credibility as a governing party and sparked a gradual loss of electoral support. Indeed, looking at Figure 12.1, it is remarkable how steady the decline in vote share has been for the Liberals since 2000 – the same year the auditor general began investigating the Liberal government's Sponsorship Program. The 2011 result was simply a continuation of this general trend, set in motion eleven years earlier, leading to the Liberal Party's worst showing in its history. The disproportionality in Canada's first-past-the-post electoral system, however, meant a far more pronounced effect in terms of Liberal seat share in the House of Commons. Indeed, whereas in 2008 the Liberals received 26 percent of the popular vote and 25 percent of the seats in Parliament, in 2011 they received 19 percent of the popular vote but just 11 percent of the parliamentary seats.[2]

The second major development in the 2000s was the merger of the Canadian Alliance and Progressive Conservatives in 2003. Since the Reform Party burst on the scene in 1993, divisions split the vote on the political right, leading to three consecutive Liberal majority governments. During

FIGURE 12.1
Historical vote share of Canadian parties, 1962-2011

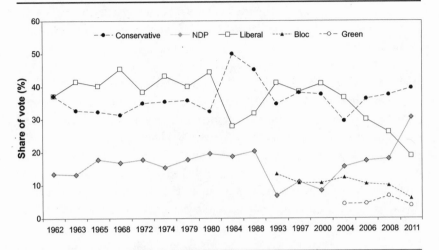

Note: Vote share for the Conservatives from 1993 to 2000 included the combined vote share of the Progressive Conservatives and the Reform Party/Canadian Alliance.

this period, although their combined vote share stayed around 35 percent, the two parties of the right were never able to secure more than 26 percent of the seats in Parliament. Following the merger, the Conservatives' vote share initially dropped in the 2004 election to below 30 percent; however, no longer suffering from the punitive effects of disproportionality, the party translated that into 32 percent of the parliamentary seats. By 2006, Stephen Harper was prime minister, and, following two minority governments, the Conservatives finally secured their coveted majority after the 2011 election.

While the Liberal sponsorship scandal and the Conservative merger set in motion the events that would lead to the NDP's historical performance, it is also evident from Figure 12.1 that the NDP did not really benefit from these changes until the 2011 election. Instead, its vote and seat shares remained fairly steady for the three elections between 2004 and 2008. The 2011 election clearly represents a tipping point for the NDP. Not only did it finally benefit from the continued decline of the Liberals but it also benefitted from a drop in support for the BQ and Greens. Taken together, the Liberals (–7), BQ (–4), and Greens (–3) lost 14 percentage points of vote share from 2008 to 2011. The NDP took almost all of this, increasing its vote share by 12.5 points. The Conservatives benefitted marginally in terms of vote share but were able to put their votes to more efficient use and win

54 percent of the seats. As we seek to understand the potential long-term changes in Canadian federal politics, it is critical to understand why the NDP was able to attract so many of the other parties' former voters. To do this, the next section seeks to differentiate between a party's core and swing supporters.

NDP Voters: The Core versus Swing Supporters

In Canada and across most advanced industrial democracies, we have seen a gradual erosion of partisan attachments in recent decades (Dalton and Wattenberg 2002). This pattern of partisan dealignment has decreased the number of loyal voters that consistently vote for the same party from one election to the next. It has also contributed to a decline in turnout, lower party membership numbers, and a public that has become increasingly disenchanted with political parties and their leaders (Dalton and Weldon 2005). Voters are making their decisions later in the campaign, many in the final days or even in the voting booth. For example, in the 2011 election, nearly 45 percent of voters report making their decision during the campaign, 11 percent on election day itself (Fournier et al. 2011). This represents a large number of potential swing voters who play a significant role in determining the overall election outcome.

This instability in voter preferences presents a growing challenge to political parties, but, as we can see in Table 12.1, it also presents opportunities to attract new voters. The table shows how NDP voters in the 2011 election recall voting in the 2008 election. Only one-third of NDP voters recall voting for the NDP in 2008, while 20 percent report voting for the Liberals.

TABLE 12.1

How NDP voters in 2011 voted in 2008 election

Party voted for in 2008	Percent
NDP	32
Liberals	21
Conservatives	9
Bloc Québécois	11
Green	6
Don't remember or did not vote	20
TOTAL	100

Source: 2011 Canadian Election Study: vote in 2011 (PES11_6); vote in 2008 (CPS11_73).

The latter indicates that nearly 1 million voters switched from the Liberals to the NDP in just three years. Similarly, 11 percent of NDP voters recall voting for the BQ in 2008. That is the national percentage. In Quebec alone, it was nearly 30 percent – almost twice as many who recall voting for the NDP in 2008. Yet the NDP did not just draw support from the Liberals and BQ. Nationally, 6 percent of NDP voters supported the Greens and 9 percent the Conservatives in the previous election. In short, it is evident that the NDP in 2011 was able to capitalize on the processes of partisan dealignment among the Canadian electorate. It remains to be seen whether the NDP can consolidate many of these first-time voters and continue to attract new ones.

We now look more broadly at the challenge Canadian federal parties face in maintaining their support and achieving electoral success, focusing on the NDP in particular. To do this, I examine more closely the respective parties' core and swing voters from the recent election.

Core voters are those who routinely vote for the same party, often out of tradition and convention rather than because of the party's current performance, and they generally make their vote decision well before the campaign. Such voters are highly coveted because they provide stability for party leaders and a strong reservoir of support in both good times and bad times (Dalton and Weldon 2007). In contrast, swing voters have no fixed party preference and are more likely to switch their vote from election to election. They represent the fluid element of each party's support base and the Canadian party system in general. They may lean towards one party, but they are by definition open to the possibility of voting for at least two different parties, possibly more.

In Table 12.2, I present three indicators of core party supporters: the percentage of 2011 party voters who also voted for the same party in 2008; the percentage who report making their decision to vote for their party before the start of the campaign; and the percentage of a party's voters who identify with that party (strongly or fairly strongly). I then combine the first two indicators – that is, respondents who both voted for the same party in the 2008 election and report making their choice before the 2011 campaign – to create a composite measure and my operationalization of core voters.[3,4]

Looking at Table 12.2, it is clear how few NDP voters in the 2011 election were core voters. Again, just 32 percent report voting for the party in 2008; also, only 35 percent claim to have made their decision to vote for the NDP before the election campaign and 33 percent identified with the party

TABLE 12.2
Identifying parties' core supporters in the 2011 election, by party (%)

Vote choice in 2011 election	Voted for party in 2008	Made decision before 2011 campaign	Identify with party	Core supporters
NDP	32	35	33	19
Liberal	69	59	71	45
Conservative	76	68	68	56
Bloc Québécois	88	74	79	66
Green	37	48	32	26
TOTAL	60	55	56	42

Note: "Core supporters" are defined as those who voted for the same party in the 2008 and 2011 elections and reported making their decision before the campaign started in 2011.
Source: 2011 Canadian Election Study: vote in 2011 (PES11_6); vote in 2008 (CPS11_73); made decision before campaign (PES11_8); identify with party (CPS11_71 and CPS11_72).

before the campaign. One can see from the final column that only 19 percent of NDP voters are defined as core voters that can be counted on to reliably vote for the party from one election to the next.[5] This represents just 6 percent of the Canadian electorate, a far cry from the 30 percent the party actually received in the election.

The NDP's small share of core voters stands in stark contrast to that of the other major political parties: 45 percent of Liberal voters, 56 percent of Conservative voters, 66 percent of BQ voters, and 26 percent of Green voters in the 2011 election are defined as core supporters. This translates to 9 percent of the electorate for the Liberals, 22 percent for the Conservatives, 4 percent for the BQ (16 percent in Quebec), and just 1 percent for the Greens. While the Liberals and BQ lost many voters to the NDP in 2011, these results show that the two parties still retain a fairly strong group of loyal supporters, especially the BQ in Quebec. The NDP is currently much more dependent on swing voters, suggesting that it may face a major challenge in increasing its result from 2011. It was, however, able to attract new voters in the first place, and this is the critical first step. Finally, we see that, with nearly half of the core voters in the entire electorate, the Conservatives appear to be in a very strong position relative to the other parties going forward.

Before more systematically examining the factors behind the NDP surge, it is informative to examine voters' own reasons for their vote choices and how these vary across parties. This is shown in Table 12.3, where I have

TABLE 12.3
Voters' key expressed reasons for vote choices in 2011 election (%)

Vote choice	Leader	Policies	Candidate	Anti-other parties	Other
NDP: core (19%)	20	43	9	12	9
NDP: new (81%)	30	24	8	22	13
Liberal	5	22	32	22	19
Conservative	20	24	17	22	18
Bloc Québécois	12	35	20	15	19
Green	11	40	4	29	16

Source: 2011 Canadian Election Study: variable PES11_8b.

also divided the NDP between its core and swing voters. For this question, respondents were asked to identify the most important reason they voted for their chosen party: the party leader, the party's policies, the party's candidate in their riding, dislike of other major parties, and any other reason.[6] As the table demonstrates, there are key differences between the NDP's core and swing voters. Core voters are far more likely to identify the party's policies, whereas a plurality of the latter point to their affinity for Jack Layton. Swing voters also express a keen dislike for the other major parties.[7]

These findings fit with the general story in the media that came out of the 2011 election and with the jump in NDP support after the leaders' debates (see also Bittner, Chapter 8, this volume). Jack Layton was extremely popular, and this surely contributed to and possibly sparked the NDP's surge. Given his death shortly after the election, one might also then assume that the NDP will simply return to its historical level of voter support in subsequent elections.

Despite many new voters identifying this as a key factor in their vote choice, however, there are also several reasons to question the importance of Layton's popularity for the NDP's success. First, Layton had been leader of the NDP since early 2003 and for three elections prior to 2011; however, as discussed above, the NDP was not able to make inroads until 2011. Second, as I show below, Layton was a popular leader among all voters, even those who voted for different parties. While new NDP voters did tend to express more fondness for Layton, the difference is relatively marginal, especially compared to Liberal and BQ voters. Third, as of March 2012, the NDP has a new leader, Thomas Mulcair. While the NDP's standing in public opinion polls eventually declined to a position behind both other major parties, early in his leadership, polls indicated that, if anything, the Mulcair-led party could even outpoll the party under Layton.[8] All these reasons suggest that Layton was as much a part of the NDP surge as he was a catalyst for it, and therefore we need to look more closely at other factors that may have affected support for the NDP in 2011.

Voting for the NDP: Short-Term Factors and the Campaign

Many factors are known to affect the calculus of Canadian voters (Anderson and Stephenson 2010). Socio-demographic cleavages, for example, have long structured vote choice among the Canadian electorate. Roman Catholics and those of non-European origin have tended to vote for the Liberals (Blais 2005; Stephenson 2010), as have women in recent decades (Gidengil et al. 2005). While these patterns have been slowly changing in recent years, especially in the 2011 election (Gidengil et al. 2012), the more basic point here is that we know such long-term factors cannot possibly account for the rapid surge in support for the NDP over the 2011 election. This includes socio-demographic cleavages, partisan attachments, and underlying core values or beliefs. Changes in these long-term factors must obviously have helped set the stage for the surge, but we need to look to more short-term factors to understand the catalyst for it.

Possible candidates to explain the NDP surge include the key issues in the campaign that may have affected vote choice (Fournier et al. 2003), voters' views of the economy and their own financial situations (Anderson

TABLE 12.4
Issue importance and vote choice in the 2011 election (%)

Respondents who favour ...	NDP (core)	NDP (new)	Liberal	BQ	Con	Green
• two-tier health care system	25	40	36	43	51	25
• scrapping gun registry	34	35	34	18	66	26
• spending more to fight crime	35	37	34	31	47	31
• closer US ties	18	23	21	25	34	13
• reducing immigration	27	25	18	31	32	15
• doing more for Quebec	27	41	20	82	13	22
• reducing income gap (strongly)	56	45	40	42	23	49
• higher corporate taxes	63	64	47	67	29	55

Source: 2011 Canadian Election Study: variables in order of above – PES11_35, PES11_27, CPS11_36, PES11_45, PES11_28, PES11_44, PES11_41, and CPS11_31.

2008), evaluations of the party leaders (Bittner 2011; Bittner, Chapter 8, this volume), and strategic considerations about which party might win the election or one's riding (Blais et al. 2001; Merolla and Stephenson 2007; Pickup 2010).

Policy Issues and Vote Choice

We start by examining the role of policy issues in Table 12.4, which lists several recent key issues in Canadian politics and from the 2011 election campaign. The numbers in the table are the percentage of voters in each party who express support for the different policy issues. The first observation from the table is that NDP voters, whether core or new, tend to have issue opinions fairly similar to those of Liberal, BQ, and Green voters. Conservative voters are the ones who consistently stand out, whether on scrapping the gun registry, spending more tax dollars to fight crime, developing closer ties to the United States, doing more for Quebec, reducing the income gap, or support for higher corporate taxes. Even on tax and welfare state issues, we see that Liberal Party voters have positions closer to those of NDP voters than to Conservative voters. This suggests a fairly clear left-right split on the key issues in Canadian politics; it also suggests that the Conservatives were able to benefit from a fragmented left in the 2011 election, much as the Liberals did from a fragmented right in the 1990s and early 2000s (Bélanger and Godbout 2010).

Looking more closely at the individual issues, however, we do find a few key differences that help to differentiate NDP voters from voters of the other left-leaning parties and Liberals. First, compared to Liberal voters (20 percent), NDP voters (41 percent) are more likely to favour doing more for Quebec. Outside of Quebec, however, it is useful to note that there is no difference between the two parties' voters on this issue. Between NDP and BQ voters, there is also a big difference on this issue, but within Quebec it is much smaller. Within this province, 70 percent of NDP voters are supportive of doing more for Quebec. This is closer to the position of BQ voters (82 percent) than it is to those of the Liberals (48 percent) and the Conservatives (51 percent).

Second, across Canada, a key issue that appears to differentiate NDP and Liberal voters is their positions on corporate taxes. This was a central issue during the campaign, largely because it was directly tied to the issue of job creation. The Conservative Party first proposed to cut the corporate tax rate from 16.5 percent to 15 percent, arguing it would help create jobs. The NDP countered with a populist message, arguing the real problem was big

TABLE 12.5
Economic voting in the 2011 election (%)

	NDP (core)	NDP (new)	Liberal	BQ	Con	Green
Economic situation – Canada (% stating "worse")	33	26	19	31	14	28
Economic situation – personal (% stating "worse")	31	28	20	19	13	27
Believe NDP government bad for economy	5	10	37	17	70	29

Source: 2011 Canadian Election Study: variables in order of table – CPS11_39, CPS11_66, PES11_52b.

business shipping jobs overseas and that companies would use the tax cut chiefly to provide their CEOs with bigger bonuses. Layton proposed to cut the tax rate of small businesses from 11 percent to 9 percent, increase the corporate tax rate to 19.5 percent, and pledged a job creation tax credit of $4,500. The Liberals got somewhat lost in this debate but did pledge to raise the corporate tax rate to 18 percent. As we can see from the bottom of Table 12.5, this message of economic populism appears to have resonated with many new NDP voters and likely contributed to the surge, especially outside of Quebec.[9]

Economic Evaluations and Vote Choice

Turning to the role of economic voting, Table 12.5 provides some additional evidence for the above interpretation. Again, the values in the table are the percentage of voters for each party who state that the Canadian economy in general or their own financial situation in particular has gotten worse since the 2008 election. One can see that NDP voters were more likely than Liberal and, especially, Conservative voters to say that the economic situation had worsened since the 2008 election. More telling is that, among those who said their financial situation had become worse since 2008, 46 percent voted for the NDP, while only 18 percent voted for the Liberals and 25 percent for the Conservatives.

The pattern is similarly favourable for the NDP in Quebec, where 53 percent who said their financial situation had gotten worse voted for the NDP and just 18 percent chose the BQ. Since the members of this group constituted more than 20 percent of the electorate, they were a large part of the NDP's support base. Moreover, their concerns about the economy were likely a key deciding factor for many former Liberal and BQ supporters in their decision to switch their vote to the NDP in 2011. We explore this possibility further below. The final row in Table 12.5, however, also highlights a potential hurdle for the NDP in expanding its support: quite a few Liberal and especially Conservative voters have reservations about the ability of the NDP to effectively manage the economy (see also Erickson 1988).

Leader and Party Images in Vote Choice

With the impact of traditional socio-political cleavages and partisan attachments waning in recent decades, scholars have increasingly pointed to the role of leadership images and general party images in shaping voting behaviour (Aarts, Blais, and Schmitt 2011). The growing importance of the media and the rise of the twenty-four-hour news cycle have made the messenger as critical as the message in contemporary politics (Wattenberg 1992), and parties whose leaders fail to connect with voters are likely to suffer at the polls. Moreover, party images tap into voter perceptions of party competence, trustworthiness, and the ability to handle key political and economic issues of concern. Independent of parties' specific policy positions, these types of valence factors appear to increasingly influence vote choice in Canada and other contemporary democracies (Zakharova, Chapter 9, this volume; Clarke, Kornberg, and Scotto 2009; Bélanger and Meguid 2008).

Table 12.6 provides an indication of how leader and party images related to voting behaviour in 2011. The values reported are the mean feeling thermometer scores (0 to 100 scale) among each party's voters. The primary goal is not to give a full overview of such factors but, rather, to assess how important Layton's likeability was to the success of the NDP (see Bittner, Chapter 8 this volume). This was perhaps the headline story coming out of the election campaign, and thus it raises serious questions about the NDP's ability to sustain support in the future. However, as discussed above, there are several reasons to doubt this view – the best evidence being that, as of 2014, the NDP continues to perform well in public opinion polls with Mulcair as leader.[10]

Moreover, we see from Table 12.6 that Layton was a rather popular leader among all voters. He had an average feeling thermometer score of 53.7, which was 8 points higher than Harper and 16 higher than Ignatieff. Not surprisingly, voters tended to rate their respective parties and leaders the highest, but Layton earned high marks from voters of the Liberal, BQ, and Green parties. Even Conservative voters had a much higher opinion of Layton than they did of the other party leaders. Yet the key takeaway from

TABLE 12.6

Rating of party leaders and party, by vote choice (100 point scale)

	NDP (core)	NDP (new)	Liberal	BQ	Con	Green	Total
Party leader							
Layton	78.5	66.7	58.2	63.6	41.9	55.3	53.7
Harper	25.2	31.6	30.7	30.0	69.4	24.8	45.7
Ignatieff	35.5	42.7	59.4	40.8	24.5	43.1	37.5
Duceppe	55.6	54.5	42.2	73.6	30.0	41.1	49.3
May	44.1	42.5	41.6	36.7	26.8	64.5	35.9
Party							
NDP	78.6	62.2	51.1	55.1	34.8	51.9	48.5
Con	27.3	35.5	34.7	28.1	70.9	31.5	48.0
Liberal	42.7	48.4	66.8	34.9	34.4	49.8	44.7
BQ	51.7	49.1	36.4	73.6	26.0	41.5	47.1
Green	38.3	38.6	35.9	36.9	22.0	65.3	32.1

Source: 2011 Canadian Election Study: variables in order of table – CPS11_23, CPS11_27; parties, CPS11_18 – CPS11_22.

this table is that, despite Layton's easily being the most liked party leader in Canada, his high marks did not always lead to a vote for the NDP. It appears many voters admired Layton, but most of them did so from afar.

We see the importance of the party over the leader for vote choice when we look at the bottom of the table. Feelings towards the party more closely align with the actual pattern of vote shares from the election. Moreover, in results from a multiple regression analysis not presented here, feelings towards the party were a much stronger predictor of vote choice than feelings towards the leaders. I should note that this does not mean Layton had a limited effect on the NDP surge: it simply indicates that affection for Layton really needed to transfer to the party as well. We can see this best when we look at the new NDP voters, who have a smaller gap between their feelings for Layton versus the NDP than do voters of other parties.

In sum, the NDP surge in 2011 appears to have resulted from a convergence of several short-term factors. With Layton as the possible catalyst that gave the NDP legitimacy, the party was able to capitalize on the more than decade-long decline in support for the Liberals. It did this with a message that included a touch of love for Quebec and a touch of economic populism, which appears to have appealed most to those who had fallen on harder economic times in recent years and who were concerned about the economic direction of the country. This finding runs counter to previous research, which suggests that the NDP has tended to suffer electorally when there is a weak economy (see Erickson 1988). There is also some evidence, however, that the NDP profited as simply the best alternative to the Conservatives or from many voters' "anyone-but-Harper" mindset. We have seen, for example, that differences on policy issues among NDP, Liberal, BQ, and Green voters are small relative to those between them and Conservative voters. We explore this possibility further in the final section, looking at evidence of strategic voting against the Conservative Party.

Strategic Voting in the 2011 Federal Election

The reality of Canada's first-past-the-post electoral system is that only one party can win representation from a riding. As is well known from Duverger's Law, such "winner-take-all" systems tend to have high disproportionality rates in the transfer of votes to seats. This tends to discourage voters from supporting third-party candidates who have little chance of winning the election and, more generally, encourages two-party competition at the district level (Duverger 1963). Thus, even if a voter supports a party on policy grounds or for another substantive reason, Duverger's Law leads to the expectation that the voter still may opt for a different party at the ballot box – a party that has a better chance of winning the election (Blais, Young, and Turcotte 2005; Godbout, Bélanger, and Mérand, Chapter 11, this volume).

While previous research has found that strategic voting in Canadian elections historically has been fairly low (about 5 percent; Blais, Young, and Turcotte 2005), there is good reason to believe it may have increased in recent years, especially in the 2011 election. The Liberals' gradual decline in support since 2000, public opinion polls showing a jump in support for the NDP during the campaign, and the possibility of a Conservative majority set the stage for voters on the left and centre-left to think twice about their vote choice. It is not possible to fully explore the extent of strategic voting in the election here. Nonetheless, we can get an initial indication of its role in the NDP surge by examining how voter perceptions about the top two parties in their riding affected the likelihood that Liberal, BQ, and Green voters from 2008 switched their votes to the NDP in 2011. If voters were more likely to switch their votes to the NDP when they thought the NDP was running in first or second place in their ridings, this would provide some evidence that voters were voting strategically. I examine this in Table 12.7.

TABLE 12.7
Vote switching of Liberal, BQ, and Green voters from 2008 to 2011,
by perception about top two parties competing in one's riding (%)

Perceived leading parties	Voted for same party in 2008 and 2011 (Liberal, BQ, and Green)	Switched vote to NDP in 2011
Con-Lib (n = 378)	59	41
Con-NDP (n = 85)	28	72
Lib-NDP (n = 119)	44	56
BQ-Con (n = 61)	32	68
BQ-Lib (n = 127)	49	51
BQ-NDP (n = 86)	51	49
Don't know (n = 241)	39	61
TOTAL (n = 1,097)	52	48

Note: Table excludes all Conservative and NDP voters in 2008 and Conservative voters in 2011.

The rows in Table 12.7 are the possible combinations of parties that the respondent perceives to be running first and second in his or her riding, excluding the Greens. The columns are the percentage of Liberal, BQ, and Green voters from 2008 who switched their votes to the NDP in 2011. The results provide some evidence that strategic voting played a role in the 2011 election, at least outside of Quebec. First, we see that Liberal, BQ, and Green voters in 2008 who thought the Conservatives and Liberals were the top two parties in their ridings in 2011 were the least likely to switch their vote to the NDP (41 percent). In contrast, those who thought the Conservatives and NDP were the top two parties were the most likely to switch to the NDP (72 percent). Second, interestingly, it appears there was little to no strategic voting in Quebec, unlike in the rest of Canada. We can see this by comparing the BQ-Liberal and BQ-NDP groups. The latter, those who believed the BQ and NDP were the top two parties in their ridings, were no more likely to switch their votes to the NDP than were those who believed the Liberals were the chief competition for the BQ.

Conclusion: Looking Forward to 2015

This chapter examines the nature of NDP support in the most recent election in an effort to understand its long-term prospects and the changing nature of the Canadian party system. The results point to several key observations. First, the NDP does have a relatively small base of core supporters and, unlike the other major parties, depended heavily on support from conversion or swing voters in the 2011 election. Indeed, over half of NDP voters in 2011 voted for a different party in the previous election, and only 35 percent claim to have made their decision before the start of the campaign. Second, at the same time, it appears that the NDP has broad appeal in the Canadian electorate and even more room to grow its support. This is especially so among voters opposed to the Conservatives and Stephen Harper. There are few differences among NDP, Liberal, and Green voters on key issues, and a relatively large number of Conservative voters in 2011 even considered the NDP as their second choice. Third, despite the enormous popularity of Jack Layton, there is limited evidence that recent NDP support can be attributed to his popularity alone; rather, the NDP profited from the steady decline in support for the Liberals since 2000. We can see this in the continued popularity of the NDP since Thomas Mulcair took over the leadership in the spring of 2012.

The 2011 election will be remembered as a breakthrough for the NDP. Long playing second fiddle to the Conservatives and Liberals, the NDP scored a historic best of 30 percent of the popular vote and rode that to Official Opposition status. It was also able to finish either first or second in 75 percent of the ridings across Canada. The key question moving forward, however, is whether the NDP will be able to solidify its support and ultimately displace the Liberals as the second major party in Canadian politics. In one sense, this seems highly unlikely. The Liberals have long been the governing party of Canada; indeed, from 1935 to 2006, it found itself out of power for just sixteen years. It is also easy to dismiss the Liberals' recent electoral declines as stemming from little more than a few poor leadership choices and the lingering effects of the sponsorship scandal. If so, we should expect to see the Liberals bounce back with a better leader and as the sponsorship scandal wanes in voters' minds. In turn, we could expect the NDP to return to its third-party status with renewed questions about its own future.

If one is willing to entertain the possibility of the NDP displacing the Liberals for even a moment, however, there is also plenty of evidence to suggest that the Liberals may be on shaky ground (see also Godbout, Bélanger, and Mérand, Chapter 11, this volume). First, history teaches us that major parties do collapse. The Progressive Conservatives are one such example, as is the British Liberal Party. The latter dominated British politics in the nineteenth and early twentieth centuries. It fell to third in the 1922 election and never recovered. Second, comparative party scholars have long known that Canada and the Liberal Party, in particular, are outliers. Canada is unique among first-past-the-post systems in terms of the number of parties competing for and winning seats in Parliament. It is also unique in having a major party that holds the ideological centre – the Liberals. There are a variety of reasons for scholars speculating that centre parties have tended to do poorly across countries (see Johnston 2008 for an overview), but the main point is that the Canadian Liberal Party has long been an outlier. With these considerations in mind, it is safe to predict that the 2015 election will be critical in determining the future of the NDP, the Liberals, and the Canadian party system more broadly.

Notes

1 Angus Reid, Leger, and Nanos all released polls on this date showing a jump in support for the NDP.

2 Only two federal elections since Confederation have produced a greater disparity between vote and seat share for the Liberals (1958 and 1984). The Liberals have long been a net beneficiary of the disproportionality in the Canadian electoral system.

3 These are variables CPS11_73 ("vote in 2008"), PES11_6 ("vote in 2011"), PES11_8 ("when respondent made the voting decision"), and CPS11_71 and CPS11_72 ("party identification" and "strength of identification").

4 I exclude party attachment from my operationalization of core voters because, while important, it is less stable and reliable as an indicator of support than actual reported voting behaviour. See also note 5.

5 If one includes party identification as an additional requirement of being a core voter, the NDP's share of core voters drops to 15 percent. Alternatively, if we consider party identification, instead of whether respondents report making their decision before the campaign, then 21 percent would be coded as core voters.

6 Variable PES11_8b in the CES 2011.

7 It is useful to note that the pattern of results in Table 12.3 were broadly consistent across Quebec and the rest of Canada.

8 For example, an Ipsos Reid poll on 23 June 2012 showed the NDP at 38 percent, Conservatives at 35 percent, and Liberals at 18 percent. It is also worth noting that many political commentators saw a big difference between the personalities of Mulcair and Layton. For example, in a story from 16 March 2012 in the run-up to the NDP leadership convention, *Maclean's* magazine ran an online story with the title "Thomas Mulcair Is Mr. Angry." "Angry" is hardly a personality characteristic that many see as positive and as contributing to electoral success, suggesting that the NDP's improved poll results may have been in spite of its new leader rather than because of him.

9   See Laycock (Chapter 5, this volume) for a discussion of the role that this economic populism has played in the NDP's historic appeals.

10 In 2014, on the Nanos Party Power Index, which is a composite measure of federal party brands, the NDP has remained very competitive with the Conservatives and it tracks not far behind the Liberals. See Nanos 2014.

References

Aarts, Kees, André Blais, and Hermann Schmitt, eds. 2011. *Political Leaders and Democratic Elections*. New York: Oxford University Press.

Anderson, Cameron D. 2008. Economic Voting, Multilevel Governance and Information in Canada. *Canadian Journal of Political Science* 41, 2: 329-54.

Anderson, Cameron D., and Laura B. Stephenson, eds. 2010. *Voting Behaviour in Canada*. Vancouver: UBC Press.

Bélanger, Éric, and Jean-François Godbout. 2010. Why Do Parties Merge? The Case of the Conservative Party of Canada. *Parliamentary Affairs* 63, 1: 41-65.

Bélanger, Éric, and Bonnie M. Meguid. 2008. Issue Salience, Issue Ownership, and Issue-Based Vote Choice. *Electoral Studies* 27, 3: 477-91.

Bittner, Amanda. 2011. *Platform or Personality? The Role of Party Leaders in Elections*. New York: Oxford University Press.

Blais, André. 2005. Accounting for the Electoral Success of the Liberal Party in Canada. *Canadian Journal of Political Science* 38, 4: 821-40.

Blais, André, Richard Nadeau, Elisabeth Gidengil, and Neil Nevitte. 2001. Measuring Strategic Voting in Multiparty Plurality Elections. *Electoral Studies* 20, 3: 343-52.

Blais, André, Robert Young, and Martin Turcotte. 2005. Direct or Indirect? Assessing Two Approaches to the Measurement of Strategic Voting. *Electoral Studies* 24, 2: 163-76.

Clarke, Harold D., Allan Kornberg, and Thomas J. Scotto. 2009. *Making Political Choices: Canada and the United States*. New York: Cambridge University Press.

Dalton, Russell J., and Martin P. Wattenberg. 2002. *Parties without Partisans: Political Change in Advanced Industrial Democracies*. Oxford: Oxford University Press.

Dalton, Russell J., and Steven A. Weldon. 2005. Public Images of Political Parties: A Necessary Evil? *West European Politics* 28, 5: 931-51.

—. 2007. Partisanship and Party System Institutionalization. *Party Politics* 13, 2: 179-96.

Duverger, Maurice. 1963. *Political Parties: Their Organization and Activity in the Modern State*. New York: Wiley.

Erickson, Lynda. 1988. CCF-NDP Popularity and the Economy. *Canadian Journal of Political Science* 21, 1: 99-116.

Fournier, Patrick, André Blais, Richard Nadeau, Elisabeth Gidengil, and Neil Nevitte. 2003. Issue Importance and Performance Voting. *Political Behavior* 25, 1: 51-67.

Fournier, Patrick, Fred Cutler, Stuart Soroka, and Dietlind Stolle. 2011. The 2011 Canadian Election Study. Dataset. http://ces-eec.org/pagesE/surveys.html.

Gidengil, Elisabeth, Matthew Hennigar, André Blais, and Neil Nevitte. 2005. Explaining the Gender Gap in Support for the New Right: The Case of Canada. *Comparative Political Studies* 38, 10: 1171-95.

Gidengil, Elisabeth, Neil Nevitte, André Blais, Joanna Everitt, and Patrick Fournier. 2012. *Dominance and Decline: Making Sense of Recent Canadian Elections.* Toronto: University of Toronto Press.

Johnston, Richard. 2008. Polarized Pluralism in the Canadian Party System. *Canadian Journal of Political Science* 41, 4: 815-34.

Merolla, Jennifer L., and Laura B. Stephenson. 2007. Strategic Voting in Canada: A Cross Time Analysis. *Electoral Studies* 26, 2: 235-46.

Nanos, Nik. 2014. Weekly Nanos Party Power Index. http://www.nanosresearch. com/library/polls/Nanos%20Political%20Index%202014-05-02E.pdf.

Pickup, Mark. 2010. Election Campaign Polls and Democracy in Canada: Examining the Evidence behind the Common Claims. In Cameron Anderson and Laura Stephenson, eds., *Voting Behaviour in Canada,* 242-78. Vancouver: UBC Press.

Stephenson, Laura. 2010. The Catholic-Liberal Connection: A Test of Strength. In Cameron Anderson and Laura Stephenson, eds., *Voting Behaviour in Canada,* 86-106. Vancouver: UBC Press.

Wattenberg, Martin P. 1992. *The Rise of Candidate-Centered Politics: Presidential Elections of the 1980s.* Cambridge, MA: Harvard University Press.

13

Future Scenarios

NDP Evolution and Party System Change

DAVID LAYCOCK and LYNDA ERICKSON

This volume traverses a wide range of dimensions and issues in the NDP experience federally, emphasizing the period following the 1988 election. Readers cannot help but be struck by the contrast between the party's recent past and current situation. The NDP went from being Canada's "nearly dead party" in 1993 to breaking through as the "newly dynamic party" in 2011 and forming the Official Opposition. These electoral high and low points reflect important changes in the federal party's internal life, its efforts to enhance its standing among Canadian voters, and its changing position in relation to evolving dynamics in the federal party system. In this concluding chapter, we review key themes from previous chapters and consider their implications.

Overlapping Themes

The 1993 electoral debacle showed how important the position of the NDP as a regionally concentrated, left-populist political force had been for defining and sustaining its status as a significant third party in the national political competition. By contrast, its 2011 breakthrough clearly revealed how much the Liberal Party had blocked its growth across the country, particularly among federalist voters in Quebec. Until 2011, the NDP had always lost the Quebec competition along the federalist axis to another party. With the advent of the Bloc Québécois, social democratic voters seemed forced to choose between a viable federalist party and a sovereign-tist social democratic party. Since 1993, voters' choices on the federalist-sovereigntist axis had trumped their preferences on the left-right axis (Carty, Cross, and Young, 2000; Gidengil et al. 2012). When this NDP-crippling forced choice no longer seemed necessary to Quebec voters on the left, the Orange Crush resulted. Straddling the federalist-sovereigntist axis had always made sense ideologically to NDP stalwarts, but never before 2011 had it made sense to more than a small minority of Quebec's left-of-centre voters.

Ideology

Several chapters in this volume underscore the federal NDP's ideological distinctiveness. One dimension of this comes through in Chapters 5 and 7, which demonstrate that, to the party's elite and members, equality is central to the NDP's ideology. In fact, as Chapter 7 demonstrates, equality far outpaced liberty as a core principle for members in both our 2009 and 1997 member surveys. Using party documents, Chapter 5 shows that the meaning of equality has changed over time. The party's understanding of the people whom it represented moved from being primarily class-based to incorporating solidarity with various disadvantaged groups, including women, ethnic minorities, the LGBT community, and future generations affected by environmental damage. This expansion of the party's egalitar-ian embrace has resulted from, and has encouraged, new social movement activist engagement in the national party organization.

One question that this raises concerns a potential clash between con-ventional (class-based) social rights claims and "new" social rights claims inside the party (Erickson and Laycock 2002). Chapter 7 provides evidence that new social rights claims do have very strong internal party support and that this is true even among trade union members. As prior champions of conventional social rights, trade unionists see connections with both unions and a wide range of social movement organizations as key to the party's mandate. As Chapter 5 notes, this is part of a broader acknowledg-ment within the party that its understanding of equality should encompass support for the types of equality rights claimed by these social movements. Party members tend not to see any conflict between older class-based equal-ity rights claims and newer equality rights claims, and they appear not to have done so for at least a decade.

Strong support for the materially underprivileged is thus a core tenet for party members, as is a continued role for organized labour within the party.

Moreover, there is little indication that support for new social rights has moved the membership to the right ideologically. Still, as François Pétry points out in Chapter 6, in the campaign context, since 2006, NDP platforms have made fewer positive references to support for trade unions than earlier ones. This reduction notwithstanding, and despite the fact that the party has moved away from strong institutional representation of trade unions in party decision-making structures and processes, both party activists and members continue to see a future for the party as an advocate of organized working-class interests.

Among the electorate, the question of the role of organized labour may be a different story. For the "swing" voters especially (Chapter 12), the NDP's union connections may have little or no appeal. As the party attempts to expand its voter base, dealing with this potential conflict between party traditions, the party members, and swing voters will be a key ideological and strategic challenge for the federal NDP.

Looking at the public face of the party, and using very different analytical tools, Laycock and Pétry both conclude in Chapters 5 and 6, respectively, that, while rightward drift in the federal party since 1993 has occurred, the NDP remains clearly on the left of the party spectrum. Despite the modernization of its appeal, its increasing emphasis on leadership, its increasing focus on "practical first steps" to assist low- to middle-income Canadians, its reduced promotion of state ownership of major industries, and the reduced profile of organized labour in its electoral appeal, the federal NDP has not effectively vacated its social democratic position. Its focus on quintessential social democratic concerns such as welfare state expansion, market regulation, and expansion of education has counterbalanced some of its shifts away from its earlier advocacy of other left-wing policy instruments (such as state ownership). As Pétry demonstrates, the NDP remains positioned on the left both in terms of the Canadian and the international partisan spectrum.

This volume presents two different but complementary approaches in support of the normative logic in positioning the party. The first, presented in Chapter 4, borrows from the comparative work of Wolfgang Merkel et al. (2008) to distinguish between three types of social democratic party policy and ideological orientations. In the first category, none of the elements of party discourse and core value commitments, policy objectives, and policy measure/instruments have changed; in the second, just party discourse and policy measures/instruments have changed; in the third, all of these key elements have changed. The first category Merkel and his colleagues label "traditional social democracy," the second "modernized social democracy," and the third "liberalized social democracy."

A close look at the chapters in this volume that advance claims about ideological change in the federal NDP shows that all are consistent with characterizing the NDP, at least since Ed Broadbent's leadership in 1975, as an instance of "modernized social democracy." In other words, while party discourse and policy instrument choice may vary over time, neither basic policy objectives nor the closely related core normative values have been substantially altered.

The second approach used in this volume to structure analysis of fundamental ideological change complements conclusions reached using the Merkel et al. (2008) approach, and it is offered in Chapter 5. Here the focus is on the logic that connects an ideology's core normative commitments and elements of its vision of how citizens, states, and civil society interact. Michael Freeden's (1996) analytical approach divides key ideological concepts into core, adjacent, and perimeter categories, placing less weight on the latter, where one finds the changing policy instrument choices made by a party. In effect, Freeden says that, so long as the core and adjacent concepts of a party's ideology do not shift substantially along with changing policy instrument choices, the party's ideology will evolve gradually, not veer in a substantially different direction. Chapter 5 contends that this is the case with the modern (post-1975) federal NDP, despite the injection of environmental themes and policies into party discourse, the expansion of its understanding of equality beyond primarily class-based concerns, the party leader's increased profile in the party, and the differential deployment and effectiveness of left-populist themes over time. In other words, none of these changes has substantially altered the key core or adjacent conceptual structure of the party's ideology. We may see a higher level of modernization, but to revert to the Merkel et al. classification, no move to the clearly distinct category of "liberalized social democracy."

A final word indirectly supportive of the approaches offered by Merkel et al. (2008) and Freeden (1996) comes from a recent study of Canadian federal elections by the CES team of Elisabeth Gidengil, Neil Nevitte, André Blais, Joanna Everitt, and Patrick Fournier. In the context of their discussion of the relationship between voters' issue preferences and their votes, they remind readers that "issues come and go, but values and beliefs are more enduring. People react to the issues of the day through the lens of their normative beliefs. Once the effects of these values and beliefs are taken into account, the issues of the day have limited independent effects"

(Gidengil et al. 2012, 99). If this is true for the consumers of ideology, it is likely also true for their producers.

By moving modestly towards the centre with its promotion of various new policy instruments, the federal NDP has come somewhat closer to – but not become as centrist as – the ideological profile and policy packages characteristic of many other social democratic parties in the Western world. This modest reorientation has not alarmed a substantial proportion of the federal party's activists, at least not to the point that they would deny the party acceptably left-wing credentials. As Chapter 7 notes, these activists placed the party further to the left than non-activist party members in each of our 1997 and 2009 surveys.

Why do party activists make such judgments? They appear to believe that a judgment regarding the party's left-right position cannot be based just on campaign strategies and advertisements. Their judgments may also reflect their appreciation of the success of new social movement and trade union resolutions and initiatives in conventions or in other party activities (such as those involved in Federal Council activities) or in the party's standing "commissions" on issues of significance to what were once called the party's "caucuses," representing the concerns of women, Aboriginal peoples, the LGBT community, visible minorities, youth, and people with disabilities.[1] As Chapter 5 argues, notwithstanding changes in party campaign strategy, election communications, and emphasis on the party's leader, these elements of party modernization have not engendered a major ideological change in federal party's central commitments.

Left populism has been a traditional source of NDP strength, allowing it to shape and insert social democratic policy options into an ideological opening created by public antagonism to economic elites, parties, and government policies that linked the former to the latter. In this volume, Chapter 1 shows that, when faced with right-populist competition from the Reform Party, the NDP faltered. Other chapters show, however, that, having effective leadership and, ironically, modernized party operations has allowed the NDP to respond to this challenge, even across a linguistic/cultural divide that had previously denied it significant support in Quebec. Absorption of the Reform/Alliance party into what quickly became a governing party also made a difference for the NDP as the resulting Conservative Party was no longer seen as a party that convincingly articulated populist grievances about elite power to a broad range of voters (Gidengil et al. 2012). This is not to say, however, that the Conservative Party does not use such populist appeals to maintain the loyalty of its "base." Such appeals were front and centre in Prime Minister Harper's speech to party loyalists at the Conservative Party's November 2013 policy convention (see Chase 2013; Flanagan 2013). The nature of the Conservative Party's communication with its base and key suburban constituencies, especially in "Ford Nation" metropolitan Toronto,[2] suggests that it can effectively challenge the NDP in claiming the populist high ground in ways that matter electorally.

Region

Many chapters in this volume underscore how region generally and, most recently, Quebec specifically have been crucial determinants of New Democratic problems and prospects. As Chapters 3, 10, 11, and 12 suggest, the NDP's traditional Quebec weakness and now its Quebec strength in federal politics have each have presented daunting challenges. In the past, even while the party affirmed Quebec's special status, optimism about its electoral chances in the province was generally crushed at election time. Now, the party's success there, with half its caucus and 36 percent of its popular votes from Quebec, means its status as the Official Opposition crucially depends upon keeping support among Québécois very high. Doing so will require a sensitivity to nationalist sentiment that somehow does not alienate the party's core and non-core voter base in the rest of the country.

As Weldon observes in Chapter 12, there is strong support among Quebec NDP voters for "doing more for Quebec," but that is not echoed among NDP voters in the rest of Canada. The social democratic values that the NDP shares with the BQ were factors in the NDP's success in Quebec. If events that trigger nationalist animosity among Quebecers do occur, it will be an easy transition for many voters to move from the NDP back to the BQ. Since the election, however, there is no evidence that BQ fortunes have revived substantially. Moreover, with its financial fortunes so negatively affected by the withdrawal of the federal per-vote subsidy, the BQ organizational structure is at risk.[3]

The flip side of the Quebec situation is that the federal party's traditional Prairie strength is now a source of weakness. Having relied on a respectable number of MPs from Manitoba and Saskatchewan until the 1990s, the party now finds itself shut out of seats in Saskatchewan and with a mere two seats in Manitoba. While the proportion of House of Commons seats allocated to those provinces is declining, the symbolism of the federal party's circumstances there is not very positive. On the other hand, in the years since 1993, the Atlantic provinces have come into play for the NDP, thanks, in part, to the Nova Scotia roots of Alexa McDonough and, in 2011, also owing to its strong showing in Newfoundland. Still, the number of NDP seats in the Atlantic region remains small, with only six of the available thirty-two seats in the party's hands.

British Columbia may be the most consistently supportive region over time for the federal party, where it currently has one-third of the province's seats. But there has been considerable variability in the number of NDP seats in British Columbia since 1993, and the party's federal prospects there are strongly affected by the popularity of its provincial counterpart, which is widely seen to have given away its best chance at holding provincial power in more than a decade with a poor campaign in spring 2013. However, it is Ontario that has been an almost continuous ground of disappointment, going back to the CCF. As the largest province in the country, with a growing number of seats, Ontario is critical to NDP fortunes. As Chapters 11 and 12 suggest, Ontario is where the case for strategic alliances with the Liberals against the Conservatives is currently strongest. But if sidelining the Liberals is central to consolidation of NDP status as *the* viable alternative to the Conservatives (Lavigne 2013), the party has a strong incentive to avoid any arrangements in Ontario or elsewhere that would sustain Liberal competitiveness.

Leadership and Organizational Factors
Contributions to this volume have shown that leadership matters a great deal to the federal NDP. More than ever, it matters to vote choice (Chapters 7, 8, and 12), to the party's campaigning (Chapters 3 and 4), and to the prospect that the NDP will sustain its pre-eminence over both the Bloc and the Liberals in Quebec (Chapters 11 and 12). This adds up to considerable significance for the party's overall future prospects, but enough other factors are involved in motivating party members and voters (Chapters 7, 8, 10, and 12) that it is best not to ignore them. As Weldon shows in Chapter 12, long-term partisans, policy issues, and the core values invoked in election campaigns are important for party success.

Modernization and the substantial finances that facilitate it also clearly matter for the federal party's future. We cannot say how much of the party's upward trend from 2004 to 2008 and its breakthrough in 2011 were due to modernization of party communications, fundraising, and national campaigns and how much was due to the slow Liberal Party collapse or, in 2011, Québécois voters' disaffection with the Bloc (see Chapters 9, 11, and 12). But it does appear that, without its additional financial resources and much better election communications/campaign work, the party would not have been able to take advantage of Liberal and Bloc decline. As Chapter 4 suggests, being able to spend the national campaign limit in 2008 and 2011 was crucial to the NDP's becoming more competitive via both television advertising and well-supported local and national campaigns.

We see in Chapter 7 that, in the party organization, party policy and core direction are crucially important to members, whose ideological commitments remain strongly in the social democratic camp. However, while there is some ambivalence among members as to whether they have enough input into party decision making, there is not widespread dissatisfaction among the troops. Moreover, few think the party leadership is too strong,· and a majority says that they can have a real influence on the party if they are actively involved. Indeed, in Chapters 2 and 5, we learn that the party did respond to internal opinion when the New Politics Initiative was launched. Substantive concerns of the NPI challengers found their way quite prominently into election materials and appeals after the NPI proposal for dissolution was turned back. And our analysis of party modernization indicates that diverse views and constituencies flourished within the party at the same time as the leader's prominence, simplification of policy messaging, and centralized campaign control all made major strides. Whether party members have permanently lost substantial ground within the NDP's democratic structures in the face of a more powerful leader and federal office is hard to ascertain at this stage since the rise of leader power and party centralization occurred during a period of intense election activity (four elections in eight years). The next election cycle and inter-election party conventions should reveal something in this respect as the party has the opportunity to take a break from perpetual election readiness.

The NDP in a Reconfigured Party System

The 2011 election ushered in a significant electoral realignment. Whether the Canadian party system has now entered a stable new long-term phase has yet to be determined (see Bittner and Koop 2013). Still, a number of features of the current configuration can be identified as important for the NDP's future prospects. First, the Conservatives have replaced the Liberal Party as the major party that wins through "coordination failure" on the other side of the left-right divide (Johnston 2009). Electorally, this Conservative advantage is augmented by the party's superior organization (Flanagan 2011) and finances (Jansen and Young 2011). Under such circumstances, the system presents the possibility that the Liberals could become a third-party "spoiler," denying the NDP a good chance of governing federally or vice versa.

The new configuration also represents the first case in which a majority federal government has been proven possible without significant support in Quebec. The addition of new House of Commons seats in western Canada and suburban Toronto means that this will soon be easier. However, the ease of ignoring Quebec in pursuit of government power is asymmetrical among viable governing parties in this system. For both the NDP and a revived Liberal Party, the road to power must travel through Quebec. One does, however, see some competitive symmetry ideologically since, as the Conservatives attempt to shift the ideological centre to the right while moderating older Reform and Alliance positions, the NDP is moderating its election appeal by focusing more on "practical first steps" than on its substantial ideological distance from the governing party (Chapters 4 and 5, this volume; Sears 2011; Topp 2010). However, this pursuit of median federal voters has not produced fundamental ideological change in any of the parties. As we argue earlier, by distinguishing between core principles and policy instruments, we can avoid the mistake of contending that one or both of the governing or Official Opposition parties have changed their ideological fundamentals to attain their success.

One key feature of the current party configuration and the ideological space it occupies is that the left-right distance between the policy choices and ideological centres of the first- and second-place parties (the Conservatives and NDP, respectively) may be greater than that between any other federal government and Official Opposition parties in Canadian history. This polarization between first- and second-place parties is a change from the dominance of brokerage politics federally, and it lands Canadian voters in unfamiliar territory. This party system configuration seems stacked against the NDP insofar as the Conservatives are "wedge issue setters" – that is, they can more readily identify and capitalize on divisive issues – and the NDP are generally "wedge issue takers." In other words, the Conservative Party can discursively frame a Conservatives versus other parties division on major economic and social issues rather easily. By contrast, the NDP has found it difficult to frame issues in terms of the NDP versus all other parties since it is attempting to connect with a good number of the same voter value preferences as the Liberals (Chapter 12, this volume; Gidengil et al. 2012).

As Mark Pickup and Colin Whelan suggest in Chapter 10, however, there may be future exceptions to the NDP's disadvantage with regard to strategic issue positioning. On social welfare issues, environmental issues, and perhaps even foreign trade issues, it has established issue ownership with increasing success and in ways that may become valuable in some future scenarios of party competition.

With its second-party status now dependent on a large Quebec caucus, the NDP will be faced with the job of minimizing damage from "coordination failures" on both the left-right axis and the federalist-sovereigntist axis, while the Conservatives can afford to virtually ignore the second challenge. As Godbout, Bélanger, and Mérand contend in Chapter 11, this double challenge for the NDP will continue so long as the SMDP electoral system continues and so long as Liberal and New Democratic Party supporters inconsistently perceive each other's left-right positional placements. NDP supporters tend to see the Liberal Party as being further to the right than Liberal supporters see their party, while Liberal supporters tend to see the NDP as further to the left than NDP supporters see their party. At the same time, Chapters 7 and 12 indicate that the NDP's non-activist members and swing voters are more willing to consider a coalition or merger with the Liberals than are its activists and core voters, thus opening up a potential rift within the party should Conservative majority governments continue.

The NDP's navigation through these fraught waters is especially tricky now that media and the public will report inconsistencies between the party's Quebec and rest-of-Canada supporters' views on powers for Quebec. The federal party's views on this matter have not changed significantly since the 2005 Sherbrooke Declaration, but if the Conservatives or Liberals make high-profile allegations that the NDP is "soft" on Quebec nationalism, many NDP supporters in western Canada will not find this easy to accept. The NDP challenge in this regard would have been complicated even more by a Parti Québécois victory in the 2014 Quebec election since a PQ government has good reasons to do what it can to shore up the BQ at NDP expense. Its proposed "charter of values" for Quebec appears to have had substantial support among some of the constituencies on which the NDP relies for continuing electoral support, so the NDP can consider itself lucky that the PQ lost power (see, e.g., Lavoie 2013). All of these aspects of the NDP's attempts to square left-right positioning with asymmetrical federalism that treats Quebec differently from other provinces leave the party relying on Thomas Mulcair's leadership more than on a strong network of deeply rooted support and activism in Quebec. As noted in Chapters

3, 11, and 12, the NDP's continued success in Quebec also relies to no small extent on continued bad luck or bad management for both the Liberals and the BQ in that province.

One way of gauging the NDP's prospects for continued and perhaps even greater success in the federal party system would be to move beyond directly electoral matters to ask whether they are enhanced because the party is now more in tune either with Canadian political culture generally or with key aspects of Canadians' political attitudes than it was before 2011. In other words, is there evidence that social democracy is gaining ground culturally? If so, then presumably the most social democratic party should gain ground politically.

For several reasons, it is difficult to make such judgments. The most obvious reason is that social and political attitudes in Quebec may be moving in ways that are different from the movement of these attitudes in the rest of Canada. The 2011 election demonstrated this gap rather starkly, when, for unusual reasons (recounted in Chapters 3, 11, and 12), the left-right axis of politics in Quebec eclipsed the national question axis. At least for now, Quebec seems more social democratic in basic political cultural terms than most other parts of Canada. This provides the NDP with an opening to become a major party. But if the political culture gap between Quebec and the rest of Canada persists, perhaps because the Conservatives make progress in their project of remaking English Canadian political culture along conservative lines, the NDP may find itself relying on a rather precarious Quebec foundation.

The other main difficulty in assessing whether social democracy is gaining ground culturally is that it is hard to translate attitudinal preferences directly into claims about significant shifts in political culture. It is easier to identify such shifts with historical hindsight, with reference to institutional and symbolic variables, than to see them actually happening. This goes beyond the problem of what sense to make of which answers to which survey questions, such as those posed by the efforts of the Manning Centre or the Broadbent Institute to frame public opinion.[4] A political cultural shift in the direction of social democracy would not just be displayed in higher numbers of respondents valuing equality more than liberty or supporting public broadcasting or national standards for health care provision. It would also be evidenced by the creation and public acceptance of new public institutions, the growth of diverse social organizations that instantiate social solidarity, increasing public acceptance of "social rights" and their symbolic expressions (such as medicare), and so on. These things develop over time as expressions of public support for broadly social democratic ways of understanding desirable patterns of interaction among individuals, civil society, collective action, and public institutions.

Complicating matters further is the distinction between policy instruments and ideological fundamentals discussed earlier. The distinction allows us to see that, even if some traditional policy mainstays of social democratic parties are removed from their electoral appeals and governing strategies, it need not mean that the underlying ideological fundamentals of these parties are being altered dramatically. In this context, the distinction reminds us that what counts as a "social democratic" view of politics and governance will change over time, particularly with respect to policy instrument choice. It is thus not wise to answer questions about whether social democracy is gaining ground in Canada primarily with reference to shifting attitudes towards the policy instruments favoured by social democrats thirty or forty years ago. In other words, showing that there is rising public support for nationalization of banks or the oil industry is not going to tell us much about whether contemporary social democracy is advancing or declining.[5]

Taken together, these complications that arise in drawing links from attitudinal to deeper cultural orientations towards politics have led authors in this volume to focus far more on the electoral than on the cultural bases of social democratic weakness and relative strength in Canada over the past twenty-five years. Seen from an electoral angle, at least on the national stage, social democracy has never been stronger in Canada. Skeptics would reply that this is an aberration caused by a "perfect storm" in Quebec in 2011 or that it is largely irrelevant because it is offset by continued Conservative Party governance at the national level. However, because we need some historical perspective and several more election cycles to see whether the NDP has federal staying power, such skepticism cannot be addressed for some time.

Strategic Challenges for the Federal New Democrats

The analyses in this volume directly raise or indirectly point to a variety of strategic challenges that the party currently faces or is likely to encounter in the near future. We spell some of these out here in an attempt to illuminate not just the NDP's challenges but also various dynamics of the newly configured federal party system.

Expanding the NDP Regional Coalition

The NDP can only grow towards viable "alternative government party" status if it sustains and builds on a regional coalition geographically similar to the one built by Brian Mulroney and the Progressive Conservatives in the 1980s. Such a coalition relies heavily on both Québécois and western Canadian support. There is no reason to believe that we will soon enter the cycles of constitutional politics that undermined the Mulroney coalition between conservative westerners and Quebec nationalists. However, it is easy to imagine conflicts between the preferences of NDP supporters in western Canada and those in Quebec being coaxed to the surface by a Liberal Party desperate to reclaim its past federalist pre-eminence in Quebec, by a Bloc Québécois desperate to reclaim soft nationalist support, and by a Conservative Party needing the failure of centre-left coordination to continue. Thus, the challenge inherent in the NDP's historic breakthrough in 2011 is to simultaneously beat the Conservative Party, the Liberal Party, and the Bloc at the distinct games each party must play. By 2011, the Conservative Party had found a "minimum winning coalition" at just under 40 percent of the popular vote (Flanagan 2011). While its popularity dropped substantially with the Senate scandals of 2013 (Visser 2013), it could well rebound with distance from those events. And the party has the advantage of doing better among likely voters than its competitors. Whether the NDP, the Liberals, and anti-Conservative civil society organizations can help sustain the decline in public trust in Stephen Harper and the "Conservative brand" before the 2015 election remains an open question.

A Liberal recovery in Quebec and partial recovery in Ontario, obtained through a reversal of most 2011 NDP gains, is the worst-case scenario for the NDP. The prospect of such a reversal presents the party with a major strategic challenge. Some combination of Justin Trudeau sustaining his early leadership popularity, successful Conservative attempts to negatively frame Thomas Mulcair, NDP difficulties in keeping Quebec and non-Quebec elements of its parliamentary caucus united on a shared view of "the national question" in Quebec, and a widespread decision among centre-left voters to use the Liberal Party as their instrument to punish the Conservatives could lead to this result.

As Chapter 11 argues, under circumstances of improved public support and increased fundraising success, the Liberals would have no incentive to merge or work in coalition with the NDP. The Conservative Party's strategic interest is in maximizing the odds of coordination failure among centre-left parties. Its best-case scenario is to keep the Liberals and the New Democrats each claiming between 20 and 30 percent of the popular vote that Conservatives have essentially written off.

For the NDP, the strategic choices are between attempting to undermine Liberal Party support among centre-left voters and keeping back channels and other potential collaborative openings available, in case a merger seems the only way to defeat the Conservatives (Adams 2013). The former choice would mean effectively supporting many Conservatives' claims about the Liberals as a party that cannot be forgiven for its past indiscretions with a leader who lacks deep political experience. On the other hand, keeping the merger option open sets a limit on how much the NDP can work to delegitimize a potential future partner.

Beyond Regional Conciliation: Keeping Old and New Party Voters Happy

As the federal NDP continues to engage public policy issues inside and outside Parliament, voters who gave it just over 30 percent of the national popular vote in 2011 will be watching for evidence that the NDP represents their interests and preferences. Which non-regional issues will pose the NDP its greatest challenge in maintaining and perhaps increasing its parliamentary standing? The challenge of reconciling core and swing voters is undoubtedly one that the federal NDP must take seriously if it is to sustain its current numbers in the House. The question is whether this is an insurmountable challenge.

Weldon's analysis in Chapter 12 shows that the NDP enjoys a much lower proportion of core voters than the Conservatives, the BQ, or the Liberals. But he also shows that, while all of the other major parties lost votes to the NDP in 2011, roughly one million voters who chose the Liberals in 2008 switched to the NDP in 2011. To the extent that policy distance considerations will shape future swing voters' decisions, reconciling core and swing voters may not be especially difficult, owing to the fact that the distance between the issue preferences of NDP and Liberal supporters is considerably closer – on all but the "national question" – than that between the Liberals and the Conservatives. The same is true of BQ and Green supporters.

So the NDP may be able to credibly stake out a claim to issue ownership on environmental questions, rebuilding social programs, a more active economic regulatory state, and carrying the anti-Harper flag. The last possibility is strengthened by the fact that the NDP finished either first or second in 75 percent of riding contests in the 2011 election. The combination of this electoral record, its ability to attract support from many swing voters, and its growing ability to claim issue ownership on electorally consequential ground (see Chapter 10) means that reconciling differences between core and swing voters may be considerably easier now for the NDP than for the Liberals.

It must be noted, however, that Weldon also points out a potential fly in this ointment. Voters' reservations about the NDP's ability to manage the economy, including those who switched to the NDP in 2011, could do much to prevent past Liberal voters who switched to the NDP in 2011 from voting NDP in the future. This perceived weakness is also identified in Pickup and Whelan's analysis of the different issue priorities among the various federal parties' core constituencies. As they note, the NDP has always had difficulty establishing issue ownership on effective economic management. If it continues to be perceived as weak on this front, the NDP may find limits to its popularity just when it needs to grow decisively past the Liberal Party. On the other hand, as Weldon points out in Chapter 12, of the CES respondents who said their financial situations had worsened since 2008, 46 percent voted NDP as compared to 18 percent Liberal and 25 percent Conservative. So this issue area may be where the NDP's choice of policy measures and instruments to champion in subsequent elections may be most critical. Whether party activists will provide Thomas Mulcair the kind of leeway in this regard that they extended to Jack Layton is thus a key question.

Another major issue that may be problematic for the party concerns the NDP's decisions regarding its traditional union support. Chapter 7 indicates a broad and relatively long-standing willingness of party members, even trade unionists, to expand party affiliations and alliances well beyond trade unions to new social movements and social justice advocacy groups. Is a further expansion of alliances along these lines consistent with an increasing NDP vote share? Declining union membership in Canada (see McFarland 2012), and the likelihood that the federal NDP's swing voters are less sympathetic to trade unions than its core voters, will both give party leaders reasons to establish greater distance between the party and organized labour.

For most of its history, the federal NDP could reaffirm its support for public- and private-sector trade unions without endangering the vote it needed to sustain its third-party status. With third-party status no longer acceptable to anyone in the party, NDP strategists have to be concerned about potential Conservative or Liberal Party suggestions that the NDP is too friendly to "big labour." Navigating a consistent course through the union alliance waters promises to be a significant challenge for the leader and activists of a party that is not interested in losing its newly won prominence in federal politics.

The NDP-Liberal Relationship: Avoiding Centre-Left Coordination Failure?

If both the New Democratic and Liberal parties fail to make significant electoral gains at the other's expense in 2015, two multi-generational enemies may attempt to overcome tremendous distrust (Adams 2013) and agree on a common consensual leader. As Godbout, Bélanger, and Mérand suggest in Chapter 11, this seems unlikely, at least until there is electoral reform federally. However, the prospect of a merger between the Alliance and Progressive Conservative parties was also considered a long shot by many before their merger. Of course, neither the NDP nor the Liberals have had as long to think about the downsides of coordination failure as did Reform/Alliance and Progressive Conservative insiders and leaders between 1993 and 2003.

The strategic challenge in relation to a merger would be to keep lines of communication open, as happened during the party's 2008 efforts to construct a Conservative-toppling coalition (Topp 2010). This would allow a group of "matchmakers" from inside Liberal and NDP ranks to get the parties to the table, allow each party to save enough face with different aspects of the collaborative outcome, and satisfy most Liberal and NDP members that desperate times – Conservative Party dominance without respite – requires radical measures. But even though Pétry points out in Chapter 6 that the ideological distance between the NDP and Liberal Party has closed over the past two decades, Chapter 11 presents good reasons for believing that the NDP and Liberals will not soon make it to merger talks at all.

What about an NDP-Green Party merger? There would be a clearer value and more basis in voter-preference for such a merger, with no long history of enmity between the two and much social movement organizational overlap. On the other hand, there may not seem much to be gained by either the NDP or the Greens here, since the Green vote shrank between 2008 and 2011, and it seems uninterested in being absorbed into a party with which it is not solidly aligned in left-right terms. In the end, however, adding even 4 percent of the popular vote to its own total would be appealing for the NDP. And since the Green Party's vote decline between 2008 and 2011 was likely more of a strategic vote loss to a party on a roll than a long-term trend, the NDP could easily lose more votes to the Greens in the next two elections. Many Green supporters are well-educated postmaterialists (Gidengil et al. 2012), so for them the dominant concerns of party competition may seem comparatively unimportant. Once again, even though the stakes are smaller for the NDP, closing the ground between them would require the NDP to finesse its relations with the Greens very carefully over the next several years. Remaining respectful competitors is a precondition of any collaboration.

Financing a Competitive Party
Party financing of both election campaigns and inter-election outreach has become more complex for the NDP as a result of changes introduced first by the federal Liberal government (in 2003) and then by successive Conservative governments (2010-14). These changes initially deprived the NDP of its key financial backer, the English-Canadian trade union movement, and forced all parties to compete for numerous modest contributions. At the same time, the quarterly public subsidies allocated to parties according to popular vote provided an important compensation for the NDP, allowing it to compete more effectively both electorally and for individual contributions.

As we see in Chapter 3, the NDP made considerable headway with fundraising after 2006, and especially after 2008. With the abolition of the quarterly subsidies, to be completed in 2014, the NDP faces a more significant challenge. To compete with the Conservative Party, the NDP will have to move its fundraising to a very different level, closing the substantial gap between it and the Conservatives in terms of both numbers of contributors and average contributor amounts. While the NDP had its best year ever in 2012, with just over 43,000 contributors donating $7.7 million, the Conservative Party's 87,000 contributors donated just over $17 million to their party (Elections Canada 2012). NDP advertising needs to be able to battle directly with that of the Conservatives not just during but also between campaigns. It must also use advertising to partially counteract the heavy newspaper editorial support that the Conservatives have had and will likely enjoy in 2015 and subsequent elections.[6]

Member-Leader-Activist Relations

The federal NDP faces several related issues with respect to the role of the leader in the party. The most obvious is whether the party led by Thomas Mulcair should attempt to maintain the kind of high profile and power for its leader, in relation to the rest of the party, that it found electorally advantageous under Jack Layton. Bittner's analysis in Chapter 8 suggests that there may be no good reason to do so if Mulcair cannot come close to matching what was, by any standard, Layton's remarkable popularity. Weldon is somewhat more cautious about the stand-alone advantages of leader popularity for the party. Chapter 7 suggests that, while NDP members showed considerable patience and willingness to accommodate Layton's outsized role in their party, there was some concern about the toll this took on members' and activists' abilities to govern their party as democratically as they would have liked. After four federal elections and a leadership race in eight years, party members can now devote more attention to where the party is going and less to election readiness and campaigning.

But the post-2011 NDP is in a dramatically different competitive position than it has ever enjoyed, and this places other constraints on intra-party activity. As the Official Opposition, the NDP can contend for the first time that it is a credible government-in-waiting. Can it afford to revert to its earlier party life, which featured wide-open ideological debate, a high profile for social movement activists, and what was, by comparison to major parties, an unusual level of intra-party democracy? Party activists may want all of these things, but whether it is possible to have them all and to remain electorally competitive with the Conservative Party remains a real question.

The party's June 2013 convention in Montreal did not devote more time to policy discussion than its 2011 convention or as much as its 2009 convention. Whether this tells us much about the state of intra-party democracy is unclear. However, it provides one indication that a recently modernized party in a newly competitive position, facing party opponents with little interest in or experience of intra-party democracy, is bound to have difficulty reverting to older models and practices of party democracy.

The NDP is now in somewhat the same position as the Conservatives were following their merger, but in a mirror image: it is more likely to move slightly more towards the centre than leftwards since it needs centre-left voters more than it needs those on its left-wing margin. And, like the radical social conservatives and staunch libertarians in the Conservative Party camp, the more radical elements in the NDP have no real electoral option. This is not to say that the left will not vocally object to any notable centrist adjustment by NDP leaders or that their complaints will go unheeded by a press looking for signs of division in a revitalized federal NDP. But taking a direct reference to socialist goals out of the party's constitution at the 2013 constitution did not trigger a significant exodus of activists, nor did it occasion more than fleeting media attention (Payton 2013). Accommodating its socialist caucus on this and other matters is far from being the party's most troubling strategic challenge (see, e.g., Azizi 2013; Weisleder 2013). And, as Chapters 4 and 7 show, many party activists over the past decade have placed a high premium on electoral success. They may decide to exercise self-restraint until such success is either achieved or stymied. Perhaps promotion of environmental, inter-generational justice and governance transparency themes on the part of Thomas Mulcair can satisfy enough New Democrat activists, without alienating potential Liberal vote switchers, to justify less openly divided internal party behaviour.

Like Alliance and Progressive Conservative Party activists ratifying their leaders' 2003 merger deal, most NDP activists seem to accept that self-restraint is a small price to pay for the exercise of political power. In the case of the NDP, the presumptive benefits offsetting this cost would be achievement of some of its medium-term egalitarian policy objectives and the novelty of remaining serious contenders to form a government in 2015 or the near future. If their party stays well behind both the Trudeau Liberals and the Harper Conservatives in polls most of the way to the 2015 election, however, the party's faithful on both its left and its centre may decide to reassert some of the power that they have currently loaned to their leader and central party organization. The sight of a fractious party would not inspire more public confidence, with the probable result that some expressions of intra-party democracy could make the NDP even less competitive.

However, the NDP's own choices are not the only determinant of its competitive position. Much obviously depends on how credible Justin Trudeau can appear as an alternative prime minister. And should public trust in the Harper Conservatives not rise significantly from the low levels resulting from the Senate scandals, both the Liberals and the NDP will face new opportunities at the same time as short-term incentives to consider a merger or strategic electoral collaboration.

Electoral Success through Liberalization?

Thinking about evolving relations between NDP leaders and activists eventually leads to a question concerning what is potentially the party's biggest strategic challenge: Should it decide to remain a "modernized" social democratic party, albeit with some minor modifications, or should it aim to become a "liberalized" social democratic party? This decision is logically and, for the party as a whole, practically prior to any decision about pursuing a merger with the Liberals.

The "strategic non-compete" option proposed by Nathan Cullen during the 2012 leadership race need not entail a decision to have the NDP make major moves to "liberalize," but Chapter 7 suggests that such a proposal could run into stiff resistance among party members, particularly those who are most active. If such opposition continued from 2009 (when the member survey was conducted) through the experience as Official Opposition and even after a serious setback in the 2015 election, it would be clear that the party is not interested in such a non-compete option. On the other hand, an NDP-Liberal Party merger option would necessarily entail liberalization of the NDP. If the NDP were to insist that the merged party remain social democratic, many Liberals would quite reasonably see this as a hostile takeover bid and reject a merger proposal. Accepting the necessity of liberalization as a condition of such a merger would very likely involve acceptance of significant changes to intra-party governance and national organization, including but moving well beyond dramatically altered relationships with provincial New Democratic parties. The prospect of such changes, in which the NDP's intra-party democracy would be an unavoidable casualty, might be enough to incline NDP members to reject such a merger. Clearly, more than distinct party cultures and multi-generational animosity towards the Liberal Party are involved in any such decision.

The party might also decide to move towards a "liberalized" mode of social democratic politics without seeking a merger. Doing so would involve emphasizing absorption of Liberal voters without having any intimate contact with what would have to be a declining Liberal Party for this strategy to make sense. It is worth remembering that the most notable instance of a party that has recently jumped from modernized to liberalized social democratic party status was Tony Blair's New Labour Party. It made no overtures to merge with the centre-left Liberal Democrats, instead adopting a raft of changes to party policy, party governance, and campaign strategy. In retrospect, these changes added up to not just a more effective appeal to Britain's median voter – including many previous Conservative and Liberal Democratic voters – but also a substantial shift in policy objectives and even underlying core values (Gamble and Wright 1999; Freeden 1999; Shaw 2007; Merkel et al. 2008).

A Canadian variant of this liberalization option would save the NDP the messiness and uncertainty of a merger process. However, it would also likely entail acting in bad faith with its party activists and core voters, unless the party conducted this liberalization over several election cycles and with explicit permission from successive party conventions. Despite the evidence presented in Chapters 4 and 7 that party activists are enthusiastic about trading their party's roles as "moral conscience" for that of federal government policy-setters, nothing in the last four party conventions of 2006, 2009, 2011, and 2013 suggests that permission for substantial liberalization would be easy to obtain. Instead, we should expect to see a party struggling with setting a new balance between intra-party democracy and electoral politics. Should the NDP sustain its position as Official Opposition in the 2015 election, it will likely have an easier time achieving a balance tilted towards the demands of electoral politics, while reversion to its traditional third-party standing in Parliament might trigger more of a contest between pro- and anti-liberalization forces within the party. Such a contest could lead the NDP to move from a "modernized" social democratic stance to a "liberalized" social democratic party identity and character. If so, its underlying core values would undergo a substantial shift along with its policy objectives and choice of policy instrument. Whether such a transformation takes place will depend on many of the variables discussed in this volume.

Many factors percolating within the Canadian party system could complicate the strategic challenges discussed above. Leadership issues in the NDP and the Liberal Party, further scandals that could rock the Conservative Party as the sponsorship scandal damaged the Liberals, and a resurgence of the Bloc Québécois all have the potential to shift the momentum and competitive dynamics in the Canadian party system to the advantage or disadvantage of the federal New Democrats. However these dynamics unfold, it is clear that the federal NDP has become a serious contender for national political power for the first time in its history. Having moved from perennial third party aiming for moral victories, policy emulation, and minority government leverage to Official Opposition with major representation from Quebec, the NDP has vaulted into the centre of Canadian political competition. We hope that this volume helps to explain how this happened, what this means, and why understanding the transformation of the New Democratic Party is now necessary to all students of Canadian politics.

Notes

1 See the party website entry on "Commissions" at http://www.ndp.ca/commissions.
2 See *Ford Nation* website, https://twitter.com/ford_nation.
3 The BQ was, among all the opposition parties except the Greens, the most heavily dependent upon this subsidy (Jansen and Young 2011).
4 See Manning Barometer poll at http://manningcentre.ca/2013poll; Broadbent Institute, *Canadian Values Are Progressive Values: A Snapshot of the Views of New and Canadian-Born Urban/Suburban Canadians, 2013* (May 2013), http://www.broadbentinstitute.ca/sites/default/files/documents/polling-en-web.pdf.
5 Jack Layton's career as a municipal and then a national politician showed that he had a nuanced understanding of the complex and evolving relationship between policy instruments and core political values. For many examples of this, recounted by Layton himself, see Layton (2004).
6 The Conservative Party obtained the vast majority of Canadian English-language daily paper editorial endorsements between 2004 and 2011. The federal NDP has only been endorsed by a major daily outside of Quebec once over that period – in 2011 by the *Toronto Star*.

References

Adams, Paul. 2013. *Power Trap: How Fear and Loathing between New Democrats and Liberals Keep Stephen Harper in Power – and What Can Be Done about It.* Toronto: Lorimer.

Azizi, Arash. 2013. The NDP Should Stay True to Its Socialist Roots. *Toronto Star,* 10 April. http://www.thestar.com/opinion/commentary/2013/04/10/the_ndp_should_stay_true_to_its_socialist_roots.html.

Bittner, Amanda, and Royce Koop, eds. 2013. *Parties, Elections, and the Future of Canadian Politics.* Vancouver: UBC Press.

Carty, R. Kenneth, William Cross, and Lisa Young. 2000. *Rebuilding Canadian Party Politics.* Vancouver: UBC Press.

Chase, Steven. 2013. Harper Assures Grassroots Conservatives He's Outsider Fighting Elites. *Globe and Mail,* 1 November. http://www.theglobeandmail.com/news/politics/harper-assures-grassroots-conservative-hes-outsider-fighting-elites/article15228311/#dashboard/follows/.

Elections Canada. 2012. Registered Party Financial Transactions Return. http://www.elections.ca/WPAPPS/WPF/EN/PP/SelectParties?act=C2&returntype=1&period=0.

Erickson, Lynda, and David Laycock. 2002. Postmaterialism vs. the Welfare State? Opinion among English Canadian Social Democrats. *Party Politics* 8, 3: 301-26.

Flanagan, Tom. 2011. The Emerging Conservative Coalition. *Policy Options* (June): 104-08.

–. 2013. Why Harper Dug in His Heels: That's Where the Money Is. *Globe and Mail*, 2 November. http://www.theglobeandmail.com/commentary/touching -base/article15232166/#dashboard/follows/.

Freeden, Michael. 1996. *Ideologies and Political Theory*. New York: Oxford University Press.

–. 1999. True Blood or False Genealogy: New Labour and British Social Democratic Thought. *Political Quarterly* 70, 1: 151-65.

Gamble, Andrew, and Tony Wright, eds. 1999. *The New Social Democracy*. London: Blackwell.

Gidengil, Elisabeth, Neil Nevitte, André Blais, Joanna Everitt, and Patrick Fournier. 2012. *Dominance and Decline: Making Sense of Recent Canadian Elections*. Toronto: University of Toronto Press.

Jansen, Harold J., and Lisa Young. 2011. Cartels, Syndicates, and Coalitions: Canada's Political Parties after the 2004 Reforms. In Lisa Young and Harold J. Jansen, eds., *Money, Politics and Democracy: Canada's Party Finance Reforms*, 82-103. Vancouver: UBC Press.

Johnston, Richard. 2009. Polarized Pluralism in the Canadian Party System. *Canadian Journal of Political Science* 41, 4: 815-34.

Lavigne, Brad. 2013. *Building the Orange Wave: The Inside Story behind the Historic Rise of Jack Layton and the NDP*. Madeira Park, BC: Douglas and McIntyre.

Lavoie, Jasmin. 2013. Charte: des milliers de Janettes se rassemblent à Montréal. *La Presse*, 26 October. http://www.lapresse.ca/actualites/montreal/201310/26/01-4703946-charte-des-milliers-de-janettes-se-rassemblent-a-montreal.php.

Layton, Jack. 2004. *Speaking Out: Ideas that Work for Canadians*. Toronto: Key Porter.

McFarland, Janet. 2012. The Weakening State of Canadian Labour Unions. *Globe and Mail*, 2 September. http://www.theglobeandmail.com/news/national/the-weakening-state-of-canadian-labour-unions/article4515873/?page=all.

Merkel, Wolfgang, Alexander Petring, Christian Henkes, and Christoph Egle. 2008. *Social Democracy in Power: The Capacity to Reform*. London: Routledge.

Payton, Laura. 2013. NDP Votes to Take "Socialism" out of Party Constitution. *CBC News*, 14 April. http://www.cbc.ca/news/politics/ndp-votes-to-take-socialism -out-of-party-constitution-1.1385171.

Sears, Robin. 2011. The Realignment Story of Campaign 41. *Policy Options* (June): 18-36.

Shaw, Eric. 2007. *Losing Labour's Soul? New Labour and the Blair Government, 1997-2007*. London: Routledge.

Topp, Brian. 2010. *How We Almost Gave the Tories the Boot*. Toronto: Lorimer.

Visser, Jon. 2013. As Scandal Grows, Stephen Harper's Conservatives Falling Far behind Justin Trudeau's Liberals: Poll. *National Post*, 24 October. http://news. nationalpost.com/2013/10/24/as-senate-scandal-grows-stephen-harpers -conservatives-falling-far-behind-justin-trudeaus-liberals-poll/.

Weisleder, Barry. 2013. Why We Fight to Keep Socialism in the NDP. *Turn Left: Voice of the NDP Socialist Caucus* (Spring): 8-11. http://www.ndpsocialists.ca/ Turn%20Left%20-%20Spring%202013%20-%20For%20Web.pdf.

Contributors

Éric Bélanger is associate professor of Political Science at McGill University and a member of the Centre for the Study of Democratic Citizenship. His research interests include political parties, public opinion, and voting behavior, as well as Quebec and Canadian politics. His work has been published in a number of scholarly journals, including *Comparative Political Studies, Political Research Quarterly, Electoral Studies,* and the *Canadian Journal of Political Science.* He is also the co-author of a book on Quebec politics, *Le comportement électoral des Québécois* (awarded the 2010 Donald Smiley Prize).

Amanda Bittner is an associate professor of Political Science at Memorial University. Her broad research interests include the effects of knowledge and information on voter decision making, as well as the institutional and structural incentives affecting voting behavior in both Canadian and comparative contexts. She is the author of *Platform or Personality? The Role of Party Leaders in Elections* (Oxford University Press, 2011) and the co-author (with Royce Koop) of *Parties, Elections, and the Future of Canadian Politics* (UBC Press, 2013).

Lynda Erickson is professor emeritus at Simon Fraser University. She has published on the topics of women and politics, public opinion and the welfare state, the economy and party support, candidates and candidate selection in Canadian elections, party leadership selection in Canada, and internal party politics in the NDP.

Jean-François Godbout is associate professor of Political Science at the Université de Montréal. Godbout's research is primarily focused on democratic processes and political institutions. He has published numerous journal articles on legislative behaviour and elections in Canada, the United States, and the United Kingdom. Godbout was a visiting research scholar at the Centre for the Study of Democratic Politics of Princeton University during the 2013-14 academic year.

David Laycock is professor of Political Science at Simon Fraser University. His research interests include the comparative study of populism, conservatism and social democracy, particularly their ideological dimensions, contemporary normative democratic theory, and public policy. His publications include *Populism and Democratic Thought in the Canadian Prairies* (University of Toronto Press, 1990), *The New Right and Democracy in Canada* (Oxford University Press, 2001), *Representation and Democratic Theory* (UBC Press, 2004), and several articles on the NDP with Lynda Erickson.

Frédéric Mérand is associate professor of Political Science and Director of the University of Montréal Centre for International Studies (CÉRIUM). His most recent publication (with Maya Jegen) is "Constructing Ambiguity: Comparing the EU's Energy and Defence Policies" in *West European Politics*.

François Pétry is a professor and the director of the Department of Political Science at Université Laval in Quebec. He is a member of the Centre for the Study of Democratic Citizenship and of the Centre for the Analysis of Public Policy. His research interests centre on the relationship between public opinion and public policy.

Mark Pickup is associate professor of Political Science at Simon Fraser University. He is a specialist in comparative politics and political methodology whose research primarily falls into three areas: (1) the economy and democratic accountability, (2) polls and electoral outcomes, and (3) conditions of democratic responsiveness. His research focuses on political information, public opinion, the media, election campaigns, and electoral institutions. His methodological interests concern the analysis of longitudinal data, with a secondary interest in Bayesian analysis.

Steven Weldon is associate professor of Political Science at Simon Fraser University. His research focuses on political representation, participation, and elections in advanced democracies, and has been published in, among others, the *American Journal of Political Science*, the *British Journal of Political Science*, *European Journal of Political Research*, and *Party Politics*.

Colin Whelan completed a BA at Simon Fraser University and an MA at the University of British Columbia focusing on the legislative impacts of Westminster committee systems. His other research interests include public opinion, political behaviour, and elections.

Maria Zakharova is a PhD candidate in the Department of Political Science at Simon Fraser University. Her primary research focus is on party valence, its sources, the ways in which it can be measured across a large number of countries and elections, and its consequences for electoral outcomes and government formation. Her most recent publication, with Paul Warwick, is "The Sources of Valence Judgments: The Role of Policy Distance and the Structure of the Left-Right Spectrum," *Comparative Political Studies* (2014).

Index